THE BOOK
OF NATURE

THE BOOK
OF NATURE

*A Sourcebook of Spiritual Perspectives
On Nature and the Environment*

Selected and Edited by

Camille Adams Helminski

*T*o *God belong the east and the west.
Wherever you turn, there is the Face of God.
Witness, God is Infinite, All-knowing.*
[Qur'an 2:115]

THE BOOK FOUNDATION

BRISTOL, ENGLAND AND WATSONVILLE, CALIFORNIA

THE BOOK FOUNDATION
www.thebook.org

Publication Design by Camille Helminski.
Cover Design by Kabir Helminski.

First Book Foundation edition published 2006.

British Library Cataloguing in Publication Data
A catalogue record of this book is available from The British Library

Library of Congress Cataloging-in-Publication Data
The Book of Nature / Selections by Camille Helminski
Bristol, England and Watsonville, California: The Book Foundation, 2006.

ISBN 1-904510-15-9 -- 9781904510154
Includes bibliographical references.
1. Islam
I. Camille Helminski II. The Book Foundation

Acknowledgments

The editor wishes to thank Nadia and Talal Zahid for their great foresight and generosity, Jeremy and Tania Henzell-Thomas for their gracious and abundant editorial assistance, and Charles Upton for his efforts in beginning the research for the *Book of Nature* and for his many contributions. We also wish to thank Marjorie Wolfe for her valiantly persistent, careful, and patient help with permissions; Michael Wolfe, Darrin Schultz, Connie Risley, my husband, Kabir, my sons, Shams and Matthew, and Lori Wood for their helpful suggestions; Hamida and Muhammad Battla for their gracious support; and the generosity of all the publishers of works that have been excerpted who are noted on the initial pages of the selections quoted. May God forgive us for our mistakes and grant good fruitfulness.

Notes on Translation

In most cases we have attempted to transliterate Arabic words as they are pronounced. In quoted material, the spelling may vary according to the custom of the author. Throughout this book, references to the Qurʾān are in brackets. These refer to the name of the *sūrah*, the *sūrah* number, and verse (*ayah*). The first time the Prophet Muḥammad ﷺ is mentioned in a paragraph, his mention is followed by the calligraphic symbol for *ṣalla Allāhu ʿalayhi wa sallam*, "May the peace and blessings of Allāh be upon him." When Muḥammad's companions are mentioned, they are followed with the symbol for *raḍiallāhu ʿanhu* (may Allāh be pleased with him) ﷜. In material that is being quoted, we have used the symbols to replace these blessings, but have not added them if they were not present in the original text.

When quoting the Qurʾān or referring in the text to God, exalted is He, we have used the masculine pronoun. Please be aware that this is merely a limitation of language and that within the universe and understanding of the Qurʾān, God is without gender and far beyond any words or manner by which we might try to describe Him/Her.

Subḥān Allāhi Rabb il-ʿālamīn!

TABLE OF CONTENTS

II. THE NATURAL WORLD

THE ELEMENTS

III. CARING FOR GOD'S CREATION

INTRODUCTION

To God belongs all that is in the heavens
and all that is on earth;
and all things are returning to God.
[*Sūrah Al ʿImrān* (The House Of ʿImrān) 3:109]

God—there is no deity but Hu,[1]
the Ever-Living, the Self-Subsisting Source of all Being.
No slumber can seize Him nor sleep.
All things in heaven and on earth belong to Hu.
Who could intercede in His Presence without His permission?
He knows what appears in front of
and behind His creatures.
Nor can they encompass any knowledge of Him
except what He wills.
His throne extends over the heavens and the earth,
and He feels no fatigue in guarding and preserving them,
for He is the Highest and Most Exalted.
[*Sūrah Al-Baqarah* (The Cow) 2:255]

---

[1] Hu: the pronoun of Divine Presence. All words in Arabic have a gender grammatically ascribed to them as they do in French and Spanish, etc. Although Allah is referred to with the third person masculine pronoun *Hu* (*Huwa*), it is universally understood that Allah's Essence is beyond gender or indeed any qualification, That which is beyond all our attempts at definition, limitless in subtle glory.

This and all verses of the *Qur'an* which introduce chapters in *The Book of Nature* are excerpted from *The Light of Dawn, Daily Readings from the Holy Qur'an,* selected and rendered by Camille Adams Helminski, Shambhala Publications, 2001, or are adapted from *The Message of the Qur'an* by Muhammad Asad, published by The Book Foundation, 2004.

1

To God belong the east and the west.
Wherever you turn, there is the face of God.
Witness, God is Infinite, All-knowing.
[*Sūrah Al-Baqarah* (The Cow) 2:115]

We have built the universe with skill and power;
and truly, it is We Who are steadily expanding it.
And We have spread wide the earth—
how well We have ordered it!
And of everything, We have created opposites
that you might bear in mind that God alone is One.
[*Sūrah Adh-Dhāriyāt* (The Dust-Scattering Winds) 51:47-49]

And We have established the night and the day as two symbols;
and then We have effaced the symbol of night
and put in place the light-giving symbol of day,
so that you might seek to obtain your Sustainer's bounty
and be aware of the passing years and of the reckoning.
For clearly, most clearly, have We spelled out everything!
[*Sūrah Al-Isrā'* (The Night Journey) 17:12]

Know that God gives life to the earth after it has been lifeless!
We have indeed made Our signs clear to you
that you might learn wisdom.
[*Sūrah Al-Ḥadīd* (Iron) 57:17]

We will show them Our signs on the farthest horizons
and within their own selves
until it becomes manifest to them that this is the Truth.
Is it not enough that your Lord is witness to all things?
Indeed! Are they in doubt concerning the Meeting with their Lord?
Ah, truly! It is He Who encompasses all things!
[*Sūrah Fuṣṣilat* (Clearly Spelled Out) 41:53-54]

2

Reading the Book of Nature

~ Charles Upton

It is of the utmost significance that in the Qur'an Allah is said to be All-Encompassing (*Muhit*), as in the verse, *But to Allah belong all things in heaven and on earth. And it is He who encompasses* (muhit) *all things.* [*Sūrah An-Nisā'* (Women) 4:26][2]

~ Seyyed Hossein Nasr

Many traditional cultures read nature like a book, knowing it as God's original scripture. Within the unfolding universe of the revelation of the Qur'an numerous chapters take their name from natural phenomenon or the *ummahs*, the communities of nature: the bee, the cow, the ant, the spider, the elephant, the fig, the light, the dawn, the night, smoke, the glorious morning light, the sun, the moon, thunder, the constellations, sand dunes, winds, gold, iron, the rocky region, Mt. Sinai, the connecting cell, woman, the human being.

From the Islamic perspective, the natural world is a tapestry woven with the "signs" of the Creator, the Arabic word for "signs," *ayat*, being the same one used to denote the "verses" of the Qur'an, thus making the correspondence between nature and scripture explicit. According to the Qur'an, *In your creation and in all the beasts scattered on the earth there are signs for people of true faith. In the alternation of night and day, and in the provision which Allah sends down from the heavens whereby he quickens the earth after its death, and in the distribution of the winds, are signs for people who are intelligent* [45:4-6]. And: *Truly the creation of the heavens and of the earth, and the succession of night and day, and in the ships which speed through the sea with what is useful to man, and in the waters which Allah sends down from the heavens . . . and in the order of the winds, and the clouds that run their appointed courses between heaven and earth, are signs indeed for people who are intelligent* [2:164].

Christianity has much the same doctrine. According to Origen, "The apostle Paul teaches us that God's invisible nature has been 'clearly

---

[2] Seyyed Hossein Nasr, *Islam and the Environment*, Ta-Ha Publishers Ltd., 1998, pp. 120-121.

perceived in the things that have been made' (Romans 1:20): what is not seen is perceived in what is seen. He shows us that this visible world contains teachings about the invisible world, and that this earth includes certain images of celestial realities. . . ." And a complementary teaching is found in Judaism—that the ability to see the signs of God in nature comes from God Himself: "It is He who gave me unerring knowledge of what exists, to know the structure of the world and the activity of the elements: the beginning and end and middle of times, the alternations of the solstices and the changes of the seasons, the cycles of the year and the constellations of the stars, the natures of animals and the tempers of wild beasts, the powers of spirits and the reasonings of men, the varieties of plants and virtues of roots; I learned both what is secret and what is manifest" (Wisdom of Solomon 7:17-21). There is probably not a single traditional Muslim philosopher or scientist who would disagree with this; in the words of Muḥammad (peace and blessings upon him), "O God, show me things as they really are."

If the natural world is a book, then we might say that the Holy Qur'an, rich with natural symbols, is in some sense like the world of nature transposed to a higher level. The Holy Book, because it was sent down from a Reality higher than nature, allows a kind of dialogue between nature and human language. The Qur'an, upon entering our consciousness, is like the world in the form of a book; the world of nature, illumined by the Qur'an, is like the Book in the form of a world.

So every visible form is a sign of God; or, to say it another way, a name. But what, exactly, is the relationship between a name and the thing being named? The Names of God are not the *parts* of God because God is One (*Al-Ahad*). So why must we say that God has ninety-nine names, or even innumerable names? Why can't we simply say that God's Name is *Allah*, and let it go at that?

The answer is that God's Names have to do with His relationship to creation. God is One but His creation is many, which is why He must show a different face and name to every creature—not because He is divided, but because every creature is different and unique. Yet all of His Names are Names of the One Reality, the Divine Essence, which exists beyond any idea, any image, or any name. In Shakespeare's words, "A

4

Rose by any other name would smell as sweet"; the scent of the rose, not the mere name "rose," is its true essence.

Yet in terms of Islam, which was sent to the human race by God Himself, the Name *Allah* and other Divine Names have an intimate connection to the Reality they name—which is why it is said that "God and His Name are One," and why the invocation of the Name of God is also an invocation of His real presence.

> *To Him belongs what is in the heavens and on earth*
> *and all between them and all beneath the soil.*
> *Whether you pronounce the word aloud or not,*
> *truly, He knows what is secret and what is yet more hidden.*
> *God—there is no god but Hu!*
> *To Him belong the Most Beautiful Names.*
> [*Sūrah Ṭā Hā* (O Man) 20:6-8]

To name something is to make it real in your consciousness. A plant or animal you don't know the name of is relatively obscure to you; it's just some animal, some plant. But when you know the name of it, everything you know about it becomes virtually present to you. "Oh, that's an *elder* tree; you can make preserves out of the berries, and its flowers are good for colds; they are used in cough drops." And the same thing is even more true of another human being; when you learn a person's name, he or she becomes more real to you.

The forms of the natural world are like words spoken by God. As God taught Adam the Most Beautiful Names, so Adam named the animals [2:31-33]. God is the only Being to Whom the name Reality belongs intrinsically; every other being only possesses reality by virtue of a free gift from That Reality. Therefore all created things are, in one sense, like Names of God. Since God is the Only Reality, all things symbolize Him—and these symbols are unveiled at the moment when human consciousness encounters the world as it really is, with no intervening ego to separate them, since God is Lord equally over the object perceived and the subject perceiving it. *We shall show them our signs on the horizons and within themselves until they are assured that this is the truth. Is not your Lord sufficient for you, since He is over all things the Witness?* [41:53]

5

To cultivate a vision of the natural world as a tapestry of symbols, as the Creator's first book in which every form is a letter, every living being a word, and every vital process a chapter, you must in a sense become profoundly naïve. We must empty ourselves of pre-conceptions and turn again to witness the Reality before us.

For instance, we may ask, "Why is the sky blue?" The scientific answer to this question involves the various wavelengths of radiant energy within sunlight, the gaseous composition of the atmosphere, the laws of refraction, etc. However, the spiritual vsisionary may engage in a different kind of refletion and arrive at a different meaning: "Because there is a higher world known as the angelic plane—the *Malakut,* a subtler and more complete reflection of God than the material world—where all is high, cool, serene and clear, where perception is pure and transparent, free from the agitation of discursive thought, where each separate object, like a bird, the sun, and the daytime moon, is a perfect expression of its enveloping matrix, which is the essence of clear perception, the essence of *air;* because this higher world exists in a relative eternity 'previous' to our experience of time, because all realities radiate their particular qualities, reflection upon reflection, into ever more constricted and literal worlds, that angelic world, through a series of spiritual, psychic, subtly material, and finally physical processes, ultimately reveals itself to our physical eyes as the luminous, blue, over-arching daytime sky." The scientific answer to "why is the sky blue?" though it may be highly illuminating, deals only with the solidified outer surface of things. . . .

According to al-Ghazali, God in His Name *Al-Khaliq,* (The Creator) conceives of creation in its essential design, like the blueprint of a building. In His Name *Al-Bari* (The Evolver) He commands that this design come into being in the material world. In His Name *Al- Muṣawwir* (The Fashioner), He shapes and molds what He has created. God as Creator sees all that will be in His universe as a single form filled with many particulars. Within the circle of "material existence" is the circle "planets"; within the circle "planets" is the circle "earth"; within the circle "earth" is "biological life"; within the circle "biological life" is the circle "trees"; within that is the circle "oak tree"; within that is the circle "this particular oak tree." In other words, creation branches—and trees are symbols of this truth. *Al-Khaliq* is like the root of the tree, *Al-Bari* like the trunk, *Al- Muṣawwir* like the branches, and the forms of the world like the leaves and fruit.

O Humankind!
Worship your Sustainer,
who has created you and those who lived before you,
so that you might remain conscious of the One
who has made the earth a resting-place for you and the sky a canopy,
and has sent water down from the sky
and with it brought forth fruits for your sustenance:
then don't claim that there is any power that could rival God,
when you grasp the truth.
[*Sūrah Al-Baqarah* (The Cow) 2:21-22]

God has hidden the sea and revealed the foam,
He has hidden the wind and revealed the dust. . . .
How could the dust rise of itself. . . .
Yet you see the dust, not the wind.
How could the foam move without the sea?
But you see the foam and not the sea, amazing!

~ Jalaluddin Rumi

The Imperishable is the Real. As sparks fly upward from a blazing fire, so from the depths of the Imperishable arise all things. To the depths of the Imperishable they again descend. Self-luminous is that Being, and formless. He dwells within all and without all. . . . From him are born breath, mind, the organs of sense, ether, air, fire, water and the earth, and he binds all these together.

~ The Upanishads[3]

---

[3] *Mundaka Upanishad*, II, i: 1-4, as reprinted in *Seeing God Everywhere*, Edited by Barry McDonald, World Wisdom, Inc. 2003, p. 33.

This world, with all its stars, elements, and creatures, is come out of the invisible world; it has not the smallest thing or the smallest quality of anything but what is come forth from thence.

~ William Law (1686-1761)[4]

The heavens declare the glory of God and the firmament shows his handiwork.

~ The Prophet David, [Psalms, 29:1]

I went to the woods because I wished to live deliberately, to front only the essential facts of life, and see if I could not learn what it had to teach, and not, when I came to die, discover that I had not lived.

~ Henry David Thoreau (1817-1862)

The book of nature, my dear Henry, is full of holy lessons, ever new and ever varied; and to learn to discover these lessons should be the work of good education.

~ Mary Martha Steerwood (1775-1851)

Read nature; nature is a friend to truth.

~ Edward Young (1683-1765)

Symbolic consciousness does not only teach us how to learn something about God by paying attention to His signs in the world around us. It also purifies our souls by breaking our attachment to the world of sense-objects. It does this by transforming these objects from material facts into *truths*.

It is possible for you to own a material object or a piece of information—but it is impossible for you to own a truth. You can never make a truth other than it is, and a truth always has both the power and the right to demand that you consider and obey it. Contemplating the

---

[4] *Selected Mystical Writings*, quoted in *A Treasury of Traditional Wisdom* by Whitall Perry (London, 1971), p. 26.

forms of the world as symbols, we contemplate God—but we need always to remember that God is also looking. As the Prophet Muḥammad ﷺ said, "Pray to God as if you saw him, because even if you don't see Him, He sees you."[5]

When my faithful servant draws near to me by his voluntary devotions, then I love him and I become the ear with which he hears, the eye with which he sees, the tongue with which he speaks, the hand with which he grasps, the foot with which he walks.

~ *Ḥadith* of the Prophet Muḥammad ﷺ[6]

---

[5] Charles Upton, contributor.

[6] A *Ḥadith* is a saying of the Prophet Muḥammad ﷺ. This *ḥadith is* noted in the *ḥadith* collection by Bukhari.

CHAPTER ONE

BASIC PRINCIPLES

This Book of blessings We have sent down to you—
so that they may meditate on its signs[7]
and that people of insight might take them to heart.
[*Sūrah Ṣād* 38:29]

A Sign for them is the earth that is dead;
We give it life and produce grain from it
of which you eat.
And We produce there orchards with date-palms and vines
and We cause springs to gush forth from within it,
that they may enjoy the fruits there.
It was not their hands that made this;
will they not then give thanks?
Limitless in His glory is God Who created in pairs
all things that the earth produces
as well as their own humankind
as well as things of which they have no knowledge.
And a sign for them is the night:
We withdraw the day from it
and see how they are plunged in darkness;
And the Sun runs his course for a period designated for him
that is determined by the will of the Almighty, the All-Knowing.
And the moon—We have measured mansions for her to pass through
until curved like a withered date-stalk she returns.
The sun is not permitted to overtake the moon
nor can the night go beyond the day,
but each moves easily in its lawful way.
[*Sūrah Yā Sīn* (O Thou Human Being) 36:33-40]

---

[7] Signs: *ayat* means both "verse" as well as "signification" or "sign."

Blessed be the One in Whose hands is sovereignty:
and He has power over all things—
He Who created death and life
that He may test which of you is best in deeds.
And He is the Almighty, the One Who is Ever Ready to Forgive,
He Who created the seven heavens in harmony;
no lack of proportion will you see
in that which the Most Compassionate has created—
just look again: can you see any flaw?
[*Sūrah Al-Mulk* (Dominion) 67:3]

And He it is who has created the heavens and the earth
in accordance with an inner truth—
and the Day He says, "Be," it is.
His word is the Truth.
And His will be the dominion
on the Day when the trumpet of resurrection sounds.
He knows all that is beyond the reach of a created being's perception,
as well as all that can be witnessed:
for He alone is Truly Wise, All-Aware.
[*Sūrah Al-Anᶜām* (Cattle) 6:73]

The Journey Towards Knowledge

~ Muhammad Asad[8]

For, indeed, it was Islam that had carried the early Muslims to tremendous cultural heights by directing all their energies toward conscious thought as the only means to understanding the nature of God's creation and, thus, of His will. No demand had been made of them to

---

[8] Muhammad Asad, *The Road To Mecca*, Dar Al-Andalus, Gibraltar, 1980, (republished by The Book Foundation in conjunction with Fons Vitae, 2004), pp. 191-192.

believe in dogmas difficult or even impossible of intellectual comprehension; in fact, no dogma whatsoever was to be found in the Prophet's message: and, thus, the thirst after knowledge which distinguished early Muslim history had not been forced, as elsewhere in the world, to assert itself in a painful struggle against the traditional faith. On the contrary, it had stemmed exclusively from that faith. The Arabian Prophet had declared that "Striving after knowledge is a most sacred duty of every Muslim man and woman," and his followers were led to understand that only by acquiring knowledge could they fully worship the Lord. When they pondered the Prophet's saying, "God creates no disease without creating a cure for it as well," they realized that by searching for unknown cures they would contribute to a fulfillment of God's will on earth: and so medical research became invested with the holiness of a religious duty.

They read the Koran verse, *We create every living thing out of water—* and in their endeavour to penetrate to the meaning of these words, they began to study living organisms and the laws of their development: and thus they established the science of biology. The Koran pointed to the harmony of the stars and their movements as witnesses of their Creator's glory: and thereupon the sciences of astronomy and mathematics were taken up by the Muslims with a fervour which in other religions was re-served for prayer alone. The Copernican system, which established the earth's rotation around its axis and the revolution of the planets around the sun, was evolved in Europe at the beginning of the sixteenth century (only to be met by the fury of the ecclesiastics, who read in it a contradiction of the literal teachings of the Bible): but the foundations of this system had actually been laid six hundred years earlier, in Muslim countries—for already in the ninth and tenth centuries Muslim astronomers had reached the conclusion that the earth was globular and that it rotated around its axis, and had made accurate calculations of latitudes and longitudes; and many of them maintained—without ever being accused of heresy—that the earth rotated around the sun. And in the same way they took to chemistry and physics and physiology, and to all the other sciences in which the Muslim genius was to find its most lasting monument. In building that monument they did no more than follow the admonition of their Prophet that "If anybody proceeds on his way in search of knowledge, God will make easy for him the way to Paradise"; that "The scientist walks in the path of God"; that "The superiority of the learned over the mere pious is like the superiority of the moon when it is full over all other stars"; and that "The ink of the scholars is more precious than the blood of martyrs."

Throughout the whole creative period of Muslim history—that is to say, during the first five centuries after the Prophet's time—science and learning had no greater champion than Muslim civilization and no home more secure than the lands in which Islam was supreme.

Sea, Earth, and Sky
~ Charles Recknagel[9]

[Professor Fuat Sezgin], a leading authority on the Golden Age of Islamic Science (from the 8th to the 16th centuries) has published thirteen volumes detailing the accomplishments of Arabic-Islamic science. He posits that it was the unusual "receptiveness" of the Muslims that enabled Muslim science to quickly become the world's dominant scientific tradition.

Sezgin says it has long been recognized that Muslim navigators undertook sea voyages over vast distances, which gave them a more complete view of geography than the ancient Greeks and Romans. But he says he believes he is the first to compile a comprehensive collection of evidence showing how Muslim cartographers combined the navigators' information with studies of astronomy and mathematics to compile maps of astonishing precision for their day. . . .

One of his greatest successes was tracking down a copy of a particularly famous map that Western scholars knew existed from Arab

---

[9] Excerpted from a 2004 feature article by Charles Recknagel, Copyright © 2006. RFE/RL, Inc. Reprinted with the permission of Radio Free Europe/Radio Liberty, 1201 Connecticut Ave. NW. Washington, DC 20036. http://www.rferl.org.

histories but which was generally assumed to be lost. That is the map of the world that Caliph al-Ma'mum, who reigned in Baghdad from 813 to 833 AD, commissioned from a large group of astronomers and geographers. "Many geographers, many astronomers, many mathematics scholars made this map. Historians of geography knew of this map, but by its name only. I [finally] found this map in an encyclopedia in Topkapi Sarai,"[10] Sezgin says. The map shows large parts of the Eurasian and African continents with recognizable coastlines and major seas. It depicts the world as it was known to the captains of the Arab sailing dhows which, with planks secured by palm-fiber ropes rather than nails, used the monsoon wind cycles to trade over vast distances. Western historians recognize that by the 9th century, Arab sea traders had reached Canton, in China.

Sezgin says the Caliph al-Ma'mum map illustrates how far the Muslim cartographers departed from earlier world views. The maps of the Greeks and Romans reveal a good knowledge of closed seas like the Mediterranean but little understanding of the vast ocean expanses beyond. "This map [shows] the Muslims knew the continents are islands, not like the Greeks' thinking that the seas are closed seas," Sezgin says. . . . He says Muslim scientists were able to make such advances because they were ready to build on the work of earlier scholars—Muslim or otherwise. . . .

"The Arabs, the Muslims, had taken from Christians, from Jews, from [Persia] without complexes. The Muslims were tolerant. The Muslims had accepted these Christians and Jews as teachers. That's very important, because the period of the reception of science was [thus just] 200 years," Sezgin says. . . .

Muslim science never disappeared. Instead, it reemerged as part of the new body of science developing in Europe as scholars there—in their turn—borrowed liberally from Muslim scholars before them. Sezgin says Portuguese and Spanish navigators used the knowledge they gained from Muslim cartographers while Iberia was under Arab domination to launch their own voyages of discovery. Those great sea journeys, including the

---

[10] The Museum of the Topkapi Palace in Istanbul, Turkey.

circumnavigation of the world and the discovery of the Americas, helped lead to a modern view of Earth as a globe containing all of the major continents.

Nothing is too wonderful to be true if it be consistent with the laws of nature.

~ Michael Faraday

Nature's laws are the invisible government of the earth.

~ Alfred A. Montapert

Nature uses as little as possible of anything.

~ Johannes Kepler

Human subtlety will never devise an invention more beautiful, more simple or more direct than does nature, because in her inventions nothing is lacking and nothing is superfluous.

~ Leonardo da Vinci

No snowflake ever falls in the wrong place.

~ Zen Proverb

Outer and Inner Space

~ Guy Murchie.[11]

When I was a child I used to think that little things were simpler than big things, but one day, wandering in the woods, I suddenly understood that the smallness of an acorn may not really make it any simpler than the oak, for it as surely contains oaks as the oak contains acorns. And ever since then, whenever space outside our world of sense seems more important or more impressive than space within the atom, I can remind myself that the differences are only relative and almost certainly illusory. Are not the crystal world of the snowflake and the symmetrical lattice of metal as real as a comet or the Milky Way? And what of the wild microscopic jungles of yeasts and bacteria that have been making bread and cheese . . . since long before man could understand fermentation? Who are we to tell our genes what they may grow or our flesh its rate of metabolism? Can an emperor banish a case of sniffles? Is the elephant master of the mouse?

To grasp the meaning of size, one must consider the fact that outer space after all is made of nothing but inner space even as great Babylon was built of little bricks or a whale is outnumbered by its billions of invisible cells. Nor is inner space closer to our reach than outer space, paradoxical though this may appear, for its true dimensions and dynamic laws are even less understood than the more classic forces of the universe outside. In actuality, both kinds of space pervade our entire world, and as truly as the great suns of the remote sky radiate with the vibrations of their atomic parts do the orbits of our inmost structure add up to the amazing complexity and bulk of this material universe.

---

[11] Guy Murchie, *Music of the Spheres*. The Riverside Press, Cambridge, 1961, p. 230.

At Whose Command?

~ Kena Upanishad[12]

Speech, eyes, ears, limbs, life, energy, come to my help. These books have Spirit for theme. I shall never deny Spirit, nor Spirit deny me. Let me be in union, communion with Spirit. When I am one with Spirit, may the laws these books proclaim live in me, may the laws live.

The enquirer asked: "What has called my mind to the hunt? What has made my life begin? What wags in my tongue? What God has opened my eye and ear?"

The teacher answered: "It lives in all that lives, hearing through the ear, thinking through the mind, speaking through the tongue, seeing through the eye. The wise man clings neither to this nor that, rises out of sense, attains immortal life.

"Eye, tongue, cannot approach it nor mind know; not knowing, we cannot satisfy enquiry. It lies beyond the known, beyond the unknown. We know through those who have preached it, have learned it from tradition.

"That which makes the tongue speak, but needs no tongue to explain, that alone is Spirit; not what sets the world by the ears.

"That which makes the mind think, but needs no mind to think, that alone is Spirit; not what sets the world by the ears.

"That which makes the eye see, but needs no eye to see, that alone is Spirit; not what sets the world by the ears.

"That which makes the ear hear, but needs no ear to hear, that alone is Spirit; not what sets the world by the ears.

"That which makes life live, but needs no life to live, that alone is Spirit; not what sets the world by the ears."

---

[12] *The Ten Principal Upanishads*, put into English by W.B. Yeats and Shree Purohit Swami. Collier Books, Macmillan Publishing Co, Inc., NY, NY, 1975, pp. 19-20.

Such is God, your Sustainer: there is no god but Hu,
the Creator of everything: then worship Him alone—
for it is He who has everything in His care.
No vision can encompass Him,
but He encompasses all human vision:
for He alone is Subtle Beyond Comprehension, All-Aware.
Means of insight have now come to you
from your Sustainer through this divine Message.
[*Sūrah Al-Anᶜām* (Cattle) 6:102-104]

CHAPTER TWO

UNITY

For with God are the keys to the Unseen:
the treasures that none knows but He.
And He knows all that is on the land and in the sea;
and not a leaf falls but He knows it;
and neither is there a grain in the earth's deep darkness,
nor anything alive or dead, but is recorded in a clear record.
And He it is who causes you to be as dead at night,
and knows what you do during the day;
and each day He brings you back to life
so that a term set by Him might be fulfilled.
In the end, to Him you must return;
and He will make you understand all that you did.
[Sūrah Al-Anʿām (Cattle) 6:59-60]

Truly, God is the One who splits the grain and the kernel apart,
bringing forth the living from the dead,
and He is the One who brings forth the dead
out of that which is alive.
This then, is God: how then can you be so deluded?
He is the One who causes the dawn to break;
and He has made the night to be a source of stillness,
and the sun and the moon for reckoning
by the order of the Almighty, the All-Knowing.
And He it is who has made the stars for you
so that you might be guided by them
through the darknesses of land and sea:
clearly have We detailed Our signs for people of inner knowing.
And He it is who has brought you all into being
out of a single soul,
and so designated for each of you a time-limit on earth
and a resting-place after death:
clearly have We detailed Our signs for people who can grasp the truth.
[Sūrah Al-Anʿām (Cattle) 6:95-98]

It is He who has created you all out of one soul.
[*Sūrah Al-Aʿrāf* (The Faculty of Discernment) 7:189]

Say: "God is the Creator of all things;
He is the One, the Supreme, the Irresistible."
[*Surah Ar-Raʿd* (Thunder) 13:16]

The Signs of God in Mathematics and Geometry: An Islamic Perspective

~ Charles Upton

Within Islam God is referred to as *Al-Ahad,* the One, and as *Al-Haqq,* the Absolute Truth and Reality. Unity is the central doctrine of Islam. The Unity of God is reflected, imperfectly but still clearly, in His creation.

In Islamic doctrine, God is said to be both incomparable (*tanzih*), and also capable of being compared (*tashbih*) with various aspects of the created world—at least up to a point. In English terminology, *tanzih* is God's *transcendence,* while *tashbih* is His *immanence.* Without *tashbih,* the signs of God could not appear in nature; without *tanzih,* nature would literally be God. In the *surah al-Fatihah* God is called Lord of the Worlds, Owner of the Day of Judgement. . . . This is *tashbih.* In the *surah al-Ikhlas,* it is said that He neither begets nor is begotten, and there is nothing to which He can be compared. This is *tanzih.*

Both *tanzih* and *tashbih* are reflected in the world of mathematics. Pythagoras, Plato, and their followers believed that mathematics and the various sciences based on it—music, geometry, etc.—were the best possible preliminary training for the understanding of eternal truths. This view of mathematics was inherited, and even further developed, by the philosophers and scientists of Islam. According to Seyyed Hossein Nasr,

21

"Any first-hand knowledge of Islamic civilization and particularly the Islamic sciences reveals the 'privileged position' of mathematics in the Islamic tradition. There are crystalline and geometric aspects to Islamic art and architecture, a love of arithmetic and numerical symbolism in both the plastic and auditory arts—especially poetry and music—an 'algebra' of language and of thought so clearly reflected in Arabic and also in many other Islamic languages, and numerous other tangible manifestations which make plain the central role of traditional mathematics in Islamic art and civilization and on the highest level in the spiritual 'style' of Islam so directly reflected in its sacred art.

This love for mathematics, especially geometry and number, is directly connected to the essence of the Islamic message, which is the doctrine of Unity (al-tawhid). God is One; hence the number one in the series of numbers is the most direct and intelligible symbol of the Source. And the series of numbers themselves is a ladder by which man ascends from the world of multiplicity to the One."[13]

Just as the eternal principles or Names of God are reflected in mathematics, so mathematical principles and relationships are reflected directly in nature: in the structure of atoms and crystals, in the design of cells, flowers and other living things, in the orbits of the planets and the revolutions of the galaxies—in fact, in virtually anything we can investigate.

You are plurality transformed into Unity.
And Unity passing into plurality:
This mystery is understood when man
Leaves the part and merges in the Whole.

~ Shabistari

---

[13] Seyyid Hossein Nasr, *Islamic Science: An Illustrated Study*, p. 75

Thou art the fire,
Thou art the sun,
Thou art the air,
Thou art the moon,
Thou art the starry firmament,
Thou art Brahman Supreme:
Thou art the waters,
The creator of all!

Thou art woman, thou art man,
Thou art the youth, thou art the maiden,
Thou art the old man tottering with his staff;
Thou facest everywhere.
Thou art the dark butterfly,
Thou art the green parrot with red eyes,
Thou art the thunder cloud, the seasons, the seas.
Without beginning art thou, beyond time, beyond space.
Thou art he from whom sprang the three worlds.

~ *The Upanishads*[114]

He it is who has made the earth a cradle for you.
[*Sūrah Ṭā Hā* (O Man) 20:53]

Behold, the heaven and the heaven of heavens is the Lord's, thy God,
the earth also, with all that is therein.

~ The Bible, Deuteronomy 10:14

---

[14] *Svetasvatara Upanishad*, IV:2-4.

THE BOOK OF NATURE

Only You

~ Levi Yitzchak of Berditchov[15]

Where I wander—You!
Where I ponder—You!
Only You everywhere, You, always, You.
You, You, You.
When I am gladdened—You!
When I am saddened, You!
Only You, everywhere, You!
You, You, You.
Sky is You!
Earth is You!
You above! You below!
In every trend, at every end,
Only You, everywhere You!

The Quest for Unity

~ Axel Reisinger[16]

What could quantum mechanics have in common with the philosophical musings of the ancient Greeks? In our age of multimillion-dollar supercolliders, it's hard to imagine that modern physics owes anything to thinkers who predate Descartes. But French physicists Etienne Klein and Marc Lachieze-Rey see an unbroken thread running from antiquity to the present—an ongoing search, throughout the history of science, for unity.

In *The Quest for Unity* the authors reveal how the quest for the One has driven all the great breakthroughs in science. They show how the Greeks searched for the fundamental element in all things; how Galileo

---

[15] Reprinted from *Seeing God Everywhere,* Edited by Barry McDonald, World Wisdom, Inc. Copyright © 2003 World Wisdom, p. 252.

[16] This selection is excerpted from pp. vii-viii, and pp. 130-131 from *The Quest for Unity, The Adventure of Physics* by Etienne Klein and Marc Lachieze-Rey, translated by Axel Reisinger, Copyright © 1999 by Oxford University Press. Used by permission of Oxford University Press, 1999.

unified the earth with the heavens by discovering valleys and mountains on the moon; and how Newton created a single theory to describe the motion of the celestial bodies. . . .Throughout the book, the authors stress the aesthetic motives of scientists, how they recognize truth through apprehension of mathematical beauty. And in tracing the quest for unity up to the present day, they illuminate the bizarre workings of quantum mechanics and the sticky definition of reality itself at the subatomic level. A grand unification of all interactions still awaits discovery—but as Klein and Lachieze-Rey show, the search itself is as fascinating as the end result may ever be.[17]

According to physicists Etienne Klein and Marc Lachieze-Rey, science could not exist without a sense that there is an underlying unity to the universe. The struggle to give conceptual expression to this unity is the central thrust of physics:

> The immenseness and diversity of the universe are awe-inspiring. The richness of the creation and the myriad forms it assumes seem far too boundless for us ever to hope to encapsulate them in a few principles. Can the world even be fathomed? The very idea of an underlying unity seems preposterous, almost insane right from the outset. The moment it is articulated, it is belied by the world itself. What could a star, a cloud, a snowflake, a living cell, an atom, and a quark possibly have in common? How could anyone reconcile the notion of unity with so many plausible and reasonable arguments that justify splintering reality into disconnected pieces? Indeed, everything points to multiplicity as an unassailable characteristic of the physical world.
>
> And yet, without Unity as a beacon, the world, indeed human thought itself, would scatter into a dust of things and ideas impossible to integrate. The very concept of universe would become senseless. The history of human thought offers a decidedly different panorama, one that is full of syntheses, bridges, unifications, and sometimes even outright fusions. The most remarkable successes have revolved around matter and its interactions. The credit goes to men of science who have managed to distill from a profusion of phenomena and

---

[17] Ibid., dust jacket introduction.

25

concepts a few guiding principles capable of organizing and unifying the infinite diversity of everyday experience. Indeed, almost every single "great physicist" recorded by history has contributed unifications that changed the reach and power of physics, transforming it into something more than a simple patchwork of disparate theories.

Galileo, for instance, reconciled the sublunar and supralunar worlds when his telescope revealed mountains and valleys on the surface of the moon. Newton created a single theory to describe the motion of the earth and that of the celestial bodies. Maxwell unified electricity and magnetism. Fraunhofer demonstrated that the physical laws discovered here on earth apply just as well to stars. Louis de Broglie established a connection between waves and particles. Perhaps the most famous case is that of Albert Einstein, who melded space and time, until then completely distinct, into a unified space-time concept. He later devoted much energy looking for a unifying theory that would encompass both the universe taken as a whole and the laws governing its elementary constituents.

But from this vantage point, does science really differ from thought itself? The longing for Unity is without a doubt a requisite for intelligibility. It is a fundamental need of man's intellect with its thirst for synthesis. At least, such was Leibniz's opinion. He felt that the One (together with being, substance, sameness, cause, perception, and reasoning) is part of the innate notions anchored in our minds, without which the data of human experience would remain incomprehensible. Immanuel Kant shared the same view. He described understanding as "the power to reduce phenomena to the unity of rules," and reason as "the ability to subjugate the rules of understanding to unity by means of principles." It would be difficult to articulate more clearly the monism pervading the pursuit of knowledge.

Be that as it may, it is in the sciences that the quest for unity has produced the most spectacular results. It continues to stimulate a considerable amount of research. During the 1970s, two types of phenomena—electromagnetism and weak interactions (the latter being responsible for, among other things, the decay of a neutron into a proton, an electron, and a third particle called antineutrino)—ostensibly quite dissimilar in their phenomenology, were formally united within the framework of a new and broader theory. The so-called *standard model* was born, providing a very elegant classification scheme of the constituents of matter into three families. This encouraging success seemed to bring us one step closer to a triumphant unification.

By all evidence, the drive toward unity and synthesis is the primary impetus behind many scientific endeavors. It seems to have been a particularly fruitful and effective tool in the field of physics. Indeed, the belief that unification is the very foundation of physics and constitutes its ultimate mission is widespread. Pierre Duhem said as much explicitly: "Every physicist naturally aspires to the unity of science." This aspiration is twofold: It reflects a drive "toward the logical unity of physical theory . . . [and] toward a theory which is a natural classification of physical laws."[18]

Yet the authors realize that while physics must seek Unity, it may never be able to perfectly express Unity. And while they do not necessarily believe in religion, they recognize that only religion could (in theory) be a perfect reflection of reality, and that physics has no business presenting itself as a religion:

The search for unification continues to be the guiding principle of physics to this day. Harmony, atomism, teleology, geometrization, sundry analogies—everything is tried, discarded, and occasionally rehabilitated. The growth of knowledge results from successful consolidations and unifications of separate disciplines, notwithstanding the many failures littering its path.

Yet, modern physics is anything but unified; it appears fragmented and compartmentalized. The prospects for an all-encompassing unity are questionable at best. Indeed, it could be argued that we have never been further from a globally unified worldview, and that is a frustrating paradox.

We are faced with an apparent contradiction. On the one hand, physics is manifestly fueled by a unifying motive. Unity often results

---

[18] Ibid., p. vii-viii.

from the discovery of new concepts or hypotheses that, almost overnight, overthrow multiplicity and install homogeneity in its place. On the other hand, the process never seems to reach its culmination. Either it cannot be pushed to its ultimate conclusion, or it succeeds only too briefly until new results bring fresh elements into the picture and force a complete reassessment of where we stand. The breadth of each discipline keeps increasing and the landscape of knowledge shifts constantly. Two branches are no sooner unified than a third begins to grow. When, in turn, it is merged with the first two, still more appear. The cycle is endless, and no magic formula can ever fundamentally change that. Will we be able to reach higher levels of understanding leading to new unifications? Probably, and it is safe to predict that it will be at the cost of further setbacks to the cause of Unity. At best, partial unifications strengthen our resolve to keep searching for further breakthroughs.

If physics works at all, it is perhaps because such unifications are amenable to mathematical treatments and formulations, which become useful tools to describe, if not the world itself, at least all the matter it contains. This process—almost dialectical in nature—is absolutely vital. Should it ever stop, science would simply wither.

Under these circumstances, should we simply give up looking for the underlying unity of diverse phenomena? The answer is a resounding no—that would be tantamount to giving up on physics itself. Yet, the irony is that unification does not necessarily lead to Unity. It weaves a fabric that is never quite finished. Rarely does it offer more than a fleeting glimpse of Unity. Interim stages are a quintessential part of science and its main stimulus; they constantly provide new incentives to press on for a better understanding of things, more novel theories, and more creative insights.

Modern physics has scored remarkable triumphs. That exposes it to the risks that inevitably come with success. In its eagerness to publicize its next anticipated achievement, it can easily degenerate into metaphysical contemplations—some are beneficial because they inspire bold hypotheses, but others are far more insidious and prone to lure it into arrogant overconfidence that it is within reach of its destiny. Only if it renounces pretensions to be a perfect reflection of reality will physics continue to thrive. Its greatest challenge is to resist the temptation to project the false self-image of a religion able to reveal the ultimate truth.[19]

The World Is a Mirror

~ Mahmud Shabistari[20]

Know that the whole world is a mirror; in each atom are found a hundred blazing suns. If you split the center of a single drop of water, a hundred pure oceans spring forth. If you examine each particle of dust, a thousand Adams can be seen. . . .

A universe lies hidden in a grain of millet; everything is brought together at the point of the present. . . . From each point along that circle thousands of forms are drawn. Each point, as it revolves in a circle, is at times a circle, at others a turning circumference.

Circles

~ Michael S. Schneider [21]

Give a young child a crayon and paper and observe what he draws. At the earliest ages children scrawl lines and zigzags. There comes a time when they discover that a line's end can meet its beginning, and they take delight in the loop. It continues endlessly around and creates an inside separate from an outside. Eventually, they come upon the circle. The circle brings the loop to perfection, so round in every direction. Children love to trace circular objects like cups and cans to achieve the fascinating perfection so hard for a young hand to draw.

---

[19] Ibid., pp. 130-131.

[20] *The Wisdom of Islam*, compiled by Nacer Khēmir, Abbeville Publishing Group, New York, N.Y., 1996.

[21] This selection is excerpted from pp. 2, 4, 8, 11-17, and 20 of *A Beginner's Guide to Constructing the Universe* by Michael S. Schneider. Copyright © 1994 by Michael Schneider. Reprinted by permission of HarperCollins Publishers Inc.

The discovery and appreciation of the circle is our early glimpse into the wholeness, unity, and divine order of the universe. Some psychologists say that the discovery of the circle arrives as the child discovers the self and distinguishes himself from another. Even as adults our attention remains hypnotically drawn to circles, toward their centers, in objects we create and those we see. We draw circles and they draw us.

Looking at a circle is like looking into a mirror. We create and respond irresistibly to circles, cylinders, and spheres because we recognize ourselves in them. The message of the shape bypasses our conscious mental circuitry and speaks directly to the quiet intelligence of our deepest being. The circle is a reflection of the world's—and our own—deep perfection, unity, design excellence, wholeness, and divine nature. Everything strives in one way or another toward unity.

There's more to a circle than just a curved line. It's a wonderful first glyph of nature's alphabet. Every circle is identical. They only differ in size. Each circle you see or create is a profound statement about the transcendental nature of the universe. Expanding from the "nowhere" of its dimensionless center to the infinitely many points of its circumference, a circle implies the mysterious generation from nothing to everything. Its radius and circumference are never both measurable at the same time in similar units due to their mutual relation to the transcendental value known as "pi" = 3.1415926 . . . When either the radius or circumference is measurable in whole, rational units, the other is an endless, irrational decimal. Thus, a circle represents the limited and unlimited in one body.

Our deepest awareness, the power that motivates all awareness, which we can call the "Power to Be Conscious," of which we are not ordinarily cognizant, recognizes its own transcendental nature in the geometry of the circle. For this reason the circle has been a universal symbol of an ideal perfection and divine state that always exists around and within us whether we acknowledge it or not. Religious art has traditionally turned to the circle to symbolize this state of divinity as "heaven," "paradise," "eternity," and "enlightenment."

Nothing exists without a center around which it revolves, whether the nucleus of an atom, the heart of our body, hearth of the home, capital of a nation, sun in the solar system, or black hole at the core of a galaxy. When the center does not hold, the entire affair collapses. An idea or conversation is considered "pointless" not because it leads nowhere but because it has no *center* holding it together.

The point is the source of our whole of wholes. It is beyond understanding, unknowable, silently self-enfolded. But like a seed, a point will expand to fulfill itself as a circle.

Nature's forms represent invisible forces made visible. The force of the circle's equal expansion works through different materials. Tap the side of a round cup of liquid, and watch as perfect concentric rings appear and converge to the center, then pass it and expand outward again. Nature delights in the principle of equal expansion in concentric ripples, splashes, craters, bubbles, flowers, and exploding stars. As you open your compass, consider that you are metaphorically repeating this first principle of the Monad, the opening of light, space, time, and power in all directions.

The second principle of the Monad is expressed by the circle's rotary motion. Unlike the still center, the circumference speaks of movement. We replicate this universal principle in our geometric constructions whenever we run the compass around its point and scribe a circle. Symbolized in nearly every culture as a wheel, the circle represents nature's universal cycles, circulations, circuits, orbits, periodicities, vibrations, and rhythms.

Because cycles are a principle of the Monad, they are all-pervasive in the universe. We are thoroughly enmeshed in cycles and periodic rhythms but notice only the most obvious, like our breath and hunger or the time or season.

All cycles have rising and declining phases. When one side goes up, the other goes down. This is true on any scale, in turning wheels and in the rising/falling pulse of an emotional burst, the changing amount of daylight through the seasons, the rise and decline of great cultures, and the life cycles of stars.

Observe a rapidly cycling bicycle wheel or ceiling fan. When it revolves slowly we can see each individual spoke or blade, but when it turns faster our nervous system just cannot register the revolutions as discontinuous, and beyond about 1,550 cycles per second the spokes and fan appear as a solid disk. Look around at any "solid" object. Be aware that the appearance of its "surface" is due to rapidly oscillating atoms, which move so fast as to give our nervous system the *impression* of a smooth surface. The same is true for our sense of hearing. A card held against turning bicycle spokes or the teeth of a turning gear will produce discrete sounds until the rapidity is such that the sound is perceived as a continuous hum. All senses are fooled by rapid cyclic vibration so that even texture, smell, and taste appear as continuous to our registration faculties.

Every process is characterized by cycles. The appearances of the entire world with all its natural and technological cycles are images rooted in the archetypal cyclic principle of the Monad represented by the geometer's turning compass. Cooperating with nature requires that we recognize the existence, and learn the ways, of its omnipresent cycles.

The third all-pervasive principle of the Monad involves the area *within* the circumference. A circle is not just the curve but the miraculous space inside, which manifests between nothingness (zero-dimensional point) and everything (infinitely many points around the circumference).

A circle expresses the most practical and efficient geometric space for natural and human creations to occur. Of all shapes a circle encloses the most space by the smallest perimeter. In other words, the most enclosure with least exposure. The Monad's third principle is maximized efficiency.

The Monad, or oneness, expressed as a point and a circle, is the foundation for our geometric construction of the universe. The three parts of the circle—center, circumference, and radius forming the space within—correspond to the three principles of the Monad: equal expansion, cycles, and efficient space. These principles, along with the Monad's wholeness, are all-pervasive and lie at the foundation of the world's objects and events, as the number one is hidden within every integer.

The Monad is knowable to us through its expression in nature's designs and human affairs as equal expansion, cycles, and efficient space. Natural structures are universally recognized as beautiful and most efficient. We, too, are part of the world's harmonious design and can't help but express the Monad's principles in the things we do and create.

Philosophy in Warm Weather

~ Jane Kenyon[22]

Now all the doors and windows
Are open, and we move so easily
Through the rooms. Cats roll
On the sunny rugs, and a clumsy wasp
Climbs the pane, pausing
To rub a leg over her head.

All around physical life reconvenes.
The molecules of our bodies must love
To exist: they whirl in circles
And seem to begrudge us nothing.
Heat, Horatio, *heat* makes them
Put this antic disposition on!

This year's brown spider
Sways over the door as I come
And go. A single poppy shouts
From the far field, and the crow,
Beyond alarm, goes right on
Pulling up the corn.

Sacred Circles

~ Black Elk[23]

You have noticed that everything an Indian does is in a circle, and that is because the Power of the World always works in circles, and everything tries to be round. In the old days when we were a strong and happy people, all our power came to us from the sacred hoop of the nation, and so long as the hoop was unbroken, the people flourished. The flowering tree was the living center of the hoop, and the circle of the four quarters nourished it. The east gave peace and light, the south gave warmth, the west gave rain, and the north with its cold and mighty wind gave strength and endurance. This knowledge came to us from the outer world with our religion. Everything the Power of the World does is done in a circle. The sky is round, and I have heard that the earth is round like a ball, and so are all the stars. The wind, in its greatest power, whirls. Birds make their nests in circles, for theirs is the same religion as ours.

Al-Tawhid, Unity

~ Charles Upton

The central doctrine of Islam is *al-tawhid,* Unity. God is One; there is no god but God. And the Unity of God is reflected in the universe, in the unity of nature's laws, as well as in the uniqueness of each object in nature. To construct circles is to make a geometrical diagram of *al-tawhid.*

The Arabic word for "heart," *qalb,* is derived from the root QLB or QBL, which embraces a number of concepts having to do with "turning." In Sufi metaphysics the Heart is the center of the psyche, the point at which it is intersected by the vertical ray of the Spirit *(ruh).* This

---

[23] Black Elk quoted from *Black Elk Speaks* by John G. Neihardt, Copyright 1961 by the John G. Neihardt Trust, University of Nebraska Press, Lincoln, Nebraska, 1979, pp. 194-195.

34

symbolic image has obvious affinities with the act of constructing a circle using a compass and a sheet of paper. The Heart is who we really are in the sight of God; it is the central point of our full and authentic humanity. Whoever wants to rise along the vertical path of the Spirit, the *axis mundi*, first has to have reached the Center, the Heart, which is another way of saying that we can't relate to God with only a part of ourselves. A line drawn from any point on the circumference of a circle so as to intersect a line passing vertically through the circle's center can never be one with the infinite elevation which the vertical line symbolizes. It must intersect the vertical line at some point short of infinity. Furthermore, it only "represents" its own point-of-origin on the circumference; it can in no way stand for the circle and the whole. But the center of the circle does stand for the whole circle, since it is the point from which the circle expands, and to which it returns. And only the central point of the circle is available to the ray of infinite elevation which symbolizes the relationship between the human form and God. It is said that God holds the Heart between His fingers, and turns it however He will. This is a way of saying that the Heart is the reality through which we can see how all the changes-of-state we experience in passing time have the same Point-of-Origin; that change on the horizontal plane is an expression of permanence on the vertical one; that the *waqt*, the present moment of spiritual time, is the manifestation of God's eternity in the created world. And just as God *turns* the Heart however He will, so the Heart is the point through which and by which the human soul *returns* to God on the spiritual Path; it is the spiritual Kaaba, the *qiblah* toward which we turn.

The Kaaba

~ Ali, Aliaa, and Aisha Rafea[24]

People in Islam have one direction all over the world when they pray. It is the Center that they focus upon. This center is called *Ka'aba* or *baytullah,* the Holy Home. They also name it *Kebia* (Direction). Turning the face to the direction of the Holy Home connotes that God's message will remain on earth and should be sought herein.

Daily practices of prayers are distributed throughout the day with the movement of the Earth around the Sun. The Sun as the Center, around which the earth revolves, symbolizes Truth as the central goal of the human being, around which his life revolves. Observing times (dawn, noon, afternoon, sunset, night) reminds man all the day long of his intimate relation to Allah.

We can also speculate upon each time of prayer. The dawn time points to the rise of light pushing away the darkness. Prayers would support man to overcome whatever darkness is enveloping his life. The noon-time symbolizes the state in which the power of Light is all prevailing. The afternoon is a stage in which the Light is about to decline. With the sunset man begins a stage of darkness. Night prayer points to a stage where man is completely encircled with darkness with no ray of light, yet he keeps seeking the Supreme Power. Praying in all times can help man focus on the ultimate goal of life which is to be attached to

---

[24]Ali, Aliaa & Aisha Rafea, *Beyond Diversities. Reflections on Revelations.* Sadek Publishing, Cairo, 2000, pp. 90-91.

The Kaaba is centered in Mecca. It is the temple which was dedicated to the One God by Abraham, and originally, before him, it is said, built by Adam, which was then later cleansed and rededicated by Muhammad. It is towards this point that all Muslims turn in prayer five times a day—towards this place of unity. The Kaaba itself is empty, indicating the pure space within the heart where we are closest to God. "Allah" is the name of God used by Arabic speaking Christians as well as Muslims. Jews, Christians, and Muslims all share the monotheistic heritage of Abraham, may peace be with them all and with all communities and their prophets and messengers of God. (C.A.H.)

Allah. With the rotation of the light and darkness, he purifies his soul and empowers his will.

Prayer restrains from shameful and unjust deeds; and remembrance of Allah is the greatest (thing in life) without doubt. [Sūrah 29:45]."

Veriditas

~ Hildegard von Bingen[25]

O most powerful path
that has entered into everything
the heights, the earth,
and the depths,
you fashion and gather everything
around you:
clouds float, air streams,
stones become wet,
waters create rivers
and the earth perspires greenness.

---

[25] Hildegard von Bingen, *Writings of Medieval Women*, Marcelle Thiebaux, translator. Copyright 1994 by Marcelle Thiebaux, Garland Publishing, NY, NY.

CHAPTER THREE

INTERDEPENDENCE

The Most Gracious!
It is He Who has taught the Qur'an.
He has created the human being.
He has taught them clear thought and speech.
The sun and the moon follow their designated paths;
and the herbs and the trees—both bow in adoration.
And He has raised high the heavens,
and He has devised a balance
so that you might not measure wrongly.
So weigh justly and don't measure lightly.
And the earth He has outspread for all creatures
with fruit on it and date-palms bearing enclosed clusters
and grain on tall stalks and sweetly fragrant plants;
which then of your Sustainer's blessings will you deny?
[*Sūrah Ar-Raḥmān* (The Most Gracious) 55:1-13]

One glorious chain of love, of giving and receiving, unites all living things. All things exist in continuous reciprocal activity—one for All, All for one. None has power, or means, for itself; each receives only in order to give, and gives in order to receive, and finds therein the fulfillment of the purpose of its existence: HaShem (YHWH/the Lord). "Love," say the Sages, "love that supports and is supported in turn. That is the character of the Universe."

~ Rabbi Samson Raphael Hirsch[26]

When one tugs at a single thing in nature, he finds it attached to the rest of the world.

~ John Muir

---

[26] Rabbi Samson Raphael Hirsch, "The Nineteen Letters," 3rd letter (end), Germany, 1808-1888. Reprinted from *The Animal's Lawsuit Against Humanity*, Fons Vitae, Lexington, KY, p. 89.

The Prophet Muḥammad ﷺ said, "You see the faithful in their mutual sympathy, love and affection, like one body. When one member has a complaint, the rest of the body is united with it in wakefulness and fever."[27]

"By Him in Whose hand my soul is, a man does not have faith until he likes for his brother what he likes for himself."

"God says, (*ḥadith qudsi*)[28] 'I am with the thought of my servant concerning Me; and I am with him when he remembers Me; and when he remembers Me within himself, I remember him within Myself; and if he remembers Me in public, I remember him in a public better than his own.' "

O you who have come to faith!
Be patient, and persevere in patience,
and keep your connection,
and remain conscious of God,
so that you might attain felicity.
[*Sūrah Al ʿImrān* (The House Of ʿImrān) 3:200]

Anthem

~ W. H. Auden

Let us praise our Maker, with true passion extol Him.
Let the whole creation give out another sweetness,
Nicer in our nostrils, a novel fragrance
From cleansed occasions in accord together
As one feeling fabric, all flushed and intact,
Phenomena and numbers announcing in one
Multitudinous ecumenical song
Their grand givenness of gratitude and joy,

---

[27] *Ḥadith* appearing in Bukhari and Muslim.

[28] *Ḥadith qudsi* are sacred sayings spoken by God through the Prophet as distinguished from the Prophet's own utterances (*Ḥadith*) or the direct revelation of the Qurʾan. (C.A.H.)

Peaceable and plural, their positive truth
An authoritative This, an unthreatened Now
When, in love and in laughter, each lives itself,
For, united by His Word, cognition and power,
System and Order, are a single glory,
And the pattern is complex, their places safe.

The Grace of Sharing

~ Ibn Kathīr

Fuhayra, freed-man of Abu Bakr, and their guide 'Abd Allah b. Urayqit al-Laythi, passed by the two tents of Umm Ma'bad al-Khuza'iyya:

"Umm Ma'bad was a good, fearless, strong woman who would sit with her legs drawn up, wrapped in her garment, at the entrance to the tent and give out food and drink. They asked her whether she had any meat or milk they could buy from her. But they obtained none from her and she told them, 'If we had anything, you would not lack for hospitality, but our people are all out of provisions and we've been suffering drought.'

"The Messenger of God ﷺ noticed a goat at the side of her tent and said, 'What about that goat, Umm Ma'bad?' She replied, 'She's a goat left over from the goats after the drought.' 'Does she give milk?' he asked. 'No, she's too dried up for that,' she replied. 'Would you permit me to milk her?' he asked. 'If she has any milk you can,' she replied.

"The Messenger of God ﷺ called to the goat and stroked it, speaking God's name, wiped her teat and again invoked God's name. Then he called for a vessel large enough to satisfy them, and the goat opened its legs and milk poured out in a copious flow until it was full. He gave (the vessel to) her to drink, and then his Companions and thereafter they all had a second drink. When they were all quenched, he drank too, saying, 'The one who pours drinks last!' He put milk in it again, left it with her, and then they departed.

He went on, "Soon her husband, Abu Ma'bad, came home, leading emaciated goats, staggering they were so weak, and their brains scarcely functioning. When he saw the milk, he was amazed and said, 'Where did this milk come from, Umm Ma'bad? We don't have a milch-camel and the goat has not been with a male.' 'Well, a man who was blessed came past us'. . . ."[29]

In our world, we need a clear awareness of the interdependent nature of nations, of humans and animals, and of humans, animals, and the world. Everything is of interdependent nature. I feel that many problems, especially man-made problems, are due to a lack of knowledge about this interdependent nature.

~ His Holiness the Dalai Lama[30]

The Tree of Life: Connecting Life and the Universe

~ Kaminaga Zenji[31]

Around the time when the autumn harvest has finished and things have settled back down somewhat in Japan, in India the rainy monsoon season that cooled the scorching earth comes to an end, the sky becomes clear,

---

[29] Imām Abū'l-Fidā' Ismāʾil ibn Kathīr, *The Life of the Prophet Muḥammad*, translated by Prof. Trevor Le Gassick (Reading, United Kingdom: Garnet Publishing Limited, 1998, 2000), Vol. II, p. 172. This and other excerpts from *The Life of the Prophet Muhammad* included within this volume are reprinted by permission from Garnet Publishing.

It is Umm Ma'bad's description of this blessed man to her husband that is one of the most well-known and beloved descriptions of Muhammad 鸞 that has come down to us. See *The Book of Character*, by Camille Helminski, p. 2.

[30] His Holiness the Dalai Lama, *The Path to Tranquility, Daily Wisdom*. Edited by Renuka Singh, Viking Arkana, member of Penguin Putnam Inc., New York, NY, 1999, p. 95.

[31] Kaminaga Zenji, *The Wealth of Asia, in Search of Common Values*, ICG Muse, Inc. NY, NY, 2001, p. 27.

41

and a period of cool weather sets in, leading to the dry season. One such fine day, I was at the foot of the Bodhi tree at the Mahabodhi Monastery in the city of Bodhgaya. This Bodhi tree was planted at the spot along the Niranjana River where Gautama Buddha attained enlightenment.

The Bodhi tree which they speak of in India refers to a pipal tree, which belongs to the mulberry family. Around the time of year described above, it is laden with small fruit more like tiny round figs than the mulberries found in Japan, each about the size of the tip of one's baby finger. Little birds seem to like this fruit, and one especially often sees common mynahs, which resemble the gray starlings (Jp., *mukudori*) seen in Japan, flying back and forth picking at them.

The big pipal tree at that great monastery, its trunk perhaps a meter or so in diameter, seemed to have grown free as a breeze under that cloudless, deep azure sky, and the rays of the morning sun of autumn were shining upon it. The twitter of the mynahs carried over the tree top. What a pleasant morning moment it was.

Opening to the Moment

~ C.A.H. with Debra Kaatz[32]

In every moment we are in relationship, but do we recognize it—how we are continually in relationship with the air we breathe, with the earth upon which we walk, with the animals and plants around us, with every human being with whom we come in contact, and with our gracious Sustainer—with Life itself. To the extent that we open to that continuous relationship, to the possibility inherent within each relationship with respect and gratitude and reverence, we are able to receive more and enabled to give more.

To go into a garden in spring, or to walk through the forest or across fields of wild flowers brings life back into the spirit. Plants

---

[32] Debra Kaatz, *Wild Flower Plant Spirits*, The Petite Bergerie Press, Sourdogues, France, 2005, p. 15.

have been used for centuries to heal the mind, body, and the spirit. Gardens have been created to nourish the soul with beauty and harmony. . . . It is from within the spirit of plants and their living essence that our understanding of their healing powers comes.

In the West we can understand using the physical plant or its extracts for medicine, but the use of plants was much more than this in ancient times. In China plants were picked for a person at a certain time that was right for both the plant as well as the person in order to change what had become imbalanced. It is this untouchable realm that we experience when we are in contemplation with nature. It is a true sense of being a part of the whole energy that surrounds us and where every movement affects something else.

The Biological Matrix

~ Michael J. Denton [33]

T he cell system as revealed by molecular biology has turned out to be a unique and peerless whole in which every component is uniquely fashioned by the laws of nature for its designated role, a three-dimensional jigsaw in which all the pieces fit together as perfectly and harmoniously as the cogs in a watch. . . .

Even above the level of the individual molecule, many of the structural materials used by living things, materials such as bone, skin, tendon, calcareous shells, chitin, and wood, which are what a structural engineer would class as composites, are also remarkable for their apparently ideal biomechanical characteristics.

A final and very remarkable aspect of the fitness of the constituents of life is that most of the key organic building blocks—sugars, amino acids,

---

nucleo-tides, etc.—can be manufactured in a relatively small number of chemical steps from a small number of readily available simple molecules. It is a remarkable fact that the great majority of the atoms used in their synthesis are derived from only three very simple molecules that are available freely and in great abundance on the surface of the earth: water, carbon dioxide, and nitrogen. Not only are the key components of life wonderfully fit for their biological roles, they are all only a very small chemical distance away from such universally available starting materials. Indeed, there are not many steps from hydrogen itself—the starting point of atom creation in the stars—to the ingredients of life.

But not only is this remarkable set of key building blocks readily synthesized from available materials, they can all be readily interconverted via a small number of chemical steps. It is fortuitous, indeed, that so many of the key molecules of life, which possess so many unique chemical and physical properties, all exist within easy chemical reach of each other. The astonishing chemical proximity of all life's constituents is surely a fact of very great and crucial significance. The fitness of the individual ingredients, such as lipids, proteins, and DNA, although remarkable enough, is insufficient in itself; it is only because all the components of life can be derived easily from simple starting materials and interconverted readily that the miracle of the cell and self-replication is possible.

Contrast this with artificial systems, even fantastically simple ones quite incapable of replication, such as a motor car or a computer or a typewriter. In the case of such artificial machines, each individual component, such as a metal rod, a silicon chip, or a plastic disc, can only be manufactured by long circuitous routes involving complex industrial processes that may involve temperatures of 1,000°C and all manner of diverse chemical processes.

The emerging picture is obviously consistent with the teleological view of nature. That each constituent utilized by the cell for a particular biological role, each cog in the watch, turns out to be the only and at the same time the ideal candidate for its role is particularly suggestive of design. That the whole, the end to which all this teleological wizardry leads—the living cell—should be also ideally suited for the task of constructing the world of multicellular life reinforces the conclusion of purposeful design. . . .

Fitness for Life's Being

We may not have final proof that the cosmos is *uniquely* fit for life as it exists on earth—because the possibility of alternative life cannot yet be entirely excluded—but there is no doubt that science has clearly shown that the cosmos is *supremely* fit for life as it exists on earth. For as we have seen, the existence of life on earth depends on a very large number of astonishingly precise mutual adaptations in the physical and chemical properties of many of the key constituents of the cell: the fitness of water for carbon-based life, the mutual fitness of sunlight and life, the fitness of oxygen and oxidations as a source of energy for carbon-based life, the fitness of carbon dioxide for the excretion of the products of carbon oxidation, the fitness of bicarbonate as a buffer for biological systems, the fitness of the slow hydration of carbon dioxide, the fitness of the lipid bilayer as the boundary of the cell, the mutual fitness of DNA and proteins, and the perfect topological fit of the alpha helix of the protein with the large groove of the DNA. In nearly every case these constituents are the only available candidates for their biological roles, and each appears superbly tailored to that particular end.

If these various constituents—water, carbon dioxide, carbonic acid, the DNA helix, proteins, phosphates, sugars, lipids, the carbon atom, the oxygen atom, the transitional metal atoms and the other metal atoms from groups 1 and 2 of the periodic table, sodium, potassium, calcium, and magnesium—did not possess precisely those chemical and physical properties they exhibit in an aqueous solution ranging in temperature from 0°C to about 75°C, self-replicating carbon-based chemical machines would be impossible. And it is not only microorganisms that the cosmic design has "foreseen." Many of the properties and characteristics of life's constituents seem to be specifically arranged for large, complex, multicellular organisms like ourselves. The coincidences do not stop at the cell but extend right on into higher forms of life. These include the packaging properties of DNA, which enable a vast amount of DNA and hence biological information to be packed into the tiny volume of the cell nucleus in higher organisms; the electrical properties of cells, which depend ultimately on the insulating character of the cell membrane, which provides the basis for nerve conduction and for the coordination of the activities of multicellular organisms; the very nature of the cell, particularly its feeling and crawling activities, which seem so ideally adapted for assembling a multicellular organism during development; the fact that oxygen and carbon dioxide are both gases at ambient temperatures; and the peculiar and unique character of the bicarbonate buffer, which together greatly facilitate the life of large air-breathing macroscopic organisms.

In short, science has revealed a *vast chain of coincidences which lead inexorably to life* on earth—not just microbial life but all life on earth, including large air-breathing organisms like ourselves—a chain of adaptations which leads from the dimensions of galaxies, through the physical conditions in the center of stars to the heat capacity of water and the atom-manipulating capacities of proteins, and on eventually to our own species and our ability to comprehend the world. From the inertial resistance we encounter when we move our hand, determined by the mass of the most distant stars, to the radioactive heat in the earth's interior which drives the great tectonic system, thus ensuring a continual replenishing of the vital elements of life—all nature, every facet of reality, is bound together into one mutual self-referential biocentric whole.

What is so particularly impressive and so highly suggestive about these life-giving adaptations is that what at first sight seem to be very trivial aspects of the chemistry and physics of a particular component turn out to be of critical significance for its biological role. Many examples have been cited . . . including the decrease in the viscosity of the blood when the blood pressure rises, which increases the blood flow to the metabolically active muscles of higher organisms; the anomalous thermal properties of water, which buffers both the planet and organisms against massive swings in temperature; the curious but critical fact that the hydration of carbon dioxide is quite slow, which prevents a fatal acidosis in the body of higher organisms in anaerobic exercise; the curious fact that it is base sequences in the major groove of the DNA which provide the electrostatic variability that can be recognized by an *alpha* helix, and so forth.

It is important also to recall that the vital mutual adaptations are in the essential nature of things and are not the product of natural selection. This was also stressed by Henderson: "Natural selection does but mould the organism without truly altering the primary qualities of environmental fitness." These are antecedent to the existence of life. The precise fit between the *alpha* helix and the large groove of the DNA are given by physics; the relationship long predated life. Similarly, the life-giving anomalous expansion of water below 4°C and on freezing and its low viscosity are given by physics. They were given before the first cell appeared in the primeval ocean. The fact that hydrogen bonds and other weak bonds have sufficient strength to hold proteins and DNA in "metastable" conformations at ambient temperatures; the fact that the majority of organic compounds are relatively stable below 100°C; the fact that oxygen, the only feasible terminal oxidant for carbon, is relatively unreactive below 50°C; the fact that the solubility of oxygen in water, the unique matrix for life, is relatively low; the fact that carbon dioxide is a gas, that bicarbonate has such excellent buffering capabilities—all these unique coincidences are in effect laws of nature, universals no less than the constants of physics. Commenting on Henderson's arguments, the great biologist Joseph Needham stressed the same point: "Since the properties of water and the . . . elements antedate the appearance of life . . . they can be regarded philosophically as some sort of preparation for life. Purposiveness, then, exists everywhere, it permeates the whole universe. . . . Restricted teleology melts away in the immensity of that discussed by Lawrence Henderson.". . .

Fitness for Becoming

The current picture of the origin of life is also compatible with the concept of a uniquely ordained path from chemistry to the cell. The growing evidence that evolution is jumpy and that major evolutionary transformations have occurred rapidly is again suggestive. The more saltational the course of evolution, the easier it is to envisage it as being the result of a built-in program. The enormous diversity of the pattern of life on earth may not represent a full plenitude of all life forms, but it appears to approach closely this ideal. The very great complexity of life, and especially its quite fantastic holistic nature, which seems to preclude any sort of evolutionary transformations via a succession of small independent changes, is perfectly compatible with the notion of directed evolution. The ease with which the evolution of the very many complex adaptations such as the eye of the lobster and the avian lung can be explained in terms of design lends further support to the notion of directed evolution.

The Argument for Design

The strength of any teleological argument is basically accumulative. It does not lie with any one individual piece of evidence alone but with a whole series of coincidences, all of which point irresistibly to one conclusion. It is the same here. Neither the thermal properties of water, nor the chemical properties of carbon dioxide, nor the exceptional complexity of living things, nor the difficulties this leads to when attempting to give plausible explanations in Darwinian terms—none of these individually counts for much. Rather, it lies in the summation of all the evidence, in the whole long chain of coincidences which leads so convincingly toward the unique end of life, in the fact that all the independent lines of evidence fit together into a beautiful self-consistent teleological whole. The evolutionary evidence is similar; it compounds. In isolation, the various pieces of evidence for direction, the speed of evolutionary change, the fantastic complexity of living things, the apparent gratuity of some of the ends achieved, are perhaps no more than suggestive, but taken together, the overall pattern points strongly to final causes. . . .

During the past fifty years advances associated with molecular biology have, as we have seen, revealed yet another set of unique mutual adaptations at the heart of life in key constituents such as DNA and protein. And over the same period advances in cosmology and astrophysics have indicated that the overall structure of the universe and the constants of physics seem also to be fine tuned for our existence.

Note also that theories or worldviews are most often accepted not because they can explain everything perfectly but because they make sense of more than any competitor does. Evolution was accepted in the nineteenth century not because it explained everything perfectly but because it accounted for the facts better than any other theory. Similarly, the teleological model of nature presented here is far more coherent and makes far more sense of the cosmos than any currently available competitor. The idea that the cosmos is a unique whole with life and mankind as its end and purpose makes sense and illuminates all our current scientific knowledge. It makes sense of the intricate synthesis of carbon in the stars, of the constants of physics, of the properties of water, of the cosmic abundance of the elements, of the existence throughout the cosmos of organic matter, of the fact that the two adjacent planets Earth and Mars appear so similar, that the atom-building process continues to uranium. No other worldview comes close. No other explanation makes as much sense of all the facts.[34]

Conclusion

In the discoveries of science the harmony of the spheres is also now the harmony of life. And as the eerie illumination of science penetrates ever more deeply into the order of nature, the cosmos appears increasingly to be a vast system finely tuned to generate life and organisms of biology very similar, perhaps identical, to ourselves. All the evidence available in the biological sciences supports the core proposition of traditional natural theology—that the cosmos is a specially designed whole with life and mankind as its fundamental goal and purpose, a whole in which all facets of reality, from the size of galaxies to the thermal capacity of water, have their meaning and explanation in this central fact.

Four centuries after the scientific revolution apparently destroyed irretrievably man's special place in the universe, banished Aristotle, and rendered teleological speculation obsolete, the relentless stream of discovery has turned dramatically in favor of teleology and design, and the doctrine of the microcosm is reborn.

---

[34] Ibid., pp. 381-385; "Conclusion, Ibid., p. 389.

Limitless in His glory is God Who created in pairs
all things that the earth produces
as well as their own humankind
as well as things of which they have no knowledge.
And a sign for them is the night:
We withdraw the day from it and see how they are plunged in darkness;
And the Sun runs his course for a period designated for him
that is determined by the will of the Almighty, the All-Knowing.
And the moon—We have measured mansions for her to pass through
until curved like a withered date-stalk she returns.
The sun is not permitted to overtake the moon
nor can the night go beyond the day,
but each moves easily in its lawful way.

[*Sūrah Yā Sīn* (O Thou Human Being) 36:36-40]

The Circularity of Existence

~ Shaykh Fadhlalla Haeri [35]

The moon has been decreed and programmed to be in its various phases, such as the lunar cycle which marks the beginning and end of each month. Since Allah is talking about purely physical realities, He gives the example of the moon, because without the moon life could not continue on earth. The moon has an enormous effect on the balance of things, upon the plants and their cycles of growth, upon the ocean-tides, upon mankind and all living beings. It rises and sheds its power and usefulness, then ends up waning like an old, yellowed branch, like the twig from which dates come, which is usually shrivelled and yellow when it has dried up (36:39). The end of the moon's appearance in the sky comes when it is spent and dead—it has done its job. What this refers to is the cycle of anything that rises up, reaches its full effulgence, and then

---

[35] Shaykh Fadhlalla Haeri, *Heart of Qur'an and Perfect Mizan. Surat Ya Sin, With Tafsir on Surat al-Fatihah* by Khwaja Abdullah Ansari. Zahra Publications, pp. 84-85.

diminishes and dies down. Everything is cyclical in its station, including man—he moves from the station of weakness to the station of physical strength, and then back again to the station of weakness.

> *It is not for the sun to overtake the moon,*
> *nor does the night outstrip the day—they each float on in an orbit.* [36:40]

> *(Lash shamsu yambaghī lahaa 'ann tudrikal qamara*
> *walal laylu sābiqun nahār. Wa kullun fī falakin yasbaḥuun)*

The sun is not allowed to surpass or bypass the moon. This means that every entity has its pre-destined, pre-measured, pre-ordained and decreed course. The night will not overtake the sun, nor move faster than it. By "overtake" it implies that the sun's light will become longer and longer. *Falak* means anything that is circular or repetitive, anything that has an up-and-down motion. *Aflak* means "the planets," because they are all in this circular movement of up-and-down, youth and age.

Yasbahun comes from the same word as *tasbih,* meaning that everything is aswim in this circularity, this repetitiveness, just like breathing itself.

Everything moves according to its own laws. Every system works within its pre-destiny, and it interacts with another system without overcoming it or confusing it. Everything in existence moves in its own orbit, existing and experienced by motion, and behind it all is the Unfathomable, Ever-Fixed, Ever-Eternal Allah, *as-Samad* (the Ever-Continuing Refuge). Everything swims in its own orbit. The best state to be in is *tasbih,* aswim in glorification. Bewildered and in awe before the revolving circularity of existence, we can do nothing but try to move in harmony with it all in glorification of its, and our, Creator.

A handful of sand contains about 10,000 grains, more than the number of stars we can see on a clear night. But the number of stars we can see is only a fraction of the number of stars that are. . . . The cosmos is rich beyond measure: the total number of stars in the universe is greater than all the grains of sand on all the beaches on the planet earth.

~ Carl Sagan, *Cosmos*, 1980

God is the Light of the heavens and the earth.
The parable of His light is,
as it were, that of a niche containing a lamp;
the lamp is enclosed in glass, the glass like a radiant star:
lit from a blessed tree—an olive-tree
that is neither of the east nor of the west—
the oil of which would almost give light
even though fire had not touched it: light upon light!
God guides to His light the one who wills to be guided;
and God offers parables to human beings,
since God has full knowledge of all things.
[*Sūrah An-Nūr* (The Light) 24:35]

Come forth into the light of things. Let nature be your Teacher.

~ William Wordsworth

Light Upon Light

~ Lynne McTaggart[36]

Against the objections of his contemporaries who believed in empty space, Aristotle was one of the first to argue that space was in fact a plenum (a background substructure filled with things). Then, in the middle of the nineteenth century, scientist Michael Faraday introduced the concept of a field in relation to electricity and magnetism, believing that the most important aspect of energy was not the source but the space around it, and the influence of one on the other through some force. In his view, atoms weren't hard little billiard balls, but the most concentrated center of a force that would extend out in space.

A field is a matrix or medium which connects two or more points in space, usually via a force, like gravity or electromagnetism. The force is usually represented by ripples in the field, or waves. An electromagnetic field, to use but one example, is simply an electrical field and a magnetic field which intersect, sending out waves of energy at the speed of light. An electric and magnetic field forms around any electric charge (which is, most simply, a surplus or deficit of electrons). Both electrical and magnetic fields have two polarities (negative and positive) and both will cause any other charged object to be attracted or repelled, depending on whether the charges are opposite (one positive, the other negative) or the same (both positive or both negative). The field is considered that area of space where this charge and its effects can be detected.

The notion of an electromagnetic field is simply a convenient abstraction invented by scientists (and represented by lines of "force," indicated by direction and shape) to try to make sense of the seemingly remarkable actions of electricity and magnetism and their ability to

---

[36] The following selection is excerpted from pp. 22-26 from *The Field* by Lynne McTaggart, Copyright © 2002 by Lynne McTaggart. Reprinted by Permission of HarperCollins Publishers, Inc.

influence objects at a distance—and, technically, into infinity—with no detectable substance or matter in between. Simply put, a field is a region of influence. As one pair of researchers aptly described it: "Every time you use your toaster, the fields around it perturb charged particles in the farthest galaxies ever so slightly."

James Clerk Maxwell first proposed that space was an ether of electromagnetic light, and this idea held sway until decisively disproved by a Polish-born physicist named Albert Michelson in 1881 . . . with a light experiment that showed that matter did not exist in a mass of ether. Einstein himself believed space constituted a true void, until his own ideas, eventually developed into his general theory of relativity, showed that space indeed held a plenum of activity. But it wasn't until 1911, with an experiment by Max Planck, one of the founding fathers of quantum theory, that physicists understood that empty space was bursting with activity.

In the quantum world, quantum fields are not mediated by forces but by exchange of energy, which is constantly redistributed in a dynamic pattern. This constant exchange is an intrinsic property of particles, so that even "real" particles are nothing more than a little knot of energy which briefly emerges and disappears back into the underlying field. According to quantum field theory, the individual entity is transient and insubstantial. Particles cannot be separated from the empty space around them. Einstein himself recognized that matter itself was "extremely intense"—a disturbance, in a sense, of perfect randomness—and that the only fundamental reality was the underlying entity—the field itself.

Fluctuations in the atomic world amount to a ceaseless passing back and forth of energy like a ball in a game of pingpong. This energy exchange is analogous to loaning someone a penny: you are a penny poorer, he is a penny richer, until he returns the penny and the roles reverse. This sort of emission and reabsorption of virtual particles occurs not only among photons and electrons, but with all the quantum particles in the universe. The Zero Point Field is a repository of all fields and all ground energy states and all virtual particles—a field of fields. Every exchange of every virtual particle radiates energy. The zero-point energy in any one particular transaction in an electromagnetic field is unimaginably tiny—half a photon's worth.

But if you add up all the particles of all varieties in the universe constantly popping in and out of being, you come up with a vast, inexhaustible energy source—equal to or greater than the energy density in an atomic nucleus—all sitting there unobtrusively in the background of the empty space around us, like one all-pervasive, supercharged backdrop. It has been calculated that the total energy of the Zero Point Field exceeds all energy in matter by a factor of 10^{40}, or 10 followed by 40 zeros." As the great physicist Richard Feynman once described, in attempting to give some idea of this magnitude, the energy of a single cubic meter of space is enough to boil all the oceans of the world."

The Zero Point Field represented two tantalizing possibilities to Hal [Hal Puthoff, the physicist who developed Zero Point Field theory in the 1980s]. Of course, it represented the Holy Grail of energy research. If you could somehow tap into this field, you might have all the energy you would ever need, not simply for fuel on earth, but for space propulsion to distant stars. At the moment, travelling to the nearest star outside our solar system would require a rocket as large as the sun to carry the necessary fuel.

But there was also a larger implication of a vast underlying sea of energy. The existence of the Zero Point Field implied that all matter in the universe was interconnected by waves, which are spread out through time and space and can carry on to infinity, tying one part of the universe to every other part. The idea of The Field might just offer a scientific explanation for many metaphysical notions, such as the Chinese belief in the life force, or *qi*, described in ancient texts as something akin to an energy field. It even echoed the Old Testament's account of God's first dictum: "Let there be light," out of which matter was created.

Portraits of Faith

~ Interviews by Laura Fisher Kaiser[37]

Sam Gon III, Director of Science, The Nature Conservancy, Hawaii
  Haipule Hawai'i practitioner and Roman Catholic:

I was always interested in the sciences, but when I began hiking in high school, I found that I was affected deeply by the landscape. That all these animals and plants could be described in Hawaiian overwhelmed me—there was obviously a long-term connection between the land and the language, which I began learning.

For the past seven years, I have been studying chants and dance with Kumu John Keolamaka'ainana Lake, a master of Hawaiian religion. Although one side of my family is Buddhist and I'm a confirmed Catholic—I'm of mixed ethnic descent—I feel comfortable both attending Mass and performing sacred Hawaiian rituals. "Loina," or traditional practice, helps you connect with the land in a very intimate way, as the ancient natives did. The winds, the trees, everything becomes living, personified. "Hana haipule," reverent acts, make you feel like you're woven into the fate of a place, and that affects my work. There's a "hana kupono"—protocol—to follow when entering a sacred space. For example, I present a chant before I go into a forest. This is my "ho'okupu," or offering. Conducting yourself in a mindful, respectful manner provides ecological and spiritual links to the landscape.

★★★

Sudaryanto, Mariculture Broodstock and Grow-Out Coordinator,
  Komodo Field Office of The Nature Conservancy, Indonesia. Muslim:

I grew up in a small village in the province of Yogyakarta, on the island of Java. I was taught how people should behave in the eyes of God and about the connection between people and nature. As the child of farmers, my life was filled with work and prayer.

---

[37] The following statements are excerpted from "Portraits of Faith," interviews by Susan Enfield Esrey, Laura Fisher Kaiser, Danielle Furlich, and Meaghan O'Neil. Edited by Laura Fisher Kaiser. Nature Conservancy (magazine), Spring 2003 issue, pp.24, 26, and 28.

I studied biology at university and developed a strong awareness of the power of God through His creation. When we learned about the smallness of bacteria, plankton that have a certain order to their body parts, the order of the cell, the atom and so forth, I experienced a feeling of wonder at the Creator.

I have a religious duty to teach other people the good knowledge I have, which Islam considers a form of charity for the public good.

★★★

Juana Londono, Project Coordinator
Fundacion Pro-Sierra Nevada de Santa Marta, Colombia. Roman Catholic:

I am from Bogotá. I was baptized and had my first communion when I was 8. I feel very privileged to have worked in the Sierra for the past 15 years and am proud of my origins. The local Kogui and Wiwa people have taught me about this huge world, in which everything grows and from which one learns. Each thing has value, in its particular context. Here, the material world does not exist alone; there is also an awareness of its origin in the spiritual world.

In the Sierra, we walk for hours between small villages—plenty of time to reflect and lose myself in thought. Beside the path, a river often flows. At first, it's just a sound, but after a while, the sound enters me and becomes part of my thoughts. The same happens with the smells, the colors, the words—everything enters my body. In these moments, I realize I am not independent of the Earth, that I am also water that shimmers, wind that blows, stone that endures. I go and return. I am not from here, nor from there. I belong to both sides. I am from wherever I feel the Earth.

When you hear thunder or see a raging river or a landslide, you understand that you are just a tiny speck in this world. Therefore, we must respect nature. I believe in what Ramon Gil, a Wiwa indigenous leader and a close friend, says: "What you breathe can feed or debilitate the forest. If you breathe hatred, violence and war, the forest dries and dies. If you breathe without any spiritual problem, the forest is fed and flourishes. And what the forest breathes, we receive. It feeds us. Respiration brings forth flowers."

CHAPTER FOUR

POWER AND BEAUTY

Do you see the seed that you sow in the ground?
Is it you that causes it to grow or are We the cause?
[*Sūrah Al-Wāqiᶜah* (That Which Must Come To Pass) 56:63-64]

We have built the universe with skill and power;
and truly, it is We Who are steadily expanding it.
And We have spread wide the earth—
how well We have ordered it!
And of everything, We have created opposites
that you might bear in mind that God alone is One.
And so, say, "Hasten to God."
[*Sūrah Adh-Dhāriyāt* (The Dust-Scattering Winds) 51:47-50]

The Most Gracious is firmly established on the throne of authority.
To Him belongs what is in the heavens and on earth
and all between them and all beneath the soil.
Whether you pronounce the word aloud or not,
truly, He knows what is secret and what is yet more hidden.
God! there is no god but He!
To Him belong the Most Beautiful Names.
[*Sūrah Ṭā Hā* (O Man) 20:5-8]

And to God belongs the dominion over the heavens and the earth;
and God has power over all things.
Truly, in the creation of the heavens and the earth,
and in the succession of night and day,
there are indeed signs for all who are endowed with insight,
and who remember God standing, and sitting,
and when they lie down to sleep,
and contemplate creation—of the heavens and the earth:
"O our Sustainer!
You have not created this without meaning and purpose.
Limitless are You in Your subtle glory!"
[*Sūrah Al ᶜImrān* (The House of ᶜImrān) 3:189-191]

Lift your head up off the table. See,
there are no edges to this garden.
Sweet fruits, every kind you can think of,
branches green and always
slightly moving.

~ Jalaluddin Rumi[38]

Listen then to Me; pay heed, pay attention is a continually
repeated refrain within the Qur'an: witness the unfolding of meaning
within yourself and upon the farthest extension of the horizon of
creation (41:53). If we look, how can we not witness the beauty and
magnificence of this creation—and who could have made it, but our
Sustainer—the Unknowable and Infinite and Sublimely Skillful and
Beneficent Source of Being? Surely it was not man that made it
thus—in shapely proportion[39] and without any flaw [Sūrah Qaf 50:6].

~ Camille Helminski

Witnessing the Beautiful and the Sublime

~ Charles Upton

Beauty and Power (*Jamal and Jalal*) are the two categories of Divine
qualities manifested in creation: sometimes blended in varying proportions
as in the beauty of a swiftly running stallion or the power of a rushing
waterfall. The Beautiful and the Sublime (or Infinitely Powerful) are the
two essential qualities of the natural world: the still reflective lake and the
erupting volcano; the dove and the cobra. Created Beauty is an expression
of the Names of God which fall under the category of Beauty (*al-Jamil*);

---

[38] Translated by Coleman Barks and John Moyne. Excerpted from "Greed and
Generosity," *The Rumi Collection*, Threshold Books, Putney, VT 1998, p. 153.
[39] Qur'an, *Surah Taghabun* 64:3.

59

Sublimity is an expression of those Names which fall under Majesty (*al-Jalal*). Without the Sublime, nature would be stagnant and cloying; without the Beautiful it would be horrendous, too much to bear. This is why a balanced relationship to the natural world—and to life itself, for that matter—requires both rigor and rapture, both war and peace, the relaxant of calm pleasure and the tonic of danger and struggle. If it's all peace, we become effete; if it's all struggle, we become barbaric. There is also Sublimity in Beauty—witness the stallion—and Beauty in Sublimity—witness the tiger. God, too, manifests as both Beauty and Sublimity, both Mercy and (Rigor) Majesty—which is why the integral vision of nature is the primary support, outside of divinely-revealed religion, for the contemplation of God.

★★★

When Muhammad ﷺ cast the idols out of the Kaaba, he was not only reminding his people that it was their duty to worship Allah, not the natural forces which are Allah's creation; he was also casting the idols of self-worship out of the temple of the human heart.

It was the Prophet's mission to remind the Arabs, and all later Muslims, that there is more to reality than what your five senses can tell you: *[God] said, "Did I not say unto you, 'verily, I alone know the hidden reality of the heavens and the earth?* [2:34] In this revelation, the ancient religion of Abraham was being renewed: *And thus we gave Abraham insight into [God's] mighty dominion over the heavens and the earth—and to the end that he might become one of those who are inwardly sure. Then, when the night overshadowed him with its darkness, he beheld a star: he exclaimed, "This is my Sustainer!"—but when it went down, he said, "I love not the things that go down." Then, when he beheld the moon rising, he said "This is my Sustainer!"—but when it went down, he said, "Indeed, if my Sustainer guide me not, I will certainly be one of the people who go astray!" Then, when he beheld the sun rising, he said, "This is my Sustainer! This is the greatest [of all]!"—but when it [too] went down, he exclaimed: "O my people! Far be it from me to ascribe divinity, as you do, to aught beside God"* [6:75-78].

We think of nature as something outside of us which also contains us, instead of realizing that the Spirit of nature—God in his Names *Al-Khaliq* (The Creator), *Al-Bari* (the Producer), *Al-Musawwir* (the Fashioner), the Life-Giver (*Al-Muyhi*), and *Al-Hafiz* (the All-Preserver)—

60

is within us as well as all around us, that He holds both us and the universe we are a part of between His two hands. He shows us His signs on the horizons *and* in our souls; He is *Al-Shahid*, the Witness over everything.

And in your own nature, and in [that of] all the animals
He scatters [over the earth] there are messages
for people who are endowed with inner certainty.
[*Sūrah Al-Jāthiyah* (Kneeling Down) 45:4]

When I Heard the Learn'd Astronomer

~ Walt Whitman

When I heard the learn'd astronomer,
When the proofs, the figures, were ranged in columns before me,
When I was shown the charts and diagrams, to add, divide, and
measure them,
When I sitting heard the astronomer where he lectured with much
applause in the lecture-room,
How soon unaccountable I became tired and sick,
Till rising and gliding out I wander'd off by myself,
In the mystical moist night-air, and from time to time,
Look'd up in perfect silence at the stars.

We can never have enough of nature. We must be refreshed by the sight of inexhaustible vigour, vast and titanic features, the sea coast with its wrecks, the wilderness with its living and decaying trees, the thunder cloud and the rain.

~ Henry David Thoreau

61

What is life? It is the flash of a firefly in the night. It is the breath of a buffalo in the wintertime. It is the little shadow which runs across the grass and loses itself in the sunset.

~ Crowfoot

String Theory

~ Brian Greene [40]

The Ancient Greeks surmised that the stuff of the universe was made up of "uncuttable" ingredients that they called *atoms*. Just as the enormous number of words in an alphabetic language is built up from the wealth of combinations of a small number of letters, they guessed that the vast range of material objects might also result from combinations of a small number of distinct, elementary building blocks. It was a prescient guess. More than 2,000 years later we still believe it to be true, although the identity of the most fundamental units has gone through numerous revisions. In the nineteenth century scientists showed that many familiar substances such as oxygen and carbon had a smallest recognizable constituent; following in the tradition laid down by the Greeks, they called them *atoms*. The name stuck, but history has shown it to be a misnomer, since atoms surely are "cuttable." By the early 1930s the collective works of J. J. Thomson, Ernest Rutherford, Niels Bohr, and James Chadwick had established the solar system-like atomic model with which most of us are familiar. Far from being the most elementary material constituents, atoms consist of a nucleus, containing protons and neutrons, that is surrounded by a swarm of orbiting electrons.

For a while many physicists thought that protons, neutrons, and electrons were the Greeks' "atoms." But in 1968 experimenters at the Stanford Linear Accelerator Center, making use of the increased capacity of technology to probe the microscopic depths of matter, found that protons and neutrons are not fundamental, either. Instead they showed that each consists of three smaller particles, called *quarks*—a whimsical name taken from a passage in James Joyce's *Finnegan's Wake* by the

---

[40] From *The Elegant Universe: Superstrings, Hidden Dimensions, and the Quest for the Ultimate Theory* by Brian Greene. Copyright © 1999 by Brian R. Greene. Used by permission of W.W. Norton & Company, Inc.

theoretical physicist Murray Gell-Mann, who previously had surmised their existence. The experimenters confirmed that quarks themselves come in two varieties, which were named, a bit less creatively, *up* and *down*. A proton consists of two up-quarks and a down-quark; a neutron consists of two down-quarks and an up-quark.

Everything you see in the terrestrial world and the heavens above appears to be made from combinations of electrons, up-quarks, and down-quarks. No experimental evidence indicates that any of these three particles is built up from something smaller. But a great deal of evidence indicates that the universe itself has additional particulate ingredients. In the mid-1950s, Frederick Reines and Clyde Cowan found conclusive experimental evidence for a fourth kind of fundamental particle called a *neutrino*—a particle whose existence was predicted in the early 1930s by Wolfgang Pauli. Neutrinos proved very difficult to find because they are ghostly particles that only rarely interact with other matter: an average-energy neutrino can easily pass right through many trillion miles of lead without the slightest effect on its motion. This should give you significant relief, because right now as you read this, billions of neutrinos ejected into space by the sun are passing through your body and the earth as well, as part of their lonely journey through the cosmos. In the late 1930s, another particle called a *muon*—identical to an electron except that a muon is about 200 times heavier—was discovered by physicists studying cosmic rays (showers of particles that bombard earth from outer space). Because there was nothing in the cosmic order, no unsolved puzzle, no tailor-made niche, that necessitated the muon's existence, the Nobel Prize-winning particle physicist Isidor Isaac Rabi greeted the discovery of the muon with a less than enthusiastic "Who ordered that?" Nevertheless, there it was. And more was to follow.

Using ever more powerful technology, physicists have continued to slam bits of matter together with ever increasing energy, momentarily recreating conditions unseen since the big bang. In the debris they have searched for new fundamental ingredients to add to the growing list of particles. Here is what they have found: four more quarks—*charm, strange, bottom,* and *top*—and another even heavier cousin of the electron, called a *tau,* as well as two other particles with properties similar to the neutrino (called the *muon-neutrino* and *tau-neutrino* to distinguish them from the original neutrino, now called the *electron-neutrino*). These particles are produced through high-energy collisions and exist only ephemerally; they are not constituents of anything we typically encounter. But even this is not quite the end of the story. Each of these particles has an *antiparticle* partner—a particle of identical mass but opposite in certain other respects such as its electric charge (as well as its charges with respect to other forces discussed below).[41]

★★★

According to string theory, if we could examine these particles with even greater precision—a precision many orders of magnitude beyond our present technological capacity—we would find that each is not pointlike, but instead consists of a tiny one-dimensional *loop*. Like an infinitely thin rubber band, each particle contains a vibrating, oscillating, dancing filament that physicists, lacking Gell-Mann's literary flair, have named a *string*.

We illustrate this essential idea of string theory by starting with an ordinary piece of matter, an apple, and repeatedly magnifying its structure to reveal its ingredients on ever smaller scales. String theory adds the new microscopic layer of a vibrating loop to the previously known progression from atoms through protons, neutrons, electrons and quarks.[42]

String Theory as the Unified Theory of Everything

In Einstein's day, the strong and the weak forces had not yet been discovered, but he found the existence of even two distinct forces— gravity and electromagnetism—deeply troubling. Einstein did not accept that nature is founded on such an extravagant design. This launched his thirty-year voyage in search of the so-called *unified field theory* that he hoped would show that these two forces are really manifestations of one grand underlying principle. This quixotic quest isolated Einstein from the mainstream of physics, which, understandably, was far more excited about delving into the newly emerging framework of quantum mechanics. He wrote to a friend in the early 1940s, "I have become a lonely old chap who is mainly known because he doesn't wear socks and who is exhibited as a curiosity on special occasions."

---

[41] Ibid., p. 7-8.
[42] Ibid., p. 14.

Einstein was simply ahead of his time. More than half a century later, his dream of a unified theory has become the Holy Grail of modem physics. And a sizeable part of the physics and mathematics community is becoming increasingly convinced that string theory may provide the answer. From one principle—that everything at its most microscopic level consists of combinations of vibrating strands—string theory provides a single explanatory framework capable of encompassing all forces and all matter.

String theory proclaims, for instance, that the observed particle properties . . . are a reflection of the various ways in which a string can vibrate. Just as the strings on a violin or on a piano have resonant frequencies at which they prefer to vibrate—patterns that our ears sense as various musical notes and their higher harmonics—the same holds true for the loops of string theory. But we will see that, rather than producing musical notes, each of the preferred patterns of vibration of a string in string theory appears as a particle whose mass and force charges are determined by the string's oscillatory pattern. The electron is a string vibrating one way, the up-quark is a string vibrating another way, and so on. Far from being a collection of chaotic experimental facts, particle properties in string theory are the manifestation of one and the same physical feature: the resonant patterns of vibration—the music, so to speak—of fundamental loops of string. The same idea applies to the forces of nature as well. We will see that force particles are also associated with particular patterns of string vibration and hence everything, all matter and all forces, is unified under the same rubric of microscopic string oscillations—the "notes" that strings can play.

For the first time in the history of physics we therefore have a framework with the capacity to explain every fundamental feature upon which the universe is constructed.[43]

★★★

And so string theory should be viewed as a work in progress whose partial completion has already revealed astonishing insights into the nature of space, time, and matter. The harmonious union of general relativity and quantum mechanics is a major success. Furthermore, unlike any

---

[43] Ibid., pp. 14-15.

previous theory, string theory has the capacity to answer primordial questions having to do with nature's most fundamental constituents and forces. Of equal importance, although somewhat harder to convey, is the remarkable elegance of both the answers and the framework for answers that string theory proposes. For instance, in string theory many aspects of nature that might appear to be arbitrary technical details—such as the number of distinct fundamental particle ingredients and their respective properties—are found to arise from essential and tangible aspects of the geometry of the universe. If string theory is right, the microscopic fabric of our universe is a richly intertwined multidimensional labyrinth within which the strings of the universe endlessly twist and vibrate, rhythmically beating out the laws of the cosmos. Far from being accidental details, the properties of nature's basic building blocks are deeply entwined with the fabric of space and time.

In the final analysis, though, nothing is a substitute for definitive, testable predictions that can determine whether string theory has truly lifted the veil of mystery hiding the deepest truths of our universe. It may be some time before our level of comprehension has reached sufficient depth to achieve this aim. . . .[44]

Flowing Strength

I find you in all these things of the world
that I love calmly, like a brother;
in things no one cares for you brood like a seed;
and to powerful things you give an immense power.

Strength plays such a marvellous game—
it moves through the things of the world like a servant,
groping out in roots, tapering in trunks,
and in the treetops like a rising from the dead.

~ Rainer Maria Rilke[45]

---

[44] Ibid., p. 18-19.

[45] Reprinted from, *Selected Poems of Rainer Maria Rilke*, translated by Robert Bly. HarperCollins, New York, NY, 1981, by permission of Robert Bly.

O sing to the Lord a new song: sing to the Lord, all the earth.
Sing to the Lord, bless His name:
show forth his salvation from day to day.
Honor and Majesty are before Him:
Strength and Beauty are in His sanctuary.
[The Bible, Psalms 96:1-2; 6]

Witnessing Power and Possessing Beauty
~ Alain de Botton[46]

Long partial to deserts, drawn to photographs of the American West (bits of tumbleweed blowing across a wasteland) and to the names of the great deserts (Mojave, Kalahari, Taklamakan, Gobi), I booked a charter flight to the Israeli resort of Eilat and went to wander in the Sinai. On the plane journey over, I talked to a young Australian woman beside me who was taking up a job as a lifeguard at the Eilat Hilton—and I read Pascal:

> When I consider . . . the small space I occupy and which I see swallowed up in the infinite immensity of spaces of which I know nothing and which know nothing of me ['l'infinie immensité des espaces que j'ignore et qui m'ignorent'], I take fright and am amazed to see myself here rather than there: there is no reason for me to be here rather than there, now rather than then. Who put me here?
> ~ Pascal, *Pensées*, 68

Wordsworth had urged us to travel through landscapes to feel emotions that would benefit our souls. I set out for the desert in order to be made to feel small.

It is usually unpleasant to be made to feel small—by doormen in hotels or by comparison with the achievements of heroes. But there may be another and more satisfying way to feel diminished. There are

---

46 Alain de Botton, *The Art of Travel*. Published by Penguin Books Ltd., 80 Strand, London. "On The Sublime" pp. 157-179; "On Possessing Beauty pp. 214-233.

intimations of it in front of *Rocky Mountains, Lander's Peak* (1863) by Albert Bierstadt, in front of *An Avalanche in the Alps* (1803) by Philip James de Loutherbourg or the *Chalk Cliffs in Rügen* (1810) by Caspar David Friedrich. What do such barren, overwhelming spaces bring us?

Two days into my Sinai trip, the group of twelve which I have joined reaches a valley empty of life, without trees, grass, water or animals. Only boulders lie strewn across a sandstone floor, as though the stamping of a petulant giant had caused them to roll off the sides of the surrounding mountains. These mountains look like naked alps and their nudity reveals geological origins normally concealed beneath coats of earth and pine forest. There are gashes and fissures that speak of the pressures of millennia, there are cross-sections through disproportionate expanses of time. The earth's tectonic plates have rippled granite as though it were linen. The mountains spread out in seeming infinity on the horizon until eventually the high plateau of the southern Sinai gives way to a featureless, baking gravel-pan described by the Bedouins as 'El Tih,' or the desert of the Wandering.

★★★

There are few emotions about places for which adequate single words exist: we have to make awkward piles of words to convey what we felt when watching light fade on an early autumn evening or when encountering a pool of perfectly still water in a clearing.

But at the beginning of the eighteenth century, a word came to prominence with which it became possible to indicate a specific response towards precipices and glaciers, the night skies and boulder-strewn deserts. In their presence, we were likely to experience, and could count on being understood for later reporting that we had felt, a sense of the sublime.

The word itself had originated around A.D. 200 in a treatise, *On the Sublime*, ascribed to the Greek author Longinus, though it languished until a retranslation of the essay into English in 1712 renewed intense interest among critics. While the writers often differed in their specific analyses of the word, their shared assumptions were more striking. They grouped into a single category a variety of hitherto unconnected landscapes by virtue of their size, emptiness or danger, and argued that such places provoked an identifiable feeling that was both pleasurable and morally good. The value of landscapes was no longer to be decided solely on formal aesthetic criteria (the harmony of colours or arrangement of lines) or on economic or practical concerns, but according to the power of places to arouse the mind to sublimity.

Joseph Addison, in his Essay on the "Pleasures of the Imagination," wrote of "a delightful stillness and amazement" that he had felt before "the prospects of an open champion country, a vast uncultivated desert, huge heaps of mountains, high rocks and precipices and a wide expanse of waters." Hildebrand Jacob, in an essay on "How the Mind is Raised by the Sublime," offered a list of places most likely to set off the prized feeling: oceans, either in calm or storm, the setting sun, precipices, caverns and Swiss mountains.

Travellers went to investigate. In 1739, the poet Thomas Gray undertook a walking tour of the Alps, the first of many self-conscious pursuits of the sublime, and reported: "In our little journey up to the Grande Chartreuse, I do not remember to have gone ten paces without an exclamation that there was no restraining. Not a precipice, not a torrent, not a cliff, but is pregnant with religion and poetry."

★★★

The southern Sinai at dawn. What then is this feeling? It is generated by a valley created 400 million years ago, by a granite mountain 2,300 metres high and by the erosion of millennia marked on the walls of a succession of steep canyons. Beside all three man seems merely dust postponed: the sublime as an encounter, pleasurable, intoxicating even, with human weakness in the face of the strength, age, and size of the universe. . . .

★★★

Why seek out this feeling of smallness—delight in it even? Why leave the comforts of Eilat, join a group of desert devotees and walk for miles with a heavy pack along the shores of the Gulf of Aqaba, to reach a place of rocks and silence, in which one must shelter from the sun like a fugitive in the scant shadow of giant boulders? Why contemplate with exhilaration rather than despair beds of granite and baking gravel pans and a frozen lava of mountains extending into the distance until the peaks dissolve on the edge of a hard blue sky?

One answer is that not everything which is more powerful than us must always be hateful to us. What defies our will can provoke anger and resentment; it may also arouse awe and respect. It depends on whether the obstacle appears noble in its defiance or squalid and insolent. We begrudge the defiance of the cocky doorman, we honour the defiance of the mist-shrouded mountain. We are humiliated by what is powerful and mean, but awed by what is powerful and noble. . . . A bull may arouse a feeling of the sublime, a piranha does not. It seems a matter of motives: we interpret the piranha's power as vicious and predatory, the bull's as guileless and impersonal.

Even when we are not in deserts, the behaviour of others and our own flaws are prone to leave us feeling small. Humiliation is a perpetual risk in the world of men. It is not unusual for our will to be defied and our wishes frustrated. Sublime landscapes do not therefore introduce us to our inadequacy. Rather, to touch on the crux of their appeal, they allow us to conceive of a familiar inadequacy in a new and more helpful way. Sublime places repeat in grand terms a lesson that ordinary life typically teaches viciously: that the universe is mightier than we are, that we are frail and temporary and have no alternative but to accept limitations on our will; that we must bow to necessities greater than ourselves.

This is the lesson written into the stones of the desert and the icefields of the poles. So grandly is it written there that we may come away from such places, not crushed, but inspired by what lies beyond us; privileged to be subject to such majestic necessities. The sense of awe may even shade into a desire to worship.

Because what is mightier than man has traditionally been called God, it does not seem unusual to start thinking of a deity in the Sinai. The mountains and valleys spontaneously suggest that the planet was built by something other than our own hands, by a force greater than we could gather, long before we were born, and set to continue long after our extinction (something we may forget when there are flowers and fast-food restaurants by the roadside). . . .

Early writers on the sublime repeatedly connected sublime landscapes with religion:

Joseph Addison, "On the Pleasures of the Imagination," 1712:
"A vast space naturally raises in my thoughts the idea of an Almighty Being."

Thomas Gray, *Letters*, 1739:
"There are certain scenes that would awe an atheist into belief without the help of any other argument."

Thomas Cole, *Essay on American Scenery*, 1836:
"Amid those scenes of solitude from which the hand of nature has never been lifted, the associations are of God the creator—they are his undefiled works, and the mind is cast into the contemplation of eternal things."

Ralph Waldo Emerson, *Nature*, 1836:
"The noblest ministry of nature is to stand as the apparition of God."

It is no coincidence that the Western attraction to sublime landscapes developed at precisely the moment when traditional beliefs in God began to wane. It is as if these landscapes allowed travellers to experience transcendent feelings that they no longer felt in cities and the cultivated countryside. The landscapes offered them an emotional connection to a greater power, even as they freed them of the need to subscribe to the more specific and now less plausible claims of biblical texts and organized religions.

★★★

The link between God and sublime landscapes is made most explicit in one book of the Bible. The circumstances are peculiar. God is asked by a righteous but desperate man to explain why his life has grown full of suffering. And God answers him by bidding him to contemplate the deserts and the mountains, rivers and icecaps, oceans and skies. Seldom have sublime places been asked to bear the burden of such a weighty, urgent question.

At the beginning of the Book of Job, described by Edmund Burke as the most sublime book of the Old Testament, we hear that Job was a wealthy, devout man from the land of Uz. He had seven sons, three daughters, 7,000 sheep, 3,000 camels, 500 yoke of oxen and 500 donkeys. His wishes were obeyed and his virtue rewarded. Then one day disaster struck. The Sabaeans stole Job's oxen and asses, lightning killed his sheep and the Chaldeans raided his camels. A hurricane blew in from the desert and wrecked the house of his eldest son, killing him and his siblings. Painful sores developed from the soles of Job's feet to the top of his head and, as he sat in the ashes of his house, he scratched them with a piece of broken pottery and wept.

Why had Job been so afflicted? Job's friends had the answer. He had sinned. Bildad the Shuhite told Job that his children could not have been killed by God unless they and Job had done wrong. 'God will not reject a righteous man,' said Bildad. Zophar the Naamathite ventured that God must have been generous in his treatment of Job: 'Know therefore that God exacteth of thee less than thine iniquity deserveth.'

But Job could not accept these words. He called them 'proverbs of ashes' and 'defences of clay.' He had not been a bad man—why therefore had bad things occurred to him?

It is one of the most acute questions asked of God in all the books of the Old Testament. And from a whirlwind in the desert, a furious God answered Job as follows:

> Who is this that darkeneth counsel by words without knowledge?
>
> Gird up now thy loins like a man; for I will demand of thee, and answer thou me.
>
> Where wast thou when I laid the foundations of the earth? declare, if thou hast understanding.
>
> Who hath laid the measures thereof, if thou knowest? or who hath stretched the line upon it?
>
> By what way is the light parted, which scattereth the east wind upon the earth?
>
> Who hath divided a watercourse for the overflowing of waters, or a way for the lightning or thunder; . . .
>
> Out of whose womb came the ice? and the hoary frost of heaven, who hath gendered it? . . .
>
> Knowest thou the ordinances of heaven? canst thou set the dominion thereof in the earth?

Canst thou lift up thy voice to the clouds, that abundance of
waters may cover thee? . . .

Hast thou an arm like God? or canst thou thunder with a voice
like him? . . .

Doth the hawk fly by thy wisdom, and stretch her wings toward
the south? . . .

Canst thou draw out leviathan with a hook? [Job 42:38-41]

Asked to explain to Job why he has been made to suffer though he
has been good, God draws Job's attention to the mighty phenomena of
nature. Do not be surprised that things have not gone your way: the
universe is greater than you. Do not be surprised that you do not
understand *why* they have not gone your way: for you cannot fathom the
logic of the universe. See how small you are next to the mountains.
Accept what is bigger than you and you do not understand. The world
may appear illogical *to Job*, but it does not follow that it is illogical *per se*.
Our lives are not the measure of all things: consider sublime places for a
reminder of human insignificance and frailty.

There is a strictly religious message here. God assures Job that he has
a place in his heart, even if all events do not centre around him and may
at times appear to run contrary to his interest. When divine wisdom
eludes human understanding, the righteous, made aware of their
limitations by the spectacle of sublime nature, must continue to trust in
God's plans for the universe.

★★★

Possessing Beauty

A dominant impulse on encountering beauty is the desire to hold on
to it: to possess it and give it weight in our lives. There is an urge to say,
"I was here, I saw this and it mattered to me."

But beauty is fugitive, it is frequently found in places to which we
may never return or else it results from a rare conjunction of season, light
and weather. How then to possess it, how to hold on to the floating train,
the halva-like bricks or the English valley?

The camera provides one option. Taking photographs can assuage
the itch for possession sparked by the beauty of a place; our anxiety about
losing a precious scene can decline with every click of the shutter. Or else

we can try to imprint ourselves physically on a place of beauty, perhaps hoping to render it more present in us by making ourselves more present in it. In Alexandria, standing before Pompey's Pillar, we could try to carve our name in the granite, to follow the example of Flaubert's friend Thompson from Sunderland ("You can't see the Pillar without seeing the name of Thompson, and consequently, without thinking of Thompson. This cretin has become part of the monument and perpetuates himself along with it. . . . All imbeciles are more or less Thompsons from Sunderland."). A more modest step might be to buy something—a bowl, a lacquered box or a pair of sandals (Flaubert acquired three carpets in Cairo)—to be reminded of what we have lost, like a lock of hair that we cut from a departing lover's mane.

★★★

John Ruskin[47] was born in London in February 1819. A central part of his work was to pivot around the question of how we can possess the beauty of places.

From an early age, he was unusually alive to the smallest features of the visual world. He recalled that at three or four: "I could pass my days contentedly in tracing the squares and comparing the colours of my carpet—examining the knots in the wood of the floor, or counting the bricks in the opposite houses with rapturous intervals of excitement." Ruskin's parents encouraged his sensitivity. His mother introduced him to nature, his father, a prosperous sherry importer, read the classics to him after tea and took him to a museum every Saturday. In the summer holidays, the family travelled around the British Isles and mainland Europe, not for entertainment or diversion, but for beauty, by which they understood chiefly the beauty of the Alps and of the medieval cities of northern France and Italy, in particular Amiens and Venice. They journeyed slowly in a carriage, never more than fifty miles a day, and every few miles stopped to admire the scenery—a way of travelling that Ruskin was to practise throughout his life.

---

[47] Ruskin published two books, *The Elements of Drawing* in 1857 and *The Elements of Perspective* in 1859, and gave a series of lectures at the Working Men's College in London, where he instructed students—mostly Cockney craftsmen— in shading, colour, dimension, perspective and framing. (A. de B.)

From his interest in beauty and its possession, Ruskin arrived at five central conclusions. Firstly, that beauty is the result of a complex number of factors that affect the mind psychologically and visually. Secondly, that humans have an innate tendency to respond to beauty and to desire to possess it. Thirdly, that there are many lower expressions of this desire for possession, including the desire to buy souvenirs and carpets, to carve one's name in pillars and to take photographs. Fourthly, that there is only one way to possess beauty properly and that is through *understanding* it, through making ourselves conscious of the factors (psychological and visual) that are responsible for it. And lastly, that the most effective way of pursuing this conscious understanding is by attempting to describe beautiful places through art, through writing or drawing them, irrespective of whether we happen to have any talent for doing so. . . .

If drawing had value even when it was practised by people with no talent, it was for Ruskin because drawing could teach us to see: to notice rather than to look. In the process of re-creating with our own hand what lies before our eyes, we seem naturally to move from a position of observing beauty in a loose way to one where we acquire a deep understanding of its constituent parts and hence more secure memories of it. A tradesman who had studied at the Working Men's College reported what Ruskin had told him and his fellow students at the end of their course: "Now, remember, gentlemen, that I have not been trying to teach you to draw, only to *see*. Two men are walking through Clare Market, one of them comes out at the other end not a bit wiser than when he went in; the other notices a bit of parsley hanging over the edge of a butter-woman's basket, and carries away with him images of beauty which in the course of his daily work he incorporates with it for many a day. I want you to see things like these."

Ruskin was distressed by how seldom people noticed details. He deplored the blindness and haste of modern tourists, especially those who prided themselves on covering Europe in a week by train (a service first offered by Thomas Cook in 1862): "No changing of place at a hundred miles an hour will make us one whit stronger, happier, or wiser. There was always more in the world than men could see, walked they ever so slowly; they will see it no better for going fast. The really precious things are thought and sight, not pace. It does a bullet no good to go fast; and a man, if he be truly a man, no harm to go slow; for his glory is not at all in going, but in being."

It is a measure of how accustomed we are to inattention that we would be thought unusual and perhaps dangerous if we stopped and stared at a place for as long as a sketcher would require to draw it. Ten minutes of acute concentration at least are needed to draw a tree; the prettiest tree rarely stops passers by for longer than a minute. . . .

In explaining his love of drawing (it was rare for him to travel anywhere without sketching something), Ruskin once remarked that it arose from a desire, "not for reputation, nor for the good of others, nor for my own advantage, but from a sort of instinct *like that of eating or drinking.*" What unites the three activities is that they all involve assimilations by the self of desirable elements from the world, a transfer of goodness from without to within. As a child, Ruskin had so loved the look of grass that he had frequently wanted to eat it, he said, but he had gradually discovered that it would be better to try to draw it: "I used to lie down on it and draw the blades as they grew—until every square foot of meadow, or mossy bank, became a *possession* [my italics] to me."

But photography alone cannot ensure such eating. True possession of a scene is a matter of making a conscious effort to notice elements and understand their construction. We can see beauty well enough just by opening our eyes, but how long this beauty survives in memory depends on how intentionally we have apprehended it. The camera blurs the distinction between looking and noticing, between seeing and possessing; it may give us the option of true knowledge but it may unwittingly make the effort of acquiring it seem superfluous. It suggests we have done all the work simply by taking a photograph, whereas properly to eat a place, a woodland for example, implies asking ourselves a series of questions like, "How do the stems connect to the roots?", "Where is the mist coming from?", "Why does one tree seem darker than another?"—questions implicitly raised and answered in the process of sketching.

★★★

Encouraged by Ruskin's democratic vision of drawing, I tried my hand during my travels. As for what to draw, it seemed sensible to be guided by the desire to possess beauty which had previously led me to take up my camera. In Ruskin's words, "Your art is to be the praise of something that you love. It may only be the praise of a shell or a stone.". . .

Drawing brutally shows up our previous blindness to the true appearance of things. Consider the case of trees. In a passage in *The Elements of Drawing*, Ruskin discussed, with reference to his own illustrations, the difference between the way we usually imagine the branches of trees before we draw them and the way they reveal themselves once we have looked more closely with the help of a pad and pencil: "the stem does not merely send off a wild branch here and there to take its own way, but all the branches share in one great fountain-like impulse. . . ."

I had seen many oak trees in my life, but only after an hour spent drawing one in the Langdale valley (the result would have shamed an infant) did I begin to appreciate, and remember their identity.

★★★

Another benefit we may derive from drawing is a conscious understanding of the reasons behind our attraction to certain landscapes and buildings. We find explanations for our tastes, we develop an "aesthetic," a capacity to assert judgements about beauty and ugliness. We determine with greater precision what is missing in a building we don't like and what contributes to the beauty of the one we do. We more quickly analyse a scene that impresses us and pin down whence its power arises ("the combination of limestone and evening sun," "the way the trees taper down to the river"). We move from a numb "I like this" to "I like this because. . . ," and then in turn towards a generalization about the likeable. Even if they are only held in exploratory, tentative ways, laws of beauty come to mind: it is better for light to strike objects from the side than from overhead; grey goes well with green; for a street to convey a sense of space, the buildings must only be as high as the street is wide.

And on the basis of this conscious awareness, more solid memories can be founded. Carving our name on Pompey's Pillar begins to seem unnecessary. Drawing allows us, in Ruskin's account, "to stay the cloud in its fading, the leaf in its trembling, and the shadows in their changing."

Summing up what he had attempted to do in four years of teaching and writing manuals on drawing, Ruskin explained that he had been motivated by a desire to "direct people's attention accurately to the beauty of God's work in the material universe." It may be worth quoting in full a passage in which Ruskin demonstrated what exactly, at a concrete level, this strange-sounding ambition might involve: "Let two persons go out for a walk; the one a good sketcher, the other having no taste of the kind. Let them go down a green lane. There will be a great difference in the scene as perceived by the two individuals. The one will see a lane and trees; he will perceive the trees to be green, though he will think nothing about it; he will see that the sun shines, and that it has a cheerful effect; and that's all! But what will the sketcher see? His eye is accustomed to search into the cause of beauty, and penetrate the minutest parts of loveliness. He looks up, and observes how the showery and subdivided sunshine comes sprinkled down among the gleaming leaves overhead, till the air is filled with the emerald light. He will see here and there a bough emerging from the veil of leaves, he will see the jewel brightness of the emerald moss and the variegated and fantastic lichens, white and blue, purple and red, all mellowed and mingled into a single garment of beauty. Then come the cavernous trunks and the twisted roots that grasp with their snake-like coils at the steep bank, whose turfy slope is inlaid with flowers of a thousand dyes. Is not this worth seeing? Yet if you are not a sketcher you will pass along the green lane, and when you come home again, have nothing to say or to think about it, but that you went down such and such a lane."

★★★

Ruskin did not only encourage us to draw on our travels, he also felt we should write, or as he called it "word paint," so as to cement our impressions of beauty. However respected he was in his lifetime for his drawings, it was his word-paintings that captured the public imagination and were responsible for his fame in the late Victorian period.

Attractive places typically render us aware of our inadequacies with language. In the Lake District, while writing a postcard to a friend, I explained—in some despair and haste—that the scenery was pretty and the weather wet and windy. Ruskin would have ascribed such prose more to laziness than incapacity. We were all, he argued, able to turn out adequate word-paintings. A failure was only the result of not asking ourselves enough questions, of not being more precise in analysing what we had seen and felt. Rather than rest with the idea that a lake was pretty, we were to ask ourselves more vigorously, "What in particular is attractive about this stretch of water? What are its associations? What is a better word for it than big?" The finished product might not then be marked by genius, but at least it would have been motivated by a search for an authentic representation of an experience.

Ruskin was throughout his adult life frustrated by the refusal of polite, educated English people to talk in sufficient depth about the weather: "It is a strange thing how little people know about the sky. We never attend to it, we never make it a subject of thought, we look upon it only as a succession of meaningless and monotonous accidents, too common and too vain to be worthy of a moment of watchfulness or a glance of admiration. If in our moments of utter idleness and insipidity, we turn to the sky as a last resource, which of its phenomena do we speak of? One says it has been wet, and another, it has been windy, and another, it has been warm. Who, among the whole chattering crowd, can tell me of the forms and the precipices of the chain of tall white mountains that girded the horizon at noon today? Who saw the narrow sunbeam that came out of the south, and smote upon their summits until they melted and mouldered away in a dust of blue rain? Who saw the dance of the dead clouds when the sunlight left them last night, and the west wind blew them before it like withered leaves?" . . .

★★★

The effectiveness of Ruskin's word-painting derived from his method of not only describing what places looked like ("the grass was green, the earth grey-brown"), but also of analysing their effect on us in psychological language ("the grass seemed *expansive*, the earth *timid*"). He recognized that many places strike us as beautiful not on the basis of aesthetic criteria—because the colours match or there is symmetry and proportion—but on the basis of psychological criteria, because they embody a value or mood of importance to us.

One morning in London, he watched some cumulus clouds from his window. A factual description might have said that they formed a wall, almost completely white, with a few indentations allowing some sun through. But Ruskin approached his subject more psychologically: "The true cumulus, the most majestic of clouds . . . is for the most part windless; the movements of its masses being *solemn*, continuous, *inexplicable*, a steady advance or retiring, as if they were *animated* by an *inner will*, or compelled by an unseen power [my italics]."

In the Alps, he described pine trees and rocks in similarly psychological terms: "I can never stay long without awe under an Alpine cliff, looking up to its pines, as they stand on the inaccessible juts and perilous ledges of an enormous wall, in quiet multitudes, each like the shadow of the one beside it—upright, fixed, *not knowing each other*. You cannot reach them, cannot cry to them—those trees never *heard* human voice; they are far above all sound but of the winds. No foot ever stirred fallen leaf of theirs. All *comfortless* they stand, yet with such *iron will* that the rock itself looks bent and shattered beside them—*fragile, weak, inconsistent*, compared to their dark energy of *delicate life* and *monotony of enchanted pride*."

Through such psychological descriptions, we seem to come closer to answering the question of why a place has stirred us. We come closer to the Ruskinian goal of consciously understanding what we have loved. . . .

And, as he had pointed out when presented with a series of misshapen drawings that a group of his pupils had produced on their travels through the English countryside: "I believe that the sight is a more important thing than the drawing; and I would rather teach drawing that my pupils may learn to love nature, than teach the looking at nature that they may learn to draw."

W hen the cherry blossoms bloomed
They brought beauty to my heart.

~ Tatasu-Jo[48]

[48] From *The Moon in the Pines, Zen Haiku selected and translated by Jonathon Clements, published by* Frances Lincoln, Ltd, © 2000. Reproduced by permission of Frances Lincoln Ltd., 4 Torriano Avenue, London NW5 2RZ. Distributed in the USA by Publishers Group West and in Canada by Raincoast Books. p. 35.

Touching the World When You Touch a Petal

~ Padma Hejmadi[49]

The mesa picks up the colors: chamisa and rabbit brush blossoming yellow everywhere, with fields of wild asters flung between them in flowing scarves of blue and purple across those illimitable distances. . . . That kind of expanse makes you breathe with your whole life. Here, the minor juxtapositions of golden sweet broom and euryops against French lavender, rosemary and blue hibiscus may seem like delusions of all that grandeur; but they try. The blue hibiscus *(Alyogyne hueglii)* may not be a hibiscus at all; but its petals have the magically faint enamel sheen of flowers in illuminated manuscripts.

Lady Murasaki's eleventh-century moon-viewing in *The Tale of Genji* floods my concept of whites along one side of the walled garden— an "Iceberg" rose; the pallor of a potato vine *(Solanum j'asminoides);* white tulips, daffodils and ranunculus; snow-in-summer, etc.—flowering in turn against a ground cover of *Lamium maculatum* massed with silvery heart-shaped leaves, and punctuated by the trunks of white birches that have to be babied along in this inhospitable zone. Then the real floods wash it all away, except the birches, to be replaced by sturdy white irises. No more combinations of moon-viewing plants and poetry.

The patio-turned-mandala makes for an open courtyard in the middle of the enclosed garden, and shamelessly mixes more cross-cultural metaphors, even if they're not always decipherable to the glancing eye. A round central bird bath stands on its mound of earth, representing the cosmic dot in Tantra. Its terra cotta continues the color of the patio tiles and evokes Tanagra figurines. Its turquoise merges into Mughal and Persian blues, blending with the lobelias planted as an integral part of the pattern. Lobelias, let's not forget, have been brought north from the southernmost tip of the African continent and named after botanist Mathias de l'Obel, physician to England's James I. ("Why do these colonial types have to keep changing names?" an indignant friend

---

[49] Padma Hejmadi, *Room to Fly, a Transcultural Memoir*, University of California Press, Berkeley, CA 1999, pp. 138-140. Reprinted by permission of the University of California Press.

demands. "Why not find out the original and stick to it?" Why not indeed: except for clumsy tongues and naming a thing to make it yours. Etymology can be a fascinating friend in the garden.)

So can fragrance. One day in early spring when orange blossoms, jasmine, roses and alyssum happen to be showing off all at the same time, our mail lady delivers a package at the door, sniffs luxuriously, and says: "Aromatherapy! I needed that."

In my language we say a dish without spices is like a child without parents. Roses without fragrance fall into the same category. The faintest scent (of violets) belongs here to the "Lady Banks" rose which threatens to take over most of the backyard, including the nearest branches of a cinnamon camphor tree. *Rosa banksiae* is originally a wild rose from the Yunnan province of China. A doughty Brit, surnamed Forrest, finds it while wandering around two hundred years ago in the Lijiang Valley— pictures of the place show it rimmed by odd-shaped smoky blue mountains—and he recruits his collectors from a village called Ulu Ky, where they use the plant as a hedge. I get lured by seeing a photograph of its graceful arching canes in that remote valley: its white petals, seven slender pointed leaflets, and curiously backward curving thorns. A more accessible thornless double variety is brought back from Canton to Kew Gardens in 1807 and . . . named after the wife of the director. Our French neighbor, who has been long familiar with this double variety, says its yellow form is cultivated in Europe, while the white I yearn for not only flourishes here but is drought-resistant. So I get it and grow it, tracing its journey from China to Kew Gardens to my neighbor's French childhood to this backyard in California. It's like touching the world when you touch a petal.

Which can happen in more ways than one. A psychotherapist I know of works with deeply traumatized immigrants from Cambodia; as one of the first steps toward stability she arranges to have her clients plant a garden. So many of us know the therapeutic value of getting our hands into the soil. I grow roses for the first time after getting some very bad news from India, about which I can do nothing—except grow roses.

Those in the front garden have to be of a variety that won't bleach or shrivel in the sun. Two identical deep reds are planted at the very entrance to the courtyard, just inside and outside the wall, so they tumble

82

contiguously over it and glow in the same tones against its creamy texture. As you enter, the eye can rest on them for a moment before moving from the range of colors beyond the courtyard to those enclosed within.

That sense of rest and continuity becomes even more necessary when trying to make a relatively small area become a fluid space. And with it comes the familiar business of connecting different aspects of that inner and outer space. During the planting we have coral-colored Indian silk cushions just inside the living room window, visible from the outside. So I grow a coral-colored climber to frame those windows. That the silk will eventually fray or fade, and the roses outlast them, makes no difference. Thinking back on what the nursery person said about gardening being an art and not a science, I realize that sometimes this isn't even a question of color and shape, texture and placement; it moves into a realm of poetry, like finding the linked syllables of a perfect phrase.

Virginia Woolf says in a letter: "After all, what is a perfect phrase? One that can mop up as much truth as it can hold." A kind of visual truth is what I'm after, to celebrate the ephemeral as well as the enduring.

W ithout a brush
The willow paints the wind.

~ Saryu[50]

The Ministry of Nature

~ Ralph Waldo Emerson[51]

Every man's condition is a solution in hieroglyphic to those inquiries he would put. He acts it as life, before he apprehends it as truth. In like manner, nature is already, in its forms and tendencies, describing its own design. Standing on the bare ground—my head bathed by the blithe air and uplifted into infinite space—all mean egotism vanishes. I become a

---

[50] From *The Moon in the Pines, Zen Haiku selected and translated by Jonathon Clements, published by* Frances Lincoln, Ltd, © 2000. Reproduced by permission of Frances Lincoln Ltd., 4 Torriano Avenue, London NW5 2RZ. Distributed in the USA by Publishers Group West and in Canada by Raincoast Books, p. 31.

[51] Excerpted from Ralph Waldo Emerson, *Essays*.

transparent eyeball; I am nothing; I see all; the currents of the Universal Being circulate through me.

Nature, in its ministry to man, is not only the material, but is also the process and the result. All the parts incessantly work into each other's hands for the profit of man. The wind sows the seed; the sun evaporates the sea; the wind blows the vapor to the field; the ice, on the other side of the planet, condenses rain on this; the rain feeds the plant, the plant feeds the animal; and thus the endless circulations of the divine charity nourish man.

But in other hours, Nature satisfies by its loveliness, and without any mixture of corporeal benefit. I see the spectacle of morning from the hilltop over against my house, from daybreak to sunrise, with emotions which an angel might share. The long slender bars of cloud float like fishes in the sea of crimson light. From the earth, as a shore, I look out into that silent sea. I seem to partake its rapid transformations; the active enchantment reaches my dust, and I dilate and conspire with the morning wind. How does Nature deify us with a few and cheap elements! Give me health and a day, and I will make the pomp of emperors ridiculous. The dawn is my Assyria; the sunset and moonrise my Paphos, and unimaginable realms of faerie; broad noon shall be my England of the senses and the understanding; the night shall be my Germany of mystic philosophy and dreams.

The presence of a higher, namely, of the spiritual element is essential to its perfection. The high and divine beauty which can be loved without effeminacy, is that which is found in combination with the human will. Beauty is the mark God sets upon virtue. Every natural action is graceful. Every heroic act is also decent, and causes the place and the bystanders to shine!

There is still another aspect under which the beauty of the world may be viewed, namely, as it becomes an object of the intellect. Beside the relation of things to virtue, they have a relation to thought. The intellect searches out the absolute order of things as they stand in the mind of God, and without the colors of affection. The intellectual and the active powers seem to succeed each other, and the exclusive activity of the one generates the exclusive activity of the other. There is something unfriendly in each to the other, but they are like the alternate periods of feeding and working in animals; each prepares and will be followed by the other. Therefore does beauty, which, in relation to actions, as ye have seen, comes unsought, and comes because it is unsought, remain for the apprehension and pursuit of the intellect; and then again, in its turn, of the active power. Nothing divine dies. All good is eternally reproductive. The beauty of nature re-forms itself in the mind, and not for barren contemplation, but for new creation.

All men are in some degree impressed by the face of the world; some men even to delight. This love of beauty is Taste. Others have the same love in such excess, that, not content with admiring, they seek to embody it in new forms. The creation of beauty is Art.

The production of a work of art throws a light upon the mystery of humanity. A work of art is an abstract or epitome of the world. It is the result or expression of nature, in miniature. For although the works of nature are innumerable and all different, the result or the expression of them all is similar and single. Nature is a sea of forms radically alike and even unique. A leaf, a sunbeam, a landscape, the ocean, make an analogous impression on the mind. What is common to them all—that perfectness and harmony—is beauty.

But beauty in nature is not ultimate. It is the herald of inward and eternal beauty, and is not alone a solid and satisfactory good. It must stand as a part, and not as yet the last or highest expression of the final cause of Nature.

Gardens Beneath which Rivers Flow

~ Charles Upton

Earth has always helped humanity remember Eden. The English word *Paradise* comes from a Persian word meaning "walled garden"; the Qur'an describes Paradise as an area of *gardens beneath which rivers flow* (i.e., a world of visible forms whose secret springs of life are in the Unseen). When witnessed in the Light of God, the earth is the very image of these gardens, her green trees and grasses the color of Paradise, which is also the color of Islam, of life and abundance. . . .

God made the universe to remind of Him. "I was a hidden treasure and loved to be known; I created the universe so that I could be known." (*Ḥadith qudsi*) And he made the human heart capable of knowing Him, just as the ear hears sounds or the eye sees light.

We have God's two books to learn from: the universe, and the Holy Qur'an. *And in your own nature, and in [that of] all the animals He scatters [over the earth] there are messages for people who are endowed with inner certainty.* [45:4]

Every Muslim has a duty to seek knowledge: of nature, of God, of other people, and of himself. He who knows himself, knows his Lord. This is why the Prophet (peace and blessings be upon him) said: "O Lord, increase me in knowledge"; and "Seek knowledge, even as far as China"; and "O Lord, show me things as they really are." And again, "He who knows himself knows his Lord."

Divine Beatitude:
Supreme Archetype of Aesthetic Experience

~ Reza Shah Kazami[52]

The experience of beauty, far from being a question of merely aesthetic sensibility, is essentially an invitation to union: union with the Divine Principle, which both projects Beauty and attracts by means of Beauty. One speaks of being entranced, enthralled, enraptured by beauty: these terms clearly indicate the spiritual potential inherent in aesthetic experience, for the individual is not fully himself in the face of a beauty that overwhelms him; indeed, a certain mode of extinction can even be said to have taken place.

Whether or not this spiritual potential will be realized depends on whether the perceiving subject is interiorized or exteriorized by his experience; that is, whether the perception of beautiful form leads one to the formless source of beauty within the heart, to the "kingdom of God

---

[52] Reza Shah Kazami, Excerpted from "Divine Beatitude: Supreme Archetype of Aesthetic Experience," within *Seeing God Everywhere, Essays on Nature and the Sacred*. Edited by Barry McDonald, Copyright 2003 World Wisdom, Inc. pp. 215-218.

that is within you," to God "who is closer to man than his jugular vein;" or whether, on the contrary, the experience of beauty gives rise to a fixation on the transient forms as such and thus to a cult of aestheticism, an art for the sake of art. In this case, the experience of beauty becomes a substitute for God, rather than a pathway to Him; it generates a *ghaflah,* a forgetfulness of God, rather than a *dhikr,* a remembrance of God . . . [53]

The born contemplative cannot see or hear beauty without perceiving in it something of God. The Divine that is contained in it allows him the more easily to detach himself from the appearances of things. As for the passional man, he sees in beauty the world, seduction, the ego, so that it takes him away from the "one thing needful."

Now all men have an existential need for beauty, for on the one hand man is "made in the image of God" *(khalaqa Allahu 'l-Adam 'ala suratihi);* and on the other, "God is Beautiful and He loves Beauty" *(inna Allaha jamilun yuhibbu 'l jamal).* The substance of man's innermost being is woven of Beauty, and like God, he loves Beauty. Consequently, love of beauty imposes itself upon man as an ontological imperative; it is far from being just a sentimental attraction.

"Beauty is in the eye of the beholder." This English saying accords perfectly with a key Platonic principle: the eye must itself be of a luminous nature for it to be able to register light; the truth must be immanent in the intellect for the intellect to be able to recognize truth. It is because beauty is of the essence of man's spirit that he is able to perceive and love beautiful forms; but it must be added that this capacity to intuit the essence in forms depends not only upon one's contemplativity, but also on the degree to which the individual's inherent beauty of soul is actualized: in other words, whether virtue and piety adorn the soul.

According to Plato again: "Beauty is the splendor of the True." Now what this implies, among other things, is that one cannot come to know the Truth without also coming to know and love Beauty, which is found in all its infinite glory only in the Truth. This same fundamental principle is implied in the *hadith qudsi:*

"I was a hidden treasure and I loved to be known, so I created the world."

---

[53] Ibid., pp. 215-216.

The fact that God loved to be known implies that man, in proportion to his coming to know God, will ineluctably come to love Him. The Truth, then, reveals the essence of Beauty, but beauty does not necessarily reveal the truth: it can both enlighten and delude, hence the drama of man's perennial quest for a beauty that is imperishable.[54]

Given the fact that the Divine Reality is at once transcendent and immanent *vis a vis* all formal beauty, it is incumbent on man to take account of both of these dimensions; one must see all beautiful things in God, and God in all beautiful things. Failure to see all beautiful things in God violates the aspect of transcendence: for it is blind to the fact that all beautiful things are prefigured in the Divine Principle which infinitely transcends the world; and failure to see the Divine Beauty in all beautiful things violates the aspect of immanence, by being blind to the fact that objects are beautiful only by virtue of the Divine Beauty that is rendered present through and by them . . . For the contemplative, every beautiful object on earth proves the Divine archetype of Beauty, and every aesthetic experience testifies to the Divine archetype of Beatitude.[55]

This intellectual certitude of the Divine source of all beatitude, of the blissful nature of ultimate Reality, can also be actualized upon contact with Revelation: that is, as a result of reflection upon and contemplation of scripture. The descriptions of God's nature as intrinsic beatitude, goodness, mercy and compassion—encapsulated in the *bismalah*[56]—can awaken the dormant knowledge of these realities within the heart of man. The descriptions of Paradise can serve as a means of Platonic remembrance: for Paradise is not only the final resting-place of man, it was also his original home. For this reason, Plato asserts that music on earth can act as a reminder of the heavenly harmonies which man heard prior to this earthly exile. And, according to the Gospel, "no man hath ascended up to Heaven but he that came down from Heaven" (St. John 3:13).

---

[54] Ibid., pp. 216-217.

[55] Ibid., p. 218.

[56] The Muslim formula of consecration: "In the name of God, the Infinitely Good, the All Merciful" (*Bismi 'Llahi ar-Rahman ar-Rahim*). (Ed. B.M.)

Of the numerous Qur'anic verses describing the felicity of Paradise, we should like to draw attention to one in particular, from the *Surah al-Baqara*. [2:25]

Whenever the dwellers of Paradise are given to eat of the fruits of the Garden they say: this is what we were given to eat before. And they were given the like thereof.

This verse establishes in a most direct manner the relationship between the earthly experience and the celestial archetype of every good. "Fruit" may be taken here to denote the varieties of beatific experience, so the dwellers of Paradise are asserting here that there is a continuity of essence between the delights offered them in Paradise and all positive, noble and beautiful experiences on earth; every mode of happiness on earth is thus a foretaste of a heavenly fruit.[57]

In the *Surah al-Rahman*, mention is made of two pairs of Gardens; following Kashani's esoteric commentary, the lower pair consists of the Gardens of the Soul and Heart, the upper pair being those of the Spirit and Essence.... For Kashani writes, in regard to the two fruits symbolizing the abodes, the date and the pomegranate:

> And the "date palm"—that which containeth food and enjoyment, the contemplation of the celestial lights and the manifestations of Divine Beauty and Majesty in the abode of the spirit, for in its garden the kernel of individuality still remaineth . . . and the "pomegranate"—that which containeth enjoyment and medicinal balm in the abode of totality, in the Garden of the Essence. It is the contemplation of the Essence through pure extinction in which there is no individuality to be fed.[58]

This extinction in the Essence is not only a posthumous possibility: the highest saints also taste it in the most sublime moments of contemplation, even in this life.[59]

---

[57] Ibid., p. 219.
[58] Translation of Dr. Martin Lings, unpublished.
[59] Ibid., p. 221.

The rivers all in Paradise
Flow with the word Allah, Allah
And every longing nightingale
He sings and sings Allah, Allah.

~ Yunus Emre

CHAPTER FIVE

COMMUNICATION

Are you not aware how God offers the parable of a good word?
It is like a good tree, firmly rooted,
reaching its branches towards the sky,
always yielding fruit, by consent of its Sustainer.
This is how God offers parables to human beings,
so that they might consider the truth.
[*Sūrah Ibrāhīm* (Abraham) 14:24-25]

Opening to the Word
~ Camille Helminski

Almost 1400 years before these days in chronological time, someone's heart opened: a man named Muḥammad, the trustworthy, received the Word of God. Such a power the delivery of this Word effected upon him that he felt as though his ribs were almost crushed in the Angel Gabriel's embrace. The command "Read!" shook him to the bone. He felt his incapacity, and responded, "But I cannot."[60] Gabriel repeated the command of His Lord:

"Recite!" In the name of Your Sustainer Who created,
created humankind from a connecting cell:
"Recite!" And your Sustainer is the Most Generous,
He Who taught by the pen,
taught humankind what it did not know![61]

The Word burst forth as such a compelling light within the heart of Muḥammad ﷺ that it had to be shared as a *guidance and a mercy to all*

---

[60] Muhammad's words were, *"Maa ana bi Qaari."* ("I am not a reciter," or " I am not one who reads.")
[61] Qur'an *Sūrah al-Iqra* 96:1-5.

humankind.[62] Continually our Creator is communicating with us, through messengers, through revelation, through the worlds of manifestation in signs and through our own hearts. We as human beings and other *ummahs*[63] have also been granted the capacity of communication each among ourselves. Through mutual communication creatures within each community of creation are able to support each other in growth and development. Sometimes this communication crosses species as the matrixes of life interweave. The more we listen and watch, the more we hear, the more we witness.

Come

~ David James Duncan[64]

I came to water too deep to wade, too deep to see bottom: a shady black pool, surface-foam eddying like stars in a nebula. And though I wanted to keep exploring, though I'd barely begun, the big pool proved a psychic magnet . . .

Its surface was a night sky in broad daylight . . .

Its depths were another world within this one . . .

The entire frenetic creek stopped here to rest . . .

I was 78 percent water myself . . .

I felt physically ordered to crawl out on a cantilevered log, settle belly-down, and watch the pool gyre directly beneath me, the foam-starred surface eddying, eddying, till it became a vision of night; water-

---

[62] Qur'an *Sūrah al-Yunus* 10:57.

[63] An *Ummah* is a community of creatures (pl. *umam*). In the Qur'an it is recognized that each species is its own community created and sustained by God. (C.A.H.)

See *Qur'an* 6:38: . . . *there is no beast that walks on earth and no bird that flies on its two wings which is not [God's] creature like yourselves: no single thing have We neglected in Our decree.*

[64] From *My Story as Told by Water*, by David James Duncan. Copyright © 2001 by David James Duncan. Reprinted by permission of Sierra Club Books, San Francisco, CA, pp. 11-12.

skipper meteors; sun-glint novas. The creek would not stop singing. I spun and spiraled, grew foam-dazed and gyre-headed. Pieces of the mental equipment I'd been taught to think I needed began falling into the pool and dissolving: my preference of light to darkness; sense of rightsideup and upsidedownness, sense of surfaces and edges, sense of where I end and other things or elements begin. The pool taught nothing but mystery and depth. An increasingly dissolved "I" followed the first verb, gravity, down. Yet depth, as the dissolved "I" sees it, is also height.

Then, up from those sunless depths, or yet also down from foam-starred heavens, a totem-red, tartan-green impossibility descended or arose, its body so massive and shining, visage so travel-scarred and ancient, that I was swallowed like Jonah by the sight. I know no better way to invoke the being's presence than to state the naked name:

Coho. An old male coho, *arcing* up not to eat, as trout do, but just to submarine along without effort or wings; just to move, who knows why, through a space and time it created for itself as it glided. And as it eased past my face not a body's length away, the coho gazed—with one lidless, primordial eye—clean into the suspended heart of me: gazed not like a salmon struggling up from an ocean to die, but like a Gaelic or Kwakiutl messenger dropped down from a realm of gods, *Tir na nOg,* world of deathlessness, world of *Ka* [water],[65] to convey, via the fact of its being, a timeless message of sacrifice and hope. The creek would not stop singing. My bagpipe heart could not stop answering. When you see a magnificent ocean fish confined in small, fresh water, it is always like a dream. And in our dreams, every object, place, and being is something inside us. Despite my smallness, ignorance, inexperience, I felt a sudden huge sense of entitlement. This creek and its music, secret world and its messenger, belonged to me completely. Or I to them.

The coho vanished as serenely as it had come, back into depth. But not before its shining eye changed the way I see out of my own. I'd glimpsed a way into a Vast Inside. A primordial traveler through water and time had said, *Come.*

---

[65] "Truly water springs up for he or she who knows the name and nature of recitation. Recitation is water." Ibid., p. 3.

A leaf, a drop, a crystal, a moment of time, is related to the whole, and partakes of the perfection of the whole. Each particle is a microcosm, and faithfully renders the likeness of the world. . . .

If the Reason be stimulated to more earnest vision, outlines and surfaces become transparent, and are no longer seen; causes and spirits are seen through them. The best moments of life are these delicious awakenings of the higher powers, and the reverential withdrawing of nature before its God.

Through all its kingdoms, to the suburbs and outskirts of things, it is faithful to the cause whence it had its origin. It always speaks of Spirit. It suggests the absolute. It is a perpetual effect. It is a great shadow pointing always to the sun behind us.

That essence refuses to be recorded in propositions, but when man has worshipped Him intellectually, the noblest ministry of nature is to stand as the apparition of God. It is the organ through which the universal Spirit speaks to the individual, and strives to lead back the individual to it.

When I behold a rich landscape, it is less to my purpose to recite correctly the order and superposition of the strata, than to know why all thought of multitude is lost in a tranquil sense of unity.

~ Ralph Waldo Emerson[66]

Listening

~ Charles Upton

When trying to tell the difference between things by naming them, we tend to rely on our eyes: we attach a particular name to a particular object we see. But to get a sense of the original Unity that exists *before* we start naming things, one thing we can do is pay more attention to what we *hear* than what we see. When we name things, we merely attach words to them; when God names things, He brings them into existence. If we stop speaking and talking to ourselves for once, and listen instead to the sounds of the world, it is as if we were listening to the sound of God's original act of creation.

---

[66] Excerpted from *Selected Essays* of Ralph Waldo Emerson, "Language," p. 61.

Listening softens the gaze. And if we listen deeply enough—if, that is, we stop talking to ourselves completely enough—then the Eye of the Heart may open, and let us see into the heart of things.

The world is God's first Book, in which every form is a letter or sentence. But the world is also an echo of God's spoken Word, in which every sound is a reverberation of the original word *Kun,* "Be!", by which He brings all things into existence. The sense of sight is related to our ability to tell things apart by naming them. The visual forms of objects appear as established facts; they seem to exist in their own right. In the face of their matter-of-fact existence, we tend to forget that, in reality, all things are signs of God.

The sense of hearing is different. It is related more to God's continuous act of creating the universe than to the catalogue of what He has already created. This is why, in Islam, the written and spoken word is emphasized over the image, and why making images of the natural world is discouraged, and why making an image of God is forbidden: because an image is always in danger of turning into an idol. Whenever we take something literally, as if it existed in its own right rather than being an act of God, we have made an idol out of it. If we see the universe as made up of *things,* we are tempted to identify with those things, to desire and possess them; and the first step toward possessing something is to define it, to give it a name. *That which you serve, apart from Him, is nothing but names yourselves have named* [12:40]. But if we see the universe as made up of *acts of God,* acts which we can no more predict, or control, or grasp with our greedy hands than the next gust of wind or the next cry of a bird, then this kind of idolatry becomes impossible to us. All we can do is wait, in attentive silence, for God's next gift. His next warning. His next command. Instead of always trying to name and define things, why not keep silent, and listen to how *God* is pleased to name and define things? Why not let *Him* teach *us* their shapes and definitions? *He taught Adam the names, all of them* [2:31]. After all, it is He, not us, who creates them.

Sound is bigger than us; it surrounds us and washes over us. We can deliberately look in a particular direction, but we can't deliberately *listen* in a particular direction. Sounds simply come to us, unpredictably, uncontrollably, from beyond what we know. This is why *hearing* is related to *obedience*—instead of judging and discriminating, we simply "hear and obey" [2:285]. To *hear* is to *heed*. With our eyes we investigate, we spy things out—but the knowledge that flows into our ears is something that is impressed upon us, not something we can grasp or locate on our own initiative.

The will of God comes into our experience through the dimension of time. We become sensitive to the will of God by paying attention to the changes that are always going on—and one of the best ways to do this is simply by listening instead of looking. If we listen deeply enough we can hear the subtle changes in the quality of passing time, like changes in the weather, or in the quality of light, or the mood we and our friends are in. If we listen deeply enough to the sounds of the world, we may almost hear the silent pressure of God's creative power—the word *Kun*—by which He brings all things into existence. *When He decrees a thing, He but says to it "Be," and it is.* [19:35]

In listening to the sounds of the world, you simply sit and attend to all the sounds within your range—birds, wind in the trees, flowing water, traffic sounds, human voices—and hear them as the voice of Allah, the vibration of the primal creative Source of the Universe, finally reaching your ears.

When you listen to the sounds of the world, you begin to see yourself as part of the world around you, a universe created by God before you were born, immensely bigger than you in space, immensely older than you in time. And you also come to understand that God's act of creating the world never ended; it is still going on. If he were to stop saying *Kun!* (Be!) for one instant, the universe and everything in it would fall into oblivion. This is one way of coming to a deeper understanding of what it means that *God is Creator, Producer, Fashioner, Lord of all Worlds.*[67]

The practice of paying attention to the natural world is a discipline in itself; it requires us to suppress our formless agitation, our obsessive planning and strategizing, as well as the images produced in our mind by fear and desire. We must never forget that heedlessness is only cured by

---

[67] *Note:* Although this kind of deep listening can be practiced anywhere, among the best places to do it, are by a stream or waterfall, or on the shore of the ocean, or in a wooded area, during a gentle wind. (Or if at night, the frogs and the crickets.) ~ C. Upton

discipline; we must also never forget that Paradise is a Garden, of which the natural world is the clearest of signs. *As for those who have attained to righteousness—what of those who have attained to righteousness? They, too, will find themselves amidst fruit-laden trees, and acacias flower-clad, and shade extended, and waters gushing and fruit abounding, never failing and never out of reach* [56:27-33].

When we go out into the natural world, into that part of the planet which is neither destroyed nor cultivated by human action—the part that "arises of itself," not by our own efforts and plans and agendas, but by the will of God—we meet a different part of ourselves. When you are in a natural, living environment, an environment that possesses life, like you do, but does not possess serious heavy ego, then you can begin to feel how your body is a part of nature, part of God's creation, one more living organism among the bugs and plants and birds. . . . *there is no beast that walks on earth and no bird that flies on its two wings which is not [God's] creature like yourselves: no single thing have We neglected in Our decree* [6:38].

Invisible Gifts

~ Camille Helminski

And [in this insight] Solomon was David's heir; and he would say:
"O you people! We have been taught the speech of birds,
and have been given [in abundance] of all [good] things:
this, behold, is indeed a manifest favour [from God]!"
And [one day] there were assembled before Solomon his hosts
of invisible beings, and of men, and of birds;
and then they were led forth in orderly ranks,
till, when they came upon a valley [full] of ants, an ant exclaimed:
"O you ants! Get into your dwellings,
lest Solomon and his hosts crush you without being aware [of you]!"

So he smiled, amused at her speech,
and he said: "O my Sustainer! So direct me that I may be grateful
for Your blessings which You have bestowed on me
and on my parents
and that I may do the good work that will please You;
and admit me by Your Grace
among the ranks of Your righteous servants."
[*Sūrah An-Naml (The Ants)* 27:15-19]

This prayer of Solomon is in response to the words of an ant, within the surah of the Qur'an conveying much of Solomon's story, as well as stories of Moses and Salih, but entitled "The Ants" in honor of these tiny creatures. Solomon offers his prayer in gratitude for his comprehension, and the compassion and admiration for all of nature which God had bestowed upon him.

The saints and prophets share this sensitive capacity with many of the native peoples who have learned to listen deeply to the animals and to the earth. Native Americans as well as saints like Francis of Assisi refer to the animals as their kindred, respecting "brother wolf," and also "sister moon," and acknowledging the need to recognize their voices and open to instruction from all that is.

And What if Rocks Speak

~ F. David Peat[68]

Native people talk of speaking to animals, trees, and rocks. As Leroy Little Bear puts it, "Trees talk to you, but you don't expect them to speak in English or Blackfoot." Part of me senses—in a very fragile and dim way—what Leroy [is] getting at. I think that part of our difficulty may be that our society, with all the intense drama of television and film, has conditioned us to think of the voice of a rock as something that will boom and reverberate into our minds like God in a biblical spectacular.

---

[68] F. David Peat, *Blackfoot Physics, A Native Journeying into the Native American Universe*, Fourth Estate Ltd, London, England, 1996 p. 288.

But what if this voice is very quiet and subtle, a gentle movement unlike the normal chattering of our thoughts; something closer to a gentle breeze than to a hurricane, to a sixth sense rather than a confrontation, a feeling rather than a thought, an emotion rather than a sentence? Silence surrounds indigenous people. Could it be that the voices of trees and rocks can only be heard within such a silence? Maybe the voices are always present, but we in the West have forgotten what it is to be still. As Therese Schroeder-Sheker put it, the angels want to sing to us, if we could only be silent long enough to hear them.

Learning Nature's Language

~ Henry David Thoreau

But while we are confined to books, though the most select and classic, and read only particular written languages, which are themselves but dialects and provincial, we are in danger of forgetting the language which all things and events speak without metaphor, which alone is copious and standard. Much is published, but little printed. The rays which stream through the shutter will be no longer remembered when the shutter is wholly removed. No method nor discipline can supersede the necessity of being forever on the alert. What is a course of history or philosophy, or poetry, no matter how well selected, or the best society, or the most admirable routine of life, compared with the discipline of looking always at what is to be seen? Will you be a reader, a student merely, or a seer? Read your fate, see what is before you, and walk on into futurity.

I did not read books the first summer [at Walden Pond]; I hoed beans. Nay, I often did better than this. There were times when I could not afford to sacrifice the bloom of the present moment to any work, whether of the head or hands. I love a broad margin to my life. Sometimes, in a summer morning, having taken my accustomed bath, I sat in my sunny doorway from sunrise till noon, rapt in a revery, amidst the pines and hickories and sumachs, in undisturbed solitude and stillness, while the birds sang around or flitted noiseless through the house, until by the sun falling in at my west window, or the noise of some traveller's wagon on the distant highway, I was reminded of the lapse of time. I grew in those seasons like corn in the night, and they were far better than any work of the hands would have been. They were not time subtracted from my life, but so much over and above my usual allowance. . . .

I had this advantage, at least, in my mode of life, over those who were obliged to look abroad for amusement, to society and the theatre, that my life itself was become my amusement and never ceased to be novel. It was a drama of many scenes and without an end.[69]

★★★

This is a delicious evening, when the whole body is one sense, and imbibes delight through every pore. I go and come with a strange liberty in Nature, a part of herself. As I walk along the stony shore of the pond in my shirt-sleeves, though it is cool as well as cloudy and windy, and I see nothing special to attract me, all the elements are unusually congenial to me. The bullfrogs trump to usher in the night, and the note of the whip-poor-will is borne on the rippling wind from over the water. Sympathy with the fluttering alder and poplar leaves almost takes away my breath; yet, like the lake, my serenity is rippled but not ruffled. These small waves raised by the evening wind are as remote from storm as the smooth reflecting surface. Though it is now dark, the wind still blows and roars in the wood, the waves still dash, and some creatures lull the rest with their notes.[70]

Versatile Words

~ Lincoln Barnett[71]

Although animal communication is limited in range, the variety of methods by which it takes place is enormous at all levels of the evolutionary ladder. Insects, the largest class of living creatures both in number of individuals and number of species, transfer information by

---

[69] Excerpted from Henry David Thoreau, *Walden*, chapter four, "Sounds."

[70] Ibid., excerpted from chapter five, "Solitude."

[71] Lincoln Barnett, *The Treasure of Our Tongue*, Knopf, NY, NY, 1962, pp. 53, 54, and 55.

means of many highly specialized organs and codes. Some involve the auditory sense. Crickets, locusts, and cicadas, for example, "talk" by stridulation—the production of sound by friction between rough, file-like surfaces or plates on legs, wings, abdomen, and thorax. . . . Much of the insect world is silent. Fireflies, glow worms, and various luminous beetles identify their kind, summon mates, and discourage predators by the emission of cold light. Many moths and butterflies possess a delicacy of olfactory sense that enables them to interpret and respond to scent stimuli at distances of more than a mile. The social insects have still more specialized systems of information transfer. . . .

The most extraordinary of all insect languages is the semantic dance of the honeybee, a phenomenon described in the classic studies of the German entomologist Karl von Frisch over several decades beginning in 1920. The remarkable feature of the dance is the quantity and accuracy of the information it conveys. When an individual bee has discovered a source of food, it returns to the hive, dusted with pollen, perfumed with nectar, and performs a dance on the vertical wall of the comb to attract the attention of its fellow workers and to announce its discovery. . . .

Of all classes of animals, birds are the most continuously vocal and, save for man, the most versatile in their vocalizing.

Caring for the Young

~ Brian J. Ford[72]

Birds show great devotion to their young. A ground-nesting plover takes risks to protect her brood. If a fox approaches she crouches low over the nest, protecting the young. If the predator approaches too closely, then she scuttles away from the nest towards the fox in order to attract its attention. Her skittering through the grass mimics the action of a mouse or a vole, and the fox takes off after her. She resists any urge to take to the

---

[72] The following selection is excerpted from *Sensitive Souls, Senses and Communication in Plants, Animals, and Microbes* by Brian J. Ford, pp. 129-131. Permission granted by Time Warner Book Group UK.

air, but manages to keep ahead of the fox as he tracks her away from the unprotected nest. Once she has led him safely away from the site of her nest, she takes to the air and flies slowly away, luring the fox onwards. Finally, she takes a circuitous route back to her young, leaving the fox bewildered, at a safe distance and facing the wrong way.

Many birds vocalize at their young—they talk to them. Often this starts before hatching. A mallard incubating her clutch of eggs will mutter sounds to the eggs. The tiny ducklings within the eggs will respond as they near the hatching time, and will utter sounds of their own. There is clearly some kind of language here, and the ducklings often initiate the exchange. Sounds have been heard coming from eggs without there having been any stimulation from outside, though the mother duck usually responds to such a message with calls of her own.

We do not know what they communicate, though there have been attempts to examine sound spectrographs or voice-prints from the sounds. It has been shown that the vocal communication peaks immediately after the hatching of the chick. There is a possibility that the sounds serve to tell the youngsters when to hatch. If eggs of a clutch are incubated, the hatchlings emerge over a period of a couple of days. A clutch of the same eggs reared by the mother will all hatch within six or eight hours, even though the chicks are of differing degrees of maturity. It may be that it is the vocalisation which coordinates this, for the chicks have to initiate the hatching processes by chipping their way out of the shell.

There are obvious benefits. A brood of ducklings hatching together allows the mother to rear them as a batch and to make sure she protects them all at once. If they were to hatch at different times, she would be neglecting one batch (eggs or hatchlings) while she cared for the other. The young get to know the mother's voice during this time, and this helps them to bond with her and to follow her when they are in the open. That is vital for the safety of a young and vulnerable duckling. It has been known for over half a century that these young birds bond to the first thing they see. Ordinarily it would be their mother, but if it is a human they see first they will bond to that person instead. They will bond to anything—even a scrubbing-brush or a mask. Since these experiments by Konrad Lorenz there have been many subsequent enquiries into this phenomenon of imprinting. It should be emphasized that in Lorenz's original papers the term was *Pragung,* meaning "stamping" or "embossing" (as in the production of medals or coinage). The translation "imprinting" is not quite right.

There is an obvious developmental benefit in being attracted to your mother. This must be what lies behind the nursery-rhyme about Mary and her little lamb, which followed her everywhere she went. The lamb had been imprinted with Mary. In reality, "imprinting" in the sense of *Pragung* is the wrong expression, for it implies permanence. In fact, birds learn to adapt to alternative objects or individuals quite quickly. In one experiment, a group of mallard ducklings were left in visual contact with a research worker for a continuous 20 hours after hatching. They became imprinted, and followed him devotedly. However, this was not the end of the experiment. In this instance the young birds were subsequently allowed to mingle with a mother mallard, who had herself hatched a clutch of eggs a few hours before. Within 90 minutes the imprinted ducklings were all following the mother mallard and her brood, and it was impossible to distinguish between the imprinted birds and the ones she had hatched herself. They showed no further predilection for the research worker who had been their surrogate parent.

Much of what we take for mechanical programming is a learning process. The imprinting of young ducks can be reversed. If imprinting phenomena are what we seek to find, then the experiments we construct are designed to demonstrate the desired effect and there is little interest in what happens later. A subsequent experiment might show that the mechanistic approach ought to be set in context with a more pliable and adaptive process of learning by experience, supplemented by unlearning through expediency. Young birds learn, and learn through their senses.

The Dolphin as Ally

~ Brian J. Ford[73]

Mother whales and dolphins are devoted to caring for their young. There is much evidence of cooperation, of care for injured individuals in the school, of attentiveness during birth. It is the dolphin, however, that has the reputation for being friendly to humankind. . . .

Brain size is irrelevant, or a shrew would be a million times less intelligent than an elephant. If there is a single criterion, it would be the ratio of the cortex to the medulla: the relationship of the outer layer of the brain to its overall volume. Humans have an extensive cortex, which is why it is folded into ridges. Dolphins have smoother brains because the ratio of surface area to volume is much the same as in other mammals. They do not have super-high intelligence or mental powers which compare with ours. Yet they can communicate verbally. Their beautiful and haunting sub-aquatic songs, and the excited clicks and chuckles they utter to their human handlers, clearly constitute a more complex language than we imagine.

Dolphins have a lengthy history of association with humans, and legends show how long they have been construed as intelligent. Their associations with humans date back to prehistory. Over 20,000 years ago paleolithic cave artists at Levano, in the Engadi Islands off the coast of Sicily, painted pictures of dolphins and men together. In Crete the dolphin was worshipped as a god. When the cult spread to mainland Greece, dolphins were respected as humans in reincarnated form. When Apollo was said to have guided ships through storm-tossed seas to the safety of Criss, near Delphio, he did so in the form of a dolphin, and it was believed that Apollo's son Icadius was saved by a dolphin after being shipwrecked. He was borne safely to dry land, and after he was set ashore the seat of Apollo was established nearby, on Mount Parnassus.

A man riding on a dolphin appeared on ancient Greek coinage and on wax seals. One legend tells of a notable musician returning home by

---

[73] The following selection is excerpted from *Sensitive Souls, Senses and Communication in Plants, Animals, and Microbes* by Brian J. Ford, pp. 40-44. Reprinted by permission of Time Warner Book Group UK.

sea after winning a competition. He was robbed of his prizes and thrown overboard by mutinous sailors. Dolphins rescued him and carried him safely to port where he was able to report the offense in time for the sailors to be captured and punished. The Greek philosopher Aristotle (384-322 B.C.) wrote on the friendship which exists between dolphins and people. Three centuries later, the *Historia Naturalis* of Pliny the Elder (A.D. 23-79) contained an account of a dolphin which regularly transported a boy across the sea to school, and added, "Ampholicians and Tarentines testify to touching dolphins which were friends of little boys." He also recounted a tale of a monkey in a shipwreck being rescued by a dolphin and transported safely to shore. A century after that, the poet Oppian described how dolphins helped fishermen near Athens to catch fish from the shore. The fish in a bay were prevented from escaping by dolphins which would drive them towards shallow water, where they could be caught by men with tridents. The dolphins would be given their allotted share by the fishermen. Some of these stories have counterparts in the modern world. It has been reported that Brazilian fishermen still cooperate with dolphins which drive schools of fish towards their nets.

Accounts of dolphins coming to the aid of people are many. During the mid-1970s a dolphin known as Beaky was regularly seen around the Isle of Man. He gave youngsters rides upon his back, trying to lift them clear of the water. Later he became known in the waters around Cornwall, where he was said to have saved several lives. One was of a diver who got into difficulties off Land's End and was borne back to his boat by the dolphin. Several swimmers claim that their lives have been saved by dolphins off the coast of Florida. A dolphin which accompanied ships across the Cook Strait in New Zealand for many years was protected by law, and a Governor's Order in Council was passed to make it an offence to harm the species. Swimming with dolphins is a form of therapy that has been used with success in treating children with mental disabilities. It has enabled autistic children to communicate and in some cases to show improvement beyond all expectation. The participation of the dolphins is itself interesting, for they clearly become involved in the process of therapy and seem to enjoy it. So great are the benefits to the young patients that one centre at Key Largo, Florida, is able to fund referred patients through health insurance.

It seems that dolphins can learn by studying their own kind. In an American marine park, a dolphin was painstakingly trained to move a buoy by pulling it. When this animal became ill and was removed from the tank, another dolphin was selected to perform the task. This dolphin preferred to move the buoy by a different method, pushing it along with its snout. As this worked just as well, the trainers allowed the animal to do this in its performance. When this second dolphin suddenly died, another in the group took over, immediately pushing the buoy along without any training. For two days in the following month this dolphin would not take part in the performance, so a fourth dolphin took over. He immediately performed by pulling the buoy along with his snout, just as the first-trained animal had done. It was concluded that the dolphins could see how to perform by watching the performer, and the memory of the different techniques stayed with them.

Dolphins show many levels of emotion. They pine for a lost mate and show distress if separated. A paper published in the *Journal of Mammalogy* recounts the depressed behaviour of a young female dolphin which, after having been caught on a hook, was placed in a marine tank to recover. She remained listless and unable to support herself to breathe, so a male was brought in as company. He spent much time in attendance, holding the female with his beak so that she could breathe in comfort, and her demeanor immediately improved. Within weeks she was well on the way to recovery and the two spent much time playing and swimming together. Three months later she became ill again, as a result of an infection of the original wound, and the male showed increasing signs of distress as her condition worsened. At her death, he uttered a loud cry. From then on he would not feed, but circled the tank aimlessly, uttering cries, until he too died three days later. It is certainly clear that dolphins care for each other when sick or disabled, and become distressed when a group member dies.

Many other mammals pine for a lost partner. They are not alone: pairing birds, such as swans, are said to do so, too, and so do some fish. That these animals feel the loss intensely is clear from their responses. Emotions are widespread in the animal world. To claim that we are the only species to suffer distress is to deny the evidence of our observations.

106

Truly God has one hundred lovingkindnesses; one of which He has sent down among man, quadrupeds, and every moving thing upon the face of the earth: by it they are kind to each other, and forgive one another; and by it the animals of the wilds are kind to their young; and God has reserved ninety-nine kindnesses, by which He will be gracious to His creatures on the last day.

~ *Hadith* of The Prophet Muhammad ﷺ[74]

[74] As quoted in *The Wisdom of Muhammad*, by Allama Sir Abdullah Al-Mamun Al-Suhrawardy, Citadel Press and Kensington Publishing Corp., NY, NY, 2001, p. 41.

CHAPTER SIX

ADAPTABILITY

He is God, the Creator, the Evolver, the Bestower of form!
To Hu belong the Most Beautiful Names.
All that is in the heavens and on earth declares His praises and glory:
for He is the Exalted in Might, the All-Wise!
[Sūrah Al-Ḥashr (The Gathering) 59:24]

Truly, God does not change men's condition
unless they change their own selves.
[Sūrah Ar-Raʿd (Thunder) 13:11]

Why not go out on a limb? That's where the fruit is.
~ Will Rogers

The water birds seem heavy
But they float.
~ Onitsura[75]

---

[75] From *The Moon in the Pines, Zen Haiku selected and translated by Jonathon Clements*, *published by* Frances Lincoln, Ltd, © 2000. Reproduced by permission of Frances Lincoln Ltd., 4 Torriano Avenue, London NW5 2RZ. Distributed in the USA by Publishers Group West and in Canada by Raincoast Books, p. 23.

Thar She Blows!

~ David Pitt-Brooke[76]

There Leviathan hugest of living creatures, on the deep
Stretched like a promontory, sleeps or swims
And seems a moving land, and at his gills
Draws in, and at his trunk spouts out a sea.

~ John Milton, *Paradise Lost,* Book 7

Milton may have been a little hazy on cetacean anatomy but he certainly had a tight grip on the one essential fact regarding whales. They're big. Blue whales, the greatest of all great whales—up to 410 metres in length and 136 tonnes—are thought to be the largest animals ever to have lived on Earth, bigger than the biggest dinosaurs. Even gray whales, though not particularly hefty as whales go, are very substantial animals at 15 metres and 30 tonnes—half again as long and twice as heavy as a fully loaded Greyhound bus.

Human beings are fascinated by cetacean superlatives. We love the exotic facts, those aspects of whale biology that make them so different from us. We relish the massiveness of blue whales with their automobile-sized hearts and culvert-sized tracheas. We're fascinated by the thought of sperm whales diving to depths of a thousand metres and staying submerged for an hour at a time while wrestling giant squid in the stygian darkness. We love the idea that great whales may communicate across thousands of kilometres of open ocean with low-frequency sound.

But these *Ripley's Believe It or Not* facts—glamorous though they may be—are essentially superficial. The truly remarkable thing about whales is not that they are so different from us, but that they are so similar. Milton notwithstanding, whales do not have gills nor do they spout seawater—they have lungs and breathe air, like us. The chief cause of death in whales isn't injury, disease or even old age, but drowning. They may be old, they may be badly injured, they way be mortally ill, but drowning is

---

[76] Excerpted from *Chasing Clayoquot, A Wilderness Almanac* by David Pitt-Brooke, Raincoast Books, Vancouver, BC Canada, 2004. (www.raincoast.com), pp. 84-86; 86-87, 88-89, 92 and 95, "Thar She Blows, the Springtime Migration of Gray Whales."

what actually kills them when they can no longer struggle to the surface for another breath. Like us, whales are warm-blooded mammals, maintaining a constant body temperature even in bitter cold water. Like us, they bear their babies in a womb and suckle them with milk. They even have some hair, like us, though the beard on a whale amounts to little more than a few bristles on the top of the snout-whiskers. . . .

Whales and human beings also share a basic terrestrial pedigree. One hundred million years ago, the distant ancestors of modern cetaceans were little mammals living along the seashore and feeding on small fish, invertebrates and such-like. They must have looked and behaved something like modern-day mink. Over eons, generation upon generation, the little beasts spent more and more time in the water. That shift in habitat must have conferred some benefit on animals willing to take the plunge. Perhaps food was more plentiful in the water, perhaps there were fewer competitors or predators.

On the other hand, spending more time in the water would also have imposed significant costs on those pioneers. The aquatic environment poses a number of rigorous challenges for land mammals. Just getting around is a problem; water is so much thicker than air.

One of the really fascinating aspects of cetacean biology is to consider the solutions that families in this branch of the class mammalia have evolved to the problems of life in a fundamentally alien medium. On the problem of getting around, for example: the de-evolution of hind limbs, the modification of front limbs into broad paddles for steering, the development of massive, powerful tails with flattened flukes for propulsion. The kinship between humans and cetaceans lends the subject a special interest; we can empathize. Looking at whales, we see ourselves mirrored back and distorted by deep waters.[77]

★★★

Every spring, pretty well the entire eastern Pacific population of California gray whales, well over twenty thousand animals, migrates the length of North America's Pacific coast, almost ten thousand kilometres. The adults have just spent three months—December, January, February, perhaps part of March—in the saltwater lagoons of Baja California, calving

---

[77] Ibid., pp. 84-86.

and mating. Now they're headed for rich summertime feeding grounds in the Bering and Chukchi seas. It is one of the world's truly remarkable natural phenomena, perhaps the greatest mammalian migration on the planet. Imagine an enormous herd of great beasts—every adult bigger than a bus—moving the length of a continent to their summer pasture. . . .

Gray whales are shallow-water whales, bottom-feeders. Unique among cetaceans, they filter small invertebrates from the sand and muck of the seafloor. On migration they hug the coast, more or less, navigating from headland to headland. And every year between late February and early May—but peaking noticeably in late March or early April—the whole procession goes right past my door. These whales are mostly in travel mode, putting the kilometres behind them. For six months they have fasted. Now they are anxious to get back north again and begin feeding in earnest. But occasionally they stop to rest and forage for a few hours in one of the shallow, sheltered waterways along the coast. The herring have just finished spawning and the gray whales are feeding at least partly on roe. In fact, some cetologists believe that the timing of gray whale migration may be determined to some extent by the progression of herring spawn from south to north. The whales exploit this rich but ephemeral food supply to help fuel their journey.

Hesquiat Harbour, at the very northern end of Clayoquot Sound, is one place where gray whales pause to rest and forage, sometimes in significant numbers. I have seen photos of the harbour showing gray whales scattered across its expanse like grazing cattle. But it's a short-lived phenomenon. One day the whales are present in extraordinary numbers, the next day they're gone.[78]

★★★

One of the problems that whales have, being big, is finding sufficient sustenance. It takes a powerful mess of food to sustain those tons of flesh and keep their metabolic fires stoked. All whales are predators but they fall into two distinct categories with very different foraging strategies. Toothed whales—orcas, sperm whales, dolphins—feed on relatively large prey that they actively pursue, seize with simple pointed teeth and gulp more or less whole.

---

[78] Ibid., pp. 86-87.

Baleen whales—gray whales, bowhead whales, blue whales—feed on relatively tiny prey, small fish and crustaceans. It seems ironic that Earth's largest predators should hunt such tiny creatures. But it makes sense for very large animals to look for sustenance at the bottom of the trophic pyramid, where a greater mass of food can be easily had, than at the top, where individual items of prey, though large, are scarce and hard to catch.

How do such large animals capture and hold such tiny prey? And, more subtly, how do they manage to eat that prey without ingesting a lot of very salty ocean as well? In short, they've managed to evolve a sort of colander in their mouths. They have given up teeth. Their gums develop a growth of baleen plates, long sheets of keratin—the protein of fingernails—hanging vertically in their cavernous mouths and overlapping like the slats of a Venetian blind. The inner edge of each plate is frayed into fibres or bristles. The mat of bristles inside the overlapping plates serves as an effective net or strainer. The size of the mesh thus formed varies between different species of whale, depending on their habitual food: coarser for larger prey, finer for smaller prey. When baleen whales have a mouthful, they use their tongues to press the seawater out of their food. The water escapes through the baleen while the food remains trapped inside.[79]

★★★

Large whales probably cannot see their own tails much of the time. In the clearest tropical waters, three-quarters of available sunlight is lost in the first ten metres. The ocean is pitch dark at depths greater than 200 metres. In the murk of cold plankton-rich waters along the west coast of Vancouver Island, visibility is even more limited: sunlight penetrates a mere 15 to 35 metres.

Whales have compensated by evolving exceptionally acute hearing. The process has been less straightforward than you might think. It wasn't just a matter of growing larger, more sensitive ears like a fox or a bat. Mammalian ears evolved to work in air. Submerged in water, we lose our capacity to determine the direction of a sound. Carried through the liquid and bone of our bodies, rather than our external ears, a sound seems to come from everywhere at once—try it in the bathtub sometime.

---

[79] Ibid., pp. 88-89.

So cetacean evolution had to substantially rework the anatomy of the skull and inner ear. The bones enclosing the middle ear, firmly attached to the rest of the skull in other mammals, float free in whales, anchored only with soft tissue. The bones inside the middle ear have been modified to capture vibrations from areas along the sides of the head, rather than from the external ear, and the whole structure is surrounded by pockets containing a mucus foam that provides acoustic insulation.

As a result, whales have excellent underwater directional hearing. The toothed whales can also generate precise high-frequency sound pulses, and evidence suggests that their brains are good at interpreting the returning echoes. In effect, they are equipped with biological sonar, active echolocation.[80]

***

Suddenly a whale surfaces right beside us. The animal is close enough that I can see its eye, surprisingly small for such a huge body. The eye is watching us. The plane[81] bobs in the spreading ripple. The whale's skin is a mottled grey encrusted with barnacles. Perhaps because they are slower moving or because they spend so much time grubbing around on the bottom, gray whales accumulate a load of external parasites, including one highly specialized species of barnacle that lives nowhere else.

The whale exhales quickly and then inhales, just as quickly. I listen through the open door. I smell the fetid odour, see the little rainbow in the droplets of exhalation. The sound of a whale breath is not what I expected. You might think that this large ponderous animal should take large ponderous breaths. Not so. Our whale gasped for air—that's the only word to describe it—a very brief, sharp exhalation followed immediately by a quick inhalation. Think of a small child paddling in cold water, mostly holding his breath, but every now and then gasping for air, while trying not to inhale any water—that is the sound of a whale breathing and it is a revelation to me, an unexpected point of kinship. A minor epiphany. I take away a stronger sense of empathy for this animal. It's one of us.[82]

---

[80] Ibid., p. 92.

[81] The author is viewing the whales from a chartered float-plane nestled momentarily on the surface of the sea. (C.A.H.)

[82] Ibid., p. 95.

The Artful Universe

~ John D. Barrow[83]

The largest dinosaur was *Brontosaurus* (which the palaeontologists now call *Apatosaurus*). At 85 tons, it was pretty close to the size limit for a land-going animal. It had little room for error if it were to stumble, or transfer too much of its weight onto one leg. (For comparison, the largest land-going creature today, the African elephant, weighs only about seven tons.) Walking up the slightest incline would have been extremely taxing for a large dinosaur, because it would then have to lift a component of its body weight against the downward force of gravity. The heavier you are, the slower you are able to move uphill. Dinosaurs alleviated the pressures on their base by spreading their load over their widely spaced legs. This aids stability; but none the less, if they fell, they would probably break their bones. Adult humans have a much shorter distance to fall if they stumble, but sometimes still break bones. Children fall shorter distances, and don't often break bones, despite constantly taking tumbles. (The fact that young bones are softer, and less brittle, than old ones also helps.) An adult may hit the floor with an energy of motion more than six times greater than that of an infant when they both stumble and fall. If adults were twice as big as they are, then walking upright would be a very dangerous business—rather like walking on stilts. . . .

When any object is placed in a liquid medium, like water, it feels a buoyancy force pushing it upwards, equal to the weight of liquid it displaces. As a result, the stress on its base is alleviated. It is no accident that the largest blue whales (at 130 tons) are enormously bigger than the biggest land-going dinosaurs ever were, or ever could have been. . . .

Water can also support you if you are small. . . . Very small creatures, like pond-skaters, can use surface tension to support their weight so long as they have their legs spread out over a few square millimetres of surface. Again, the surface force increases more slowly with increasing size than

---

does the weight of a creature; there is thus a maximum size, and weight, that can be supported in this way. It works only if you are very small. Humans would need legs spread over about seven kilometres in order to walk on water, like Hilaire Belloc's Water beetle;

> The water beetle here shall teach
> A sermon far beyond your reach:
> He flabbergasts the Human Race
>   By gliding on the water's face
>   With ease, celerity, and grace;
>   But if he ever stopped to think
>   Of how he did it, he would sink.

If you want to fly, then it also pays to be small. Your wings must generate enough lift to overcome the pull of gravity. As you get bigger, the power required to support your weight grows faster than the power your muscles can exert. Consequently, there is a maximum size for a flying creature. The largest birds that can hover in still air for long periods are humming-birds; they vary between about 2 and 20 grams in weight. In fact, they can even take off vertically. Of course, there are far bigger birds. At the top of the tree are the largest Kori bustards, weighing about 12 kg. But they stay aloft by soaring, riding wind-currents, or thermal draught. Likewise, when you see a kestrel hovering over a point on the ground, it is not hovering; it is flying against the wind—just strongly enough to ensure that it remains stationary relative to the ground. It is not strong enough to support its own weight by hovering in still air.

These examples reveal something of the ongoing terrestrial battle between strength and weight, which pits the force of gravity against the intermolecular forces of electromagnetic origin. It was these same forces that first determined the inevitable sizes of habitable planets with atmospheres, the strength of gravity at their surfaces, and, hence, the sizes of complex living things that can exist on their surfaces. Our size is not an accident. It is, within quite narrow bounds, imposed by the invariant strengths of the forces of Nature. But the consequences of our size for our development, our culture, and our abilities are deep and wide. They shed light upon how we have outstripped other living things in controlling natural resources.

The battle between strength and size is displayed by a simpler struggle: that waged between volume and the surface area enclosing it. Watch a rolling snowball as it accretes snow and grows bigger. Its radius increases; so both its volume and surface area grow as well. But, whereas its volume grows according to the cube of its radius, its surface area increases only in proportion to the square of the radius: its surface area cannot keep pace with the growth in its volume. This losing battle that surface area fights with volume as size increases imposes many vital constraints upon the sizes of living things. As your volume increases with growth, so your heat-generating organs increase in volume and energy output. But your ability to keep cool depends upon how much heat can escape from your exposed surface. Small creatures have a relatively large surface area for their volume; large creatures possess a relatively small one. In cold climates small creatures will therefore be at a disadvantage, unable to generate enough heat from eating to keep warm. This is why babies need to be wrapped up so much more thoroughly than adults in cold conditions. Large animals, by contrast, will be at an advantage in the cold. Hence we find large animals—polar bears, rather than small mice—at the Poles, and the average size of birds increases between the Equator and the Poles. The smallest shrews are about as small as animals can be without being thermodynamically at great risk in an environment that occasionally cools to a few degrees below their body temperatures. Small animals can combat this risk of exposure by huddling together for warmth. They share their body heat, and reduce their exposed surfaces by mimicking the geometry of a larger creature. Small animals can also adopt other strategies for reducing their heat losses: growing fur, for example.

Journeying

~ Bruce Chatwin

All animal migrations have been conditioned by shifting zones of climate, and, in the case of the green turtle, by the shift of the continents themselves.

There were theories of how birds fix their position by the height of the sun, the phases of the moon, and the rising and setting of stars; and of how they make navigational adjustments if blown off course by a storm. Certain ducks and geese can "record" the choruses of frogs beneath them, and "know" that they are flying over marsh. Other night-fliers bounce their calls on to the ground below, and, catching the echo, fix their altitude and the nature of the terrain.

The howls of migrating fish can pass through the sides of a ship, and wake up sailors from their bunks. A salmon knows the taste of its ancestral river. Dolphins flash echo-locating clicks onto submarine reefs, in order to steer a safe passage through . . . when a dolphin "triangulates" to determine its position, its behaviour is analogous to our own, as we name and compare the "things" encountered in our daily lives, and so establish our place in the world.[84]

Languages of Plants

~ Brian J. Ford[85]

Plants have a vast vocabulary of signals and responses. They can detect the signs of a change in their environment and adjust their metabolisms to anticipate its effects. They have finely tuned senses for signs of environmental stress which can compensate for its effects. Plants are able to detect the signals that herald change in the leafy canopy above them, and alter

---

[84] Excerpted from *Songlines*, by Bruce Chatwin, pp. 272-273.

[85] The following selection is excerpted from *Sensitive Souls, Senses and Communication in Plants, Animals, and Microbes* by Brian J. Ford, pp. 239-241. Reprinted by permission of Time Warner Book Group UK.

their architecture in order to retain their fair share of light. Plants can detect changes in the total amount of light reaching them, and can also sense changes in the spectrum of the light. The most obvious method is for the plant to respond to the amount of light energy, sometimes even by twisting the leaf to avoid too much light, and so adjust the extent of photosynthesis within the leaf. However, we also believe that plants have specific light sensors which act as "eyes." They detect the nature and extent of the light, but consume very little of its energy.

This may be regarded as a sense of "sight," quite distinct from a mere response to the effects of light energy on the rate of metabolism of the plant cells. Plants detect light in colour. They have sensors specifically for ultraviolet, blue, red and far-red radiation. These sensors provide them with a rich and detailed impression of their situation. Plants use the ratio of red to far-red radiation to control their rate of growth. By changing the speed at which stems elongate, a plant seems to be able to avoid future deleterious effects on its development. In particular, changes in light quality can forewarn the plant about future changes before any shading by neighbours has occurred, and we have seen that plants detect wind, too. Changes in calcium ions, Ca^{+2}, trigger alterations in gene expression which modify the way the plant grows. The metabolism, the expression of genes and the rate of growth of the plant are an integrated response to all this sensory input.

Meanwhile, plant roots adjust to the availability of nutriment, and favour areas where nourishment is most abundant. Their sensing of the availability of food and water allows the plant to adjust its rate of nutriment uptake. Not only can they sense gradients of moisture in the soil, but they change their rate of growth in the presence of nearby roots. It seems that they are able to control their growth in order to avoid too much competition for scarce supplies of raw materials. There are mycorrhizal associations between plants and fungi, in which a fungus colonises the roots of a host plant (sometimes even penetrating inside the host plant cells, but causing no disease). These relationships bring a number of benefits. Not only do the fungi process wastes in the soil and recycle them as foodstuffs for the growing plant, but the interchange of compounds between fungus and plant provides many opportunities for communication and the transmission of warning signals.

118

Plants have many of the senses possessed by humans. They have sight, as far as they need it; they have a sense of touch (sometimes to an extraordinary degree); can sense temperature, and—through gravity—they can tell "up" from "down," or "left" from "right." Twiners can (usually) tell clockwise from anticlockwise. Plants can remember stimuli, and tell one form of stimulus from another. They can communicate, and they cooperate to survive. If plants required more intelligence, they would have developed it. As it is, their senses and the limits of their sentience are exactly what they require. Some of the senses in the plant world are already more highly developed than ours (the sense of touch, for example). No longer should science regard a green plant as a simple organism which endures what it must, and adjusts like a chemical system. We owe plants respect, for on green plants we all rely for survival. They are not our subjects; plants are our cousins.

The Creative Tongue
~ Lincoln Barnett[86]

The fundamental feature of human language is that it has to be learned. Animal sounds are inborn and remain uniform within species, with only slight variations, wherever its members exist around the world. The fact that human language is acquired rather than innate is apparent in the multiplicity of man's tongues. If language did not have to be learned, there would be only one language and all men would speak alike. But each linguistic community has its own separate vocal code within which the relationship between the sound and the meaning of every word is a matter of local convention. That is why human children have to learn to talk: learning to talk is a matter of learning the meanings their parents attach to the vocal sounds they make. Language is learned slowly and often with great effort, especially if the effort is made after infancy. . . .

Perhaps the supreme attribute of human language is its limitless creativity. Alone of all creatures on earth, man can say things that have

---

[86] Lincoln Barnett, *The Treasure of Our Tongue*, pp. 68 and 70.

never been said before—and still be understood. . . . Man has the capacity to create every time he speaks. It is within his power to coin new words, invent new phrases, evolve new modes of expression, invoke new ideas and concepts, seek new responses, by the process of arranging and rearranging familiar elements in accordance with the rules accepted by all speakers of his tongue. Language is thus, in one sense, a wondrously flexible system within which man spins tapestries of thought. It is also a living organism that changes constantly and will never cease to change as long as men have tongues.

CHAPTER SEVEN

CREATIVITY
AND TRANSFORMATION

Praise be to God
Who originally created the heavens and the earth;
Who made the angels messengers with wings—
two or three or four;
Hu[87] *adds to creation as Hu pleases: for God has power over all things.*
What God out of His mercy bestows on humankind,
none can withhold;
what He withholds, none can grant separately from Him,
for He is the Exalted in Power, the All-Wise.
O people! Call to mind God's grace to you!
Is there a creator other than God to give you sustenance
from heaven or from earth?
There is no god but Hu

[*Sūrah Al-Fāṭir* (The Originator) 35:1-3]

And it is We who have built the universe with [Our creative] power; and, verily,
it is We who are steadily expanding it.[88]
And the earth have We spread out wide—
and how well have We ordered it!
And in everything have We created opposites,
so that you might bear in mind [that God alone is One].
[*Sūrah Adh-Dhāriyāt* (The Dust-Scattering Winds) 51:47-49]

---

[87] Hu: the pronoun of Divine Presence. All words in Arabic have a gender grammatically ascribed to them as they do in French and Spanish, etc. Although Allah is referred to with the third person masculine pronoun Hu (Huwa), it is universally understood that Allah's Essence is beyond gender or indeed any qualification, That which is beyond all our attempts at definition, or description, limitless in subtle glory, the Divine Reality permeating and encompassing all that is. ~ C.A.H

[88] The phrase *innā la-mūsiʿūn* clearly foreshadows the modern notion of the "expanding universe"—that is, the fact that the cosmos, though finite in extent, is continuously expanding in space. ~ Muhammad Asad.

121

God is He who has created seven heavens,
and, like them, [the many aspects] of the earth.
Through all of them flows down from on high, unceasingly,
His [creative] will,[89]
so that you might come to know that God has the power
to will anything,
and that God encompasses all things with His knowledge.
[*Sūrah Aṭ-Ṭalāq* (Divorce) 65:12]

It is God who has raised the heavens without any supports
that you could see,
and is established on the throne of His almightiness;
and He [it is who] has made the sun and the moon
subservient [to His laws], each running its course for a term set [by Him].
He governs all that exists.
Clearly does He spell out these messages,
so that you might be certain in your innermost [self]
that you are destined to meet your Sustainer [on Judgment Day].
And it is He who has spread the earth wide
and placed on it firm mountains and running waters,
and created thereon two sexes of every [kind of] plant;[90]
[and it is He who] causes the night to cover the day.

---

[89] Lit., "the command." The verbal form *yatanazzalu* implies recurrence and continuity; its combination with the noun *al-amr* reflects the concept of God's unceasing creative activity. ~ M. Asad

[90] Lit., "and out of all [kinds of] fruits He made thereon [i.e., on earth] pairs (*zawjayn ithnayn*)." The term *zawj* denotes, according to the context, either "a pair" or "one of a pair." Whenever the dual form *zawjān* is followed by the additional numerical definition *ithnān* ("two"), it invariably signifies "a pair comprising both sexes." Thus, the above phrase states that there are two sexes to every kind of plant: a statement fully in accord with botanical science. (Usually the male and female organs of reproduction exist together in one and the same flower of a particular plant, e.g., cotton; alternatively, they are placed in separate flowers of one and the same plant, e.g., in most of the cucurbitaceae; and, in some rare cases, e.g., the date-palm, in entirely separate, uni-sexual plants of the same species.) ~ M. Asad

Truly, in all this there are messages indeed for people who think!
And there are on earth [many] tracts of land close by one another
[and yet widely differing from one another];
and [there are on it] vineyards, and fields of grain,
and date-palms growing in clusters from one root or standing alone,
[all] watered with the same water:
and yet, some of them have We favoured above others
by way of the food [which they provide for man and beast].[91]
Truly, in all this there are messages indeed
for people who use their reason!
But if you are amazed [at the marvels of God's creation],
amazing, too, is their saying, "What! After we have become dust,
shall we indeed be [restored to life] in a new act of creation?"
[*Sūrah Ar-Ra*ᶜ*d* (Thunder) 13:2-5]

*R*emain ever vigilant regarding that day
when hearts and eyes will be transformed.
[*Sūrah An-Nūr* (The Light) 24:37]

Moment by Moment

~ Jalaluddin Rumi[92]

God brought the earth and heavenly spheres into existence
through the deliberation of six days.
even though He was able through *"Be, and it is"*[93]
to bring forth a hundred earths and heavens.
Little by little until forty years of age
that Sovereign raises the human being to completion,
although in a single moment He was able
to send fifty flying up from non-existence.

---

[91] Stress is laid on the multiformity of plants—and their varying beneficence to man and animal—as some of the signs of God's purposeful, creative activity. ~ M. Asad

[92] Jalaluddin Rumi, *Mathnawi*, III, 3500-3508, Translated by Camille and Kabir Helminski, *Jewels of Remembrance*, p. 34.

[93] Qur'an, Surah Yā Sīn 36: 82.

Jesus by means of one prayer could make the dead spring to life:
is the Creator of Jesus unable
to suddenly bring full-grown human beings
fold by fold into existence?
This deliberation is for the purpose of teaching you
that you must seek God slowly, without any break.
A little stream which moves continually
Doesn't become tainted or foul.
From this deliberation are born felicity and joy:
this deliberation is the egg;
good fortune is the bird that comes forth.

We are often sad and suffer a lot when things change, but change and impermanence have a positive side. Thanks to impermanence, everything is possible. Life itself is possible. If a grain of corn is not impermanent, it can never be transformed into a stalk of corn. If the stalk were not impermanent, it could never provide us with the ear of corn we eat. If your daughter is not impermanent, she cannot grow up to become a woman. Then your grandchildren would never manifest. So instead of complaining about impermanence, we should say, "Warm welcome and long live impermanence." We should be happy. When we can see the miracle of impermanence, our sadness and suffering will pass.

Impermanence should also be understood in the light of inter-being. Because all things inter-are, they are constantly influencing one another. It is said that a butterfly's wings flapping on one side of the planet can affect the weather on the other side. Things cannot stay the same because they are influenced by everything else, everything that is not itself.[94]

~ Thich Nhat Hanh

---

[94] Thich Nhat Hanh, *No Death, No Fear, Comforting Wisdom for Life,* Riverhead Books, a member of Penguin Putnam Inc. NY, NY, 2002, p. 41.

Moon in which the snow drifts into the tents of the Hoga
Moon in which the geese come home
Little frog moon
Moon in which nothing happens
Moon in which they plant
Moon in which the buffalo bulls hunt the cows
Moon in which the buffalo bellow
Moon in which the elk bellow
Moon in which the deer paw the earth
Moon in which the deer rut
Moon in which the deer shed their antlers
Moon in which the little black bears are born

~ Omaha Native American Moon Calendar[95]

The creation of a thousand forests is in one acorn.

~ Ralph Waldo Emerson

Metamorphosis

~ May Sarton[96]

Always it happens when we are not there—
The tree leaps up alive into the air,
Small open parasols of Chinese green
Wave on each twig. But who has ever seen
The latch sprung, the bud as it burst?
Spring always manages to get there first.

Lovers of wind, who will have been aware
Of a faint stirring in the empty air,
Look up one day through a dissolving screen
To find no star, but this multiplied green,
Shadow on shadow, singing sweet and clear.
Listen, lovers of wind, the leaves are here!

---

[95] Reprinted from *Changing Light: the Eternal Cycle of Night and Day* by Ruth Gendler, HarperCollins Publishers, NY, NY, 1991, p. 25.
[96] "Metamorphosis" from *Collected Poems 1930-1993* by May Sarton. Copyright © 1993,1988, 1984, 1980, 1974 by May Sarton. Useed by permission of W. W. Norton & Company, Inc.

In the Forest, Leaves Are Always Falling

~ Camille Helminski

In the forest, leaves are always falling. Butterflies flit through, and leaves as colorful tumble to the forest floor. Tomorrow, or perhaps this moment, new ones unfurl.

Continually the letting go of life prepares the way for further fruitfulness. Leaves become soil; earth nurtures seeds; trees sprout and leaves and fruit surge into abundance, death and life.

Each seed knows its own fruition; deeply embedded meaning and purpose make their way forth into the fingertips of branches longing for light and air, moisture and space. Openings emerge, blossom in momentary splendor, and drop to earth, allowing new seed to mature. After the blossoming comes the bowing so that further fruitfulness might return. Seeds burst open and fall or are blown to their destination; and a living forest, a rejoicing meadow grows.

Innately, all of nature is *Muhklisin*, sincere in devotion, as *ihklas,* one who is purely devoted, pure of any other focus but God.

Continually transforming, continually praising—even rock.

A papaya cannot suddenly become a breadfruit or a tomato. It is what it is intended to be. How it develops and its ultimate fruitfulness may be open to circumstance—to weather and the forces of nature, to foraging animals, microbes of disease, insects or man's needs—but essentially, it always follows the course of its original patterning. In its very nature and its fulfillment it praises its Creator.

> "Of the names of God, *Al-Khāliq* is the one who creates from nothing, creating at the same time the states, the conditions, and sustenance of all that He has created. . . .
>
> *Al-Bāri* is the one who orders His creation with perfect harmony—not only each thing harmonious within itself, but everything in accordance with everything else. This infinite-seeming universe works like a clock. All is for one and one is for all. See how everything in you is connected, working together, and how when a part fails, all else is affected. The functions of one and all depend upon each other. . . .

Al-Muṣawwir is the perfect artist who gives everything the most unique and beautiful form. He is the one who, without using any model, shapes everything in the most perfect shape. No two things are the same—look at your fingerprints. Each and every creation is a choice creation, an expression of Allah's infinite beneficence and wisdom."[97]

Four Wings and a Prayer

~ Sue Halpern[98]

This would be my second trip to Mexico to see monarchs. The first had been three years before, when my daughter was nine months old. That was how I would always remember the trip, with a certain amount of distance, as if I had been watching myself there: a woman in a foreign country with a small baby in her arms. We had been at a meeting, my husband and I, and at the end of it, as a kind of reward, we were to be taken into the mountains to a monarch butterfly preserve. Those words, *butterfly preserve,* meant nothing to me. I could not make them into a coherent image the way I could, say, Walt Disney World, where I had never been, either, or Glacier National Park, or Victoria Falls. What would a butterfly *preserve* look like?

We took a bus, and then a truck, and then we walked. At ninety-five hundred feet, where the climb began, the air was not so thin that you noticed, yet, how high you were. Other things were more obvious and would have taken your breath away even at sea level: the skinny little boys, for instance, who were selling things—recapped bottles of beer and snapshots of clustered monarchs and handkerchiefs embroidered by their

---

[97] Sheikh Tosun Bayrak al-Jerrahi al-Halveti, *The Most Beautiful Names.* Threshold Books, VT, 1985, pp. 19-21.

[98] The following selection is excerpted from *Four Wings and a Prayer,* by Sue Halpern, Vintage Books (Random House) 2002, pages 6-8, 9, 10, 11-12, 18-19, 32-35, 73-80. (Copyright © by Sue Halpern 2001) www.vintagebooks.com and is reprinted by permission.

mothers or grandmothers or sisters. The handkerchiefs cost a quarter, and though they were made by hand, all of them looked alike: a white cotton square with scalloped edges and an orange-and-black monarch butterfly sewn into one of the corners. That was the other thing that brought me up short: the butterflies. They were underfoot. I was used to seeing butterflies in the air, or on flowers, but there, at the entrance to El Rosario, thousands of wings torn from their bodies lay in the dirt. They were like cairns in the forest, pointing upward, and so we climbed, my husband, our daughter, and I, and the little boys fell away, and I could hear myself breathing, and my heart in my ears, and when I looked up again, what I was seeing made so little sense that I turned it into something else, something I understood— autumn leaves, falling through the air. That was what it sounded like, too. Millions of leaves, ripped and ripping from their moorings. The sound was overwhelming. It woke the baby in my arms, who opened her eyes to this sight. The three of us stood there, looking and looking, and gradually it occurred to me, gradually it registered, that though there were millions of them, they were not leaves at all, they were butterflies, monarch butterflies, the butterflies of my backyard. They were in the air, and so heavy on the branches of the pine trees that the branches bent toward the ground, supplicants to gravity and mass and sheer enthusiasm.

We moved on. As we hiked we saw even more butterflies, more than would seem possible, twenty or thirty million. Every available place to roost was taken. Even the baby became a perch. There were butterflies on her shoulder and shoes, butterflies in her hair. Somehow she knew not to touch them, and not to be afraid. We found a rock at the edge of the forest, and the baby and I sat down. The clamor of butterfly wings was as constant and irregular as surf cresting over rocks. I watched my daughter watching the butterfly resting on her shoelace, watched her reach down and wait until the butterfly crawled up the ladder of one of her fingers, climbed over the hump of knuckles, and rested on the back of her hand. She was completely silent, as if she had lost her voice. Her eyes were wide open, and so was her mouth, and for twenty minutes, maybe longer, the two of us just sat, eleven thousand feet up the side of a mountain, and paid attention. If I were a more religious person I would have called that place, and that moment, holy, or blessed. But my vocabulary did not typically include those words. Still, unbidden, they were the ones that came to mind. . . .[99]

All of us have experiences that could change our lives if "we let them": love, offered suddenly, turning from the mantelpiece, as Delmore Schwartz put it. And that, oddly, was the way it was with me and the butterflies. Not love, exactly, offered suddenly, but a similar quickening of heart and desire—in this case a desire to *know*, if knowledge was not only information and understanding but experience. I could feel those butterflies tugging on my imagination as if it were a loose sleeve.[100]

★★★

Monarch butterflies never fly at night. They can't. Once the ambient temperature drops below fifty-five degrees, they become sluggish, unable to flap their wings. The wings, which are commonly—and erroneously—described as solar panels, don't store energy but instead absorb it directly from the sun and air. Pick a monarch off a tree in the early morning and put it on your palm and it will sit there as if it were tame. Until the sun warms the air, the monarch is stuck paralytically, making it breakfast for certain steel-gutted birds. This is crucial because every autumn, monarchs do something no other butterflies do: they migrate unimaginably long distances. Monarchs born east of the Rockies typically go to Mexico. Those born to the west go for the most part to the California coast. They travel forty-four miles a day on average, but sometimes as many as two hundred, and all of it by day. Unlike songbirds, which often migrate in the dark to elude predators, monarchs are limited to flying out in the open when it is sunny enough for them, and warm enough, and not too windy.[101]

★★★

"Keep your eyes open," [my friend and guide for this trip, Bill Calvert,] said. "If you ever see a butterfly flying under these conditions—

---

[99] Ibid., pp. 6-8.

[100] Ibid., p. 9.

[101] Ibid., p. 10.

THE BOOK OF NATURE

overcast, with no wind—it'll wreak havoc with all the existing theories."
I understood implicitly that he would like this. Rules, even scientific
rules, were anathema to him. But it wasn't going to happen; it was a
biological impossibility. Thermoregulation was one of the few sure things
that scientists knew about monarch migration. The rest—how the
butterflies knew when it was time to leave their summer breeding
grounds for their overwintering sites thousands of miles away, and
how, navigationally speaking, they got to those sites—had stymied
them for decades. And so had this: how did monarch butterflies from
the eastern United States and Canada, *millions of them,* end up every
year in the same unlikely spot, a remote and largely inhospitable fifty
acres of oyamel fir forest ten thousand feet up the southwestern flank
of Mexico's Transverse Neovolcanic Mountains?

This last question—how do monarchs find their way back to the
same oyamel trees year after year?—remains one of the great
unsolved mysteries of animal biology. Monarchs are not guided by
memory, since no single butterfly ever makes the round trip. Three
or four generations separate those that spend one winter in Mexico
from those that go there the next. A monarch butterfly born in
August where I live, in the Adirondack Mountains of New York
State, for instance, will probably fly all the way to Mexico, spend the
winter there, and leave in March. Then it will fly north, laying eggs
(if it is female) on milkweed along the Gulf Coast in Texas and
Florida before dying. The butterflies born of those eggs will continue
northward, breeding and laying more eggs along the way. So will
their offspring. By August another monarch, four generations or so
removed from the monarch that left my land for Mexico the previous
summer, will emerge from its chrysalis hidden among the raspberry
canes and do the same thing. It will head south, aiming for a place
it's never been, an acre or two of forest on the steep slopes of the
Neo-volcanics. . . .[102]

When birds migrate, they do so primarily because of food.
Winter comes, and mosquitoes and berries and other food sources

---

[102] Ibid., pp. 11-12.

dwindle or become less accessible. Birds fly south, and the landscape becomes one big commissary. This is oversimplified, of course, but even schematically, what birds do is nothing like what butterflies do. Monarchs do not leave their northern breeding grounds because the flowers have withered. They leave for the same reason the flowers wither: the climate changes. The monarch butterfly, which is, genetically, a tropical species, cannot survive sub-freezing temperatures. And when monarchs are wet, they are even more vulnerable. If they are going to reproduce, they have to move to a more hospitable place—or, as is really the case, a less hospitable place. At ten thousand feet, the Neovolcanics are not the Bahamas for butterflies; the overwintering sites are not warm. Rather, they have the right microclimate for monarch survival, warm enough so the monarchs don't freeze and cool enough so they don't drain their finite supply of energy, the lipids stored in their bellies. Monarchs spend an average of 135 days at the overwintering colonies, days of entropy when food may be sought but is not much available.

But they need food; they need energy, both to fly long distances and to survive the winter. Intuitively one might expect the butterflies to bulk up in the north, the way we might fill up the gas tank before driving cross-country. The problem is that a loaded gullet may actually require more energy to transport. And it may cause drag. So the question of when a monarch obtains its winter food supply is an important one, both because it may suggest how the butterflies find their way to Mexico (do they, for instance, follow the asters and the black-eyed Susans?) and because it may have implications for conservation (what happens if wildflowers are replaced by roads or subdivisions or wheat fields?). Besides, it is just plain interesting: science for science' sake.

This last, more than the others, appealed to Bill Calvert: the questions, one begetting another—no, begetting many others. We would drive, and I would ask Calvert, who has devoted his life to studying monarch butterflies, how high monarchs flew, and if they followed corridors of wildflowers when they headed south, and if predation was greater during migration or remigration, and invariably he would smile and tell me that I had asked a good question and say, "But that's the thing, no one knows the answer." In my knapsack I was carrying around a book called *The End of Science,* about how scientists were closing in on a unifying theory to explain *everything,* and it seemed pretty clear to me, in talking with Bill Calvert, that the physicists were going to be able to tell us how the world worked, and we still wouldn't know how a single monarch butterfly found its way from Canada to Mexico, or the answers to the hundreds of questions raised by its flight. . . .[103]

So what is danger? For me it is a feeling, sensual and percussive and paralytic. For a butterfly it may be this, too; we can't begin to know—but it is also a constant condition, like weather. Indeed, weather itself presents one of the greatest dangers in a butterfly's life, and particularly that of a migrating monarch butterfly, which covers thousands of miles through uplands and lowlands, across water and along coasts, in its journey south and then north again. Too cold and the monarch can't fly, might freeze. Too hot and it gets overheated, can't fly. Too hot and there might not be enough water. Too much wind, grounded. Wind from the southeast, stalled. Wind from the west, blown seaward. Hurricanes. Tornadoes. Snow. All present dangers, and not just to monarchs, but to their habitat as well. Of the 106 known species of milkweed, only about a dozen are used by monarchs as sites on which to lay their eggs. The milkweed is essential, for it provides the cardiac glycosides—the poisons—that are ingested by monarch caterpillars and that in turn make monarch butterflies poisonous to most birds. Although perhaps hardier than the monarchs themselves, milkweed plants nonetheless need adequate rain, but not too much rain, and adequate sunshine, but not too much sunshine, in order to grow. They are weather-dependent, too. The absence of suitable habitat for breeding, migrating, or overwintering breaks a link in the chain and puts monarchs at risk. . . .

To call people predators is perhaps a stretch, but only if you assume that predation requires intent. For the most part, people are monarch butterfly predators not by design but by default, as when they mow a highway median strip at the wrong time and eliminate thousands of acres of accessible milkweeds; or when they plant genetically modified corn infused with a toxin aimed at killing corn borers, which also, through its pollen, kills monarch caterpillars; or when they spray crops with

---

[103] Ibid., pp. 18-19.

herbicides and pesticides; or when they cut down trees in the Mexican overwintering sites, thinning the protective canopy and altering the microclimate it creates, which together allow the butterflies to survive both the cold and the breakfast-time raids of orioles and other birds of this particular emetic appetite. It's the same old ecological story: everything is connected.

The fact that the process is circular, not linear, poses its own danger, too. What I mean is this: it's easier to identify problems that arise in causal relationships and then to address, if not remove, them. If your boyfriend hits you, for example, you can leave him and no longer be in the path of his blows; it may not be that simple a relationship to leave, but you understand what you have to do. With monarchs, however, there are many potential "batterers," few of whom actually mean to hurt the butterflies. The loggers in Mexico may be thinking only of the money that a truckload of oyamel fir trees will get them, the corn it will buy or the heat it will furnish; monarchs may never enter into the calculation. But the loss of the trees puts them in jeopardy. The farmers in the midwestern United States who plant genetically altered corn may be thinking only about increased crop yields, not how far the pollen travels or whether monarch caterpillars will ingest it and die. The road crews in New York State may be thinking only about driver safety when they raze the weeds and grasses along the highway, not realizing that in so doing they are eliminating a major food source and breeding ground for migrating monarchs.

And if culpability is difficult to assign, changing these practices may be even harder. How easy it is to feel insignificant when you're part of something so much bigger than yourself, to just go on about your business as if your particular actions had no consequences, or even as if your particular aggregate actions had no obvious consequences—if you're a farmer in Iowa, say, or a tree cutter in Michoacan, and you know that even if you personally don't do that thing that is destructive to monarchs or to monarch habitat or to monarch larvae, someone else, somewhere else, might. And then who will know whose fault it is that the web is coming undone?[104]

---

[104] Ibid., pp. 32-36.

★★★

The monarchs looked good. Only a few were tattered or bird-bitten, only a few were thin. Most were bright orange, with full bellies and minimal wear and tear to their wings. They had flown thousands of miles, but there was no way to tell that from looking at them. They had come through just fine.

Although we didn't say so, we were also looking for tags—tiny dots of paper the size of the circle spit out from a hole punch. They would be stuck to the underside of the hind wing. The tags had a sequence of letters and numbers on them—QS498 or N6304—and some other information as well. The tags asked people who found the butterflies, or sighted them, to report their findings to Monarch Watch, at the University of Kansas, which had been tracking the monarch butterfly migration since 1992 and posting the data on the Internet. We looked, but our looking was reflexive. Of the hundred thousand butterflies that were tagged that year fewer than two hundred were ever found, and only forty-six of them in Mexico. We were in the midst of fifteen million butterflies. We knew the odds and looked anyway. I had tagged twenty monarch butterflies myself, months before in northern New York, and it was these that I was looking for. I had looked in Austin, and in Ciudad Maiz, and in Tula. I had looked in Morelia and in Jamauve. I would look till I left Mexico. . . .

The monarch I was really hoping to find had left my yard on the twenty-sixth of August. My daughter had found it near the end of July feeding on the milkweed near the basketball hoop, having deduced it was there from a pile of caterpillar scat and then carefully turning over leaf after leaf until she located it three plants over. She was thrilled. It was as if her intelligence alone had put it there: she thought it should be there, and there it was! To the extent that there was ownership, this caterpillar was hers. It was only about a week old when we brought it to the back porch, put it in the cage we had made from a cardboard box and an old screen, and named it Junior to distinguish it from some of the others there—Biggie, Itsy, and Bitsy among them.

I told myself I was doing this for my daughter's sake, so she could witness the metamorphosis from caterpillar to butterfly. I could describe it to her, or show her pictures or even a video, but none was in real time. Each condensed the experience to the point where *amazing* and *remarkable* and *awesome* were the only words that seemed appropriate. And while it was all of those things, they all missed the nuanced, constant, incremental, and very-rarely-awesome-in-its-particulars way that that remarkable and amazing transformation was occurring. In any case, it was only partly true that it was for my daughter's sake. I wanted to see it. Metamorphosis, like resurrection, is a powerful symbol. But what was happening in the cardboard box was not symbolic at all. It was nature investing symbolism with its power.

"Raising" monarchs, as many schoolchildren know, is a blessedly simple task. Supply the caterpillars with fresh milkweed and water daily and watch them grow. In three weeks an individual monarch caterpillar will increase its weight three thousand times and outgrow its skin over and over again, molting five times. When it unzips its striped cuticle for the fifth time, though, it does not acquire a new skin. Instead it seems to turn inside out altogether, and when it is done there is a pale-green chrysalis studded with five gold dots, and no sign at all of the caterpillar that was there.

On the porch we were seeing this with Junior. On August 6 she crawled to the top of the cardboard box, secreted a gluey white liquid, and anchored herself to it. The glue was liquid silk, spun and deposited by Junior's spinnerets. When it was made, she backed up to it and grabbed on with her anal claspers till she was securely fastened. Then she hung there like a health nut in inversion boots, her body forming a perfect J. This step was critical. A few weeks before, Biggie had fallen to the bottom of the box after his chrysalis was made. When he emerged, full-grown, his wing was crumpled and he was unable to fly. He was the monarch that was eaten by mice in our kitchen.

That night, the night of the chrysalis, my daughter told me a story at bedtime. "This will be a little scary and a little sad," she warned me. "Once there was a little girl who woke up with spots all over her. That's the scary part. Soon she made a J and then died. That's the sad part. But she didn't really die because when she came out of her chrysalis she was a beautiful butterfly."

That "died but didn't really die" part was as good a description as any of what was happening inside the acorn-shaped shell that Junior had made. She had gone into it a caterpillar and she would, if all went well, emerge as something completely different—a butterfly. In between she was neither, her larval self having dissolved into a viscous genetic stew that would reconstitute itself into the constituent parts of a butterfly.

After my daughter fell asleep, I opened a book called *The World of the Monarch Butterfly* and copied this into my notebook:

"The change of form and function affects every part of the insect's being, from its senses to the way it moves and feeds. Buds of tissue in the thorax grow and develop into wings. The larva's leaf-nibbling jaws dissolve and new adult mouth parts grow, later fitting together to make a hollow tube through which the adult butterfly will draw nectar. The long intestine shrinks to match the new diet, and sex organs appear for the first time. Long, delicate antennae develop on the insect's head, and the twelve simple eyes of the caterpillar are replaced by the two huge compound eyes of the adult. All these changes are finely co-ordinated, so none comes too soon or too late."

Inside her green envelope, this was happening to Junior. I didn't know this for sure, of course, since the chrysalis was opaque, but this was what was supposed to be happening, having happened countless times before. The accountability of nature offers its own path to knowledge. I might never have seen a monarch butterfly emerge from a chrysalis, but I could assume it would. It was knowledge that I could count on, that we all do count on—the background knowledge (the sun will rise, the tides will ebb, the trees will bud) that lets us live our lives so exclusively in the foreground.

On August 25 I had the first direct evidence that the metamorphosis not only was occurring but was almost complete: Junior's chrysalis was no longer green, it was black. Then I shined a light on it and saw that it wasn't black at all, it was transparent. The black I was seeing was part of a wing. I could see it, too.

Junior was reborn at 8:23 A.M. Her wings were stubby, condensed, and her abdomen was enormous. She looked like a mutant. A pair of long, articulated legs that ended in pincers grasped her recently vacated apartment. Then her abdomen started to heave, pumping fluid through her veins. Her wings opened to full size like a pocket umbrella whose button had been pushed.

I brought the box outside and let it sit in the sun. Junior clung to her chrysalis and swayed in the breeze like a piece of clothing on the line. Her proboscis yoyoed in and out. At 9:25, an hour into her new life. Junior spread her wings for the first time. They were a deep, almost red, orange. And it really was a new life, at least as against how I had imagined her living it (heading south, wintering in Mexico, mating, heading north, laying eggs, dying), for when her wings were fully expanded, I saw that she was not a she at all. Junior was a male.

Two hours later, when his wings were fully hardened, I gave him his tag and held him up to the sun. I said a short prayer that was really just a wish and waited for him to take off. It's so easy to impute emotions to wild creatures, and even easier to have personal feelings for them. It was more than twenty-four hundred miles from my yard to the Neo-volcanics, and I really wanted Junior to make it. He pumped his wings a few times and peered over the edge of my palm like a diver contemplating the deep end of the pool. Then, without warning, he took off. His wings flapped confidently and he moved like a finch, undulating through the air. What was I to him? I wondered. Probably a tree, I thought, as he circled around me three times before landing in the grass near the pond, then high-jumping to a low branch of a white pine. There he sat for what seemed to me, who was just sitting, too, to be a long time. I went inside. Fifteen minutes later he was out of sight. Gone.

So it was Junior I was looking for when I scanned a roost with my binoculars. Junior I was hoping to find every time I pulled a monarch from Bill Calvert's net and measured its wingspan. Junior I knew I had absolutely no chance of finding, yet continued to look for, which was, when I thought about it, the acknowledgment of, the recognition of, belief, which is its own kind of story.[105]

---

[105] Ibid., pp. 73-80.

Unconscious Came a Beauty

~ May Swenson[106]

Unconscious
came a beauty to my
wrist
and stopped my pencil,
merged its shadow profile with
my hand's ghost
on the page:
Red Spotted Purple or else Mourning
Cloak,
paired thin as paper wings, near black,
were edged on the seam side poppy orange,
as were its spots.

UNCONSCIOUS

CAME A BEAUTY

I sat arrested, for its soot haired
body's worm
shone in the sun.
It bent its tongue long as
a leg
black on my skin
and clung without my
feeling,
while its tomb stained
duplicate parts of
a window opened.
And then I
moved.

---

[106] "Unconscious Came a Beauty" by May Swenson. Used with permission of the Literary Estate of May Swenson. *American Poetry, Twentieth Century, Vol.2.* New York, NY: Literary Classics of the United States, 2000, p. 889.

CHAPTER EIGHT

ENDURANCE
AND REJUVENATION

How many are the creatures that do not carry their own sustenance?
It is God Who feeds them and you:
for He is the One Who Hears and the One Who Knows.

[*Sūrah Al-ʿAnkabūt* (The Spider) 29:60]

Are you not aware of your Sustainer [through His works]?—
how He causes the shadow to lengthen [towards the night]
when, had He so willed,
He could indeed have made it stand still:
but then, We have made the sun its guide;
and then, [after having caused it to lengthen,]
We draw it in towards Ourselves[107] *with a gradual drawing-in.*
And He it is who makes the night a garment for you,
and [your] sleep a rest,
and causes every [new] day to be a resurrection.
And He it is who sends forth the winds
as a glad tiding of His coming grace;
and [thus, too,] We cause pure water to descend from the skies,
so that We may bring dead land to life thereby,
and give to drink thereof to many [beings] of Our creation,
beasts as well as humans.

[*Sūrah Al-Furqān* (The Standard Of True And False) 25:45-49]

---

[107] I.e., "We cause it to contract in accordance with the 'laws of nature' which We Ourselves have instituted." As in so many other instances in the Qur'ān, the abrupt change from the third-person pronoun "He" to "We" is meant to illustrate the fact that God is undefinable, and that it is only the inadequacy of human speech—and, hence, of the human mind—that makes it necessary to refer to the Supreme Being by pronouns which in reality are applicable only to finite, created "persons". ~ M. Asad

The Lord is my shepherd. I shall not want.

He makes me to lie down in green pastures;

He leads me beside the still waters. He restores my soul;

He leads me in the paths of righteousness for His name's sake.

Yea though I walk through the valley of the shadow of death

I will fear no evil, for You are with me.

[The Bible, Psalm 23: 1-4]

Sailing Homeward

~ Chan Fang-Sheng (5th Century)[108]

Cliffs that rise a thousand feet
Without a break,
Lake that stretches a hundred miles
Without a wave,
Sands that are white through all the year,
Without a stain,
Pine-tree woods, winter and summer
Ever-green,
Streams that for ever flow and flow
Without a pause,
Trees that for twenty thousand years
Your vows have kept,
You have suddenly healed the pain of a traveller's heart,
And moved his brush to write a new song.

---

[108] Excerpted from *Translations from the Chinese* by Arthur Waley. Copyright 1919, 1941 by Alfred A. Knopf, Inc. Copyright renewed 1947 by Arthur Waley.

You Ask Why

~ Li-Po[109]

You ask why I made my home in the mountain forest,
And I smile, and am silent,
And even my soul remains quiet:
It lives in the other world
Which no one owns.
The peach trees blossom.
The water flows.

Fertility

~ Herman Hesse[110]

On the slope behind the house today
I cut through roots and rocks and
Dug a hole, deep and wide,
Carted away from it each stone
And all the friable, thin earth.
Then I knelt there a moment, walked
In the old woods, bent down again, using
A trowel and both my hands to scoop
Black, decaying woods-soil with the warm
Smell of fungi from the trunk of a rotting
Chestnut tree—two heavy buckets full I carried
Back to the hole and planted the tree inside;
Carefully I covered the roots with peaty soil,
Slowly poured sun-warmed water over them,
Mudding them gently until the soil settled.
It stands there, young and small,
Will go on standing when we are gone

---

[109] Li Po (8th century), excerpted from *Translations from the Chinese* by Arthur Waley, copyright 1919 by Arthur Waley, 1941 by Alfred A. Knopf, Inc. Copyright renewed 1947 by Arthur Waley.

[110] Herman Hesse, "Page from a Journal," as quoted by Kate Farrell, *Art and Nature, An Illustrated Anthology of Nature Poetry*, Metropolitan Museum of Art, 1992.

And the huge uproar, endless urgency and fearful delirium
   of our days forgotten.
The foehn will bend it, rainstorms tear at it,
The sun will laugh, wet snow weigh it down,
The siskin and the nuthatch make it their home,
And the silent hedgehog burrow at its foot.
All it has ever experienced, tasted, suffered:
The course of years, generations of animals,
Oppression, recovery, friendship of sun and wind
Will pour forth each day in the song
Of its rustling foliage, in the friendly
Gesture of its gently swaying crown,
In the delicate sweet scent of resinous
Sap moistening the sleep-glued buds,
And in the eternal game of lights and
Shadows it plays with itself, content.

Rain Stirrings

~ Elspeth Huxley[111]

At this time of year Mount Kenya seemed to move closer to us, the base became more purple, the outlines darker, the crest more white. By eight o'clock the peak had always disappeared behind a cloudy muffler. . . . The long rains which in those days were expected on 25 March exactly, arrived punctually at two o'clock in the afternoon. A deluge of enormous chilly drops beat with a noise like thunder on Mrs. Nimmo's iron roof, turned our surroundings into a mess like melted chocolate, poured in rivers down every slope, and swept through the unglazed windows. . . .

Rain had stirred the people on the farm . . . They carried on their heads boxes of bright-leaved coffee trees, dumped them in the shamba and hurried back to the nurseries for more. . . . shamba-boys placed each

---

[111] Elspeth Huxley, excerpted from *The Flame Trees of Thika: Memories of an African Childhood*, London: Penguin 1962, Viking Penguin and Chatto and Winduss: Copyright © 1959, renewed by Elspeth Huxley.

seedling carefully in a hole and packed in the chocolate mud, which they pressed down with their naked feet.

There was an art to planting young coffee, because if the little tap-root was not put in absolutely straight, if it had the least kink in it, the tree would die. . . . Robin would not allow me to plant any trees, I suppose because he did not trust me with the tap roots; however, I was allowed to help scoop moist earth around the seedlings, and press it in with my fingers, which had all the delight of making mud pies with the added pleasure of utility; for children are bored with pointless things and, when they play, attempt by pretence to add the dimension of reality to their actions. Now there was no need to pretend, the mud pies had a purpose and so the making of them was delightful, at least until I grew tired.

Chasing Clayoquot, A Wilderness Almanac

~ David Pitt-Brooke[112]

It's raining steadily now and a breeze from the south ruffles the water. Fortunately it's not cold. It does feel a little odd, sitting calmly in the open, getting rained on. One's natural impulse is to head for cover. (What's the expression? *Too dumb to get out of the rain.*) But it's not uncomfortable once I get used to the idea. In fact, the sight and sound of rain on the water is unexpectedly soothing, almost meditative. It echoes the musical tinkle of the birds talking among themselves. They have calmed down, too. Most are standing quietly, one foot tucked up. Occasionally they rouse to shake the water off their feathers.

I feel increasingly content simply being here, present, not doing anything in particular. In fact, I can't think of a time I've felt more thoroughly engaged with the natural world, part of the whole. The birds seem to think so, too. They had moved away when we took our places,

---

[112] Excerpted from *Chasing Clayoquot, A Wilderness Almanac* by David Pitt-Brooke, Raincoast Books, Vancouver, B.C., Canada, 2004, p. 112.

but now they're back. Before long I have western sandpipers foraging within arm's length. A tiny least sandpiper is feeding a couple of centimetres from my right boot. I feel accepted. And so we possess ourselves in patience, waiting for events to come to us.

A fallen flower
Flew back to its perch
A butterfly.

~ Moritake [113]

---

[113] From *The Moon in the Pines, Zen Haiku* selected and translated by Jonathon Clements, published by Frances Lincoln, Ltd, © 2000. Reproduced by permission of Frances Lincoln Ltd., 4 Torriano Avenue, London NW5 2RZ. Distributed in the USA by Publishers Group West and in Canada by Raincoast Books, p. 31.

Australian Flowers

~ Jessie Ackermann[114]

During the summer months the country, in aspect, reaches the very acme of all desolation. Every blade of grass withers to a dismal and forlorn yellow; not a real yellow, but burnt and hopeless, a sort of this-is-the-end-of-me shade. Flowers disappear, and the very stalks drop off at the roots; disagreeable sand-storms smite one right and left; the hot winds, like an escaped breath from the nether world, circle about in fiendish delight. This, however, is greatly to be desired—even at 108 or 114 degrees in the shade—when compared with the humid parts where the wilted people droop with the whole surroundings.

This may all seem most uninviting, but the very vastness of it is compelling. I have stood under the blighting sun when the semi-tropical rays get into the very blood and bones, with dead sheep and dying cattle on every hand; when the over-heated sand came stinging its way over hands and face, until I seemed rooted to the place, unable to move. This awful warring of the elements carries a strange spell in its track. The possibilities of it all are overpowering. Comparatively few people have been in those places where Father Time whets his scythe and Death is double-armed with fatal darts, for such scenes are limited to certain sections, and are not liable to frequent recurrence.

It is rather remarkable how soon the discomforts of the dry season are forgotten with the coming of the rain. The feeling which prevailed among the ancient Egyptians at the moment of the overflow of the Nile, and prompted long watches, which were spent listening for the voice of the Sphinx, is, as it were, reflected in Australia when the rains, which alone assure a bountiful harvest, set in. I have known members of a family to wire the news to others of the household travelling thousands of miles away, "It rains! It rains!"

In a single week of rain the whole country begins to burst into life— and such life! Never was a greater transformation brought about in less time! A month later, no one would recognise a single locality. Everything

---

[114] Jessie Ackermann, *Australia From a Woman's Point of View*, Cassell and Company, Ltd. London, NY, Toronto and Melbourne, 1913, pp. 12-15.

springs into beauty. Shrubs, plants, grasses, creepers, and carpet upon carpet of endless variety of wild flowers, colour the earth from one end of the island almost to the other. In fact, wild flowers in winter are the great feature of Australia.

Scientists declare that most of the flora is distinctively Australian. These primitive types exist elsewhere in fossil form only, as belonging to the past ages of a country. Bacon says, "God Almighty first planted a garden." Perhaps this was the spot! There are three thousand families, not to speak of family branches of wild flowers, and nearly three hundred known specimens of orchids, which, although delicate and fragile to look upon, seem hardy and vigorous. The colouring is faint and tint-like rather than decided, and the fantastic-fringed forms are among the wonders of the floral kingdom. Then there are the rugged, sturdy, almost bold families which fairly force themselves upon notice, and demand attention whether one will or not. The Kangaroo Paw is a compelling, saucy-looking, haughty-headed flower, with monkey-like hair—a real outstanding growth upon the stem, which shades into grey as it nears the blossom. Hair is not peculiar to it alone, for there are many hairy plants to be found, especially in desert places.

The sand is as productive of plant-life as the richer forms of soil. In the northern part I have seen miles and miles literally covered with pink, yellow, red, blue, and variegated flowers, some of which take rootage in cracks in the rocks, where they thrive in a scanty supply of yellow sand. At a picnic not far from a large city, I gathered nearly two hundred varieties of flowers without leaving one hill.

The people are flower enthusiasts—not one class, but almost everybody. Children roll in flowers, caress, fondle, and gather them from the beginning to the end of the season. Flower excursions are arranged by the Government and form a most popular outing. These take place on the half-holidays, and frequently are repeated on Sundays, when whole families leave the city and spend the day with the flowers in the country. I never saw such a sight in my life. I have spent hours at a time at stations, merely watching the crowds, trying to study the relation of flowers to the people. What a day they have had! The older ones read or visit; but the children! The joy and happiness of those droves of youngsters as they romp and roll and tumble about amongst a multitude of blossoms is a delight simply to contemplate. A flower show in a great city can in no way compare with these open-air, admission-free exhibitions, where every flower-voice invites the weary and heavy laden, the toilsome and discouraged, to come and rest in Nature's bowers. By night the baskets are filled, bunches are tied up, and men and women are decorated with them wherever a stem can be thrust or a festoon hung. These gay, happy crowds plunder the fields, but soon every trace of their pillage will be covered with brighter freshness, and the scene repeats itself, until the earth refuses, for a time, to array herself in her festive garb.

If it rains during the night, no one sees the rain,
for then every soul and breath is asleep;
but the freshness of every beautiful rose-garden
is clear evidence of the rain that was not seen.

~ Jalaluddin Rumi[115]

Rejuvenation

~ Muhammad Asad[116]

All through the night Zayd seems to be restless with pain. He awakens long before dawn, and his sudden movement stirs me also from my uneasy sleep.

"I see only one camel," he says: and when we look around, we discover that one of the beasts—Zayd's—has indeed disappeared. Zayd wants to set out on mine to search for it, but his injured foot makes it difficult for him even to stand, not to speak of walking and mounting and dismounting.

---

[115] Jalaluddin Rumi, *Mathnawi* VI, 2724-2725, *Jewels of Remembrance*, translated by Camille and Kabir Helminski, Threshold Books, p. 166.
[116] Muhammad Asad, *The Road to Mecca*, Fons Vitae and The Book Foundation, pp. 22-31.

"Thou rest, Zayd, and I shall go instead; it won't be difficult to find my way back by retracing my own tracks."

And in the breaking dawn I ride away, following the tracks of the lost dromedary which wind across the sand valley and disappear behind the dunes.

I ride for one hour, and another, and a third: but the tracks of the strayed animal go on and on, as if it had pursued a deliberate course. The forenoon is well advanced when I stop for a short halt, dismount, eat a few dates and drink from the small water-skin attached to my saddle. The sun stands high, but somehow it has lost its glare. Dun-coloured clouds, unusual at this time of year, float motionless under the sky; a strangely thick, heavy air envelops the desert and softens the outlines of the dunes beyond their usual softness.

An eerie stir over the summit of the high sand hill in front of me catches my eye—is it an animal? The lost camel perhaps? But when I look more carefully, I see that the movement is not above but in the dune crest itself: the crest is moving, ever so slightly, ripplingly, forward—and then it seems to trickle down the slope toward me like the crest of a slowly breaking wave. A murky redness creeps up the sky from behind the dune; under this redness its contours lose their sharpness and become blurred, as if a veil had suddenly been drawn across; and a reddish twilight begins to spread rapidly over the desert. A cloud of sand whirls against my face and around me, and all at once the wind begins to roar from all directions, crisscrossing the valley with powerful blasts. The trickling movement of the first hilltop has been taken up by all the sand hills within sight. In a matter of minutes the sky darkens to a deep, rust-brown hue and the air is filled with swirling sand dust which, like a reddish fog, obscures the sun and the day. This is a sandstorm, and no mistake.

My crouching dromedary, terrified, wants to rise. I pull it down by the halter, struggling to keep myself upright in the wind that has now assumed the force of a gale, and manage to hobble the animal's forelegs and, to make it more secure, a hind leg as well. Then I throw myself down on the ground and draw my *abaya* over my head. I press my face against the camel's armpit so as not to be choked by the flying sand. I feel the animal press its muzzle against my shoulder, no doubt for the same reason. I can feel the sand being heaped upon me from the side where I am unprotected by the dromedary's body, and have to shift from time to time to avoid being buried.

I am not unduly worried, for it is not the first time that I have been surprised by a sandstorm in the desert. Lying thus on the ground, tightly wrapped in my *abaya,* I can do nothing but wait for the storm to abate and listen to the roar of the wind and the flapping of my cloak—flapping like a loose sail—no, like a banner in the wind—like the flapping of tribal banners carried on high poles by a beduin army on the march: just as they flapped and fluttered nearly five years ago over the host of Najdi beduin riders—thousands of them, and I among them—returning from Arafat to Mecca after the pilgrimage.

★★★

When the storm finally subsides, I shake myself free of the sand that has been heaped around me. My dromedary is half buried in it, but none the worse for an experience that must have befallen it many times. The storm itself, it would seem at first glance, has not done us any damage apart from filling my mouth, ears and nostrils with sand and blowing away the sheepskin from my saddle. But soon I discover my error.

All the dunes around me have changed their outlines. My own tracks and those of the missing camel have been blown away. I am standing on virgin ground.

Now nothing remains but to go back to the camp—or at least to try to go back—with the help of the sun and the general sense of direction which is almost an instinct with someone accustomed to travelling in deserts. But here these two aids are not entirely reliable, for sand dunes do not allow you to go in a straight line and so to keep the direction you have chosen.

The storm has made me thirsty, but, not expecting to be away from camp for more than a few hours, I have long ago drunk the last sip from my small water-skin. However, it cannot be far to the camp; and although my dromedary has had no water since our last stop at a well some two days ago, it is an old campaigner and can be relied upon to carry me back. I set its nose toward where I think the camp must lie, and we start at a brisk pace.

An hour passes, a second, and a third, but there is no trace of Zayd or of our camping ground. None of the orange-coloured hills presents a familiar appearance; it would be difficult indeed to discover anything familiar in them even if there had been no storm.

Late in the afternoon I come upon an outcrop of granite rocks, so rare in the midst of these sand wastes, and recognize them immediately: we passed them, Zayd and I, yesterday afternoon, not long before we made camp for the night. I am greatly relieved; for though it is obvious that I am way beyond the place where I hoped to find Zayd—having probably missed him by a couple of miles or so—it seems to me that it should not now be difficult to find him by simply going in a southwesterly direction, as we did yesterday.

There were, I remember, about three hours between the rocks and our night camp: but when I now ride for three more hours, there is no sign of the camp or of Zayd. Have I missed him again? I push forward, always toward southwest, taking the movement of the sun carefully into account; two more hours pass, but still there is no camp and no Zayd. When night falls, I decide it is senseless to continue further; better rest and wait for the morning light. I dismount, hobble the dromedary, try to eat some dates but am too thirsty: and so I give them to the camel and lie down with my head against its body.

It is a fitful doze into which I fall: not quite sleep and not quite waking, but a succession of dream states brought about by fatigue, broken by a thirst that has gradually become distressing; and, somewhere in those depths which one does not want to uncover to oneself, there is that grey, squirming mollusc of fear: what will happen to me if I do not find my way back to Zayd and to our water-skins?—for, as far as I know, there is no water and no settlement for many days' journey in all directions.

At dawn I start again. During the night I calculated that I must have gone too far to the south and that, therefore, Zayd's camp ought to be somewhere north-northeast of the place where I spent the night. And so toward north-northeast we go, thirsty and tired and hungry, always threading our way in wavy lines from valley to valley, circumventing sand hills now to the right, now to the left. At noon we rest. My tongue sticks to the roof of my mouth and feels like old, cracked leather; the throat is sore and the eyes inflamed. Pressed to the camel's belly, with my *abaya* drawn over my head, I try to sleep for a while, but cannot. The afternoon

150

sees us again on the march, this time in a more easterly direction—for by now I know that we have gone too far west—but still there is no Zayd and no camp.

Another night comes. Thirst has grown to be torment, and the desire for water the one, the overpowering thought in a mind that can no longer hold orderly thoughts. But as soon as dawn lightens the sky, I ride on: through the morning, through noonday, into the afternoon of another day. Sand dunes and heat. Dunes behind dunes, and no end. Or is this perhaps the end—the end of all my roads, of all my seeking and finding? Of my coming to the people among whom I would never again be a stranger . . . ? "O God," I pray, "let me not perish thus . . ."

In the afternoon I climb a tall dune in the hope of getting a better view of the landscape. When I suddenly discern a dark point far to the east, I could cry with joy, only I am too weak for that: for this must be Zayd's encampment, and the waterskins, the two big waterskins full of water! My knees shake as I remount my dromedary. Slowly, cautiously, we move in the direction of that black point which can surely be nothing but Zayd's camp. This time I take every precaution not to miss it: I ride in a straight line, up sand hills, down sand valleys, thus doubling, trebling our toil, but spurred by the hope that within a short while, within two hours at the most, I shall reach my goal. And finally, after we have crossed the last dune crest, the goal comes clearly within my sight, and I rein in the camel, and look down upon the dark something less than half a mile away, and my heart seems to stop beating: for what I see before me is the dark outcrop of granite rocks which I passed three days ago with Zayd and revisited two days ago alone . . . For two days I have been going in a circle.

★★★

When I slide down from the saddle, I am entirely exhausted. I do not even bother to hobble the camel's legs, and indeed the beast is too tired to think of running away. I weep; but no tears come from my dry, swollen eyes.

How long it is since I have wept. . . . But, then, is not everything long past? Everything is past, and there is no present. There is only thirst. And heat. And torment.

I have been without water for nearly three days now, and it is five days since my dromedary has had its last drink. It could probably carry on like this for one day more, perhaps two; but I cannot, I know it, last that long. Perhaps I shall go mad before I die, for the pain in my body is ensnarled with the dread in my mind, and the one makes the other grow, searing and whispering and tearing. . . .

I want to rest, but at the same time I know that if I rest now I shall never be able to get up again. I drag myself into the saddle and force the dromedary with beating and kicking to get up; and almost fall from the saddle when the animal lurches forward while rising on its hind legs and, again, when it lurches backward, straightening its forelegs. We begin to move, slowly, painfully, due west. Due west: what a mockery! What does 'due west' amount to in this deceptive, undulating sea of sand hills ? But I want to live. And so we go on.

We plod with the rest of our strength through the night. It must be morning when I fall from the saddle. I do not fall hard; the sand is soft and embracing. The camel stands still for a while, then slides down with a sigh on its knees, then on its hind legs, and lies crouched by my side with its neck stretched on the sand.

I lie on the sand in the narrow shadow of the dromedary's body, wrapped in my *abaya* against the heat outside me and the pain and thirst and dread within me. I cannot think any more. I cannot close my eyes. Every movement of the lids is like hot metal on the eye-balls. Thirst and heat; thirst and crushing silence: a dry silence that swathes you in its shroud of loneliness and despair and makes the singing of blood in your ears and the camel's occasional sigh stand out, threateningly, as though these were the last sounds on earth and you two, the man and the beast, the last living beings, doomed beings, on earth.

High above us, in the swimming heat, a vulture circles slowly, without ever stopping, a pinpoint against the hard paleness of the sky, free and above all horizons. . . .

My throat is swollen, constricted, and every breath moves a thousand torturing needles at the base of my tongue—that big, big tongue which should not move but cannot stop moving in pain, backward, forward, like a rasp against the dry cavity of my mouth. All my insides are hot and intertwined in one unceasing grip of agony. For seconds the steely sky becomes black to my wide-open eyes.

152

My hand moves, as if of its own, and strikes against the hard butt of the carbine slung on the saddle-peg. And the hand stands still, and with sudden clarity the mind sees the five good shells in the magazine and the quick end that a pressure on the trigger could bring. . . Something in me whispers: Move quickly, get the carbine before you are unable to move again!

And then I feel my lips move and shape toneless words that come from some dark recesses of my mind: "We shall try you . . . most certainly try you . . ." and the blurred words slowly assume shape and fall into pattern—a verse from the Koran: *We shall most certainly try you with fear and hunger and with the lack of possessions and labour's fruits. But give the good tiding to those who remain steadfast and, when calamity befalls them, say: "Behold, to God we belong and unto Him do we return."*

Everything is hot and dark; but out of the hot darkness I sense a cooling breath of wind and hear it rustle softly—wind rustling, as if in trees—over water—and the water is the sluggish little stream between grassy banks, near the home of my childhood. I am lying on the bank, a little boy of nine or ten years, chewing a grass stalk and gazing at the white cows which graze nearby with great, dreamy eyes and the innocence of contentment. In the distance peasant women work in the field. One of them wears a red head-kerchief and a blue skirt with broad red stripes. Willow trees stand on the bank of the stream, and over its surface glides a white duck, making the water glitter in its wake. And the soft wind rustles over my face like an animal's snort: oh, yes, it is indeed an animal's snort: the big white cow with the brown spots, come quite close to me and now nudges me, snorting, with its muzzle, and I feel the movement of its legs by my side. . . .

I open my eyes, and hear the snort of my dromedary, and feel the movement of its legs by my side. It has half raised itself on its hind legs with uplifted neck and head, its nostrils widened as if scenting a sudden, welcome smell in the noon air. It snorts again, and I sense the excitement rippling down its long neck toward the shoulder and the big, half-raised body. I have seen camels snuffle and snort like this when they scent water after long days of desert travel; but there is no water here.... Or—is there? I lift my head and follow with my eyes the direction toward which the camel has turned its head. It is the dune nearest us, a low summit against the steely bleakness of the sky, empty of movement or sound. But there *is* a sound! There is a faint sound like the vibration of an old harp, very delicate and brittle, high-pitched: the high-pitched, brittle sound of a beduin voice chanting on the march in rhythm with the camel's tread—just beyond the summit of the sand hill, quite near as distances go, but—I know it in a fraction of an instant—far beyond my reach or the sound of my voice. There are people there, but I cannot reach them. I am too weak even to get up. I try to shout, but only a hoarse grunt comes from my throat. And then my hand strikes, as if of its own, against the hard butt of the carbine on the saddle . . . and with the eye of my mind I see the five good shells in the magazine. . . .

With a supreme effort I manage to unsling the weapon from the saddle-peg. Drawing the bolt is like lifting a mountain, but finally it is done. I stand the carbine on its butt and fire a shot vertically into the air. The bullet whines into the emptiness with a pitifully thin sound. I draw the bolt again and fire again, and then listen. The harplike singing has slopped. For a moment there is nothing but silence. Suddenly a man's head, and then his shoulders, appear over the crest of the dune; and another man by his side. They look down for a while, then turn around and shout something to some invisible companions, and the man in front clambers over the crest and half runs, half slides down the slope toward me.

There is a commotion around me: two, three men—what a crowd after all that loneliness!—are trying to lift me up, their movements a most confusing pattern of arms and legs. . . . I feel something burning-cold, like ice and fire, on my lips, and see a bearded beduin face bent over me, his hand pressing a dirty, moist rag against my mouth. The man's other hand is holding an open waterskin. I make an instinctive move toward it, but the beduin gently pushes my hand back, dunks the rag into the water and again presses a few drops onto my lips. I have to bite my teeth together to prevent the water from burning my throat; but the beduin pries my teeth apart and again drops some water into my mouth. It is not water: it is molten lead. Why are they doing this to me? I want to run away from the torture, but they hold me back, the devils. . . . My skin is burning. My whole body is in flames. Do they want to kill me? Oh, if only I had the strength to get hold of my rifle to defend myself! But they do not even let me rise: they hold me down to the ground and pry my mouth open again and drip water into it, and I have to swallow it—and, strangely enough, it does not burn as fiercely as a moment ago—and the wet rag on my head feels good, and when they pour water over my body, the touch of the wet clothes brings a shudder of delight. . . .

And then all goes black, I am falling, falling down a deep well, the speed of my falling makes the air rush past my ears, the rushing grows into a roar, a roaring blackness, black, black. . . .

★★★

Black, black, a soft blackness without sound, a good and friendly darkness that embraces you like a warm blanket and makes you wish that you could always remain like this, so wonderfully tired and sleepy and lazy; and there is really no need for you to open your eyes or to move your arm; but you do move your arm and do open your eyes: only to see darkness above you, the woollen darkness of a beduin tent made of black goat hair, with a narrow opening in front that shows you a piece of starry night sky and the soft curve of a dune shimmering under the starlight. . . . And then the tent-opening darkens and a man's figure stands in it, the outline of his flowing cloak sharply etched against the sky, and I hear Zayd's voice exclaim: "He is awake, he is awake!"—and his austere face comes quite close to my own and his hand grips my shoulder. Another man enters the tent; I cannot clearly see him, but as soon as he speaks with a slow, solemn voice I know he is a Shammar beduin.

Again I feel a hot, consuming thirst and grip hard the bowl of milk which Zayd holds out toward me; but there is no longer any pain when I gulp it down while Zayd relates how this small group of beduins happened to camp near him at the time when the sandstorm broke loose, and how, when the strayed camel calmly returned by itself during the night, they became worried and went out, all of them together, to search for me; and how, after nearly three days, when they had almost given up hope, they heard my rifle shots from behind a dune. . . .

And now they have erected a tent over me and I am ordered to lie in it tonight and tomorrow. Our beduin friends are in no hurry; their waterskins are full; they have even been able to give three bucketfuls to

155

my dromedary: for they know that one day's journey toward the south will bring them, and us, to an oasis where there is a well. And in the meantime the camels have fodder enough in the *hamdh* bushes that grow all around.

After a while, Zayd helps me out of the tent, spreads a blanket on the sand, and I lie down under the stars.

II. THE NATURAL WORLD

CHAPTER NINE

THE NATURAL WORLD

The Cosmos and the Natural Order

~ Seyyed Hossein Nasr[117]

*We have not revealed unto thee this Quran
that thou shouldst be distressed,
But as a reminder unto him who feareth;
A revelation from Him Who created the earth
and the high Heavens, The All-Compassionate,
who is established on the Throne.
Unto Him belongeth whatsoever is in the heavens
and whatsoever is in the earth,
and whatsoever is between them,
and whatsoever is beneath the sod.*
[*Sūrah Ṭā Hā* (O Man) 20:2-6]

The Cosmos and Revelation

The revelation that comes from Him to Whom belong the heavens and the earth and all that is between them and below the earth also addresses itself to all these realms of the cosmic hierarchy as well as to man. The Quran is, in a sense, a Revelation unto the whole of creation, and one of its primary functions is to awaken in man an awareness of the Divine Presence in that other primordial revelation which is the created order itself. Primordial man saw the phenomena of nature *in divinis,* as the story of Adam in paradise reveals. Islam, in bestowing upon man access to this primordial nature and in addressing itself to the primordial man within every man, unveils once again the spiritual significance of nature and the

---

[117] This selection, "The Cosmos and the Natural Order" by Seyyid Hossein Nasr is excerpted from *Islamic Spirituality: Foundations,* edited by Seyyid Hossein Nasr, the Crossroad Publishing Company, NY, NY, 1987, chapter 18, pp. 345-357. All footnotes in this article are by Seyyid Hossein Nasr.

ultimately theophanic character of the phenomena of the created order. It enables man to read once again the eternal message of Divine Wisdom written upon the pages of the cosmic text.

Islamic spirituality is therefore based not only upon the reading of the written Quran (*al-Qur'ān al-tadwīnī*) but also upon deciphering the text of the cosmic Quran (*al-Qur'ān al-takwīnī*) which is its complement.[118] Nature in Islamic spirituality is, consequently, not the adversary but the friend of the traveler upon the spiritual path and an aid to the person of spiritual vision[119] in his journey through her forms to the world of the Spirit, which is the origin of both man and the cosmos. The Quranic Revelation created not only a community of Muslims but also an Islamic cosmic ambience in which the signs of God (*āyāt Allāh*) adorn at once the souls of men and women and the expanses of the skies and the seas, the birds and the fish, the stars and the creatures living in the bosom of the earth. As the text of the Quran is woven of verses (*āyāt*), which are the words of God, so are the events in the souls of men and the phenomena of nature so many *āyāt* of the Supreme Author, Who caused the reality of all things to be written upon the Guarded Tablet (*al-Lawḥ al-Maḥfūẓ*) by the pen (*al-Qalam*). As the Quran itself bears witness, *We shall show them our portents [āyāt] upon the horizons and within themselves, until it becomes manifest unto them that it is the Truth* [41:53], and also, *And in the earth are portents for those whose faith is sure. And (also) in yourselves. Can ye not see?* [51:20-21].[120] The inner relation between man, the cosmos, and

---

[118] Traditional Islamic commentaries refer to the Quran revealed in Arabic as *tadwīnī*, that is, put together as a book, and to the cosmos as *takwīnī*, that is, as the book of existence itself. The eighth/fourteenth-century Sufi 'Azīz al-Dīn Nasafī writes concerning the book of nature, "Each day destiny and the passage of time set this book before you, surah for surah, verse for verse, letter for letter, and read it to you . . . like one who sets a real book before you and reads it to you line for line, letter for letter, that you may learn the content of these lines and letters"; see his *Kashf al-ḥaqā' iq*, trans. F. Meier in "The Problem of Nature in the Esoteric Monism of Islam," in *Spirit and Nature: Papers from the Eranos Yearbooks*, trans. R. Manheim (Princeton, NJ: Princeton University Press, 1954) 203.

[119] These are the people to whom the Quran refers as *ūlu' l-absār*, the "possessors of vision."

[120] "The Quran and the great phenomena of nature are twin manifestations of the divine act of Self-revelation. For Islam, the natural world in its totality is a vast fabric into which the 'signs' of the Creator are woven. It is significant that the word meaning 'signs' or 'symbols', *āyāt*, is the same word that is used for the

Revelation is clearly demonstrated in the use of the same term (*āyah*, pl. *āyāt*) to designate the verses of the sacred Book, the inner reality of man, and the verses written upon the pages of the cosmic book.... To the extent that man turns to the spiritual world within, nature unveils her inner message to him and acts as both support and companion in his spiritual journey.

Since all levels of cosmic existence belong to God, all creatures also praise Him with their very existence. The Quran says, "*The seven heavens and the earth and all that they contain praise Him, nor is there anything that does not celebrate His praise, though ye understand not their praise. Behold, He is clement, forgiving*" [17:44]. Also, *Hast thou not seen that unto God prostrate themselves whatsoever is in the heavens and whatsoever is in the earth—the sun and the moon and the stars and the hills and the trees and the beast and many of mankind?* [22:18].[121]

The Breath of the Compassionate

According to a Sufi doctrine expounded especially by Ibn ʿArabī, the very substance of the universe consists of the Breath of the Compassionate (*nafas al-Raḥmān*) breathed upon the archetypal realities (*al-aʿyān al-thābitah*).[122] The very substance of things is, therefore, the breath that issues from the Divine Compassion (*al-Raḥmah*) while every creature praises the Lord through its very existence. The sage hears in the existence of every creature of nature the invocation (*dhikr*) of His Name and in the qualities of the created order reflections of His Attributes. He sees upon the face of all things the sign of His Oneness, according to the well-known Arabic poem: "In every creature there exists a sign (*āyah*) from

---

'verses' of the Quran. Earth and sky, mountains and stars, oceans and forests and the creatures they contain are, as it were, 'verses' of a sacred book. *'Indeed Allah disdaineth not to coin the similitude of a gnat or of something even smaller than that'* [2:26]. Creation is one, and He who created the Quran is also He who created all the visible phenomena of nature. Both are the communications from God to man" (G. Eaton, *Islam and the Destiny of Man* [Albany, NY: Stare University of New York Press, 1985] p. 87).

[121] See Eaton, *Islam and the Destiny of Man*, p.91.

[122] On this doctrine, see T. Burckhardt, *An Introduction to Sufi Doctrine*, trans. D. M. Matheson (Lahore: M. Ashraf, 1959) chap. 9.

Him, Bearing witness that He is Unique."[123] The Quran emphasizes the Divine Origin of all the order that is observed in the universe. *"He it is who appointed the sun a splendour and the moon a light, and measured for her stages, that ye might know the number of the years and the reckoning. God created not [all] that save in truth (bi'l-ḥaqq). He detaileth the portents (āyāt) for people who have knowledge"* [10:6]. The Muslim mind is, in fact, much more impressed by the order and regularity of the natural order than by those extraordinary events that break that order, that is, miracles. It is just as miraculous that the sun does rise every morning from the east as it would be if it were to rise suddenly from the west. Islam does, however, accept the existence of miracles and believes that a day will come when, according to a *hadith,* the sun will rise from the west.

Moreover, the world is created in truth and by the truth (bi'l-ḥaqq) and not in vain. *We created not the heaven and the earth and all that is between them in play* [21:16]. The study of nature can therefore reveal an aspect of Divine Wisdom provided that study does not divorce the world from its Divine Principle. The Islamic view of nature permitted and encouraged the cultivation of the sciences of nature but never as profane knowledge.[124] Even particular branches of the Islamic sciences such as physics and botany possessed a spiritual aspect as well as a rational one. Being created in truth, nature reflects the Truth on its own level of reality and this Truth can be contemplated by the sage gazing upon a flower as well as by a student of the traditional sciences studying the works of the Muslim scientists, who carried out their study of the natural order always in the light of discovering the vestiges of the Hand of the Divine Artisan.

The Fragility of the World

While it emphasizes that God has created the world by the truth, the Quran also asserts over and over again, especially in the last chapters, the fragility of the created order. A day will come when all the earth, from the mightiest mountain to the lowliest rock will be rendered unto dust before the Majesty of God. *"And thou seest the mountains, which thou deemest so firm, pass away as clouds pass away"* [27:88]. The spiritual

---

[123] *Wa fī kulli shay' in lahū āyatun tadullu 'alā annahu' wāḥidun.*

[124] See the introduction of Nasr, *Science and Civilization;* also idem, *Islamic Science: An Illustrated Study* (London: World of Islam Festival Trust, 1976) part I.

significance of nature resides not only in conveying the message of the One through its beauty, harmony, order, and the symbolism of its forms, but also in being witness to the grandeur of the One Who alone abides while all else passes away. To stand before a mighty mountain and to meditate upon its passing away before the Divine Majesty are to gain a glimpse of that Divine Face which alone subsists while all else dies and perishes, according to the verse, "*Everything perishes save His Face*" [28:88]. But this fragility of the natural order is not as immediate as that of the world of man, and Islamic spirituality emphasizes over and over again that in the span of the ordinary life of humanity the works of man perish while the order of nature abides. Islam has always inculcated the importance of man's being the custodian of nature and has instructed man not to struggle to destroy it but rather to live with it in peace, aware that if man seeks to annihilate and subdue nature he will inevitably fail and that it is always nature that will have the final word.

We must tread carefully upon the earth, treating it with the same respect that we show to the Book of Allah, for although *He hath made the earth humbled to you*, and although we are free *to walk in its tracts and eat of His providing*, yet: *Are ye assured of Him that is in heaven that He might not cause the earth to swallow you? For behold! The earth is quaking* [67:15-16].[125]

Nothing is farther removed from traditional Islamic spirituality than the raping of the earth in the name of man's earthly welfare and without consideration of the welfare of the whole of creation.

Nature as Support in the Spiritual Life

Virgin nature is a source of grace in that in its bosom the Muslim contemplative senses the presence of God and the resonance of the world of the Spirit. He hears the prayer of creatures and sees reflected in their complete surrender to the Divine Will the perfection of the state of *islam*, which itself is complete surrender to the Will of God. The saint is the person whose will is perfectly integrated into and in harmony with the Divine Will and is therefore, in a sense, the counterpart of the creatures of nature whose very life is in accordance with His Will. The prayer of the saint is in fact the prayer on behalf of all creation and for all creation in

---

[125] See Eaton, *Islam and the Destiny of Man*, p. 91.

the same way that the Muslim canonical prayer addresses God using the plural form of the subject to emphasize that man prays as representative of the whole of creation.[126]

Nature, moreover, is the sanctuary in which the supreme Muslim rite of ṣalāt takes place. These canonical prayers can be performed anywhere in nature, for the whole earth was sanctified by God to allow Muslims to pray on it.[127] The mosque does not in fact seek to create a "supernatural" space but to recreate within the man-made ambience of the urban environment, the harmony, tranquillity, peace, and equilibrium that characterize virgin nature. Being the creation of the Divine Artisan, virgin nature is the supreme work of art, a source of inexhaustible beauty, and the ally of man in quest of God. She remains an ever present witness to the cosmic and metacosmic reality of the truth of Islam, and although man may waver in his faith and religious practice, she abides in her perfect surrender to the One in her perpetual state of being *muslim*.

Nature is also a source for gaining knowledge of God's Wisdom as reflected in His creation. The laws, activities, energies, forms, forces, and rhythms of nature reveal a knowledge that possesses a spiritual significance lying beyond the domain of nature itself. In fact, nature is also the source of metaphysical knowledge in the sense that there exists a symbolic science of nature that is of a metaphysical character. There is, moreover, an immediate knowledge of a purely spiritual character imparted by nature to those qualified to receive such a knowledge. For the contemplative, nature provides not only such a knowledge but also an aid for the spiritual life. In her embrace man is already freed from the pettiness of the human world and savors the foretaste of paradise. The grandeur of nature—the incredible beauty of her forms and harmony of rhythms and cycles—can help to melt the hardened heart and untie the knots in the soul so that man comes to see nature as the counterpart of that primordial revelation of which the Arabic Quran is the final crystallization in the life of present humanity.

---

[126] As already mentioned, at the heart of the canonical prayers stands the *Surāt al-fātiḥah,* in which man addresses God in these terms; *iyyāka na'budu wa iyyāka nasta'īn* ("Thee only *we* serve; to Thee alone *we* pray for succour").

[127] See S. H. Nasr, *Islamic Art and Spirituality* (Albany, NY: State University of New York Press, 1987) chap. 3.

Islamic Cosmological Sciences

The spiritual significance of nature in Islam cannot be understood fully without considering the Islamic cosmological sciences which reveal the imprint of the One upon the manifold and relate the world of multiplicity to its Unique Origin. Islamic cosmology acts as a bridge between the metaphysical teachings of the Quranic Revelation and the particular sciences and provides the framework whereby particular branches of knowledge can be sacralized and integrated into the supreme knowledge of the *Shahādah*. It might be said that if all metaphysical knowledge is contained in the first *Shahādah, Lā ilāha illa' Llāh,* all cosmological knowledge is, in a sense, contained in the second *Shahādah, Muḥammadun rasūl Allāh.* Inasmuch as Muḥammad also means all that is positive in the cosmos, the second *Shahādah* means esoterically that all that is positive in the universe comes from—that is, is *rasūl* of—God, and that is precisely the ultimate function of Islamic cosmology.[128]

The root of all Islamic cosmology is to be found in the Quran, and the earliest Islamic cosmological studies must be sought in the works of the Quranic commentators of the first few generations of Islamic history. There are, however, many cosmological schemes developed by Muslims on the basis of Quranic teachings but using languages as diverse as letter symbolism and the hierarchy of light.[129] The Quran itself contains the principles of several cosmological schemes as found in such verses as the Throne Verse (*āyāt al-kursī*) and the Light Verse (*āyāt al-nūr*).[130] These verses have been the subject of

---

[128] See T. Burckhardt, *The Mirror of the Intellect,* ed. W. Stoddart (Cambridge: Quintessential Books, 1987).

[129] On Islamic cosmology, see S. H. Nasr, *Islamic Cosmological Doctrines;* idem, "Philosophy and Cosmology," in *The Cambridge History of Iran,* vol.4, ed. R. N. Frye (Cambridge: University Press, 1975) 419-41.

[130] The *āyāt al-kursī* is as follows: *God—there is no god but He, the Living, the Everlasting. Slumber seizes Him not, neither sleep; to Him belongs all that is in the heavens and the earth. Who is there that shall intercede with Him save by His leave? He knows what lies before them and what is after them, and they comprehend not anything of His knowledge save such as He wills. His Throne comprises the heavens and earth; the preserving of them oppresses Him not; He is the All-high, the All-Glorious* [2:255]. As

numerous commentaries by nearly all classes of Quranic commentators ranging from theologians to philosophers to Sufis. Some of the most important works of Quranic cosmology, such as the *Mishkāt al-anwār* of al-Ghazzālī and *Tafsīr āyāt al-nūr* of Ṣadr al-Dīn Shīrāzī, are in fact commentaries upon the Light Verse and certain *ḥadīths* that complement this verse.[131] The Throne (*al-'arsh*), the Pedestal (*al-kursī*) the Supreme Spirit (*al-Rūḥ*), the four archangels, the eight angels holding the Throne, and other aspects of the cosmic and angelic realities described in the Quran and *Ḥadīth* literature comprise the foundation of Islamic cosmology, providing spiritual significance for the universe in which the Muslim lives and breathes.

The goal of Islamic cosmology is to provide a science that displays the interrelation of all things and the relation of the levels of the cosmic hierarchy to each other and finally to the Supreme Principle. Thereby it provides a knowledge that permits the integration of multiplicity into Unity, a goal which is no more than a commentary upon the Quranic verse, *Verily we belong to God and to Him is our return* [2:156]. By virtue of the integrating and synthesizing power inherent in the Islamic tradition, various schools of Islamic thought developed different cosmologies over the centuries, drawing from many diverse sources. These cosmologies differ in their language and form but not in content, which is always the assertion of the Unity of the Divine Principle, which is the origin of the cosmos, the reality of the hierarchy of cosmic and universal existence, and the interdependence and interrelation of all orders of cosmic reality and various realms of nature. These cosmologies may in fact be described as so many versions of what one might call a *cosmologia perennis*.[132]

---

for the *ayat al-nur*, it asserts, *God is the Light of the heavens and the earth; the like of His Light is as a niche wherein is a lamp (the lamp in a glass, the glass as it were a glittering star) kindled from a Blessed Tree, an olive that is neither of the East nor of the West whose oil well nigh would shine, even if no fire touched it; Light upon Light; God guides to His Light whom He will. And God strikes similitudes for men, and God has knowledge of everything* [24:35].

[131] Of special significance is the series of *hadiths* dealing with the veils of light and darkness and the hierarchy of angels.

[132] The goal of Islamic cosmology was shared by other traditional cosmologies

Some of the earliest cosmological schemes in Islam are to be found in circles that were involved in the study of Pythagorean and Hermetic texts being translated into Arabic from the second [*hijrah*]/eighth [C.E.] century on. A cosmology based on the symbolism of numbers and the language of alchemy and astrology is already to be found in the writings of the first major Islamic alchemist, Jābir ibn Hayyān, who lived in the second/eighth century.[133] This type of cosmology was often combined with the symbolism of letters related to the science of *jafr*, which is of purely Islamic origin, inextricably related to the Arabic language and the structure of the Quran itself. In such cosmological schemes, each letter or number signifies a grade of being, a particular existent within the cosmic or metacosmic hierarchy, while the cosmic dimensions of the alchemical natures and qualities are brought out. . . .

Ibn Sīnā was also interested in the symbolism of letters and numbers, and the more esoteric cosmology associated with such esoteric sciences as *al-jafr* as can be seen in his *Risālat al-nayrūziyyah*. Moreover, toward the end of his life, he turned toward what he called "the Oriental philosophy" (*al-ḥikmat al-mashriqiyyah*), in which cosmology became not a theoretical scheme but a plan to enable the traveler upon the path of spiritual perfection to journey through the cosmic crypt, to be liberated from all limitation, and thereby to gain spiritual freedom.[134] This later cosmology of Ibn Sīnā is a prelude to the cosmology that was to be expanded a

---

and sciences, without which Islam would not have integrated some of these cosmologies and cosmological sciences into its intellectual world. That is why one can speak of a *cosmologia perennis* as one can speak of a *philosophia perennis*. See T. Burckhardt, "Cosmology and Modern Science," in *The Sword of Gnosis*, ed. J. Needleman (Boston, MA: Arkana Paperbacks, 1986) 102ff.; and Nasr, "The Role of the Traditional Sciences in the Encounter of Religion and Science—An Oriental Perspective," *Religious Studies* 20 (1984) 519-41.

[133] There are numerous cosmological treatises in the Jābirean corpus, and whether they are all by him or his school is not of consequence here. On the name of these treatises, see P. Kraus, *Jābir ibn Ḥayyān, Contribution à l'historie des idées scientifiques dans l'Islam* (2 vols.; Cairo: Institut francais d'archeologie orientale, 1942-43); and H. Corbin "Le Livre du Glorieux de Jābir ibn Ḥayyan," *Eranos Jahrbuch* (Ascona) 18 (1950), 47-114.

[134] See Nasr, *Islamic Cosmological Doctrines*, chap. 15.

century and a half after Ibn Sīnā by Suhrawardī, the founder of the School of Illumination (ishrāq).[135] Ishrāqī cosmology is based on the symbolism of light. The Supreme Principle is called by Suhrawardi the "Light of lights" (nūr al-anwār), and there issues from this transcendent source the longitudinal and latitudinal hierarchies of light which govern every aspect of cosmic existence. The cosmos itself consists, in fact, of grades of light, and matter is nothing more than the absence of light. Every light is but a faint glimmer of that Light which as the Quran asserts is neither of the east nor the west and which is the Light of the heavens and the earth according to the Quranic verse, *God is the Light of the heavens and the earth* [24:35]. . . .

The Spiritual Significance of Cosmology and Nature

The spiritual significance of all Islamic cosmologies is to provide a knowledge of the cosmos so as to transform the cosmic reality from opacity to transparency, from a veil to the means of unveiling the Divine Reality, which the cosmos veils and unveils by its very nature. The goal is to provide a map of the cosmic labyrinth so as to enable man to escape from the prison of all limitative existence. The goal is to reveal Unity (al-tawḥīd) as reflected in the world of multiplicity and hence to aid man to realize Unity. In order to realize God, some men may be able to fly directly to the Divine Empyrean without concern for the cosmic reality that surrounds them. But Islamic spirituality provides the means for those human beings whose inner nature is such that they must read the pages of the cosmic book before being able to put this book away and experience the moment described in the Quran as follows: *On the day when We shall roll up heaven as a scroll is rolled for the writings* [21:104].

The role of the natural order and the sciences related to it are, however, not limited to the intellectual significance of the cosmological sciences. Nature is also the foretaste of the beatitude of the Islamic paradise. The Quranic description of paradise includes animals and plants,

---

[135] On Suhrawardī and his cosmology, see S. H. Nasr, *Three Muslim Sages: Avicenna, Suhrawardī, Ibn 'Arabī* (Cambridge, MA: Harvard University Press, 1964) chap. 2; H. Corbin, *En Islam iranien* (4 vols.; Paris: Gallimard, 1970) vol. 2.

and there are those Muslim sages such as Mullā Ṣadrā who have spoken of the resurrection of all of creation at the Day of Judgment. The Muslim contemplative experiences in the bosom of nature something of the delights of paradise and sees in the beauty of nature, in the majestic mountains that uphold the earth, in the stars that adorn the heavens, and in the seas that hide the treasures of creation in their infinite expanse, reflections of the Face of the Beloved. The experience of virgin nature is related to that beatific vision whose subject transcends all that is created. Islamic spirituality brings into being that "creation-consciousness" which enables man to see in nature the theophany of the Divine Names and Qualities and to hear in the flight of the bird soaring toward heaven the prayer of creation to the Divine Throne, for, as the Quran asserts, *Seest thou not that it is God whom all things in the heavens and earth praise—and the birds in flight outstretched? Each knoweth its [mode of] prayer and praise to Him, and God is aware of all that they do* [24:41].

THE ELEMENTS

EARTH

AIR

FIRE

WATER

CHAPTER TEN

EARTH

And We have spread the earth out wide;
set upon it firm and immovable mountains;
and produced upon it all kinds of things in balance.
And We have provided there means of subsistence for you
and for those whose provision does not depend on you.
[*Sūrah Al-Ḥijr* 15:19-20]

And in the mountains are areas
that are white, and red of various shades, and black intense in hue.
Even so among people and crawling creatures and cattle
are those of various colors.
Those among His Servants who have knowledge stand in awe of God:
for God is Almighty, Often-Forgiving.
[*Sūrah Al-Fāṭir* (The Originator) 35:27-28]

God has caused you to grow gradually from the earth,
and in the end He will return you to it
and then raise you forth anew.
And God has unfolded wide the earth for you
that you might move about there on spacious paths.
[*Sūrah Nūḥ* (Noah) 71:17-20]

And He has set upon the earth
mountains standing firm lest it should shake with you;
and rivers and roads, that you may guide yourselves,
and signs and means of orientation;
for by the stars men find their way.
Is then He Who creates like one who cannot create?
Will you not listen to counsel?
If you were to count the favors of God
never would you be able to compute them:
for God is Oft-Forgiving, Most Merciful.
[*Sūrah Al-Anʿām* (Cattle) 6:15-18]

Say: "All praise is due to God,
and peace be upon those servants of His whom He chose
[to be His message-bearers]!"
Is not God far better than anything
to which men ascribe a share in His divinity?[136]
Nay—who is it that has created the heavens and the earth,
and sends down for you water from the skies?
For it is by this means
that We cause gardens of shining beauty to grow—
it is not in your power to cause its trees to grow!
Could there be any divine power besides God?
[*Sūrah An-Naml* (The Ants) 27:59-60]

Have they, then, never considered the earth—
how much of every noble kind [of life] We have caused to grow upon it?
In this, behold, there is a message,
even though most of them will not have faith.
[*Sūrah Ash-Shuᶜarā'* (The Poets) 26:7-8]

On the earth are signs for those with inner certainty,
just as within your own selves: will you not then see?
And in heaven is your sustenance
and all that which you are promised.
Then by the Sustainer of heaven and earth, this is the Truth—
as true as the fact that you are able to speak.
[*Sūrah Adh-Dhāriyāt* (The Dust-Scattering Winds) 51:21-23]

And We bestowed Our grace upon David:
"O you Mountains! Sing with him the praises of God!"
[*Sūrah Sabā'* (Sheba) 34:10]

---

[136] Lit., "Is God better, or that to which they ascribe. . . ," etc.: thus including, by implication, not only deified beings or forces of nature, but also false social and moral values to which custom and ancestral tradition have lent an almost "religious" sanction. ~ M.Asad

The Prophet Muḥammad said that, "The earth has been created for me as a mosque and as a means of purification." (Clean dust may be used for ablutions before prayer if clean water is not available.) So there is a sacrality to the earth which is a fit place for human's service to God whether in formal ceremonies or in daily life.

~ Frederick M. Denny[137]

To see a world in a grain of sand,
And Heaven in a wild flower,
Hold infinity in the palm of your hand,
And Eternity in an hour.

~ William Blake[138]

Abu Shāma stated, "The Messenger of God used to see strange visions before his mission."

On this same subject there is the material in the *sahih* collection of *Muslim*, on the authority of Jābir b. Samura, who said that the Messenger of God ﷺ stated, "I know a rock in Mecca that would greet me before I received my mission. I still know it now."

~ Ibn Kathīr[139]

---

[137] Frederick M. Denny, "Islam and Ecology: A Bestowed Trust, Inviting Balanced Stewardship," *Earth Ethics* 10, no.1 (Fall 1998) Copyright 1998 Center for Respect of Life and Environment.

[138] Excerpted from William Blake's "Auguries of Innocence."

[139] Excerpted from the Ḥadith collection of Imām Abū'l-Fidāʾ Ismāʾil ibn Kathīr, *The Life of the Prophet Muḥammad,* translated by Prof. Trevor Le Gassick (Reading, United Kingdom: Garnet Publishing Limited, 1998, 2000), Vol. I, p. 282.

No matter how sophisticated you may be, a huge granite mountain cannot be denied—it speaks in silence to the very core of your being. ~ Ansel Adams

The surface geography and subterranean geology of the earth contribute to its uniqueness in subtle ways that make our existence and behavior patterns possible. The arrangement of the continental land masses relative to the axis of rotation is an interesting example. The early spread of humanity's influence after the development of agriculture was more easily accomplished over continents that straddled lines of constant seasonal climate, than over those land masses that ran across a whole range of climatic variations. . . .

The internal composition of the earth also has profound implications for us. All our fuels are fossilized gases, liquids, and solids, extracted from beneath its surface. ~ John D. Barrow[140]

Essential Salt

~ C.A.H. with Mark Kurlansky[141]

Salt is essential to human survival and to that of animals. Sodium chloride is the most basic and usual form of salt we ingest. In prehistoric days, animals instinctively located salt pools and human beings followed their tracks. *Salt, a World History* reveals some interesting facts:

Chloride is essential for digestion and in respiration. Without sodium, which the body cannot manufacture, the body would be unable to transport nutrients or oxygen, transmit nerve impulses, or move muscles, including the heart . . .

---

[140] John D. Barrow, *The Artful Universe*, op. cit., p.122-123.

[141] Camille Helminski with excerpts from Mark Kurlansky, *Salt, a World History*, Penguin Books, Penguin Putnam Inc. NY. NY, 2002, pp. 6, 7, 9, 12, 48-49.

On every continent, once human beings began cultivating crops, they began looking for salt to add to their diet. How they learned of this need is a mystery. . . .[142]

Almost no place on earth is without salt. But this was not clear until revealed by modern geology and so for all of history until the twentieth century, salt was desperately searched for, traded for, and fought over. For millennia, salt represented wealth. . . .[143]

In 1352, Ibn Batuta, the greatest Arab-language traveler of the Middle Ages, who had journeyed overland across Africa, Europe, and Asia, reported visiting the city of Taghaza, which, he said, was entirely built of salt, including an elaborate mosque. . . .

Taghaza was not the earliest report of buildings made of salt. The first century A.D. Roman, Pliny the Elder, writing of rock salt mining in Egypt, mentioned houses built of salt. . . .

In ancient Taghaza, salt was quarried from the near surface in 200-pound blocks loaded on camels, one block on each side. The powerful animals carried them 500 miles to Timbuktu, a trading center because of its location on the northernmost crook of the Niger River, which connects most of West Africa. In Timbuktu, the goods of North Africa, the Sahara, and West Africa were exchanged, and the wealth from trade built a cultural center, . . . a center of learning. [144]

For thousands of years salt provided the main means of preserving food, because salt preserves.

In both Islam and Judaism, salt seals a bargain because it is immutable. . . . Loyalty and friendship are sealed with salt because its essence does not change.[145]

---

[142] Ibid., pp. 6 and 9.

[143] Ibid., p. 12.

[144] Ibid., pp. 48-49.

[145] Ibid., pp. 6 and 7.

If your mind becomes firm like a rock and no longer shakes
In a world where everything is shaking,
Your mind will be your greatest friend
And suffering will not come your way.

~ Buddha[146]

The Grand Canyon

~ John Muir[147]

In a dry, hot, monotonous forested plateau, seemingly boundless, you come suddenly and without warning upon the abrupt edge of a gigantic sunken landscape of the wildest, most multitudinous features, and those features, sharp and angular, are made out of flat beds of limestone and sandstone forming a spiry, jagged, gloriously coloured mountain-range countersunk in a level grey plain. It is a hard job to sketch it even in scrawniest outline; and, try as I may, not in the least sparing myself, I cannot tell the hundredth part of the wonders of its features—the side-canyons, gorges, alcoves, cloisters and amphitheatres of vast sweep and depth, carved in its magnificent walls; the throng of great architectural rocks it contains resembling castles, cathedrals, temples and palaces, towered and spired and painted, some of them nearly a mile high, yet beneath one's feet. All this, however, is less difficult than to give any idea of the impression of wild, primeval beauty and power one receives in merely gazing from its brink. The view down the gulf of colour and over the rim of its wonderful wall, more than any other view I know, leads us to think of our earth as a star with stars swimming in light, every radiant spire pointing the way to the heavens.

---

[146] *Theragatha*, excerpted from *The Pocket Buddha Reader*, edited by Anne Bancroft, Shambhala Publications, Boston, MA, p. 73.
[147] Excerpted from *John Muir, The Eight Wilderness Discovery Books*, pages 999-1012. Joint publication of The Mountaineers (US) and Baton Wicks (UK). John Muir (1838-1914), the son of a Scottish immigrant, was largely responsible for the establishment of several of the great national parks of North America.

But it is impossible to conceive what the canyon is, or what impression it makes, from descriptions or pictures, however good. Naturally it is untellable even to those who have seen something perhaps a little like it on a small scale in this same plateau region. One's most extravagant expectations are indefinitely surpassed, though one expects much from what is said of it as "the biggest chasm on earth"—"so big is it that all other big things—Yosemite, the Yellowstone, the Pyramids, Chicago—all would be lost if tumbled into it." . . .

Every feature of Nature's big face is beautiful—height and hollow, wrinkle, furrow, and line—and this is the main master-furrow of its kind on our continent, incomparably greater and more impressive than any other yet discovered, or likely to be discovered, now that all the great rivers have been traced to their heads.

The Colorado River rises in the heart of the continent on the dividing ranges and ridges between the two oceans, drains thousands of snowy mountains through narrow or spacious valleys, and thence through canyons of every colour, sheer-walled and deep, all of which seem to be represented in this one grand canyon of canyons.

It is very hard to give anything like an adequate conception of its size; much more of its colour, its vast wall-sculpture, the wealth of ornate architectural buildings that fill it, or, most of all, the tremendous impression it makes. According to Major Powell, it is about two hundred and seventeen miles long, from five to fifteen miles wide from rim to rim, and from about five thousand to six thousand feet deep. So tremendous a chasm would be one of the world's greatest wonders even if, like ordinary canyons cut in sedimentary rocks, it were empty and its walls were simple. But instead of being plain, the walls are so deeply and elaborately carved into all sorts of recesses—alcoves, cirques, amphitheatres and side-canyons—that, were you to trace the rim closely around on both sides, your journey would be nearly a thousand miles long. Into all these recesses the level, continuous beds of rock in ledges and benches, with their various colours, run like broad ribbons, marvellously beautiful and effective even at a distance of ten or twelve miles. And the vast space these glorious walls enclose, instead of being empty, is crowded with gigantic architectural rock-forms gorgeously coloured and adorned with towers and spires like works of art. . . .

176

Of all the various kinds of ornamental work displayed—carving, tracery on cliff-faces, mouldings, arches, pinnacles—none is more admirably effective or charms more than the webs of rain-channelled taluses. Marvellously extensive, without the slightest appearance of waste or excess, they cover roofs and dome-tops and the base of every cliff, belt each spire and pyramid and massy, towering temple, and in beautiful continuous lines go sweeping along the great walls in and out around all the intricate system of side-canyons, amphitheatres, cirques and scallops into which they are sculptured. From one point hundreds of miles of this fairy embroidery may be traced. It is all so fine and orderly that it would seem that not only had the clouds and streams been kept harmoniously busy in the making of it, but that every raindrop sent like a bullet to a mark had been the subject of a separate thought, so sure is the outcome of beauty through the stormy centuries. Surely nowhere else are there illustrations so striking of the natural beauty of desolation and death, so many of nature's own mountain buildings wasting in glory of high desert air—going to dust. See how steadfast in beauty they all are in their going. Look again and again how the rough, dusty boulders and sand of disintegration from the upper ledges wreathe in beauty the next and next below with these wonderful taluses, and how the colours are finer. . . . We oftentimes see Nature giving beauty for ashes—as in the flowers of a prairie after fire—but here the very dust and ashes are beautiful.

Gazing across the mighty chasm, we at last discover that it is not its great depth nor length, nor yet these wonderful buildings, that most impresses us. It is its immense width, sharply defined by precipitous walls plunging suddenly down from a flat plain, declaring in terms instantly apprehended that the vast gulf is a gash in the once unbroken plateau, made by slow, orderly erosion and removal of huge beds of rocks. Other valleys of erosion are as great—in all their dimensions some are greater— but none of these produces an effect on the imagination at once so quick and profound, coming without study, given at a glance. . . .

No other range of mountainous rock-work of anything like the same extent have I seen that is so strangely, boldly, lavishly coloured. The famous Yellowstone Canyon below the falls comes to mind; but, wonderful as it is, and well deserved as is its fame, compared with this it is only a bright rainbow ribbon at the roots of the pines. Each of the series of level, continuous beds of carboniferous rocks of the canyon has its own characteristic colour. The summit limestone-beds are pale yellow; next below these are the beautiful rose-coloured cross-bedded sandstones; next there are a thousand feet of brilliant red sandstones; and below these the red wall limestones, over two thousand feet thick, rich massy red, the greatest and most influential of the series, and forming the main colour-fountain. Between these are many neutral-tinted beds. The prevailing colours are wonderfully deep and clear, changing and blending with varying intensity from hour to hour, day to day, season to season; throbbing, wavering, glowing, responding to every passing cloud or storm, a world of colour in itself, now burning in separate rainbow bars streaked and blotched with shade, now glowing in one smooth, all-pervading ethereal radiance like the alpenglow, uniting the rocky world with the heavens.

The dawn, as in all the pure, dry desert country is ineffably beautiful; and when the first level sunbeams string the domes and spires, with what a burst of power the big, wild days begin! The dead and the living, rocks and hearts alike, awake and sing the new-old song of creation. All the massy headlands and salient angles of the walls, and the multitudinous temples and palaces, seem to catch the light at once, and cast thick black shadows athwart hollow and gorge, bringing out details as well as the main massive features of the architecture; while all the rocks, as if wild with life, throb and quiver and glow in the glorious sunburst, rejoicing. Every rock temple then becomes a temple of music; every spire and pinnacle an angel of light and song, shouting colour hallelujahs.

★★★

In cool, shady amphitheatres at the head of the trail there are groves of white silver fir and Douglas spruce, with ferns and saxifrages that recall snowy mountains; below these, yellow pine, nut pine, juniper, hop-hornbeam, ash, maple, holly-leaved berberis, cowania, spiraea, dwarf oak and other small shrubs and trees. In dry gulches and on taluses and sun-beaten crags are sparsely scattered yuccas, cactuses, agave, etc. Where springs gush from the rocks there are willow thickets, grassy flats and bright, flowery gardens, and in the hottest recesses the delicate abronia, mesquite, woody compositae and arborescent cactuses.

178

The most striking and characteristic part of this widely varied vegetation are the cactaceae—strange, leafless, old-fashioned plants with beautiful flowers and fruit, in every way able and admirable. While grimly defending themselves with innumerable barbed spears, they offer both food and drink to man and beast. Their juicy globes and disks and fluted cylindrical columns are almost the only desert wells that never go dry, and they always seem to rejoice the more and grow plumper and juicier the hotter the sunshine and sand. Some are spherical, like rolled-up porcupines, crouching in rock-hollows beneath a mist of grey lances, unmoved by the wildest winds. Others, standing as erect as bushes and trees or tall branchless pillars crowned with magnificent flowers, their prickly armour sparkling, look boldly abroad over the glaring desert, making the strangest forests ever seen or dreamed of. *Cereus giganteus,* the grim chief of the desert tribe, is often thirty or forty feet high in southern Arizona. Several species of tree yuccas in the same deserts, laden in early spring with superb white lilies, form forests hardly less wonderful, though here they grow singly or in small lonely groves. The low, almost stemless *Yucca baccata,* with beautiful lily flowers and sweet banana-like fruit, prized by the Indians, is common along the canyon-rim, growing on lean, rocky soil beneath mountain-mahogany, nut pines and junipers, beside dense flowery mats of *Spiraea cespitosa* and the beautiful pinnate-leaved *Spiraea millefolia.* The nut pine (*Pinus edulis*) scattered long the upper slopes and roofs of the canyon buildings, is the principal tree of the strange dwarf Coconino Forest. It is a picturesque stub of a pine about twenty-five feet high, usually with dead, lichened limbs thrust through its rounded head, and grows on crags and fissured rock tables, braving heat and frost, snow and drought, and continuing patiently, faithfully fruitful for centuries. Indians and insects and almost every desert bird and beast come to it to be fed.

***

The whole canyon is a mine of fossils, in which five thousand feet of horizontal strata are exposed in regular succession over more than a thousand square miles of wall-space, and on the adjacent plateau region there is another series of beds twice as thick, forming a grand geological library—a collection of stone books covering thousands of miles of shelving, tier on tier, conveniently arranged for the student. And with what wonderful scriptures are their pages filled—myriad forms of successive floras and faunas, lavishly illustrated with coloured drawings, carrying us back into the midst of the life of a past infinitely remote. And as we go on and on, studying this old, old life in the light of the life beating warmly about us, we enrich and lengthen our own.

Renewal

~ Dayton Fandray[148]

Sometimes a person just needs to step back and get some perspective. On one's life. On one's career. On a world that seems, on occasion, to make no sense at all. . . . Getting off the train, I head straight for the edge of the canyon, dragging my suitcase with me. I thought I had remembered what it was like to stand here, feeling nothing but the whisper of the breeze that flits like a wraith among the rocky outcrops, but I was wrong. Here, at the very edge of the Grand Canyon, the world as I know it ends abruptly. My first impression is one of impossibly empty space, as if the earth itself has melted away. And, in a sense it has. The Colorado River, which sparkles below me in the afternoon sun, is eating away at the earth even as I stand here. It has left behind these impossibly steep cliffs and the buttes and mesas that rise from the floor of the canyon like so many medieval castles, once impenetrable but fallen now into ruin. I realize here that every visit to the Grand Canyon is like seeing it for the first time. Human memory is just too frail to hold it. . . .

At every lookout, I find myself gazing into a subtly different canyon. All it takes is a slight change of angle, a shift in the light and shadows, to turn a rock formation you saw 10 minutes ago into a bewildering new discovery. . . . I hike a bit. I linger on an accommodating rock. I look and listen. . . . The next morning I wake up refreshed and ready to face a world that makes sense to me once again.

---

[148] Excerpted from "Grand Canyon Grandeur," Alaska Airlines magazine, September 2004, pp. 41, 43, 45.

Mountain Christening

After a hard climb
Through a dry river-bed,
Its scoured stones glistening
Like a white chain to the horizon,
Descending between its links
The long concerto of a stream
Where the listening mountains incline,
Rising against the steep fall of soft bog,
Searching for our grip
In the shimmer of scree.
At last on the summit
Of the Beanna Beola,
Overlooking three valleys,
Delighted to be so high
Above the lives where we dwell,
Together for a while
From other sides of the world,
Sensing each other,
Strangely close, where few reach.
Suddenly, your voice
Calling out my name.
I call yours.
The echoes take us
To the heart of the mountains.
When the silence closes,
You say: Now that they
Have called our names back
The mountains can
Never forget us.[149]

---

[149] "Mountain Christening" from *Conamara Blues* by John O'Donohue, published by Doubleday. Reprinted by permission of The Random House Group, Ltd.

From the Garden of Abu Mahmoud

~ Naomi Shihab Nye

. . . He stooped to unsheathe an eggplant
from its nest of leaves,
purple shining globe,
and pressed it on me.
I said No, no, I don't want
to take things before they are ripe,
but it was started already,
handfuls of marble-sized peaches,
hard green *wish-wish* and delicate lilt
of beans. Each pocket swelled
as he breathed mint leaves,
bit the jagged edge.

He said every morning found him here,
before the water boiled on the flame
he came out to this garden,
dug hands into earth saying, *I know you*
and earth crumbled rich layers
and this result of their knowing—
a hillside in which no inch went unsung.
His enormous onions held light
and the trees so weighted with fruits
he tied the branches up.

And he called it *querido, corazon,*
all the words of any language
connecting to the deep place
of darkness and seed. He called it
ya habibi in Arabic, my darling tomato,
and it called him governor, king,
and some days he wore no shoes. [150]

---

[150] Excerpted from "The Garden of Abu Mahmoud" from *19 Varieties of Gazelle,*

The garden of love is green without limit
And yields many fruits other than sorrow or joy.
Love is beyond either condition . . . it is always fresh.

~ Mevlana Jalaluddin Rumi, *Mathnawi*

The Garden

~ Shaykh Fadhlalla Haeri[151]

Everything, in reality, is a sign. Allah is saying, "Wherever you look there is a sign," and in particular He says, "And one sign for them is the earth which previously was dead, dormant before the throb of life arose in it, and then from it We created seeds." There is this cyclical movement from the earth, so that we may eat from it and be sustained by it, and also be able to read its multiplicity of signs in order to wake up to the One Reality behind them.

In the elliptical, circular and repetitive way of the Qur'an, each time a sign is repeated, it is viewed from a slightly different angle, either in time or in space. Here we are again reminded that the earth after its creation was once dead, that it cooled down from it molten metallic state, then after that cooling came the advent of water and rain, and the creation of dust on top of the rocks which were formed during the earlier melting state. From that dead state, then, Allah says, "We brought it to life, and began to animate it as a sentient thing." Geologists say that this process took several hundred million years.

Wa akbrajna minha habban
(And bring forth grain from it) [36:33]

Poems of the Middle East, by Naomi Shihab Nye. Greenwillow Books, 2002, pages 20-21. Copyright © 2002 Naomi Shihab Nye. Used by permission of HarperCollins Publishers.
[151] *Heart of Qur'an and Perfect Mizan, Surat Ya Sin. (Surah 36)* With *Tafsir* on *Surat al-Fatihah* by Khaja Abdullah Ansari. *Tafsir* by Shaykh Fadhalla Haeri. Zahra Publications, pp. 75-79.

Habb means "grain," "seed." The seed of anything originates from within itself, and again there exists the duality. We have the tree and the seed, just like the chicken and the egg—which came first? The creation has come about and it hangs on the two ends of the balance, creation and destruction. From the plant comes the seed, and the seed, in turn, reproduces the plant,

Faminhu ya'kulun
(So they may eat of it)

And from it, men derive their physical nourishment.
And We make gardens of palm-trees and grapevines in it,
and We make springs flow forth in it— [36:34]

Jannah is a garden, either a physical garden or a garden in the Unseen. Usually, when the Qur'an talks about gardens that are fed by underground rivers, it implies the "state" of being in a garden, the state of inner tranquility, peace, satisfaction, complete contentment and joy that accompanies a person present in a garden. So *jannah* means both an outer, visible garden, and an inner state, as though we were in Paradise. Clearly, here the reference is to a physical garden of this world.

wa ja'alna fiha jannatin
(And We make it in gardens . . .) [36:34]

And in the earth, after its creation and rebirth, after it cooled down, there were created gardens *min nakhilin wa 'a'nab* (of palm-trees and grapevines), which represent the different types of gardens which flower forth on this earth. *Nakhl*, the date-palm, is the highest, most sophisticated plant we have, in the same way that the fungus, or mushroom, is the lowest, being the link between so-called "dead" matter and living matter. The date-palm, on the opposite end of the scale, occupies a place between the plant kingdom and the human kingdom. *A'nab* (grapevines) is a general word meaning anything like berries, or grapes, etc.

The date-palm is a very highly elevated plant—it has a heart. If we try to drown the tree, it will not die unless the water goes above a certain height. But if we immerse the whole tree for half a day in water, it dies. People also say that it has the rudiments of consciousness. It is a common practice in the oldest palm groves in the east that if a female plant does not produce dates after about four or five years, they threaten her. There was once a very beautiful palm-tree, but it would not produce dates, so one day a man came along with a sword and said, "It's no use, I'll have to cut her down!" And another man said, "Look, just leave her alone until next year." They took their little drama all very seriously, and the following year the tree produced dates. It is a very special, noble tree, and it is referred to in many *hadiths* of the Prophet Muḥammad 🕮 in which he said of them that they are *ummatukum*, they are "your community."

Wa fajjarna fiha minal-'uyun
(*And We make springs flow forth*) [36:34]

Fajjarna ("We detonate. We break open") springs from the earth, both the sweet and the salty, the good and the bad, indicating all the dualities, the total creational effulgence that manifests in doubles, in opposites, in complementary pairs throughout existence.

So they may eat the fruit of it, and their hands did not make it —
so will they not be grateful? [36:35]

There are two ways of looking at this *ayah*. The first meaning is, "They eat from the fruit of it and sustain themselves by these fruits, and what has come through their hands by the permission of Allah," by the permission of nature, working along the natural path, from the fruits, or from the products of the fruits, whether dried fruits or products of the pressing of fruit, such as vinegar or syrup.

The second meaning is, "And this is nothing their hands have accomplished, not independently. They are not independent, so can they not be in gratitude for this amazing garden?" This is a prelude to the final Garden. Gardens on this earth are a preparation for the full Garden, they are all a foretaste of that final Garden, as if people were being introduced to the final Garden gradually in this world.

Our entry into the Garden is through *shukr* (gratitude), because the door of increase is *shukr;* when we are in gratitude we no longer have expectations and desires. At the moment of gratitude, for that split second, we are desireless, open, and our hearts are clear. In that way, our 'Iman increases, and we are flooded with the *nur* (Light) of Allah by which we can see His manifestations in the creation.

One's inmost consciousness is like the root of a tree;
And just as the hard wood sprouts leaves
On the tree, in souls and minds
The leaves grow according to the root.
From the trees of faithfulness wings soar to heaven:
Its root is fast in the earth and its branch is in the sky.
[*Sūrah Ibrahim* 14:24]

~ Jalaluddin Rumi[152]

Leaf Patternings

~ Leila Ahmed[153]

It was as if there were to life itself a quality of music in that time, the era of my childhood, and in that place, the remote edge of Cairo. There the city petered out into a scattering of villas leading into tranquil country fields. On the other side of our house was the profound, unsurpassable quiet of the desert.

There was, to begin with, always the sound—sometimes no more than a mere breath—of the wind in the trees, each variety of tree having its own music, its own way of conversing. I knew them all like friends ... although none more intimately than the two trees on either side of the corner bedroom I shared with Nanny. On one side was the silky, barely perceptible breath of the mimosa, which, when the wind grew strong, would scratch lightly with its thorns at the shutters of the window facing the front of the house, looking out onto the garden. On the other side was the dry, faintly rattling shuffle of the longleaved eucalyptus that stood by the window facing the street. On hot nights the street lamp cast the shadows of the slender twirling eucalyptus leaves onto my bedroom wall,

---

[152] *Mathnawi* III, 4386-4388, excerpted in *Jewels of Remembrance,* translations by Camille and Kabir Helminski, Threshold Books, p. 46.
[153] Leila Ahmed, *A Border Passage,* Penguin Books, Penguin Putnam Inc., New York, NY 1999, pp. 3-4.

my own secret cinema. I would fall asleep watching those dancing shadows, imagining to myself that I saw a house in them and people going about their lives. . . .

I loved the patterns of light cast by leaves on the earth and I loved being in them, under them. The intricate, gently shifting patterns that the flame tree cast where the path widened toward the garden gate, fading and growing strong again as a cloud passed, could hold me still, totally lost, for long moments.

Befriending Trees

~ Kevin Lax and Patrick Tyler

The "Father of Old Trees," [Liao Shou-yi], has long been one of Taipei's greatest admirers of old trees. "Trees are Taipei City's oldest residents," says the sixty-year-old elementary school teacher. Liao's passion to preserve these old residents began in the 1960s when he started to plant trees and have an appreciation for trees around the city. He believed that through public appreciation, people would come to nurture and love these old trees.

Over the past decade, Liao has climbed Taipei's nearby mountains in search of old trees and has documented their existence. With his assistance, the Taipei City Government currently has on record more than a hundred trees that are over a hundred years old.

Liao has also formed the "Taiwan Tree Lovers' Archive Workshop" to promote the concept of planting and appreciating trees in various schools and communities. With this project, he hopes the public will come to understand the correlation between trees, water resources, and the environment.

In addition, Liao is promoting "Ten Tree Actions" on campuses to encourage a younger generation of tree admirers to plant, love, protect, save, preserve, harmonize, record, and appreciate these giant old residents. Students are asked to select a "perfect ancient tree" on school grounds to cement their appreciation of trees.

The avid tree lover has also compiled the book, *Community Walkways and Ancient Trees*, in which he proposes the establishment of walking trails in each community centered on ancient trees to integrate the lives of old trees and Taipei's residents.[154]

★★★

Wangari Maathai, a Kenyan woman who started an environmental movement that has planted 30 million trees in Africa and who has campaigned for women's rights and greater democracy in her home country, was awarded the 2004 Nobel Peace Prize. She is the first African woman to win the peace prize. . . . Maathai, 64, born in Nyeri, Kenya, founded the Green Belt Movement in 1977, to organize poor women in rural Kenya to plant millions of trees to combat deforestation and to replenish the source of fuel for village cooking fires. . . .

Asked if the committee had stretched the limits of the prize that already recognizes human rights advocacy and peacekeeping, Mjoes [the Nobel committee chairman], a physician and former president of Tromsoe, replied, "It is clear that with this award, we have expanded the term "peace" to encompass environmental questions related to our beloved Earth."

He added, "Peace on earth depends on our ability to secure our living environment."[155]

---

[154] "Protecting Taipei's Trees" by Kevin Lax excerpted from "Discover Taipei," January-February 2003. Department of Information, Taipei City Government, pp. 7-9 and pp.5-6.

[155] Patrick E. Tyler, "Kenyan awarded Nobel Peace Prize," The New York Times, Saturday, October 9, 2004. Accessed through International Herald Tribune, October 8, 2004. www.iht.com/articles/542775. html.

Deep Ecology: "Wisdom Related to Action"

~ Peter Reed and David Rothenberg[156]

The mark the land has left on Norwegian culture is deeper than regional differences in speech and dress, though less easy to demonstrate....Patience, tenacity, courage, and strong kinship ties are also said to be the bequest of a landscape that split people into small communities and only grudgingly yielded them a living. But a "rugged individualism," a sense of living every day on the frontier, was not the whole story: nature was a challenge, to be sure, but nothing one could expect to triumph over. Philosopher Gunnar Skirbekk writes: "One must learn that nature is not always something that can be conquered. We ourselves are small and vulnerable, and we must understand that we do not stand outside of nature as all-powerful engineers, but that we belong to nature, as a part of the whole."[157] In fact, Skirbekk continues, Norway is a "state that to a great degree builds its national identity on nature." Nature precedes human culture, and culture precedes the individual. Rather than try to extract glittering generalizations about Norwegian culture and nature, it is best to let Norwegians speak for themselves. . . .[158]

In Norway, at least, there was a development that Nils Faarlund later elaborates as "deep romanticism"—a true entrance into the awe of nature for its own sake as the greatest of possible wonders. Henrik Wegerland was so admired in his own time (the mid-nineteenth century) for the very

---

[156] Excerpts from *Wisdom in the Open Air: The Norwegian Roots of Deep Ecology* edited by Peter Reed and David Rothenberg, "Deep Ecology from Summit to Blockade" by Peter Reed and David Rothenberg, pp. 6., 9, 20-22; "Arne Naess" pp. 65, 67-70, 76-77; "Nils Faarlund pp. 156-157, 168-169, University of Minnesota Press, Minneapolis, Minnesota, Copyright © 1993. Reprinted by permission of the University of Minnesota Press. Footnotes by P. R. and D. R.

The term "deep ecology" first appeared in a short article entitled "The Shallow and the Deep, Long Range Ecology Movement: A Summary" Inquiry 16 (1973): 95-100.

[157] Gunnar Skirbeck, "Nasjon org nature, eit essay om den norske verematen" (Nation and Nature: An essay on the Norwegian way of being), in *Ord og bilde: En essaysamling*, ed. Asbjorn Aarnes (Oslop: Stenerson, 1981), p. 23.

[158] Reed and Rothenberg, op.cit., p. 6.

reason that he saw the great in the little; "divine ideas lifted up on the weak straws of the grass . . . from tiny gnat-sparks and mammal flames to the conflagration of suns"[159]:

Concealed there is a spirit in the dimmest grain of dust
Just as the word
Slumbers hidden in the idea.

And the "idea" slumbers hidden in nature, what Wergeland called the "mirror of innocence." Nature can speak directly to the Creator as nothing else can. And humanity can stand on and with it as participant and equal.

This can scarcely be called a conception of nature that comes entirely from the poet, but one that comes from a nature that is itself stirring and vivid, so linked to people's lives. Literary historian Harald Beyer speaks of a triad of inspiration for all Norwegian literature, the mountains, the sea, and the forests:

A literature that has grown up among mountains may lack luxuriance and gaiety, but it has the advantages of seriousness and greater perspective. . . Such a [vision] may bubble away in the aimless backwash of the eddying fjord, but more often it finds its way to the open sea . . . . Whether by contrast or association, these two features have the deepest possible significance for Norwegian writing. But to these we must add a third feature, the forest. The forest generally calls upon the mystical. In the woods the poet can dream of hidden and secret forces.[160]

Contrast among the three is the essence. There is a trend in Norwegian literature that is essentially dramatic, with change and decision at the center of things, with shifting identities linked so closely to a nature of *mangfold*, diversity.

Tarjei Vesaas is a twentieth-century master of deceptive simplicity in language, drawn from the Earth. He describes what this type of identity means, linking all of the three elements Beyer describes. The following

---

[159] In Harald Beyer, *A History of Norwegian Literature* (New York: NYU Press 1956), p. 126.
[160] Ibid., pp. 4–5.

excerpt from a poem, "Snow and Fir Forests,"[161] describes the Norwegian sense of place with a language that is as cleanly etched as the pattern of snow on trees that it seeks to evoke:

> Talk of what home is —
> snow and fir forests
> are home.
> From the first moment
> they are ours.
> Before anyone has told us,
> that it *is* snow and fir forests,
> they have a place in us—
> and since then it is there
> always, always.
> . . .
> Come home.
> go in there
> bending branches—
> go on till you know
> what it means to belong.[162]

***

Go into the forests around Oslo on Sunday and you may be one of about a hundred thousand other people who had the same idea. Every weekend about one-quarter of Norway's largest city can be found on the paths and lakes of Oslomarka, a green lung that is 80 percent of the city's official area—large enough to hide the other 99,999 hikers.

They travel on skis, foot, bicycle, sled, or baby carriage, depending on season, age, and temperament. The reason for this weekly migration isn't really that the city proper is a horrible place to live. City dwellers, in fact, head for the hills no more (and no less) frequently than their rural counterparts. Wherever they live, Norwegians have an exceptionally strong interest in outdoor recreation: 90 percent of the population gets out to the forests, mountains, or coast at least once a year, and the average

---

[161] Translated by the editors from the original, "Snø og granskog," Tarjei Vesaas, in Dikt i samling (Oslo: Glydendal, 1969), p. 11.

[162] Reed and Rothenberg, op. cit., pp. 8-9.

person gets out more than sixty times a year. On any day of the week almost a fourth of the population spends about two hours doing some form or other of outdoor recreation. A typical Norwegian idyll is a holiday at a small cabin in the country. And the dream is a reality for many: there is about one vacation cabin for every thirteen Norwegians.

"*H gh ph tur*"—to go for a hike—is something of a national hobby. Norwegians are supposed to be "born with skis on their feet," and there's a palpable peer pressure to get out into the woods fairly frequently—otherwise one is not *really* Norwegian.

"To go skiing," writes Gunnar Skirbekk, "is not only healthy, it is good. If you go on a skiing trip through Norwegian nature, you are a good person. The moral undertone is there, and cannot be ignored."[163] The late King Olav's skiing trips rated headlines in Norwegian dailies, and instead of going south to the sun during their spring break, nearly half of Norwegian vacationers go north to catch the last of winter's snow. And as if this were not enough, statistics show that most Norwegians would prefer to get out into nature even more than they do.

It is easier to do this in Norway than almost anywhere else. Since the earliest settlement in Norway, access to key natural resources, such as streams, lakes and forests, was too important to allow them to be fenced off by private landowners. Similarly, overland travel was difficult enough already without its being further hindered by closing off private lands. There grew up, accordingly, a tradition of *allemannsferdselsrett*: a legal right of anyone to hike through private property and to use rivers and lakes for recreation. The eventual rise of a capitalist economy was bound to collide with this tradition. First threatened were coastal areas, where private landowners were determined to seal off sections of the beach for their exclusive use. Conflicts between recreationists and farmers also became serious, and in 1957 a comprehensive outdoor recreation law was drafted to settle the conflict.[164]

The 1957 *Friluftsloven* codified the tradition of free travel explicitly. Hikers and campers are today entitled to walk or camp nearly anywhere

---

[163] Gunnar Skirbekk, "Nasjon og natur," p. 20.

[164] The earliest codification of this tradition, however, was made as far back as 1687.

they like, on private or public lands, provided they do not damage the area. Deep ecologists Sigmund Kvaløy and Nils Faarlund have since been active in setting limits to the kinds of recreation that can legitimately take place in these areas, arguing for uses that do not rely on motorized transport and the products of a technological society. But however one travels through the Norwegian countryside, the freedom of movement guaranteed by law is virtually unknown outside of Scandinavia, and is a legal illustration of the importance of outdoor recreation in the Norwegian lifestyle.

With this in mind, it is not surprising that interest in outdoor activities is mobilized into political activism when recreation areas are threatened. The history of Oslomarka is a good example. Landscape artist Peter Balke claimed as early as 1873 that he knew of no other capital city in the world blessed with such beautiful natural surroundings, but warned that without the political will to preserve them these riches would soon be squandered. The Oslo Municipal Outdoor Recreation Council was sympathetic, and they eventually bought up 270 square miles of farmsteads and forests for recreational use.

But the city government soon faced a dilemma: a growing Oslo required a larger and larger area for outdoor activities, but at the same time required land for housing and corridors through which to feed in electric current. The result was inevitably compromise—and not always in the interest of the forest. When in 1946 a new powerline was to slash through Oslomarka, it sparked a demonstration of thirty thousand angry citizens, probably the largest single protest in postwar Norway. That show of support for the woods around Oslo resulted in a rerouted corridor and a comprehensive plan for the management of the area. Subsequent planning has succeeded in reducing logging activities in the forest and establishing inviolate residential boundaries.

The history of Oslomarka is more than just a quaint example of how a city saved some woodlands for Sunday strolls. Like the "People's Park" movement in America, it is symbolic of how a devotion to outdoor recreation can come to dominate the political agenda of a municipality— or a country. Deep ecologist Nils Faarlund, for example, will argue later in this volume that not only is *friluftslivpolitikk* rooted in a Norwegian tradition of "nature-life," but it is also a tool for the transformation to an ecologically sensitive society.[165]

As professor of philosophy from 1936-1970, [Arne Naess's] career has been crucial in shaping the whole higher education system in Norway, with its stress on a basic grounding in philosophy and the history of ideas for all students, and a particular concern with linking academics with the present problems in the outside world of our century. This concept also forms the backbone of deep ecology, the term he invented, for a "wisdom related to action." . . .[166]

It is impossible to understand Naess's philosophies without realizing his deep connection to nature, which led him naturally toward ecophilosophy. He describes some of these first encounters:

> From when I was about four years old until puberty, I could stand or sit for hours, days, weeks in shallow water on the coast, inspecting and marvelling at the overwhelming diversity and richness of life in the sea. The tiny beautiful forms which "nobody" cared for, or were even unable to see, were part of a seemingly infinite world, but nevertheless my world. Feeling apart in many human relations, I identified with nature.
>
> From the age of eight a definite mountain became for me a symbol of benevolent, equal-minded, strong "father," or of an ideal human nature. These characteristics were there in spite of the obvious fact that the mountain, with its slippery stones, icy fog and dangerous precipices, did not protect me nor care for me in any trivial sense. It required me to show respect and take care.
>
> When fifteen years old I managed through sheer persistency of appeals to travel alone in early June to the highest mountain region of Norway—Jotunheimen. At the foot of the mountain I was stopped by deep rotten snow and I could find nowhere to sleep. Eventually I came across a very old man who was engaged in digging away the snow surrounding and in part covering a closed cottage belonging to an association for mountaineering and tourism. We

---

[165] Reed and Rothenberg, op.cit, pp. 20-22.
[166] Ibid., p. 65

stayed together for a week in a nearby hut. So far as I can remember, we ate only one dish: oatmeal porridge with dry bread. The porridge had been stored in the snow from the previous autumn—that is what I thought the old man said. Later I came to doubt it. A misunderstanding on my part. The porridge was served cold, and if any tiny piece was left over on my plate he would eat it. In the evenings he would talk incidentally about mountains, about reindeer, hunting, and other occupations in the highest regions. But mostly he would play the violin. It was part of the local culture to mark the rhythm with the feet, and he would not give up trying to make me capable of joining him in this. But how difficult! The old man's rhythms seemed more complex than anything I had ever heard!

Enough details! The effect of this week established my conviction of an inner relation between mountains and mountain people, a certain greatness, cleanness, a concentration upon what is essential, a self-sufficiency; and consequently a disregard of luxury, of complicated means of all kinds. From the outside the mountain way of life would seem Spartan, rough, and rigid, but the playing of the violin and the obvious fondness for all things above the timberline, living or "dead," certainly witnessed a rich, sensual attachment to life, a deep pleasure in what can be experienced with wide open eyes and mind. These reflections instilled within me the idea of modesty—modesty in man's relationships with mountains in particular and the natural world in general. As I see it, modesty is of little value if it is not a mutual consequence of much deeper feelings, a consequence of a way of understanding ourselves as part of nature in a wide sense of the term. This way is such that *the smaller we come to feel ourselves compared to the mountain, the nearer we come to participating in its greatness.* I do not know why this is so.[167]

It is easy to see that Naess would, in time, try to discover "why this is so" by elaborating a philosophical system that leads from the self into

---

[167] Assembled from Arne Naess, "How My Philosophy Seemed to Develop," pp. 210-213, and "Modesty and the Conquest of Mountains," in *The Mountain Spirit*, ed. Michael Tobias and Harold Drasdo (New york: Overlook Press, 1979) by Reed and Rothenberg, *Wisdom in the Open Air*, pp. 13-16.

the world of nature, through norms and hypotheses. Like Gandhi, he chooses Self-realization as the central norm or key word, and proceeds to enter a system in which one's identity and sense of place are only enhanced by greater understanding of the universe:

> It is often said that the discovery that the Earth is not the center of the universe has made man smaller, diminishing his status. I have always felt that I grew bigger and bigger with the extensions in time, space, and cultural diversity. The universe is my universe, not my ego's but that of the great Self we have in common. This is metaphysics, but through philosophical research it can be developed in the direction of clarity and cognitive responsibility. From the fundamental norm "Self-realization," plus hypotheses about the world, I derive a set of principles for "green politics." In this way abstract problems of philosophy are connected with concrete issues of contemporary political conflict.[168]

And these principles are what Arne refers to as an "ecosophy." This is one's own personal "philosophy," a code of values and a view of the world that guides one's own decisions in regard to the natural world. Arne Naess introduces simply one ecosophy, which he chooses to call ecosophy T. One is not expected to agree with all of its values and paths of derivation, but to learn the means for developing one's own systems or guides, say, ecosophies X, Y, or Z.

For Arne Naess, ecosophy T serves as the grounds for supporting the principles espoused by the now worldwide deep ecology movement. Arne introduced the term in several short paragraphs that begin an article published in the interdisciplinary journal *Inquiry* in 1973:

> The emergence of ecologists from their former relative obscurity marks a turning point in our scientific communities. But their message is twisted and misused. A shallow, but presently rather powerful movement, and a deep, but less influential movement, compete for our attention. I shall make an effort to characterise the two.

---

[168] See Naess, "How My Philosophy Seemed to Develop," p. 225.

1. *The Shallow Ecology movement:* Fight against pollution and resource depletion. Central objective: the health and affluence of people in the developed countries.

2. *The Deep Ecology movement:*

a. Rejection of the man-in-environment image in favour of *the relational, total-field image.* Organisms as knots in the field of intrinsic relations. An intrinsic relation between two things A and B is such that the relation belongs to the definitions or basic constitutions of A and B, so that without the relation, A and B are no longer the same things. The total field model dissolves not only the man-in-environment concept, but every compact thing-in-milieu concept— except when talking at a superficial or preliminary level of communication.

b. *Biospherical egalitarianism—in principle.* The "in principle" clause is inserted because any realistic praxis necessitates some killing, exploitation, and suppression. The ecological field worker acquires a deep-seated respect, even veneration, for ways and forms of life. He reaches an understanding from within, a kind of understanding that others reserve for fellow men and for a narrow section of ways and forms of life. To the ecological field worker *the equal right to live and blossom* is an intuitively clear and obvious value axiom. Its restriction to humans is an anthropocentrism with detrimental effects upon the life quality of humans themselves. This quality depends in part upon the deep pleasure and satisfaction we receive from close partnership with other forms of life. The attempt to ignore our dependence and to establish a master/slave role has contributed to the alienation of man from himself.[169]

Intrinsic Value: Will the Defenders of Nature Please Rise[170]

Things may have value, people say, without having value for humans. "Animals have equal rights, but humans take away the right" is a common [response]. When asked what they think about

---

[169] Reed and Rothenberg, op.cit., pp. 67-70.
[170] An essay by Arne Naess included in *Wisdom in the Open Air* by Reed and Rothenberg, pp. 76-77.

the prediction that a million species may be wiped out if policies are not changed, it is pathetic to see how this idea elicits horror, indignation and despair. . . .

Are the experts really narrowly utilitarian in their views, and are they really in favor of present environmental policies? In an attempt to find out I recently sent a long personal letter to 110 people who influence national environmental policy in Norway. About one out of four has responded, some with long, interesting essays. The respondents include high-level personnel in the Departments of Finance, Justice, and Energy—persons with comprehensive educations in various branches of natural science and technology. The experts were asked to react to the following eight points, which, incidentally, I call "the platform of deep ecology," or rather, one formulation of such a platform.

1. The flourishing of human and nonhuman life on Earth has inherent value. The value of nonhuman life forms is independent of the usefulness of the nonhuman world for human purposes. *The great majority indicated their agreement.*

2. Abundance and diversity of life forms are values in themselves and contribute to the flourishing of human and nonhuman life on Earth. *The great majority agrees.*

3. Humans have no right to reduce this abundance and diversity except to satisfy vital needs. *The great majority* tend *to agree. Many comment on the term "vital."*

4. The flourishing of human life and cultures is compatible with a substantial decrease in the human population, and the flourishing of non-human life requires such a decrease. *The great majority agree.*

5. Present human interference with the nonhuman world is excessive, and the situation is rapidly worsening. *The great majority agree.*

6. Policies must therefore be changed. The changes in policies affect basic economic, technological, and ideological structures. The resulting state of affairs would be deeply different from the present and would make possible a more joyful experience of the connectedness of all things. *The great majority tend to agree. Some find the last sentence rhetorical and doubtful.*

7. The ideological change is mainly that of appreciating life quality rather than adhering to an increasingly higher standard of living. There will be a profound awareness of the difference between big and great. *The great majority tend to agree.*

8. Those who subscribe to the foregoing points have an obligation, directly or indirectly, to participate in the attempt to implement, the necessary changes. *The great majority agree. . . .*

★★★

[Nils] Faarlund, [another] deep ecologist and mountaineer, calls for a nonaggressive, environmentally sensitive approach to being in nature—*friluftsliv,* a way of tuning our lifestyles and society so that they are in harmony with nature.

To some, the word *friluftsliv* translates as "outdoor recreation," but to Nils, it is something more: it is nothing less than an agent of paradigm shift, the clearest way toward resolution of our ecological crises. . . .

Faarlund's attitude has always been that the journey is more important than the destination. He tries (with mixed success) to avoid the massive equipment purchases and corporation sponsorship that make modern mountaineering seem like a business enterprise. More important than reaching the top of the mountain is to learn from the people in the region and to respect their customs, even when this means *not* climbing to a "sacred" summit. . . .

For Faarlund, outdoor life is not competitive, but a reintroduction to an old friend—free nature. *Friluftsliv* is thus a descendant of the Romantic attitudes to nature in nineteenth-century urbanized Norway. And naturally, Romantic attitudes are seen as archaic in our fast-paced, technological world. Nils is not alone, though, in calling for their rehabilitation. Gunnar Breivik, the only philosopher employed full time at the *idrettshogskole,* sees *friluftsliv* as belonging to the traditions of rural Norway, not only a practice of city folk seeking release from urban pressures. Small farmers and fishermen, though living much closer to free nature, also found joy in wandering about in the mountains—activities that, though connected to their "jobs," also had an element of pure lark.

Faarlund prefers to see this not as *friluftsliv,* but as its absence: such cultures had achieved a harmony with nature and did not need a reintroduction to it. The point of living outdoors should be to help us understand the bankruptcy of our city-dependent lifestyle, and lead us back to the kind of intimate contact with nature enjoyed by these people.

The main point is clear: *friluftsliv* is a shift in perspective. It is a rejection of a paradigm that sees man as a vacationer in favor of one that presents free nature as man's true *home*.

What Faarlund points out, then, is that we often underestimate the influence that being in free nature has on our minds and our lifestyles. And it is never, never enough to talk about being in nature. We need to step out into it. And after the first step can come another, and another. . . .[171]

★★★

A Way Home:[172]

Most of these actions are aimed at changing political institutions, and they can be useful; still, activism instead of re-activism, policy design instead of policy protest, is better. Avalanche victims don't live for long.

In any mountain accident, though, one's chances for survival are highest if competent comrades are nearby. And it is the same for cultural rescue attempts. Personal, grassroots contact is the way. Recreating the feeling of being *home* in free nature is the best prevention and *"friluftsliv-activists"* can introduce others to a joyous encounter with free nature.

Personal friendships with nature are going to form the backbone in the efforts needed to rescue a nature in distress. Friendship with nature needs the same conditions for growth as human friendships: nearness (not objectivity), caution (without fear), intimacy (without pressure), and persistence (not endurance).

Conclusions: Carl Gustav Jung argues throughout his work in psychology that fundamental to all humans is a recollection of archetypes. Having lived for more than a hundred thousand generations in an environment where the nonhuman, rather than the human, was dominant, it should hardly be surprising that many of our archetypes involve free nature. To understand ourselves, then,

---

[171] Reed, Peter and David Rothenberg, excerpts from the introduction "Deep Ecology from Summit to Blockade" from *Wisdom in the Open Air*, pp. 156-7.

[172] Excerpted from "A Way Home" an essay by Nils Faarlund, included in *Wisdom in the Open Air* by Reed and Rothenberg, pp. 168-9.

to realize our potential for being a human being, we must communicate intimately with that which is—in some sense—the most *inhuman:* wild, undeveloped nature. *Friluftsliv,* in challenging us to respond in body, mind, and spirit with the rhythms of the natural environment, is our best opportunity for that development.

It is a paradigm shift: away from a dominant, "objective" view of nature and toward an emotive identity with it characteristic of Romanticism. By using the Romantic tradition as an example I do not mean we should become "romantic about the past." Rather, I mean that the search for a more multisided relationship with nature need not occur exclusively in Eastern traditions or in the "new physics." We have the roots for such a relationship in our traditional cultures, and we have not completely lost them!

More than just an individual pastime, this is a tradition inspiring an active response to an ecological crisis. It points toward a new way of living with other people and with our planet. Deemphasizing interhuman competition in outdoor activities weakens one of the driving forces behind our ecologically destructive social and political systems. *Friluftsliv,* then is a poor "media event" in the eyes of the networks. In its proper perspective, though, it is more significant than an event at the Olympics—as much social movement as body movement. It is a step toward replacing the barriers keeping us from our true home by a lifestyle in which there is no need to seek this home. In this sense, the goal of *friluftsliv* is to make itself unnecessary.

"There is no way leading to peace," wrote Gandhi, "Peace is the way." *Friluftsliv* is not an armed battle, not a sports event, not an academic discipline but a move toward lasting cultural change. It is a process.

Perhaps a slow process, though the growing disaffection with a "normally" polluted environment could make the green wave crest sooner than we think. If it is slow, we must persevere; the motto for mountain climbing in Hemsedal seminars is "Don't let go the hold!" But *friluftsliv* is in many senses its own reward. Not a solemn attempt to go out and be miserable in nature, it is a lifestyle that nourishes hope and emanates strength.

The Way Is the Goal

Encountering free nature is an experience of joy.

There is no force stronger than joy.

Joy is the way Home.

CHAPTER ELEVEN

AIR

It is God Who sends the winds, and they raise the clouds;
then He spreads them in the sky as He wills
and breaks them into fragments
until you see rain-drops flow forth;
then, when He has made them reach those of His servants that He wills,
see how they rejoice!

[*Sūrah Ar-Rūm* (The Byzantines) 30:48]

And He it is who sends the winds
as joyous news of His coming grace—
so that, when they have brought heavy clouds
We may drive them towards dead land and cause rain to descend;
that by it We may cause all manner of fruitfulness to spring forth.
Even so shall We cause the dead to emerge—
perhaps you will remember.

[*Sūrah Al-Aʿrāf* (The Faculty Of Discernment) 7:57]

Consider the winds that scatter the dust far and wide,
and those that lift and bear away heavy burdens,
and those that flow with ease and gentleness,
and those that distribute by command—
truly, that which you are promised is true;
and, truly, judgement must come to pass.

[*Sūrah* Adh-Dhāriyāt (The Dust-Scattering Winds) 51:1-6]

[And God sets forth as an example to those who have faith]
Mary, the daughter of ʿImran, who guarded her chastity,
and We breathed into her of Our spirit,
and she witnessed to the truth of the words of her Sustainer
and of His revelations and was one of those devoted.

[*Sūrah At-Taḥrīm* (Prohibition) 66:12]

Clouds come
Clouds go
Above the maple leaves
At the waterfall.

~ Soseki[173]

Just for a moment, flowers appear
On the empty, nearly-spring tree.
Just for a second, wind
Through the wild thicket thorns.

~ Lalla[174]

Flowers from an unknown tree
Filled me with their fragrance.

~ Basho[175]

---

[173] Jonathan Clements, *The Moon in the Pines, Zen Haiku.* London: Frances Lincoln, Ltd., 2000, p. 37.

[174] *Lalla, Naked Song,* Translations by Coleman Barks, Maypop Books, Athens, GA 1992, p. 20.

[175] Jonathan Clements, *op.cit.,* p. 44.

The Wind Blows from the Sea

~ Papago Indian[176]

By the sandy water I breathe in the odor of the sea;
From there the wind comes and blows over the world.
By the sandy water I breathe in the odor of the sea;
From there the clouds come and the rain falls over the world.

The Bird

~ Edwin Muir[177]

Adventurous bird walking upon the air,
Like a schoolboy running and loitering, leaping and springing,
Pensively pausing, suddenly changing your mind
In all the crystalline world was there to find
For your so delicate walking and airy winging
A floor so perfect, so firm and so fair,
And where a ceiling and walls so sweetly ringing,
Whenever you sing, to your clear singing?
The wide-winged soul itself can ask no more
Than such a pure, resilient and endless floor
For its strong-pinioned plunging and soaring and upward and
    upward springing.

---

[176] "The Wind Blows From the Sea," Anonymous, Papago Indian.
[177] Edwin Muir, *Collected Poems*. Copyright ©1960 by Willa Muir.

And I have felt
A presence that disturbs me with the joy
of elevated thoughts; a sense sublime
Of something far more deeply interfused,
Whose dwelling is the light of setting suns,
And the round oceans and the living air,
And the blue sky, and in the mind of man:
A motion and a spirit, that impels
All thinking things, all objects of all thought,
And rolls through all things.

~ William Wordsworth[178]

One cannot force or grasp a spiritual experience because it is as delicate as the whisper of the wind. But one can purify one's motivation, one's body, and train oneself to cultivate it.

~ Tsultrim Allione[179]

The Prophet said, "Fragrant zephyrs from the Divine arise in the course of your days. Beware of these moments and catch them on the wing."

~ Jalaluddin Rumi *Mathnawi* I:1951-1952

Awake O north wind;
And come, thou south: blow upon my garden
That the spices of it may flow out.
[The Bible, Song of Solomon 4:16]

---

[178] William Wordsworth, excerpt from "Lines Composed a Few Miles above Tintern Abbey."
[179] *Women of Wisdom,* Arkana, imprint of Routledge & Kegan Paul Inc. NY, NY, © Tsultrim Allione 1984, p. xv.

Who Has Seen the Wind?

~ Christina Rossetti[180]

Who has seen the wind?
  Neither I nor you:
But when the leaves hang trembling
  The wind is passing through.

Who has seen the wind?
  Neither you nor I:
But when the trees bow down their heads
  The wind is passing by.

Watching the Weather

~ A.B.C Whipple[181]

Aristotle may have coined the word—"meteorology," which meant "talk about weather." Strolling with his students in the Lyceum gardens in the fourth century B.C., the great Athenian philosopher and man of science mused about the causes of thunder and lightning, of wind and storm, and put his conclusions on paper in *Meteorologica*, the first published work on the subject. Although his views may now seem quaint, they were accepted as gospel for about 2,000 years.

To the deductive logic of Aristotle, his student Theophrastus added a long list of natural observations by which, he said, the weather could be foretold. Included in his *Book of* Signs were 80 manifestations that he

---

[180] Christina Rossetti, "Who Has Seen the Wind?" p. 144 of *Art and Nature, An Illustrated Anthology of Nature Poetry*, Selected by Kate Farrell, The Metropolitan Museum of Art, A Bullfinch Press Book/Little, Brown and Company Boston, 1992.

[181] A.B.C. Whipple, *Planet Earth: Storm*. Time-Life Books, Alexandria Virginia, 1982, pp. 41 and 49.

believed to be harbingers of rain, 45 of wind, and 50 of storm. Many were fanciful . . . But other omens had a basis in nature. "The plainest sign," Theophrastus wrote, "is that which is to be observed in the morning, when, before the sun rises, the sky appears to be reddened over; and it indicates rain." In nature, a lurid dawn is caused by the diffusion of the sun's rays in air heavily laden with water particles and modern research indicates that rain does indeed result about 70 percent of the time.

By thus applying their considerable powers of reasoning to the witnessed workings of nature, the ancient Greeks, both in the principles enunciated by Aristotle and in the aphorisms of Theophrastus, gave birth to the science of meteorology. . . .

★★★

[For centuries, the infant science slept. It was not until the 17th century that a student of Galileo, Evangelista Torricelli, invented the first rudimentary barometer to measure the changes in air pressure, ushering in a new era for the science of meteorology.]

With the subsequent refinement of these 17th Century instruments, meteorologists of the future could at last begin to understand the nature of storms. These would be men with keen powers of observation, with the patience to collect and analyze enormous amounts of data and with the ability to make intuitive leaps of logic.

★★★

[And yet, native peoples around the globe continue to share an instinctive knowledge of the winds of change. . . .]

The Opening of the Wind

~ Juliette de Bairacli Levy[182]

My friends the Bedouins so love the wind, that as well as being called People of the Black Tents (of Kedar), they are also called People of the Wind (*Howwa*)—their beloved *Howwa*. How well they know where to set

---

[182] Juliette de Bairacli Levy, *Traveler's Joy*, pp. 57-59, and prayer on p. 231.

their black tents so as to get all the fresh airs from the winds in the hot, dry climates. The Bedouins adjust their tent flaps through the day, closing here and opening there, like sailors working their canvas sails to take the maximum of wind.

In Tennyson's beautiful poem about King Arthur, *Idylls of the King,* I would not be happy with the weather promised for that immortal land of Avillion to which the dying King is to be taken:

Avillion,
Where falls not hail, or rain, or any snow,
Nor ever wind blows loudly.

I think that the ballad of The Wraggle-Taggle Gypsy is the better life: "She would out in the street with her bare, bare feet, all out in the wind and weather, O!"

I like the old-fashioned weather sayings. They are weather-wise and true for most parts of the world except where freak climates are found. . . . Here are some of the sayings I remember:

"When March winds blow we shall have snow." "March comes in like a lion, and goes out like a lamb." "Cast not a clout [coat] till May is out." "April showers bring forth May flowers." "August's sun is never done." "When December skies glow there will be snow." "Red in the morning, shepherd's warning, red sky at night, shepherd's delight." "Dull harvest moon, rain soon." "When the blackberries color, we'll have true summer." . . .

The Gypsies and the Bedouins are people with great weather sense, but despite having been so much with them I learned almost no weather lore, because their deep knowledge of this is instinctive, an inherited talent. What such people know about weather is, to me, possessing true education. On days when the sky would be filled with rain-clouds, and I would be longing for rain for my parched gardens, Ali the Bedouin, after a quick look at the sky, often predicted that no rain would fall for months, and no rain did fall.

I remember in a recent exploration of the Sinai region of Israel in December, where there had been a drought for nearly two years, friends and I gave a Bedouin a lift in our car as he told us he wanted to move some of his camels to higher ground urgently. We asked him what was the urgency, and he astonished us by saying that there would be heavy rain within three days and that could mean floods in the valleys. The Israel official weather forecasts heard on the car radio had made no mention of coming rain, and the sun as ever glared down on us from a cloudless sky. I decided that we should heed the Bedouin's rain warning and get away within the three days. Rain was not mentioned on the radio until it actually came down in torrents, flooding areas of the Sinai, exactly within the days that the Bedouin had foretold. As we came into Jerusalem from the Sinai, snow came along also!

A Prayer for Travelers

O God, who did call Abraham to leave his home, and did protect him on all his wanderings, grant to those who now travel by land, mountain, sea or river, a prosperous journey, a quiet time, and a safe arrival at their travels' end.

Be to them a shadow in the heat, a refuge in the tempest, a protection in adversity.

~ Priest's Prayer Book, 1870

Air Dances

~ Theodor Schwenk[183]

As water on the one hand absorbs gases, so on the other it is prepared to relinquish its liquid form for a time and become vaporous. There is in the lower layers of the earth's atmosphere no air that does not contain water. Indeed, the water contained in the air is the incentive for all meteorological events in the atmospheric mantle of the earth. Nearly all the different kinds of precipitation consist of water that has previously evaporated into the air. As it comes into contact with the air it dissolves into it until the saturation point of the air is reached. Every waterfall dissolves at its edges into an infinite number of the tiniest droplets,

---

[183] Theodor Schwenk, *Sensitive Chaos, The Creation of Flowing Forms in Water and Art*, preface by Jacques Cousteau. Rudolf Steiner Press, www. rudolfsteinerpress. This revised translation © Rudolf Steiner Press, Sussex England, 1996. pp. 101-102, 105-106. 110-112, 113.

forming an inconceivable expanse of surface at which the two elements meet, and there the water surrenders itself to the air. The opposite process may be observed wherever water cascades and pours over stones into a pool. Air is then swept into the water, sparkling in white bubbles and creating great surfaces of contact at which the water can "breathe." So air takes part in the streaming movements of water, just as, in the play of clouds, water vapours join in the movements of the air.

Thus air and water mingle in an intermediate region; they move mainly according to the laws of liquid flow. Air complies to a great extent with these laws, only fully asserting its own nature under certain circumstances. We may therefore expect to find in air many of the forms of movement familiar to us in water, though often on a larger scale or at greater speeds. . . .

Everywhere in nature the elements of air and water mingle in manifold interplay. Every system of rivers, every lake, every sea, is an organic totality with its own circulation, and to each of these belongs the air space above it. Every river, lake, or sea-coast makes itself felt in the air above it, up to a great height. On misty days a pilot can often see the courses of the rivers as banks of mist below him; but also on days without mist he can tell by the behaviour of his machine when he is flying over a river or lake, or whether he is over a wood or an open stretch of field, for their borders have an effect in the air above.

The air space above a piece of land forms a totality with it, and the air moves accordingly. In summer, air descends over the cool lakes and woods, and ascends over the warmer fields. If there is considerable cooling at night it can happen that the open country becomes cooler than neighbouring woods or stretches of water, so that the movements of air are reversed in a rhythm of day and night. The air is always ascending over the warmer land and descending over the cooler. Circulations arising in the air spaces over a tract of land express something of its life and belong to it entirely.

There are circulations like this in the whole atmosphere of the earth. What takes place on a small scale over woods and lakes occurs on a large scale over the oceans; and what takes place over fields and meadows is repeated over the continents. In winter the relationship is reversed on the small as well as on the large scale, because in winter water is warmer than dry land.

These ascending and descending movements of air form the great areas of the earth into a vast organism. The rhythm of day and night in the circulation over a small landscape has its equivalent in the rhythms of the seasons of summer and winter over the whole planet. In the warm season of the year, the air rises over the continents and falls over the seas; in the cold season this movement is reversed. An ascending movement of air is among other things connected with the formation of regions of low pressure, and descending air with regions of high pressure. In this way, towards summer, a great region of low pressure spreads out over the Central Asian continent, which towards winter becomes transformed into a region of high pressure centred over Asia. These processes are an integral part of the great seasonal breathing of the earth. . . .

In connection with the movements of air we have just described there is also an expansion and contraction according to heat or cold which occurs in the rhythms of the seasons. The meteorologists speak of the "breathing of the continents." . . .

The realization that these rhythms are extra terrestrial is becoming increasingly widespread. The sequence of cyclones is today considered to be connected with events on the sun, and these, for instance solar activity (sun spots), are considered to be due to the effect on the sun of the interweaving movements of the planets. May not the great cosmic events in the universe have their effect in the "sensitive" surfaces of contact in the atmospheric mantle of our earth? The laws of the heavens address themselves to these membranes as though speaking into delicate ears. Organs are created, and the earth, with its oceans and continents and its landscapes, becomes a great organism. The earth, like a living creature, is received into the still greater living community of the celestial world. If it were possible to look down on land and sea from a great height, we would be able to experience the creation of vortices in the belts of low pressure through the confluence of different masses of air. Where different streams of air meet, waves arise along the surface of contact and then curl in; this all happens in enormous dimensions over the continents and oceans. Sometimes one single such "vortex" has the dimensions of a whole continent.

On the earth we do not experience these spacious movements; we only notice the daily ups and downs of the weather as it passes. Great processes like the battle between different masses of air, for instance, between cold, polar air and warm, humid sea air streaming in from the south, appear to us as the varied, dramatic events of our daily weather. A visible expression of these processes taking place above us is the formation and dissolution of the clouds and the varied kinds of precipitation, which dictate the character of the weather. We have here not only movements which through their interplay create moving forms, but there also occur differences in temperature and, connected with these, the expansion and contraction of the air and the release and absorption of water. This last process is the main incentive for meteorological events, because in it large quantities of heat are absorbed or released, according to the ruling of the celestial universe, which plays its part in the process.

The vagaries of the weather are a play with the intermingling of water in the atmosphere. It absorbs great quantities of heat in the warm regions of the earth and either carries this warmth to more northerly latitudes in the form of warm currents in the oceans, or as water vapour in the great air currents of the planet. Where the water meets with cold air it separates out again like a warm breath in the cold winter air, and becomes visible as mist, cloud, or precipitation. In this way it releases the huge quantities of heat it had absorbed in warmer regions.

★★★

Many of the elements of form and movement which we described in connection with water can be found again in connection with the formation of clouds. Waves and rhythmically arranged ridge formations arise when the wind blows across a thin layer of cloud, curling vortices arise at the moving edge of clouds; there are sources and sinks and great and small spiralling surfaces. The little tufts of altocumulus or cirro-cumulus clouds, for instance, show where there is an upwelling current. Air rises in each little flake of cloud and falls again at its edge. A great variety of small air circulations spreads out in a field of "fleecy" clouds. If a wind arises that drives the whole field onwards, they arrange themselves in rows, turn into scales that seem to push over one another like ice floes in a river, and create forms that are familiar to us from the varied kinds of ridges and ribs made by water in sand.

Mysterious Air

~ David Abram[184]

Let's sit down here . . . on the open prairie, where we can't see a highway or a fence. Let's have no blankets to sit on, but feel the ground with our bodies, the earth, the yielding shrubs. Let's have the grass for a mattress, experiencing its sharpness and its softness. Let us become like stones, plants, and trees. Let us be animals, think and feel like animals. Listen to the air. You can hear it, feel it, smell it, taste it. *Woniya wakan*—the holy air—which renews all by its breath. *Woniya, woniya wakan*—spirit, life, breath, renewal—it means all that. *Woniya*—we sit together, don't touch, but something is there; we feel it between us, as a presence. A good way to start thinking about nature, talk about it. Rather talk to it, talk to the rivers, to the lakes, to the winds as to our relatives.

~ John Fire Lame Deer

What a mystery is the air, what an enigma to these human senses! On the one hand, the air is the most pervasive presence I can name, enveloping, embracing, and caressing me both inside and out, moving in ripples along my skin, flowing between my fingers, swirling around my arms and thighs, rolling in eddies along the roof of my mouth, slipping ceaselessly through throat and esophagus to fill the lungs, to feed my blood, my heart, my self. I cannot act, cannot speak, cannot think a single thought without the participation of this fluid element. I am immersed in its depths as surely as fish are immersed in the sea.

Yet the air, on the other hand, is the most outrageous absence known to this body. For it is utterly invisible. I know very well that there is something there—I can feel it moving against my face and can taste it and smell it, can even hear it as it swirls within my ears and along the bark of trees, but still, I cannot see it. I can see the steady movement it induces in the shapeshifting clouds, the way it bends the

---

[184] From *The Spell of the Sensuous* by David Abram, copyright © 1996 by David Abram. Used by permission of Pantheon Books, a division of Random House, Inc.

branches of the cottonwoods, and sends ripples along the surface of a stream. The fluttering wing feathers of a condor soaring overheard; the spiraling trajectory of a leaf as it falls; a spider web billowing like a sail; the slow drift of a seed through space—all make evident, to my eyes, the sensuous presence of the air. Yet these eyes cannot see the air itself.

Unlike the hidden character of what lies beyond the horizon, and unlike the unseen nature of that which resides under the ground, the air is invisible in principle. That which today lies beyond the horizon can at least partly be disclosed by journeying into that future, as that which waits under the ground can be somewhat unearthed by excavations into the past. But the air can never be opened for our eyes, never made manifest. Itself invisible, it is the medium through which we see all else in the present terrain.

And this unseen enigma is the very mystery that enables life to live. It unites our breathing bodies not only with the under-the-ground (with the rich microbial life of the soil, with fossil and mineral deposits deep in the bedrock), and not only with the beyond-the-horizon (with distant forests and oceans), but also with the interior life of all that we perceive in the open field of the living present—the grasses and the aspen leaves, the ravens, the buzzing insects and the drifting clouds. What the plants are quietly breathing out, we animals are breathing in; what we breathe out, the plants are breathing in. The air, we might say, is the soul of the visible landscape, the secret realm from whence all beings draw their nourishment. As the very mystery of the living present, it is that most intimate absence from whence the present presences, and thus a key to the forgotten presence of the earth.

Nothing is more common to the diverse indigenous cultures of the earth than a recognition of the air, the wind, and the breath, as aspects of a singularly sacred power. By virtue of its pervading presence, its utter invisibility, and its manifest influence on all manner of visible phenomena, the air, for oral peoples, is the archetype of all that is ineffable, unknowable, yet undeniably real and efficacious. Its obvious ties to speech—the sense that spoken words are structured breath (try speaking a word without exhaling at the same time), and indeed that spoken phrases take their communicative power from this invisible medium that moves between us—lends the air a deep association with linguistic meaning and with thought. Indeed, the ineffability of the air seems akin to the ineffability of awareness itself, and we should not be surprised that many indigenous peoples construe awareness, or "mind," not as a power that resides inside their heads, but rather as a quality that they themselves are inside of, along with the other animals and the plants, the mountains and the clouds.

According to Robert Lawlor, a researcher who has lived and studied among the indigenous cultures of Australia, Aboriginal peoples tend to consider the visible entities around them—rocks, persons, leaves—as crystallizations of conscious awareness, while the invisible medium between such entities is experienced as what Westerners would call "the unconscious," the creative but unseen realm from which such conscious forms arise. Thus, the Alcheringa, or Dream-time—that implicit realm of dreamlike happenings from whence the visible present is continually emerging—resides not just within the hills and landforms of the surrounding terrain, but also in the invisible depths of the air itself, in the thickness of the very medium that flows within us and all around us. This leads Aboriginal Australians to accord awesome significance to various atmospheric phenomena. Flashes of lightning are experienced as violent discharges from the depths of the Dreaming. Birds, who wing their way through the invisible, are often experienced as messengers of the unconscious, while the rainbow (the Rainbow Snake, who arcs upward across the sky and then dives back into the earth) is felt to personify all the most implacable, dangerous, and yet life-giving forces in the land. For the rainbow is perceived as the very edge of the Dreaming, as that place where the invisible, unconscious potentials begin to become visible.[185]

★★★

The Navajo identification of awareness with the air—their intuition that the psyche is not an immaterial power that resides inside us, but is rather the invisible yet thoroughly palpable medium in which we (along with the trees, the squirrels, and the clouds) are immersed—must seem at first bizarre, even outrageous, to persons of European ancestry. Yet a few moments' etymological research reveal that this identification is not nearly so alien to European civilization as one might assume. Indeed, our English

---

[185] Ibid., pp. 225-227.

term "psyche"—together with all its modern offspring like "psychology," "psychiatry," and "psychotherapy"—is derived from the ancient Greek word *psyche*, which signified not merely the "soul," or the 'mind" but also a "breath," or a "gust of wind." The Greek noun derived from the verb *psychein*, which meant "to breathe," or "to blow." Meanwhile, another ancient Greek word for "air, wind, and breath"—the term *pneuma*, from which we derive such terms as "pneumatic" and "pneumonia"—also and at the same time signified that vital principle which in English we call "spirit."

Of course, the word "spirit" itself, despite all of its incorporeal and non-sensuous connotations, is directly related to the very bodily term "respiration" through their common root in the Latin word *spiritus*, which signified both "breath" and "wind." Similarly, the Latin word for "soul," *anima*—from whence have evolved such English terms as "animal," "animation," "animism," and "unanimous" (being of one mind, or one soul), also signified "air" and "breath." Moreover, these were not separate meanings; it is clear that anima, like psyche, originally named an elemental phenomenon that somehow comprised both what we now call "the air" and what we now term "the soul." The more specific Latin word *animus*, which signified "that which thinks in us," was derived from the same airy root, *anima*, itself derived from the older Greek term *anemos*, meaning "wind."

We find an identical association of the "mind" with the "wind" and the "breath" in innumerable ancient languages. Even such an objective, scientifically respectable word as "atmosphere" displays its ancestral ties to the Sanskrit word *atman*, which signified "soul" as well as the "air" and the "breath." Thus, a great many terms that now refer to the air as a purely passive and insensate medium are clearly derived from words that once identified the air with life and awareness! And words that now seem to designate a strictly immaterial mind, or spirit, are derived from terms that once named the breath as the very substance of that mystery.

It is difficult to avoid the conclusion that, for ancient Mediterranean cultures no less than for the Lakota and the Navajo, the air was once a singularly sacred presence. As the experiential source of both psyche and spirit, it would seem that the air was once felt to be the very matter of awareness, the subtle body of the mind. And hence that awareness, far from being experienced as a quality that distinguishes humans from the rest of nature, was originally felt as that which invisibly joined human beings to the other animals and to the plants, to the forests and to the mountains. For it was the unseen but common medium of their existence.

But how, then, did the air come to lose its psychological quality? How did the psyche withdraw so thoroughly from the world around us, leaving the cedar trees, the spiders, the stones, and the storm clouds without that psychological depth in which they used to dwell (without, indeed, any psychological resonance or even relevance)? How did the psyche, the spirit, or the mind retreat so thoroughly into the human skull, leaving the air itself a thin and taken-for-granted presence, commonly equated, today, with mere empty space? Read on.

Wind, Breath, and Speech

Like so many ancient and tribal languages, Hebrew has a single word for both "spirit" and "wind"—the word *ruach*. What is remarkable here is the evident centrality of *ruach*, the spiritual wind, to early Hebraic religiosity. The primordiality of *ruach*, and its close association with the divine, is manifest in the very first sentence of the Hebrew Bible:

When God began to create heaven and earth—the earth being unformed and void, with darkness over the surface of the deep and a wind [*ruach*] from God sweeping over the water . . .

At the very beginning of creation, before even the existence of the earth or the sky, God is present as a wind moving over the waters. Remember the similar primordiality of the wind in the Navajo telling: "Wind existed first . . . and when the Earth began its existence Wind took care of it." And breath, as we learn in the next section of Genesis, is the most intimate and elemental bond linking humans to the divine; it is that which flows most directly between God and man. For after God forms an earthling (*adam*), from the dust of the earth (*adamah*), he blows into the earthling's nostrils the breath of life, and the human awakens. Although *ruach* may be used to refer to the breath, the Hebrew term used here is *neshamah*, which denotes both the breath and the soul. While *ruach* generally refers to the wind, or spirit, at large, *neshamah* commonly signifies the more personal, individualized aspect of wind, the wind or breath of a particular body—like the "Wind within one" of a Navajo person. In this sense, *neshamah* is also used to signify conscious awareness. . . .

218

The ancient Hebrews were . . . among the first communities to make sustained use of phonetic writing, the first bearers of an alphabet. Moreover, unlike the other Semitic peoples, they did not restrict their use of the alphabet to economic and political record-keeping, but used it to record ancestral stories, traditions, and laws. They were perhaps the first nation to so thoroughly shift their sensory participation away from the forms of surrounding nature to a purely phonetic set of signs, and so to experience the profound epistemological independence from the natural environment that was made possible by this potent new technology. To actively participate with the visible forms of nature came to be considered idolatry by the ancient Hebrews; it was not the land but the written letters that now carried the ancestral wisdom.

Yet although the Hebrews renounced all animistic engagement with the visible forms of the natural world (whether with the moon, or the sun, or those animals—like the bull—sacred to other peoples of the Middle East), they nevertheless retained a participatory relationship with the invisible medium of that world—with the wind and the breath.[186]

The Power of Letters

Yet this sense of the written text as an animate, living mystery is nowhere more explicit than in the Kabbalah, the esoteric tradition of Jewish mysticism. For here it is not just the text as a whole but the very letters that are thought to be alive! Each letter of the *aleph-beth* is assumed by the Kabbalists to have its own personality, its own profound magic, its own way of organizing the whole of existence around itself. Because the written commandments were ostensibly dictated to Moses directly by God on Mount Sinai, so the written letters comprising that first Hebrew text— the twenty-two letters of the *aleph-beth*—are assumed to be the visible traces of divine utterance. Indeed, some Kabbalists claimed that it was by first generating the twenty-two letters, and then combining them into such utterances as "Let there be light," that God spoke the visible universe itself into existence. The letters, that is, are sensible concretions of the very powers of creation. . . .

★★★

---

[186] Ibid., pp. 237-240; and "The Power of Letters," Ibid., p. 245.

The teaching of the great thirteenth-century Kabbalist Abraham Abu-lafia asserted that the spoken vowels and the written consonants are as interdependent "as the soul and the body." To combine the vowels—the sounded breath—with the visible consonants was akin to breathing life into a clump of clay, as *YHWH* had lent his breath to the earthen Adam.

Finally, we must acknowledge the vast importance within the Jewish mystical tradition, of the breath itself. In the thirteenth-century Zohar, the most important of all Kabbalistic texts, the central figure, Rabbi Shim'on bar Yohai, insists that the union between humans and God is best effected through the medium of the breath. According to Rabbi Shim'on, King Solomon learned from his father, King David, the breathing techniques involved in invoking the holy breath, the inspiration of the divine. "By learning and practicing the secrets inherent in the breath, Solomon could lift nature's physical veil from created things and see the spirit within." In a manner startlingly reminiscent of a Navajo or a Lakota ceremony, Rabbi Shim'on's son, El'azar, begins a prayer session by exhorting "the winds to come from all four directions and fill his breath," and instructs his companions to circulate the air inhaled from all four directions interchangeably within their bodies. Elsewhere in the Zohar, one of Rabbi Shim'on's companions speaks of "the soul-breath" sent from *YHWH* to enter the body of the righteous person at birth. Much like the "wind within one" of the Navajo people, "the soul-breath that enters at birth directs and trains the human being and initiates him into every straight path. This sense of the breath as medium between the individual and the divine is exemplified in a commentary on prayer by a nineteenth-century Hasidic master (Hasidism was a vibrant wave of Jewish mysticism that swept East European Jewry in the eighteenth and nineteenth centuries):

> If prayer is pure and untainted,
> surely that holy breath
> that rises from your lips
> Will join with the breath of heaven
> that is always flowing
> into you from above. . . .

Thus that part of God
which is within you
is reunited with its source.

Yet the sacred breath enters not just into human beings (providing awareness and guidance), it also animates and sustains the whole of the sensible world. Like the wind itself, the breath of God permeates all of nature. In a classic text entitled "The Portal of Unity and Faith," the eighteenth-century Hasidic master Schneur Zaiman of Ladi describes how the syllables and letters of God's creative utterances, such as "Let there be light," or "Let the waters bring forth swarms of living creatures," gradually generate, through a concatenated series of permutations and numerical substitutions, the exact names, and hence the exact forms, of all natural entities (in Hebrew a single term, *davar*, means both "word" and "thing"). Yet without the continual outflow of God's breath, which Schneur Zaiman calls "the Breath of His Mouth," all of the letters that stand within the things of this world—all the letter combinations embodied in particular animals, plants, and stones—would return to their undifferentiated source in the divine Unity, and the sensible world, along with all sensing beings, would be extinguished. Just as the consonantal letters of a traditional Hebrew text depend, for their communicative power, upon the sounded breath that animates them, so the divine letters and letter combinations that structure the physical universe are dependent upon the divine breath that continually utters them forth. All things vibrate with "the Breath of His Mouth."[54]

And it is by virtue of this continual breath that nature is always new; the world around us is a continual, ongoing utterance! Thus, the activity of speech, like breathing, links humans not just to God but to all that surrounds us, from the stones to the sparrows. This is simply illustrated in another Hasidic commentary on prayer:

See your prayer as arousing the letters
through which heaven and earth
and all living things were created.
The letters are the life of all;
when you pray through them,
all Creation joins with you in prayer.

All that is around you can be uplifted;
even the song of a passing bird
may enter into such a prayer.[187]

★★★

In the world of modernity the air has indeed become the most taken-for-granted of phenomena. Although we imbibe it continually, we commonly fail to notice that there is anything there. We refer to the unseen depth between things—between people, or trees, or clouds—as mere empty space. The invisibility of the atmosphere, far from leading us to attend to it more closely, now enables us to neglect it entirely. Although we are wholly dependent upon its nourishment for all of our actions and all our thoughts, the immersing medium has no mystery for us, no conscious influence or meaning. Lacking all sacredness, stripped of all spiritual significance, the air is today little more than a conveniently forgotten dump site for a host of gaseous effluents and industrial pollutants. Our fascination is elsewhere, carried by all these other media— these newspapers, radio broadcasts, television networks, computer bulletin boards—all these fields or channels of strictly human communication that so readily grab our senses and mold our thoughts once our age-old participation with the original, more-than-human medium has been sundered.

As a child, growing up on the outskirts of New York City, I often gazed at great smokestacks billowing dark clouds into the sky. Yet I soon stopped wondering where all that sooty stuff went: since the adults who decided such things saw fit to dispose of wastes in this manner, it must, I concluded, be all right. Later, while learning to drive, I would watch with some alarm as the trucks roaring past me on the highway spewed black smoke from their gleaming exhaust pipes, but I quickly forgave them, remembering that my car, too, offered its hot fumes to the air. Everybody did it. As the vapor trails from the jets soaring overhead seemed to disperse, perfectly, into the limitless blue, so we assumed that these wastes, these multicolored smokes and chemical fumes, would all cancel themselves, somehow, in the invisible emptiness. . . .

---

[187] Ibid., p. 247.

Today the technological media—the newspapers and radios and televisions—are themselves beginning to acknowledge and call attention to the changes underway in the air itself. It is through these secondary media that we recently learned of the massive buildup in the upper atmosphere of manufactured chemical compounds that every year burn an ever-widening hole in the stratospheric ozone layer above Antarctica, while thinning the rest of that protective layer worldwide. From these media we also learn of the drastic increase in atmospheric carbon dioxide since the onset of the Industrial Revolution, and we hear over and again that this surfeit of carbon dioxide, along with other heat-absorbing gases, is already promoting a substantial warming of the earthly climate, a change which in turn endangers the survival of numerous ecosystems, numerous animal and plant species already stressed, many to the edge of extinction, by the ever-burgeoning human population.

Nevertheless, such published and broadcast information, reaching us as it does through these technological channels, all too often remains an abstract cluster of statistics; it does little to alter our intellectual detachment from the sensuous earth until, returning from a journey, we see for ourselves the brown haze that now settles over the town where we live, until we feel the chemical breeze stinging the moist membranes that line our nose, or until we watch, with alarm, as gale-force winds rip the awning off our storefront. Or perhaps, after recovering from our fifth fevered illness in a single winter, we realize that our bodily resistance has been dampened by the increased radiation that daily pours through the exhausted sky, or by airborne fallout from the latest power-plant failure across the continent.

Phenomenologically considered—experientially considered—the changing atmosphere is not just one component of the ecological crisis, to be set alongside the poisoning of the waters, the rapid extinction of animals and plants, the collapse of complex ecosystems, and other human-induced horrors. All of these, to be sure, are interconnected facets of an astonishing dissociation—a monumental forgetting of our human inherence in a more-than-human world. Yet our disregard for the very air that we breathe is in some sense the most profound expression of this oblivion. For it is the air that most directly envelops us; the air, in other words, is that element that we are most intimately in. As long as we experience the invisible depths that surround us as empty space, we will be able to deny, or repress, our thorough interdependence with the other animals, the plants, and the living land that sustains us. We may acknowledge, intellectually, our body's reliance upon those plants and animals that we consume as nourishment, yet the civilized mind still feels itself somehow separate, autonomous, independent of the body and of bodily nature in general. Only as we begin to notice and to experience, once again, our immersion in the invisible air do we start to recall what it is to be fully a part of this world.

For the primordial affinity between awareness and the invisible air simply cannot be avoided. As we become conscious of the unseen depths that surround us, the inwardness or inferiority that we have come to associate with the personal psyche begins to be encountered in the world at large: we feel ourselves enveloped, immersed, caught up within the sensuous world. This breathing landscape is no longer just a passive backdrop against which human history unfolds, but a potentized field of intelligence in which our actions participate. As the regime of self-reference begins to break down, as we awaken to the air, and to the multiplicitous others that are implicated, with us, in its generative depths, the shapes around us seem to awaken, to come alive. . . .[188]

---

[188] Ibid., pp. 258-260.

CHAPTER THIRTEEN

FIRE

Have you ever considered the fire which you kindle?
Is it you who have brought into being the tree
which feeds the fire, or is it We Who cause it to grow?
It is We Who have made it a reminder
and a comfort for those who wander in the wilderness.
Then celebrate the limitless glory
of the Name of your Sustainer, the Most High.
[*Sūrah Al-Wāqiʿah* (That Which Must Come To Pass) 56:71–74]

Does man not see that it is We Who created Him from sperm?
Yet witness! He stands in open opposition!
And he makes likenesses for Us and forgets his own creation:
he says, "Who can give life to decomposed bones?"
Say: "He will give them life Who created them in the beginning!
For He is supremely skilled in every kind of creation!
The same Who produces for you fire out of the green tree;
witness, how you kindle your own fires from it!
Is not He Who created the heavens and the earth
able to create their like?"
Of course! For He is the Creator Supreme in skill and knowledge!
Truly, when He intends a thing, His command is "Be" and it is!
So glory to Him in Whose hands is the dominion of all things;
and to Him will you all return.
[*Sūrah Yā Sīn* (O Thou Human Being) 36:77-83]

Don't you see how God has created the seven heavens in harmony
and made the moon a light in their midst
and made the sun a glorious lamp?
[*Sūrah Nūḥ* (Noah) 71:15-16]

225

And among His Signs He shows you the lightning
by way both of fear and of hope
and He sends down rain from the sky
and with it gives life to the earth after it is dead:
truly, in that are signs for those who are wise.
[*Sūrah Luqmān* 30:24]

So I call to witness the rosy glow of sunset,
the night and its progression,
and the moon as it grows in fullness;
surely, you shall travel from stage to stage.
What then is the matter with them
that they do not have faith in the unfolding?
[*Sūrah Al-Inshiqāq* (The Splitting Asunder) 84:16-20]

He is the Sustainer of the Worlds.
He established the mountains standing high above it
and bestowed blessings on the earth,
and measured all things there to give them nourishment
in due proportion,
in four aeons in accordance with the needs of those who seek.
And He comprehended in His design the sky which had been as smoke.
He said to it and to the earth: "Come together willingly or unwillingly."
They said: "We come in willing obedience."
So He completed them as seven heavens in two aeons
and He assigned to each heaven its duty and command.
And We adorned the lower heaven with lights
and provided it with protection.
Such is the Command of the Almighty, the All-Knowing.
[*Sūrah Fuṣṣilat* (Clearly Spelled Out) 41:9-12]

226

In the Name of God, the Infinitely Compassionate and Most Merciful
Consider the sky and the night-visitor.
And what will explain to you what the night-visitor is?
It is the star of piercing brightness.
There is no soul that does not have a protector over it.
[*Sūrah Aṭ-Ṭāriq* (That Which Comes In The Night) 86:1-4]

Of all the ways you can think of, none has the sixteenth part of the value of loving-kindness. Loving-kindness is a freedom of the heart which takes in all the ways. It is luminous, shining, blazing forth.

Just as the stars have not a sixteenth part of the moon's brilliance, which absorbs them all in its shining light, so loving-kindness absorbs all the other ways with its lustrous splendor.

Just as when the rainy season ends and the sun rises up into the clear and cloudless sky, banishing all the dark in its radiant light, and just as at the end of a black night the morning star shines out in glory, so none of the ways you can use to further your spiritual progress has a sixteenth part of the value of loving-kindness. For it absorbs them all, its luminosity shining forth.

~ Buddha[189]

The knowledge of Unity is like fire—
It enflames everything it comes upon,
And by this very act purifies it.

~ Al-'Alawi[190]

---

[189] Itivuttaka Sutta, *The Pocket Buddha Reader*, edited by Anne Bancroft, Shambhala Publications, pp. 17-18.
[190] Shayikh Ahmad al-'Alawi, as quoted in *Two Who Attained*, by Leslie Cadavid, Lexington, KY: Fons Vitae, 2005, p. 104.

Alchemy

~ Charles Upton

This is alchemy: man is both the substance to be refined, and the refiner, God is both the Refiner, and the Fire.

Al-Ghazali classified alchemy as among the "intellectual sciences"; unlike such things as magic and sorcery, it is permissible to Muslims. We usually think of alchemy as an early precursor to chemistry, and that's certainly true as far as it goes. But there is more to this craft than simple chemistry. According to Seyyed Hossein Nasr (who, besides being a master of Islamic history and doctrine, earned a degree from the Massachusetts Institute of Technology), in his *Islamic Science: An Illustrated Study,*

> A few practicing alchemists were reported early in [the 20th] century in such areas as the Maghrib. But few realize that in those centers of the Islamic world where the traditional arts are still alive—in such cities as Yazd and Isfahan in Persia—alchemy still survives on a much larger scale than is outwardly suspected. Its dispensations . . . make the continuity of such arts as the weaving of traditional cloth possible.
>
> A few real masters of the art survive along with many amateurish aspirants. The masters are well-hidden and usually veil their activity by some kind of outward occupation such as shopkeeping or the practice of medicine. Yet they are not wholly inaccessible to those who really seek them. To meet with one of these masters is to be faced with the blinding evidence that alchemy is not simply a proto-chemistry, for in their presence one feels not as if one were in the presence of an ordinary chemistry teacher but as if one were bathing in the sun on a cool autumn day. They exhibit a spiritual presence, intelligence and inner discipline which proves that they are concerned above and beyond all charcoal-burning with the transformation of the base metal of the soul and the unveiling of the gold or the sun which shines at the center of man's being, were he only to lift the veil which eclipses it before the outer eye. (pp. 204-205)

In the history of Islam, alchemy has always been related to the traditional crafts, to medicine, and to art. As to the question of whether base metal can really be transmuted into gold, on rare occasions, by alchemists in their workshops, it was always debated and has not yet been settled. What we can be sure of is that the symbols and metaphors of alchemy relate directly to the purification and integration of the human soul—which means that in one of its aspects, alchemy is a form of traditional psychotherapy. In this special psychotherapy, however, unlike the modern brand, we do not "adjust" to society or our natural passions, but to our *fitrah,* the eternal form of Humanity in the mind of God.

When a field is ploughed and sown and fertilized, when iron is extracted from ore and transformed into steel by the addition of carbon, a kind of alchemy is being done. Alchemy works with nature to transform nature, to bring it to a higher level of organization, closer to spirit.

The alchemy of being and essence is to separate them within the mind, and then reunite them on a higher level. This separation and reunion is what all true art does, to break us free from our stale habits of perception.

The world appears not as a set of material objects and forces, but as a pattern composed of the living signs of God's presence. *Wherever you turn, there is the face of God.* [2:115]

If we always think we know *what* things are, we may forget to realize *that* they are. Our world will become matter-of-fact, boring, literal — opaque to the Light of God. This is a state of mind the alchemists symbolized as *lead,* where being and essence, or Source (God) and His manifestation (nature) are chaotically mixed or crushed together. In the art of alchemy, these two must first be separated, and then reunited in a higher level, so that essence *reveals* being instead of hiding it. This is the state the alchemists symbolized as *gold.* When we see nature as the signs of God, we live in just this kind of world. To stop viewing the world as a materialistic machine and start seeing it as a carpet woven with the signs of God is to transmute lead into gold.

This is the alchemy which all true art serves. As the human substance is purified through the remembrance of God, nature becomes a vision of the signs of God.

229

Inside water, a waterwheel turns.
A star circulates with the moon.

We live in the night ocean wondering,
What are these lights?

~ Jalaluddin Rumi[191]

Why Newton Played with Sunbeams

~ Nechaev and Jenkins[192]

Back in the year 1660 the young scientist Isaac Newton, living in the peaceful town of Cambridge, used to spend days at a time doing the strangest thing—catching the reflections of sunbeams!

He sat for hours all alone in a dark room fussing at something, now and then muttering aloud to himself. Perhaps he was seeking an escape from the heat and was trying to keep cool in a darkened room? Hardly! He had carefully covered up every crack and the room was like a hot-house. He had a heavy wig on his head, in the fashion of the day, and the sweat was rolling down his face. Outside a fresh breeze was blowing.

Why was he sitting in this suffocating room?

He was catching the reflections of sunbeams on a piece of paper.

The shutters of all the windows were tightly closed so that no light could get in. In one of the shutters Newton had made a small, round hole about the size of your little finger. A narrow bar of sunlight came into the dark room through this little hole. Newton was walking quietly about the room, now holding his palm in the beam, now a sheet of paper, then letting the beam cross over to the opposite wall. A clear, bright reflection leapt from his hand to the wall, from the wall to the paper, from the paper to Newton's black doublet.

---

[191] Jalaluddin Rumi, Translated by John Moyne and Coleman Barks. *Unseen Rain*, Threshold Books, Putney, VT, p. 35.

[192] Nechaev and Jenkins, *The Chemical Elements, The fascinating story of their discovery and of the famous scientists who discovered them,* published by: Tarquin Publications, Stradbroke, Diss, Norfolk. Sections 4, 5 & 6, pp. 53-60.

Was it possible that the young scientist could have been playing a childish game?

Newton was certainly not amusing himself. He was engaged in serious work. He was performing an experiment.

He had a triangular prism in his hand, just a piece of common glass with three equal facets. From time to time he held this little piece of glass in the beam of sunlight.

As soon as the glass cut the path of the sunbeam the round white circle of sunlight on the wall disappeared and in its place a long, many-coloured strip appeared.

"Where did the white light go?" Newton asked in bewilderment the first time he observed this inexplicable change.... He repeated the experiment over and over. And every time the same thing happened: without the prism the sun rays were an ordinary white, but when they passed through the prism they came out painted all colours of the rainbow....

Newton called this coloured strip the spectrum.

The upper edge of the spectrum was always red. The red merged imperceptibly into orange, the orange into yellow, the yellow into green, the green into blue. At the very bottom of the spectrum came indigo and violet.

Newton racked his brain for a long time trying to discover where the spectrum came from. As soon as the sun showed itself in the morning he closed the shutters and began to catch the vari-coloured rays; and he remained in his self-imposed prison until evening, squinting in the light, the wonderful, coloured spectrum still dancing before his eyes.

He thought about it constantly, day and night, and finally he found the answer.

The light of the sun is not really white, he concluded. It only looks white to us. In reality a shower of brilliant, multi-coloured rays is pouring down from the sky and when the rays are all together our eyes cannot distinguish one from another. Therefore the sun's light appears to be white. But when these mingled rays pass through a prism, the prism scatters them and we see each one by itself....

Newton's explanation must have seemed very strange at first. It was difficult to grasp the idea that white light is really not white at all; that the sun shining down from the sky overhead is not a brilliant white sun, but a wonderful multi-coloured one which is at one and the same time red and yellow and green and violet.

But this unbelievable statement is nevertheless true. Remember how transparent dewdrops and raindrops gleam with brilliant colours in the sunlight!

Newton carried out scores of experiments in his darkened room before he reached the conclusion that the white light of the sun is really a mixture of rays. And his proofs were so convincing that it was hard to dispute him. He not only split up the white, mixed light into its component colours, he also reversed the operation and, passing the coloured rays through another prism, showed that by recombining they came out white again.

He devised the following experiment too: he painted all the colours of the sun's rays on a circular piece of wood, then whirled it rapidly on its axis. The whirling wheel appeared to be white, when as a matter of fact it was all striped with colour and there was not a single speck of white on it.

Spectral Analysis

~ Camille Helminski[193]

Building on Newton's discoveries and using a similar method of observation of candle light and lamplight as well as sunlight, in 1814 a German optician, Fraunhofer, discovered that the rays which shone most brightly in artificial light were exactly those that were missing in the sun's light. He documented over 500 dark lines of absence of color within the sun's spectra. These lines came to be referred to as "Fraunhofer's lines," but no one was able to explain what caused them until years later, when Kirchhoff and Bunsen were able to carry the process further.

From a simple cigar box and two old telescopes Kirchoff built a spectrascope that similarly enabled them to view the light spectra. Then Bunsen labored to prepare clean specimens of salts and crystals to

---

[193] Camille Helminski with excerpts from Nachaev and Jenkins, op. cit. p. 60.

examine. With a great deal of patience and perseverance, they were able to document the identifying colors of different elements and learned to recognize which elements were present in a specimen by the color of the flame which was emitted when it was subjected to fire.

> Each bright line stood out separately, each in its place. The two yellow lines of sodium stood out the clearest. But the violet line of potassium, the red line of lithium, and the deep blue of strontium all came out distinctly in the different parts of the broad, many-coloured strip of the spectrum.

> Just as a person may be picked out in a crowd by the sound of his voice, so every element in the mixture could be identified by the coloured ray which its flaming vapours gave out. The prism distributed to its own position on the spectrum the rays sent out by each different element so that no colour could conceal another.[194]

It was the fire that revealed the essence of the matter, in beautiful colors elucidating their qualities. Even so when the human being is subjected to the fire of difficulties, he or she shows "what he or she is made of." It is often that fire of difficulty which burns away the imperfections, rendering the soul purer, more resplendent in its essential qualities.

So, Truly with every difficulty comes ease.

[*Sūrah Ash-Sharḥ* (The Opening-up Of The Heart) 94:5]

---

[194] Ibid., p. 60.

Aurora Borealis

~ John Muir[195]

My bed was two boulders, and as I lay wedged and bent on their up-bulging sides, beguiling the hard, cold time in gazing into the starry sky and across the sparkling bay, magnificent upright bars of light in bright prismatic colours suddenly appeared, marching swiftly in close succession along the northern horizon from west to east as if in diligent haste, an auroral display very different from any I had ever before beheld. Once long ago in Wisconsin I saw the heavens draped in rich purple auroral clouds fringed and folded in most magnificent forms; but in this glory of light, so pure, so bright, so enthusiastic in motion, there was nothing in the least cloud-like. The short colour-bars, apparently about two degrees in height, though blending, seemed to be as well defined as those of the solar spectrum.

How long these glad, eager soldiers of light held on their way I cannot tell; for sense of time was charmed out of mind and the blessed night circled away in measureless rejoicing enthusiasm.

In the early morning after so inspiring a night I launched my canoe feeling able for anything, crossed the mouth of the Hugh Miller fiord, and forced a way three or four miles along the shore of the bay, hoping to reach the Grand Pacific Glacier in front of Mount Fairweather. But the farther I went, the ice-pack, instead of showing inviting little open streaks here and there, became so much harder jammed that on some parts of the shore the bergs, drifting south with the tide, were shoving one another out of the water beyond high-tide line. Farther progress to northward was thus rigidly stopped, and now I had to fight for a way back to my cabin, hoping that by good tide luck I might reach it before dark. But at sundown I was less than half-way home, and though very hungry was glad to land on a little rock island with a smooth beach for the canoe and a thicket of alder bushes for fire and bed and a little sleep. But shortly after sundown, while these arrangements were being made, lo and behold another aurora enriching the heavens! and though it proved to be one of

---

[195] John Muir, *The Eight Wilderness Discovery Books*, published jointly by The Mountaineers, Seattle, 1992, and Baton Wicks (UK), pp. 862-864.

the ordinary almost colourless kind, thrusting long, quivering lances toward the zenith from a dark cloudlike base, after last night's wonderful display one's expectations might well be extravagant and I lay wide awake watching.

On the third night I reached my cabin and food. Professor Reid and his party came in to talk over the results of our excursions, and just as the last one of the visitors opened the door after bidding good-night, he shouted, "Muir, come look here. Here's something fine."

I ran out in auroral excitement, and sure enough here was another aurora as novel and wonderful as the marching rainbow-coloured columns—a glowing silver bow spanning the Muir Inlet in a magnificent arch right under the zenith, or a little to the south of it, the ends resting on the top of the mountain-walls. And though colourless and steadfast, its intense, solid, white splendour, noble proportions and fineness of finish excited boundless admiration. In form and proportion it was like a rainbow, a bridge of one span five miles wide; and so brilliant, so fine and solid and homogeneous in every part, I fancy that if all the stars were raked together into one windrow, fused and welded and run through some celestial rolling-mill, all would be required to make this one glowing white colossal bridge.

After my last visitor went to bed, I lay down on the moraine in front of the cabin and gazed and watched. Hour after hour the wonderful arch stood perfectly motionless, sharply defined and substantial-looking as if it were a permanent addition to the furniture of the sky. At length while it yet spanned the inlet in serene unchanging splendour, a band of fluffy, pale grey, quivering ringlets came suddenly all in a row over the eastern mountain-top, glided in nervous haste up and down the under side of the bow and over the western mountain-wall. They were about one and a half times the apparent diameter of the bow in length, maintained a vertical posture all the way across, and slipped swiftly along as if they were suspended like a curtain on rings. Had these lively auroral fairies marched across the fiord on the top of the bow instead of shuffling along the under side of it, one might have fancied they were a happy band of spirit people on a journey making use of the splendid bow for a bridge. There must have been hundreds of miles of them; for the time required for each to cross from one end of the bridge to the other seemed only a minute or less, while nearly an hour elapsed from their first appearance until the last of the rushing throng vanished behind the western mountain, leaving the bridge as bright and solid and steadfast as before they arrived. But later, half an hour or so, it began to fade. Fissures or cracks crossed it diagonally through which a few stars were seen, and gradually it became thin and nebulous until it looked like the Milky Way, and at last vanished, leaving no visible monument of any sort to mark its place.

I now returned to my cabin, replenished the fire, warmed myself, and prepared to go to bed, though too aurorally rich and happy to go to sleep. But just as I was about to retire, I thought I had better take another look at the sky, to make sure that the glorious show was over; and, contrary to all reasonable expectations, I found that the pale foundation for another bow was being laid right overhead like the first. Then losing all thought of sleep, I ran back to my cabin, carried out blankets and lay down on the moraine to keep watch until daybreak, that none of the sky wonders of the glorious night within reach of my eyes might be lost.

I had seen the first bow when it stood complete in full splendour, and its gradual fading decay. Now I was to see the building of a new one from the beginning. Perhaps in less than half an hour the silvery material was gathered, condensed, and welded into a glowing, evenly proportioned arc like the first and in the same part of the sky. Then in due time over the eastern mountain-wall came another throng of restless electric auroral fairies, the infinitely fine pale-grey garments of each lightly touching those of their neighbours as they swept swiftly along the under side of the bridge and down over the western mountain like the merry band that had gone the same way before them, all keeping quivery step and time to music too fine for most ears.

While the gay throng was gliding swiftly along, I watched the bridge for any change they might make upon it, but not the slightest could I detect. They made no visible track, and after all had passed the glowing arc stood firm and apparently immutable, but at last faded slowly away like its glorious predecessor.

Excepting only the vast purple aurora mentioned above, said to have been visible over nearly all the continent, these two silver bows in supreme serene supernal beauty surpassed everything auroral I ever beheld.

W alking along
My shadow beside me
Watching the moon.
~ Sodo[196]

Lo! [While lost in the desert,] Moses said to his family:
"Behold, I perceive a fire [far away];
I may bring you from there some tiding,
[as to which way we are to pursue]
or bring you a burning brand so that you might warm yourselves."
But when he came close to it, a call was sounded:
"Blessed are all who are within [reach of] this fire, and all who are near it!
And limitless in His glory is God,
the Sustainer of all the worlds!"
[*Sūrah An-Naml* (The Ants) 27:7-9]

"Within reach of it," "near it," thus Zamakhsharī explains the expression *ḥawlahā* (lit., "around it"). According to some of the earliest commentators, quoted by Ṭabarī, the "fire" (*nār*) is in this context synonymous with "light" (*nūr*), namely, the illumination which God bestows on His prophets, who—one may presume—are *a priori* "near it" by virtue of their inborn spiritual sensitivity. Alternatively, the phrase *man fī 'n-nār wa-man ḥawlahā* may be understood as referring to God's Own light, which encompasses, and is the core of, all spiritual illumination.

~ Muhammad Asad[197]

---

[196] From *The Moon in the Pines, Zen Haiku selected and translated by Jonathon Clements*, published by Frances Lincoln, Ltd, © 2000. Reproduced by permission of Frances Lincoln Ltd., 4 Torriano Avenue, London NW5 2RZ. Distributed in the USA by Publishers Group West and in Canada by Raincoast Books, p. 76.

[197] Muhammad Asad, *The Message of the Qur'an*, commentary on 27:8.

Ring of Fire, Exploring
the Last Remote Places of the World

~ Lawrence Blair with Lome Blair[198]

It was really a scent, the aroma of spice, which first drew the West's attention to the Eastern islands. Exotic substances began arriving in medieval Venice, brought through overland trading routes and via Arab mariners across the Indian Ocean. Spices, together with tales of phoenixes . . . filtered into the bloodstream of the sleeping Europeans. Nutmeg, cloves, cinnamon, and curry-powders enabled us, for the first time in history, to preserve and stockpile food across the seasons. With insurance against hunger came the ability to plan ahead, and a different structuring of time emerged. The ability to store more food than we could eat at once also meant being able to buy and sell it in real quantity—and the merchant cities arose. The resultant economics was to lead directly to the Renaissance, and thence to the Industrial Revolution. No sooner had we caught the first heady whiff of the East and altered the chemistry of our food with it than we made a quantum leap in our cultural and artistic range as well. The Age of Discovery was launched. . . .[199]

★★★

In the summer of 1883, from the Sunda Straits between Java and Sumatra, the volcano of Krakatoa suddenly blew eleven cubic miles of ash and rock into the stratosphere, sending a shockwave seven times around the globe. The dying ripples of its massive tidal wave lapped up the English Channel, and the volcanic debris, wreathing the planet, altered weather and harvest patterns around the world for years afterwards. Despite Kipling's dictum that "Never the twain shall meet," the East had reached out and touched the West—with a premonition, perhaps, of the planetary holism which was to grip our minds less than a century later

---

[198] Lawrence Blair with Lorne Blair, *Ring of Fire, Exploring the Last Remote Places of the Earth*, copyright © 1988 by Lawrence Blair and Lorne Blair, published by Bantam Books, NY, NY, 1988.
[199] Ibid., p. 33.

when we walked on the moon, looked back, and for the first time saw the whole earth rising as a single bubble of life. It was also a foretaste of the explosive energy which, within a life-span, would be ours to control or abuse.

Within a few decades, forests and animals had returned to the shattered islands which were all that remained of Krakatoa's outer rim; and from the waters between them emerged an ominous smoking mound, sometimes growing at a rate of more than three feet a month. The locals call it "Anak Krakatoa"—"Child of Krakatoa." It has actually raised and submerged its sulphurous head five times since its first appearance in 1925, and when Lome and I reached it in September of 1983 it was nearly 300 feet high and so active that the government had denied us landing permits. Under these circumstances we were obliged to reach it at night, in a small open boat crewed by two very anxious and expensive local fishermen.

We approached the crackling silhouette through floating fields of pumice which rattled against our wooden hull, and when we stepped into the surf to haul our boat on to the beach, as black as the night around us, our bare feet sank into sand too hot for comfort. Moving like ants in a sand-trap we gasped slowly up the near-vertical rim of the secondary crater, into a storm of ash which masked the gathering dawn.[200]

★★★

We had read in our Admiralty Pilot that the temperature of the sea round here could vary very suddenly by hundreds of degrees. Ships are advised to give the islands a wide berth as the seabed is constantly shifting and massive magnetic anomalies cause compasses to swing wildly round the rose.

By the time we reached the volcano's outer lip it was deafeningly noisy. It was erupting rhythmically at about eight-minute intervals, which were preceded by two separate and terrifying sounds. First, as the whole island trembled like jelly, from way beneath us came what sounded like a giant rustling great sheets of brown wrappingpaper. This was followed by the bowling-alley racket of stones and boulders ricocheting off the walls of the crater as they ascended from a great depth to gush out over our heads

---

[200] Ibid., p. 29.

in billowing clouds of debris and smoke. Our equipment, clothes and bodies were penetrated by the finest, hardest black dust. Every so often a football-sized boulder would thud into the ash nearby.[201]

★★★

As the sun rose, the sky became perfectly clear and blue all around us, except for directly overhead where the island was creating its own weather. It wore a personal mushroom cloud which fired sheet-lightning directly down into its crater, with thunder so head-shattering that it was hard to convince the body it had nothing to worry about. With each blast came a drizzle of hot stinging ash, which settled on our eyelashes and blistered their roots. We had difficulty in breathing, our hair stood on end, and the tape-recorder and camera electronics began initiating a synch-pulse all their own, transforming our voices into a sort of demonic rasping.

Our shooting permits, after what had been eleven months of filming, were due to expire that evening and, though shot at the very end, the sequence on Anak Krakatoa was intended to introduce the very beginning of our whole ten years of adventure films. This was indeed a place of power, shunned as studiously by modern shipping as by local fishermen, and yet it was also a chance to pay homage to the mysteries moving beneath the surface of this strange island region. Here, at the site of the most devastating explosion in human memory, we wished to demonstrate both the unity and the fragility of the earth by blowing soap bubbles across the crater. One might hardly suspect that so simple a task for so few seconds of film could prove so practically trying and, on reflection, so symbolic of our whole chain of adventures, attempting to keep aloft and alive a consecutive string of luminous mirrors against rather ridiculous odds. Considerable effort was spent first on locating the appropriate soap powder and the pharmaceutical glycerine, and then on experimenting with proportionate mixtures and blowing techniques for producing the strongest bubbles. But these glistening globes, though blown by the panting thousands, lived in that rain of ash only for frustrating fractions of a second.

---

[201] Ibid., p. 30.

Standing on Anak Krakatoa we could see and feel the fragility of the world, for we also stood at the gateway to its oceanic hemisphere. Krakatoa is merely the first of a whole chain of active volcanoes which arc down through the Indonesian islands and round the Pacific to form what geologists call the Ring of Fire. To pass beyond it is to cross the threshold into another dimension which, for all its pragmatic gifts to the West over the centuries, remains as mysteriously little-known to us now as it was for the first explorers.[202]

Living amongst the Indonesians, where the pursuit of wisdom virtually amounts to a national pastime, the elements of Earth, Air, Fire, Water and Ether became real for me in a way they had never been in the writings of the Gnostics or Pythagoreans. Expressed in their paintings and sculpture and stories, these elements are seen as the successive thresholds, or levels of initiation, which the warrior of consciousness must broach on his path to enlightenment.[203]

Engendering Life

~ Camille Helminski[204]

Fire is a means of purification and renewal. For centuries, before antibiotics and other modern medical methods of healing, wounds were cauterized or seared with red-hot metal to reduce the risk of infection and encourage healing. Air in hospitals was cleansed by flaming alcohol; many traditions use the burning of incense to cleanse the air and atmosphere as well as to make it fragrant for worship.

Sometimes it is only fire that allows new life. Forest fires—though they can be devastating—also regulate undergrowth, making space for new seeds to sprout. There is a species of pine tree in California that only

---

[202] Ibid., p. 33.

[203] Ibid., p. 23.

[204] C.A.H. with excerpts from *Planet Earth, Volcano*, George Daniels, editor, Time-Life Books, Alexandria VA, 1982, p. 7.

releases its seeds after the cones have been heated by fiery temperatures. And on the banks of lava flows one discovers delicate ferns nestling in crannies, opening the way for restoration of greenness. It is the fire of the sun that provides us with the light and warmth for continued life.

Volcanoes are among nature's mightiest engines, builders of the land, makers of the sea, producers even of the atmosphere.

The eruptions of volcanoes are the source of the primeval and continuing regeneration of mountains and plains. The ocean floor, science now knows, is the result of millions of years of slow but ceaseless volcanic extrusions emanating from a 30,000-mile-long chain of deep-sea rift valleys.

A volcano's noxious ash and gases are essential to life on earth. The billions of tons of mineral-rich ash that fall to earth after an eruption are transformed in time into the most fertile of soils. Volcanologists calculate that, judging by their present rate of activity, volcanoes could have accounted for nearly a quarter of the oxygen, hydrogen, carbon, chlorine and nitrogen in the biosphere, and may, in fact, have been the primal source for most of the earth's air and water.

*And call to mind Our servants Abraham and Isaac and Jacob,
[all of them] endowed with inner strength and vision:
for, truly, We purified them by means of a thought most pure:
the remembrance of the life to come.*

[*Sūrah Ṣād* 38:45-46]

CHAPTER THIRTEEN

WATER

And there is not a thing but its storehouses are with Us;
but We only send it down in appropriate measures.
And We send the fertilizing winds,
then cause the rain to descend from the sky
and so provide you with water
though you are not the guardians of its stores.
And, truly, it is We Who give life and who give death:
it is We Who shall remain after all else passes away.
[*Sūrah Al-Ḥijr* 15:21-23]

And your God is the One God: there is no deity save Him,
the Most Gracious, the Dispenser of Grace.
Truly, in the creation of the heavens and of the earth,
and the succession of night and day:
and in the ships that speed through the sea with what is useful to man:
and in the waters which God sends down from the sky,
giving life thereby to the earth after it had been lifeless,
and causing all manner of living creatures to multiply thereon:
and in the change of the winds, and the clouds
that run their appointed courses between sky and earth:
[in all this] there are messages indeed for people who use their reason.
[*Sūrah Al-Baqarah* (The Cow) 2:163-164]

And when his people asked Moses for water,
We inspired him, "Strike the rock with thy staff!"—
whereupon twelve springs gushed forth from it,
so that all the people knew whence to drink.
And We caused the clouds to comfort them with their shade,
and We sent down unto them manna and quails,
[saying:] "Partake of the good things
which We have provided for you as sustenance."
[*Sūrah Al-Aʿrāf* (The Faculty Of Discernment) 7:160]

Let man, then, consider [the sources of] his food:
[how it is] that We pour down water, pouring it down abundantly;
and then We cleave the earth [with new growth], cleaving it asunder,
and thereupon We cause grain to grow out of it,
and vines and edible plants, and olive trees and date-palms,
and gardens dense with foliage,
and fruits and herbage, for you and for your animals to enjoy.
[*Sūrah 'Abasa* (He Frowned) 80:24-32]

It is God Who has given freedom to the two bodies of flowing water:
one palatable and sweet and the other salty and bitter;
yet He has made a barrier between them,
a threshold which they cannot cross.
It is He Who has created the human being from water
and endowed relationships of lineage and marriage:
for your Sustainer's power extends over all things.
[*Sūrah Al-Furqān* (The Standard Of True And False) 25:53-54]

It is He Who sends down rain from the sky:
from it you drink and with it plants grow
on which you feed your cattle.
With it He produces for you grain, olives,
date-palms, grapes, and all kinds of fruit:
truly, in this is a sign for people who reflect.
[*Sūrah An-Naḥl* (The Bee) 16:10-11]

The heart is comforted by true words,
just as a thirsty man is comforted by water.

~ Jalaluddin Rumi[205]

---

[205] Jalaluddin Rumi, *Mathnawi* [VI, 4276] translated by Camille and Kabir Helminski, *Jewels of Remembrance*, p. 188.

Water in the Qur'an

~ M.A.S. Abdel Haleem [206]

We made from water every living thing.
[*Sūrah Al –Anbiyā'* (The Prophets) 21:30]

In this concise and powerful statement the Qur'an sums up and draws attention to the vital importance of water. In perusing the pages of the Qur'an, one finds that water is a major theme. The word "water" *(ma')* occurs over 60 times, "rivers" over 50, and "the sea" over 40; while "fountains," "springs," "rain," "hail," "clouds," and "winds" occur less frequently. The Qur'an, however, is not a science text book and does not discuss the chemistry and physics of water, rather it is a book *for the guidance of mankind.* Thus, as we shall see, it treats the theme of water in its own way and for its own objectives. Water is shown not merely as an essential and useful element, but one of profound significance and far-reaching effect in the life and thinking of individual Muslims and of Islamic society and civilisation. . . .

Water is one of the most precious resources on earth. The verse quoted above explains in the Qur'an's characteristic way, how vital it is for all living things. The Qur'an talks about two kinds of water, . . . *one palatable and sweet, the other salty and bitter* . . . [25:53], pointing out some of their qualities and benefits, a division which we will conveniently follow here.

Fresh Water

It will be seen that in regard to the theme of water, Qur'anic material and the way it is treated is lively, exciting and particularly intimate to man. Accordingly, references to fresh water are more extensive in the Qur'an than those to salt water. Although the Qur'an states:

---

[206] "Water in the Qur'an," by M.A.S. Abdel Haleem, excerpted from *Islam and the Environment*, Edited by Harfiyah Abdel Haleem. Ta-Ha Publishers Ltd., London, England. Copyright © 1998 Harfiyah A. Haleem. Published in Ramadan 1419 AH/ December 1998 CE., pp. 102-117. Reprinted by permission from Ta-Ha Publishers Ltd.

Allah is the Creator of all things and He is guardian over all things [39:62] and *He created everything and ordained it in due proportion* [25:2],

it does not simply state that Allah *created* fresh water: That would be rather abstract. Instead, it involves the reader in what he or she can "observe" of the processes that generate water and produce its benefits:

It is Allah who drives the winds that raise the clouds and spreads them along the sky as He pleases and causes them to break up so that you can see the rain issuing out from the midst of them [30:48].

The Qur'an frequently speaks of the winds and the clouds:

In the marshalling of the winds, and in the clouds that are driven between earth and sky: surely in these there are signs for people who have sense [2:164].

It is He who shows you the lightning, inspiring you with fear and hope and raises the heavy clouds [13:12].

It is He Who drives the winds, glad tidings heralding His mercy, and We send down pure water from the sky [25:48].

Do they not see how we drive the rain to the barren land and bring forth therewith crops of which their cattle eat, and they themselves? Have they no eyes to see with? [32:27].

Qur'anic statements about fresh water constantly remind us that its origin is with Allah and not man. Thus the statements begin with (He is Allah . . . , it is He Who . . .]. This is further emphasized by a most significant statement in this context: *He sends down from the sky . . .* , immediately removing the source of water from the realm where men could claim they have made it and pointing out that He brought it down from that higher source. The unbelievers are thus challenged in the Qur'an:

Consider the water that you drink. Was it you that brought it down from the rain cloud or We? If We had pleased, We could make it bitter: why then do you not give thanks? [56:68-70].

The repetition of *"from the sky"* also draws attention to the surface paradox that the sky contains water held there by His power and at will He *"brings it down,"* the Qur'an never saying "it falls."

Water being of such vital importance, human beings are reminded, "you are not the holders of its stores"; rather *There is not a thing but with Us are the storehouses of it, and We do not send it down except in a known measure* [15:21].

246

Benefits

The benefits of this gift from Allah are often pointed out. Drinking is naturally a high priority:

And We send the water from the sky and give it to you to drink [15:22].

We provided you with sweet water [77:27].

We send down pure water from the sky, that We may thereby give life to a dead land and provide drink for what We have created—cattle and men in great numbers [25:48-49].

In this instance, and in some others, cattle occur first—a sobering thought! They are also important in being, themselves, a source of drink and food for man.

Giving life to a dead land is a frequent expression that shows the beneficial effect of water in the Qur'an.

There is a sign in the water which Allah sends down from the sky and with which he gives life to the earth after its death, dispersing over it all manner of beasts [2:164].

It is He Who sends down water from the sky in due measure and thereby We quicken the dead land [43:11].

The earth is revived to produce what benefits man and beast. The Qur'an repeatedly enumerates such products, detailing the observable phases they go through, and inviting the reader to look upon them:

It is He Who sends down water from the sky and with it brings forth the buds of every plant. From these We bring forth green foliage from which We bring forth the thick-clustered grain, palm-trees laden with clusters of dates within reach, vineyards and olive groves and pomegranates [which are] alike and different. Look upon their fruits when they bear fruit and upon its ripening, surely in these there are signs for true believers [6:99].

Water is driven to the dead land, caused to fall on it

. . . and with it we bring forth all manner of fruit [7:57]

. . . fruits of different hues . . . [35:27]

. . . watered with one water, yet We make some excel others in taste [13:4].

Water has a dramatic and beautifying effect on earth which men are directed to observe:

Do you not see that Allah sends down water from the sky and then the earth becomes green on the morrow [22:63].

You see the earth barren and lifeless, but when We send down water upon it, it thrills and swells and puts forth every joyous kind of growth [22:5].

It is indeed a "blessed" element that gives rise to such beauty and sustenance:

We send down blessed water from the sky with which We brought forth gardens with harvest grain and lofty date-palms with ranged clusters, a sustenance for men [50:9-11].

As mentioned earlier, the Qur'an deals with material very intimate to man, things taken perhaps too much for granted for him to reflect upon them. By pointing such things out and enumerating their phases and stages, the Qur'an refreshes people's sensitivity to them and invites reflection on them:

Let man reflect on the food he eats: how We pour down the rain in torrents; We open the soil for the seed to grow;

How We bring forth the corn, the grapes and the fresh vegetation, the olive trees and the palm trees, the thickets, the fruit-trees and the green pastures, for you and your flocks to enjoy [80:24-32].

Cleanliness

For Muslims, water serves another daily-recurring important function—cleansing and purification:

He sends down water from the sky to cleanse you [8:11].

Muslims are ordered: *Cleanse your garments* [74:4]. The Prophet said, "Cleanliness is part of faith," and in the Qur'an the instruction to cleanliness is a favour that warrants thanksgiving:

O you who believe, when you rise to pray, wash your faces and your hands as far as the elbow, wipe your heads, and your feet to the ankle. If you are polluted, cleanse yourselves . . . Allah does not wish to burden you, but desires to purify you and to perfect His favour to you and that you may give thanks [5:6].

The Prophet urged his followers to cleanse themselves particularly for such a gathering as the Friday prayer "even if a glass of water would cost a dinar," and the Qur'an stresses:

[Allah] loves those who purify themselves [9:108].

Understandably, emphasis is placed noticeably on water from the sky because of its vital importance for drinking and irrigation, but water on and in the ground is not neglected:

From it also channels flow, each according to its measure [13:17],

and: *He leads it through springs in the earth* [39:21]

One of the stores of fresh water provided by Allah is in the ground. He *"lodged it in the earth"* [22:18]. That Allah does not make this water soak away irretrievably and disappear is a favour, which is made clear by contemplating his power to do this if He so wishes:

Say: "Think: if all the water that you have were to sink down into the earth, who would give running water in its place"[67:30]; *We could take it [drinking water] all away* [18:23]

If We willed, We could make it bitter [56:70].

. . . Water is not simply there, it does not fall by itself, nor does the earth revive itself or plants come out by themselves. It is He who does it "with" or "by means of" water . . . emphasising over and over again the instrumentality of this vital element.

Connected with fresh water are rivers, which recur in the Qu'ran over fifty times. They are the vessels of abundant "running" water; the epithet forms a collocation with "river" in the Qur'an, emphasised by the noticeable juxtaposition of the mountains "standing firm" on earth, with the rivers [16:15; 27:61]. The fundamental importance of rivers for cooling, irrigation and beautification is borne out in the frequent statements about Paradise in the Qur'an *"underneath which rivers flow"* [5:119 and elsewhere]. Paradise is almost always connected with running rivers and *"is better and more lasting"* [87:17]. This makes water more significant to Muslims than perhaps any other people in the world.

Sea Water

In the language of the Qur'an and classical Arabic in general a large perennial river is called *bahr*, which is the same word used for sea. In a number of cases the Qur'an compares fresh and sea water, talking of them as *al-bahrayn* (the two *bahrs*). The majority of translators render this as *"the two seas"* which is clearly confusing to the reader. Yusuf 'Ali opts for *"the two bodies of flowing water"* which is preferable. Both of them are signs of Allah's power and grace. He subjected them to man for the common benefits he derives from them.

From each you eat tender fish and bring up ornaments to wear, and you see the ships plough their courses through them, so that you may seek His bounty and may be thankful [35:12].

These benefits are mentioned many times in the Qur'an, and here again we usually find the key statement *It is Allah/It is He who subjected the sea to you so that . . .* [45:12]. The benefit of using the sea for transportation is strongly emphasised in the Qur'an. It is a sign of honour:

We have honoured the children of Adam; and provided them with transport on land and sea . . . [12:70].

This is fitting for Muslims who are urged in the Qur'an to travel and seek the bounty of Allah [4:100; 73:20]. Islam, which encourages travel, has set aside for the wayfarer a share in the *zakah* (regular charitable contributions). The Qur'an reminds people:

It is He Who conveys you on the land and the sea [10:22].

Ships float and run on the sea by His command and He keeps the ships from sinking and the sky from falling, except by His own will [22:65].

The sea is "*kept filled*" to perform its functions [52:6]. It contains a prodigious volume of water:

Say: if the waters of the sea were ink with which to write the words of my Lord, the sea would surely be drained before His words were finished [18:109].

This boundless sea, with all that it contains, is encompassed by Allah's knowledge:

And He has knowledge of all that land and sea contain [6:59].

He delivers men from darkness and harm on the sea when they call upon him humbly and in secret:

Say: Who delivereth you from the darkness of the land and sea? Ye call upon Him humbly and in secret, (saying): If we are delivered from this (fear) we will be truly thankful [6:63].

And when harm toucheth you upon the sea, those that ye call upon (for succour) fail, save for Him (alone) [17:67].

The vital difference between fresh water and sea water is emphasized in the Qur'an:

The two are not alike, the one fresh, sweet and pleasant to drink from while the other is salty and bitter [35:12].

Had he wished, he would have made (drinking-water) bitter [56:65].

The two kinds of water meet, yet He has set a barrier between them which they do not overrun. [25:53]

Thus people may continue to have sea water and fresh water on earth.

Language

It will have become clear from the earlier part of this article that the language the Qur'an employs in talking about water is full of liveliness and movement: the winds "drive" the clouds; He "sends down" water which "revives" the earth, "leads it through" springs and "flowing" rivers, He "splits" the earth and with water "brings forth" plants and fruits, etc. The movement indicated is quick, using the conjunction of speed: the *a* of *ta 'qib* (following on the heels) and the conjunction of surprise: *idha* of *fuja 'iyah* (surprise) [30:48; 41:39]. He sends down water and the earth "becomes green on the morrow." This is intensified by personification, the earth is "barren and lifeless" and "lowly" but when He sends down water on it "it thrills and swells," the effects of the rain are "the marks/prints of Allah's mercy":

He sends the winds, harbingers pacing along close in front in between the two hands of His approaching mercy [25:48].

He sends water so that you may taste His mercy [30:46].

He sends down saving rain for them when they have lost all hope and spreads abroad His mercy [42:28].

Such emotionally charged situations are used with fresh water and also when talking about the sea:

It is He Who conveys you on the land and sea, until when you are in the ships, and they sail, carrying them in a pleasant wind, a violent wind overtakes them, and billows surge upon them from every side, and they fear that they are encompassed, then they pray to Allah with all fervour: Deliver us from this peril and we will be truly thankful [10:22].

In discussing water in the Qur'an, the intensity and richness of the language is enhanced by the employment of *iltifat* which, in this case, involves a sudden shift, for a desired effect, from the singular to plural while continuing to refer to the same person. The shift occurs at a significant point in the sentence. Thus we read:

It is He who drives the winds, glad tidings heralding His mercy, and We

251

send down pure water from the sky, that We may give life thereby to a dead land and provide drink to what We have created—cattle and men in great numbers [25:48-9].

The shift from the third person singular "He" to the divine "We" brings majesty and grace to the statement at the significant point of bringing the water down and giving life by it. In a verse that concerns Allah's power in giving various colours to fruits, mountains, men, beasts and cattle, the shift again occurs at the significant point in the context:

Did you not see how Allah sent down water from the sky and We produced with it fruits of diverse hues [35:27]. . . .

Arab classical rhetoricians and critics in their enthusiasm about the feature of *iltifat* in Arabic described it as a sign of "the bold nature of the Arabic language." Actually, the statement should be corrected to read "the bold nature of the Qur'anic language" because the majority and most significant examples such critics cited were from the Qur'an and there is no better place from which to understand the real function of *iltifat* than in the verses about water in the Qur'an.

Qur'anic statements about water are intense, very intimate to man, his food, drink, his survival and that of his animals, his plants and his crops. Sometimes, as we have seen, he is made to contemplate life without water, or with too much of it. Here, in contrast with the benign, blissful nature of water manifested in such adjectives as "purifying" "blissful," "fresh," "saving," "mercy," man is reminded of the destructive side of water, when, instead of being sent down in due measure it is "loosed," made to "rise high," and "*billows surge from every direction*"; *when nothing could provide protection from the flood* [11:43]; when:

We opened the gates of heaven with pouring water and caused the earth to gush forth with springs [54:11].

Man is regularly directed to "look," "observe," "think" and "contemplate." On very numerous occasions, verses end with *In this there are signs for people who think/ who hear/ who have sense. ; Can they not see, will they not give thanks?* Thus water in the Qur'an is far from being a mere element: it is a subject of profound significance, and man's senses, emotions, and reason are constantly brought into play in discussing it.

252

Purposes of Referring to Water

The theme of water in the Qur'an serves chiefly three purposes:

It is used as a proof of Allah's existence, unity and power. This is indicated by such statements as *"of His signs,"* *"in this there are signs,"* *"It is Allah / He that"*:

Who is it that sent down water for you from the sky with which We caused to bring forth joyous orchards? Try as you may you cannot cause such trees to grow, was it another god beside Allah? [27:60]

And consider the water that you drink. Was it you that brought it down from the cloud or We? [56:68-69]

It is also used as a proof of Allah's care. This is always indicated by the prepositions "for you," "to you" which accompany statements about sending down, bringing forth, subjecting, *"for you and your flocks to enjoy,"* *"out of this mercy"* and is implied in the contemplation of the opposite as already noted.

Water, with its effects, is further used in the Qur'an as a proof of the Resurrection. The unbelievers frequently argued in the Qur'an how, when they have died and been turned into *"dust and bones,"* *can they be restored to life?* [56:47]. Among the answers the Qur'an gives to this type of logic is the effect of water on the dry and barren earth:

He that gives it life will restore the dead to life. [41:30]

Likewise you shall be brought forth. [30:19]

In fact the Qur'an uses the very same verb for *"bringing forth"* people out of their mother's womb [16:78] and *"bringing forth"* plants from the earth [46:99] and *"bringing forth"* people from the earth at the resurrection. Likewise the same verbal root is used in *"making every living thing from water,"* *"giving life to earth"* and *"He who gave it life will give life to the dead."* Such a linguistic method enhances the pattern of persuasion used in the Qur'an.

The belief in Allah's existence, unity, power and care and in the resurrection are fundamental in Islam. Employing water to prove them gives it deeper significance and explains the frequent reference to it in the Qur'an.

Guidance on the Use of Water

The Qur'an provides practical teaching about the use of water. Since it is Allah Who made from water every living thing, and it is He Who sent down fresh water from the sky out of His grace and mercy and gave it lodging in the earth, such a vital resource should not be monopolized by the powerful and privileged and kept from the poor. References in the Qur'an to water distribution "provide the basis upon which much legal thought was formulated" in Islamic law.

Tell them that water is to be divided between them [54:28-29].

The Prophet said: "People are co-owners in three things: water, fire, and pasture." (*Hadith:* Abu Dawud)

"Allah does not look with favour upon three kinds of people. One of these is . . . a man who has surplus water near a path and denies the use of it to a wayfarer. . . ." (*Hadith:* al-Bukhari)

"He who withholds water in order to deny the use of pasture, Allah withholds from him His mercy on the day of resurrection." (*Hadith:* Bukhari, Muslim, Tirmidhi, Abu Dawud Ahmad)

The following *hadith* exemplifies the virtue of sharing water, even with a dog: While a man was walking, he became thirsty. He went to a well and drank from it. Afterwards he noticed a dog sniffing at the sand because of thirst. The man said to himself, "This dog is suffering what I have suffered," so he filled his shoe with water and held it for the dog to drink. He then thanked Allah who bestowed upon him forgiveness for his sins. The Prophet's companions asked, "Are we also rewarded for (kindness to) animals?" He answered, "There is a reward for (kindness to) every living thing." (*Hadith:* al-Muwatta)

Muslim jurists in general recognise the urgent nature of man's need for water as well as the necessity to provide water for animals. A man who is thirsty is permitted to fight another, though without the use of any weapon, if the other has water and denies him the right to quench his thirst.[130] A tradition records that 'Umar made some owners of water pay the *diya* (blood money) for a man who died of thirst after they had refused his request for water.

In addition to the prohibition on monopoly of water, there is the prohibition on excess and wastefulness in using water:

Eat and drink but do not be excessive; He loves not the extravagant. [7:31]

Do not squander (your substance) wastefully, for the wasteful are the devil's brothers [17:26].

The Prophet said: "Excess in the use of water is forbidden, even if you have the resources of a whole river." (*Hadith:* Tirmidhi)

It is forbidden, moreover, to pollute water. Out of His grace, Allah sent it down from the sky "pure," "to cleanse you with it" [25:47; 8:11]. Thus in Islamic law it is forbidden to urinate in water. We have seen earlier that Qur'anic statements about water normally contain "for you," "to you," or "so that you." Statements about the sea and large rivers, too, are always accompanied by the purpose Allah intended for them. Thus:

It is He Who subjected the sea to you, so that you may eat of its tender fish and bring up from it ornaments with which to adorn yourselves, and you see the ships ploughing their courses through it, that you may seek His bounty and render thanks to Him [16:34].

Polluting rivers and seas goes against the functions and purposes stated for them in the Qur'an; it is corruption:

Corruption doth appear on land and sea because of (the evil) which men's hands have done [35:41].

Allah created the earth:

And blessed it and measured therein its sustenance [4:10].

Pollution that disturbs plant, animal, or sea life disturbs the balance of Allah's "measurement" and is a long way from "rendering thanks" for the blessing of water.

Thus in Islam, refraining from monopolising water, wasting or polluting it is not merely a matter of being wise, civilised, or showing good conduct as a citizen—it is, above that, an act of worship.

Water in Islamic Society

It was natural that Qur'anic teaching should have a far-reaching effect on Islamic life, shown in the attitude of the Muslims to water, whether related to this world or the world to come, in the rituals, the law, in Islamic art and architecture and in Islamic civilisation in general. We have already mentioned the stress on cleansing one's body and clothes which is a condition observed several times a day for one of the "pillars" of Islam. It is no wonder that public baths became known, before the advent of modern civilisation, as an important feature of Islamic cities, recorded in great numbers in classical writings. Drinking fountains (*sabil*) also became an architectural feature of Islamic cities with calligraphic

Qur'anic references to drinking in Paradise adorning their facades; so did
watering places for animals. Religious endowments, with elaborate and
exquisitely detailed deeds, many of which have survived, were made to
ensure the continued maintenance of such institutions.[131] Traditional
Islamic gardens, with water as an essential element, were inspired by the
descriptions of Paradise in the Qur'an underneath whose trees *rivers flow*.

From the Qur'an, Muslims learn that water is a sign of Allah's
existence, unity, power and care. It is the essence of life, and sustenance,
an instrument of cleanliness and beauty. It is not to be monopolized,
wasted or polluted, and it is an essential feature of the best that Muslims
aspire to in the life to come.

Whoever devotes himself solely to God for 40 days,
springs of wisdom will pour forth from his heart upon his tongue.
~ The Prophet Muhammad ﷺ[207]

Waves of the Sea

~ Sa'd ud-Din Mahmud Shabistari[208]

What is the sea whose shore is speech? What is the pearl to be
found in its depths?

The sea is Being and speech is its shore;
Shells are words, pearls are Heart-knowledge.
With every wave are tossed thousands of royal pearls
Revealed from texts, traditions, and prophecies.
Thousands of waves surge from It at every moment,
Yet It is never made less by even one drop.
The existence of Knowledge comes from that deep sea;
Its pearl is nestled in a covering of sounds and words.
When inner meanings descend to this [sensible] realm,
They must reveal themselves in allegory and metaphor.

---

[207] *Kalemat-e Maknuneh Fayze Kashani*, p. 247.
[208] Sa'd ud-Din Mahmud Shabistari, *The Garden of Mystery* (*Gulshan-i raz*),
translated by Bob Darr, Sausalito, CA: Real Impressions, 1998, p. 68.

And the Rains Came

~ Padma Hejmadi[209]

A conch shell blows for somebody's morning prayer; children and neighbors come around, peering through the windows at this weird anomaly of a woman closeted with her typewriter, under a sky illimitably full of sun. Subservient to my monkey, I want to scratch and ask for peanuts.

Outside, the hills around town change all day, from blue to lavender to a deep drenched purple and then, after dark, to the exact tinge you see in the smudges of fatigue beneath a child's eyes. It is June; we are waiting for the monsoon to break. It has passed Sri Lanka. It has rounded the tip of our southern coast. Then the wind drops. How to describe it? Day following hot, breathless day; the inexorable parching, all color drained from the earth and the sky and the hills; the unspoken anxiety in everyone's eyes: "Please don't let the rains fail, please don't let the crops fail, please let our bellies be filled . . ."

The wind picks up, reaches Cochin on the west coast, gets as far as Bombay, and then stops again.

Early morning, my mother and I go up to the roof to watch a cloud above the mountains—small, purple-grey, no bigger than the proverbial man's hand. And there it stays. "You might as well get back to work," my mother says.

In my workroom, at some point I realize I have to turn on the light. Clouds have massed overhead. Suddenly, a breath of coolness courses through the trees . . . there's a roll of thunder (incredible timing) . . . and then down comes the rain. A roar rises from the whole neighborhood, as if from one throat. Street vendors put down their baskets, college students put down their books, everyone links arms and goes singing and dancing and clapping down the street. Children rush out into the yard or up onto the roof, whirling round and around like little dervishes, arms flung wide open, lifting their heads to drink the new rain as it falls.

---

[209] Padma Hejmadi, *Room to Fly, a Transcultural Memoir,* University of California Press, Berkeley, CA 1999, pp. 39-40. Reprinted by permission of The University of California Press.

In the spring rain
All things grow beautiful.
~ Chiyo-Ni [210]

Every man with a sense of the subtle is aware of the effect of what is mentioned on the soul, whether it be something serious or light-hearted. If we admit this, then we are bound to admit also that the name of God has an influence on the soul, as do other names, each to its own degree. . . . Do not lose sight of the fact that a name is as noble as that which is named, insamuch as it bears its imprint in the folds of its secret essence and meaning.

~ al-'Alawi[211]

Remembrance of God is the greatest.
[*Sūrah Al-ᶜAnkabūt* (The Spider) 29:45]

Truly, in remembrance of God, hearts find rest.
[*Sūrah Ar-Raᶜd* (Thunder) 13:28]

---

[210] From *The Moon in the Pines, Zen Haiku selected and translated by Jonathon Clements, published by* Frances Lincoln, Ltd, © 2000. Reproduced by permission of Frances Lincoln Ltd., 4 Torriano Avenue, London NW5 2RZ. Distributed in the USA by Publishers Group West and in Canada by Raincoast Books, p. 14.

[211] Shaykh Ahmad al-'Alawi as quoted in *Two Who Attained*, op.cit., p. 51

Miraculous Messages from Water

~ Masaru Emoto[212]

Water is a very malleable substance. Its physical shape easily adapts to whatever environment is present. But its physical appearance is not the only thing that changes; its molecular shape also changes. The energy or vibrations of the environment will change the molecular shape of water. In this sense water not only has the ability to visually reflect the environment but it also molecularly reflects the environment. Mr. Emoto has been visually documenting these molecular changes in water by means of his photographic techniques. He freezes droplets of water and then examines them under a dark field microscope that has photographic capabilities. His work clearly demonstrates the diversity of the molecular structure of water and the effect of the environment upon the structure of the water.

~ Stacy Sharpe

We start out life being 99 percent water, as fetuses. When we are born, we are 90 percent water, and by the time we reach adulthood we are down to 70 percent. If we die of old age, we will probably be about 50 percent water. In other words, throughout our lives we exist mostly as water.

From a physical perspective, humans are water. When I realized this and started to look at the world from this perspective, I began to see things in a whole new way.

First, I realized that this connection to water applies to all peoples. Therefore, what I am about to say applies to everyone, all over the world.

I believe I am also starting to see the way that people should live their lives. So how can people live happy and healthy lives? The answer is to purify the water that makes up 70 percent of your body.

---

[212] Masaru Emoto, *The Hidden Messages of Water*, copyright 2004 by Beyond Words Publishing, Inc. Hillsboro, Oregon, pp. xv-xvii, xxv-xxvi, pp. 39-46. Originally published 2001 as Mizu Wa Kotae Wo Shitteiru by Masaru Emoto, Sunmark Publishing, Tokyo, Japan. Stacy Sharpe is quoted from www.wellnessgoods.com/messages.asp

Water in a river remains pure because it is moving. When water becomes trapped, it dies. Therefore, water must constantly be circulated. The water—or blood—in the bodies of the sick is usually stagnant. When blood stops flowing, the body starts to decay, and if the blood in your brain stops, it can be life threatening.

But why does blood become stagnant? We can see this condition as the stagnation of the emotions. Modern researchers have shown that the condition of the mind has a direct impact on the condition of the body. When you are living a full and enjoyable life, you feel better physically, and when your life is filled with struggles and sorrow, your body knows it. So when your emotions flow [positively] throughout your body, you feel a sense of joy, and you move towards physical health.

Moving, changing, flowing—this is what life is all about.

★★★

If we consider that before we became human beings, we existed as water, we get closer to finding the answer to the basic question of what a human being is. If we have a clear understanding of water, we will better understand the human body, and even unlock the mystery of why we were born and exist as we do.

So just what is water? Your first answer might be that it is life force. If we lose 50 per cent of the water in our bodies, we can no longer maintain life. Water carried by blood and bodily fluids is the means by which nourishment is circulated throughout our bodies. This flow of water enables us to live active lives. Water serves as the transporter of energy throughout our bodies.[213]

★★★

Water is the mirror of the soul. It has many faces, formed by aligning itself with the consciousness of human beings. What gives water its ability to reflect what is in people's souls? In order to answer that question, I would first like to make sure that you understand this fact: Existence is vibration.

The entire universe is in a state of vibration, and each thing generates its own frequency, which is unique. . . . My years of research into water have taught me that this is the fundamental principle of the universe.

---

[213] Ibid., pp. xv-xvii.

It can be said in just three words, but for people who have never heard them, these are very difficult words to understand.

You might think, *Existence is vibration? Even this table? This chair? My body? How can everything that can be seen and touched be vibration?* It is indeed difficult to believe that things that you can pick up with your hands and examine—things like wood, rocks, and concrete—are all vibrating.

But now the science of quantum mechanics generally acknowledges that substance is nothing more than vibration. When we separate something into its smallest parts, we always enter a strange world where all that exists is particles and waves.

Let's imagine that you could reduce your body to microscopic size, and that you set off on an exploration to discover the secrets of this universe called you. You would soon see that each thing consists of nothing more than atoms, each atom being a nucleus with electrons rotating around it. The number and shape of these electrons and their orbits give each substance a particular set of vibrational frequencies. You would discover that whatever the substance, nothing is solid. Instead there is only a nucleus surrounded by an endlessly rotating wave.

Everything is eternally moving and vibrating—on and off, at an incredible speed.

According to the *Hanyashingyo*, the Buddhist Wisdom and Heart Sutra, "That which can be seen has no form, and that which cannot be seen has form," We can now say that this strange contradiction, spoken ages ago by the Buddha, has been proved true by modern science.

Our eyes can see objects, but they can't see vibration. However, I'd like you to ask yourself if you haven't had an experience similar to the following:

You are talking with someone in a room, and the mood is warm, friendly, and free-flowing. Then another person enters the room. The moment they open the door, you notice a change in the atmosphere, and now instead of warmth filling the room, the space is encased in a dark and cold mood.

You look at the new arrival's face and see a haggard expression and humped-over shoulders, someone who looks like they are just tired with life. What could be the cause of this pain? Maybe a broken heart, a mistake at work, or just general disgust with life—I'll leave it up to you.

What I want you to think about is why the mood in the room changed the moment that the door was opened.

Human beings are also vibrating, and each individual vibrates at a unique frequency. Each one of us has the sensory skills necessary to feel the vibrations of others.

A person experiencing great sadness will emit a sadness frequency, and someone who is always joyful and living life fully will emit a corresponding frequency. A person who loves others will send out a frequency of love. . . .

All things vibrate, and they vibrate at their own frequencies. When you understand this, you will significantly broaden your understanding of the universe. With this understanding, your eyes will open to things you have never seen before—things previously pushed to the back of your consciousness—and these discoveries and feelings will give new life to your soul.

The fact that everything is in a state of vibration also means that everything is creating sound.

This doesn't mean that we can hear every sound, although there are some people who apparently hear the voices of trees and who can communicate with plants. Whether we can hear the sound or not, we can say that the unique frequency of all objects can be interpreted as sound.

It is said that the human ear is generally capable of hearing frequencies from approximately 15 Hz to 20,000 Hz (Hz, or Hertz, indicates the number of cycles of the repetitive waveform per second). Actually, it's a good thing that our ears have such limits—otherwise we probably wouldn't be able to sleep at night.

The natural world is indeed well designed—everything is in balance. And as sound is created, there is a master listener to receive the sound: water.

Let me ask you to think about why crystal formation would be affected by music, and why completely different results would be reached depending on the spoken and written words water was exposed to. The answer is found, again, in the fact that everything is vibration. Water—so sensitive to the unique frequencies being emitted by the world—essentially and efficiently mirrors the outside world.

Music and spoken words are vibration, they are easily understood and interpreted by just about anyone. Sounds like the chant created by a human voice at a Buddhist funeral create a healing frequency.

But how can we interpret the phenomena of crystal formation being affected by words written on paper and shown to water? The written words themselves actually emit a unique vibration that the water is capable of sensing. Water faithfully mirrors all the vibrations created in the world, and changes these vibrations into a form that can be seen with the human eye. When water is shown a written word, it receives it as vibration, and expresses the message in a specific form. (You might think of letters as being a visual code for expressing words.)

But what, fundamentally, are words? The Old Testament states, "In the beginning there was the Word." This would mean that before the creation of the universe, there existed "the Word." My interpretation of this is that "the Word" created human beings, and human beings then learned words from nature.

In primeval times, when people lived within nature, they needed to protect themselves, and so they were sensitive to the frequencies and sounds generated by nature, in order to detect danger before it could sneak up on them.

The sound of the wind blowing, the sound of water flowing, the sound of an animal walking through the grass—the ability to understand these sounds and relay them to others using one's voice was required for survival. It is likely that these attempts at language were simple messages of a few words, but with the development of culture and accumulation of experience, our vocabulary expanded.

Why, then, are the languages that people speak so diverse? This is quite easy to understand if you consider that language is learned from the vibrations of the natural environment. The natural environment varies greatly with location, and each environment will create different vibrations. The volatile weather climate of Europe and the humid islands of Asia all create different vibrations that flow out of nature. In Japan, there are four distinct seasons, and so the Japanese language reflects this with a beautiful lexicon of weather related words.

Water exposed to the words "Thank you" formed beautiful geometric crystals, no matter what the language. But water exposed to "You fool" and other degrading words resulted in obviously broken and deformed crystals.

According to the Bible, before the Tower of Babel all people spoke the same language. Perhaps this is telling us that even though location and natural environ-ment differ, the fundamental principles of nature are the same.

We can surmise that when a complete geometric crystal is formed, water is in alignment with nature and the phenomenon we call life. The crystals do not form in water that has been polluted by the results of our failure to remember the laws of nature. When we tried taking photographs of crystals from Tokyo's tap water, the results were pitiful. This is because the water is sanitized with chlorine, thus damaging the innate ability of water to form crystals.

When water freezes, the particles of water link together to form the crystal nucleus, and when the nucleus grows in a stable way into a hexagonal shape, a visible water crystal appears.[214]

★★★

Learning about water is like an exploration to discover how the cosmos works, and the crystals revealed through water are like the portal into another dimension. . . . I particularly remember one photograph. It was the most beautiful and delicate crystal that I had so far seen—formed by being exposed to the words "love and gratitude." It was as if the water had rejoiced and celebrated by creating a flower in bloom. It was so beautiful that I can say that it actually changed my life from that moment on.

Water had taught me the delicacy of the human soul, and the impact that "love and gratitude" can have on the world.

In Japan, it is said that words of the soul reside in a spirit called *kotodama* or the spirit of words, and the act of speaking words has the power to change the world. We all know that words have an enormous influence on the way we think and feel, and that things generally go more smoothly when positive words are used. . . . Words are an expression of the soul. And the condition of our soul is likely to have an enormous impact on the water that composes as much as 70 per cent of our bodies. . . .

---

[214] Ibid., pp. 39-46, and the following section: Ibid., pp. xxv-xxvi.

Human vibrational energy, thoughts, words, ideas and music, affect the molecular structure of water, the very same water that comprises over seventy percent of a mature human body and covers the same amount of our planet. Water is the very source of all life on this planet; its quality and integrity are vitally important to all forms of life. The body is very much like a sponge and is composed of trillions of chambers called cells that hold liquid. The quality of our life is directly connected to the quality of our water. . . .

Water has a very important message for us. Water is telling us to take a much deeper look at our selves. When we do look at ourselves through the mirror of water, the message becomes amazingly, crystal, clear. We know that human life is directly connected to the quality of our water, both within and all around us.

~ Stacy Sharpe[215]

All the rivers run into the sea; yet the sea is not full;
unto the place from which the rivers come,
thence they return again.

~ The Bible, Ecclesiastes 1:7

And [remember] when Moses prayed for water for his people
and We replied, "Strike the rock with thy staff!"—
whereupon twelve springs gushed forth from it,
so that all the people knew whence to drink.
[And Moses said:] "Eat and drink the sustenance provided by God,
and do not act wickedly on earth by spreading corruption."
[Sūrah Al-Baqarah (The Cow) 2: 60]

---

[215] "How Water reflects Our Consciousness" by Stacy Sharpe, regarding *Miraculous Messages from Water*, quoted from www.wellnessgoods.com/messages.asp.

Sacred Springs

~ Juliette de Bairacli Levy[216]

Water is the true staff of life for the traveler, not bread. Man and animal can live a year and more without bread, but not many weeks without water. The human body is seventy-five percent water.

Travelers should be very concerned with the provision of clean sweet water, as many of the common ills of those who voyage far and long from home are caused by unclean water.

The nomad American Indians, the first true ecologists, blamed the decline of their people on the loss of their supplies of pure water: "The water of the Missouri River is not pure as it used to be, and many of the creeks are no longer good for us to drink" (Okute, an old Teton Sioux).

The Gypsies know and cherish every spring of water of every region they inhabit as nomads. The first thing I search for when I arrive in any new area are the springs. This world possesses a multitude of water springs, both sweet and mineral; it is worthwhile finding out their sites.

★★★

In hot climates, where cold drinks are so important for the well-being of the family (and where there is no electricity and therefore no refrigerator), much attention is given to the drinking water. Into the water jugs every morning are put sprigs of fragrant herbs such as sweet basil or mint or bee balm. Or crushed leaves from the lemon tree, or pieces of borage herb. Or slices of cucumber. These all give a cool taste to water.

In the Middle East there is a sweet-scented white blossom, which resembles white, satin-covered buttons. Three or four blossoms are used to scent a two-pint jar of water. It is called "Fil," and is often known as "the Water-Flower" because of its popular use in water jars.

In the summer heat of the Canary Islands, the country people know how to keep water, milk and fruits cool when no refrigeration is available. They use only clay or glass containers, never plastic. Wet cloths are

---

[216] Juliette de Bairacli Levy, *Traveler's Joy*, Woodstock, VT: Ash Tree Publishing, 1994. pp. 18-19 and 23-25.

draped over them to exclude all hot air. They stand on earth or stone; if on wood, it is kept damp. The earth conducts away the heat.

Other plant-life associated with water is the hazel or willow shrub or tree. A forked branch from either often gives water-divining powers to sensitive hands. With hazel or willow, travelers may be able to find water in arid regions. I know many of the world's wells which owe their existence to water-divining. These two shrub trees so love water that often they will tremble at its nearness in the ground over which they are being carried in a human hand, and then bend towards that element.

In deserts and other dry regions, rainwater is always looked upon as a blessing, and it should be collected and stored. Though it must be said of rain that it can only be used for drinking when it falls from skies where the air is not polluted. Because rain is a very pure and sensitive form of water, it also absorbs matter from the air through which it falls, and can soon become saturated with such impurities as chimney smoke and fumes from kerosene stoves, toxic exhausts from passing vehicles, and so on. Rain will also heavily absorb atomic fallout, and therefore after atomic bomb explosions by countries which possess such lethal and antihuman weapons, warnings often are given on radio programs that rainwater should not be used for drinking.

Water from the sky, in the form of hail or snow, can also be utilized as drink and food, provided, like the rainwater, it is from uncontaminated skies. A mixture of either can be made with added honey or sugar, and fruit juices. This is really a good food for children, much used by the Gypsies, but I like it! and so do other adult travelers.

★★★

Palestinian Shepherd's Prayer

Water! Rain! Streams!
O Lord, the streams!
For the watering of the fattening sheep,
O Lord, rain and clouds
For the watering of the cows and horses,
O Lord, a pouring
For the fulfillment of the wheat,
For the birth of the robust, golden, children.

O Lord, a deluge
For the refreshment of ourselves,
Body and soul.

When travelers have access to wells of sweet water, whether on one's own private property, or a rented place, or public wells, do not pollute such water, for it is mankind's heritage of life and health. Love the wells.[217]

A lake is the landscape's most beautiful and expressive feature. It is earth's eye; looking into which the beholder measures the depth of his own nature. The fluviatile trees next the shore are the slender eyelashes which fringe it, and the wooded hills and cliffs are its overhanging brows.

~ Henry David Thoreau, *Walden*

The Great Sea

~ Eskimo[218]

The great sea
Has sent me adrift,
It moves me as the weed in a great river,
Earth and the great weather
Move me,
Have carried me away
And move my inward parts with joy.

---

[217] Ibid., pp. 23-25.

[218] Excerpted from "Divine Beatitude: Supreme Archetype of Aesthetic Experience," *Seeing God Everywhere, Essays on Nature and the Sacred*. Edited by Barry McDonald, Copyright 2003 World Wisdom, Inc., p. 169.

An Expedition to the Pole

~ Annie Dillard[219]

I have put on silence and waiting. I have quit my ship and set out on foot over the polar ice. I carry chronometer and sextant, tent, stove and fuel, meat and fat. For water I melt the pack ice in hatchet-hacked chips; frozen salt water is fresh. I sleep when I can walk no longer. I walk on a compass bearing toward geographical north.

I walk on emptiness; I hear my breath. I see my hand and compass, see the ice so wide it arcs, see the planet's peak and curving and its low atmosphere held fast on the dive. The years are passing here. I am walking, light as any handful of aurora; I am light as sails, a pile of colorless stripes; I cry "heaven and earth indistinguishable!" and the current underfoot carries me and I walk.

The blizzard is like a curtain; I enter it. The blown snow heaps in my eyes. There is nothing to see or to know. I wait in the tent, myself adrift and emptied, for weeks while the storm unwinds. One day it is over, and I pick up my tent and walk. The storm has scoured the air; the clouds have lifted; the sun rolls round the sky like a fish in a round bowl, like a pebble rolled in a tub, like a swimmer, or a melody flung and repeating, repeating enormously overhead on all sides.

My name is Silence. Silence is my bivouac, and my supper sipped from bowls. I robe myself mornings in loose strings of stones. My eyes are stones; a chip from the pack ice fills my mouth. My skull is a polar basin; my brain pan grows glaciers, and grease ice, and floes. The years are passing here.

Far ahead is open water. I do not know what season it is, know how long I have walked into the silence like a tunnel widening before me, into the horizon's spread arms which widen like water. I walk to the pack ice edge, to the rim which calves its floes into the black and green water; I stand at the edge and look ahead.

---

[219] Excerpted from pp. 60-61 (359 words) from *Teaching a Stone to Talk: Expeditions and Encounters* by Annie Dillard. Copyright © 1982 by Annie Dillard. Reprinted by permission of HarperCollins Publishers.

That Day

~ Denise Levertov[220]

Across a lake in Switzerland, fifty years ago,
light was jousting with long lances, fencing with broadswords
back and forth among cloudy peaks and foothills.
We watched from a small pavilion, my mother and I,
enthralled.
            And then, behold, a shaft, a column,
a defined body, not of light but of silver rain,
formed and set out from the distant shore, leaving behind
the silent feints and thrusts, and advanced
unswervingly, at a steady pace,
toward us.
            I knew this! I'd seen it! Not the sensation
of deja vu: it was Blake's inkwash vision,
'The Spirit of God Moving Upon the Face of the Waters'!
The column steadily came on
across the lake toward us; on each side of it,
there was no rain. We rose to our feet, breathless—
and then it reached us, took us
into its veil of silver, wrapped us
in finest weave of wet,
and we laughed for joy, astonished.

---

[220] By Denise Levertov, from *This Great Unknowing: Last Poems*, p. 14. Copyright © 1998 by The Denise Levertov Literary Trust, Paul A. Lacey and Valerie Trueblood Rapport, Co-Trustees. Reprinted by permission of New Directions Publishing Corp.

THE COMMUNITIES

CREATURES OF THE AIR

CREATURES OF THE SEA

CREATURES OF THE LAND

THE HUMAN UMMAH

CHAPTER FOURTEEN

CREATURES OF THE AIR

*A*nd your Sustainer inspired the bee to build its cells
in hills, on trees, and in dwelling places,
then to eat of all that the earth produces
and to skillfully find the spacious paths of its Lord.
There issues from within their bodies a drink of varied hues
containing healing for human beings:
truly, in this is a sign for those who reflect.
[*Sūrah An-Naḥl* (The Bee) 16:68-69]

*H*ave, then, they never considered the birds,
enabled to fly in mid-air,
with none but God holding them aloft?
In this, behold, there are messages indeed for people who will have faith!
[*Sūrah An-Naḥl* (The Bee) 16:79]

*A*re you not aware that it is God whose limitless glory
all creatures in the heavens and on earth praise,
even the birds as they outspread their wings?
Indeed, each of them knows how to pray to Him and glorify Him;
and God has full knowledge of all that they do:
for God's is the sovereignty of the heavens and the earth,
and with God is all journeys' end.
[*Sūrah An--Nūr* (The Light) 24:41-42]

*A*nd the birds celebrate Our praises with David.
[*Sūrah Al-Anbiyā'* (The Prophets) 21:79]

Don't they observe the birds above them
spreading their wings and folding them in?
None can uphold them except the Most Gracious:
truly, it is He Who watches over all things.
No; who is there who can stand with you like an army
except the Most Merciful?
Those who deny the Truth are only deluding themselves.
Or who is there who can provide you with sustenance
if He were to withhold His provision?
[*Sūrah Al-Mulk* (Dominion) 67:19-21]

Doves of Peace

~ Camille Helminski

For many of the Prophets, doves have been companions of peace, harbingers of blessing and connection with the Divine Sustenance. It was a dove that brought the Prophet Noah the olive branch, a sign (*āyāh*) of fertile land and fresh hope at the ebbing of the great flood. The Prophet Solomon loved the doves that sang to him, reminding him of his Beloved.

O my dove, in the clefts of the rock,
in the secret places of the stairs, let me see thy countenance
let me hear your voice, for sweet is your voice,
and your countenance is comely.

[Song of Solomon 2:14]

Faridu'd-Din Attar sings to us of the dove's qualitites, comparing it to the Prophet Moses, in his *Conference of the Birds*:

Bravo, well-done O Dove of the quality of Moses!
Arise cooing away in knowledge of the Divine,
Turned for the soul's sake man recognitive of music:
The musical notes, the Creation's thanksgiving,
Like Moses seeing the fire from afar,
Inevitably, the Ring-Dove on the mountain of Sinai,

273

Be distant from the brutish Pharoah:
Come to the trysting place and be the bird of the Blessed Mountain.

★★★

Moses had the status, as one who had spoken with God Almighty and also conversed with the Prophet [Muhammad], of the Perfect Man endowed with Divine Perfection, so that . . . he might converse with God in the language of the heart and the soul. Birds of the dove family are noted for closeness to man and, especially the turtle-dove, for their being the emblem of "connubial attachment and constancy." Perhaps, however, as the bird of Mount Sinai, the poet had the rock-dove in mind; but the whole Colomban species is notable for gentle cooing and, of course, for "homing," hence the reminder . . . that the dove should "hasten home," i.e., to the appointed place. . . .

It should be observed that Pharoah stands for the concupiscent carnal spirit that constantly lies in wait to ambush travelers . . . and deprive them of the sight of the only Reality. The bird of Sinai, the Blessed Mountain, means the guide for the soul's ascent to the pinnacle where the wayfarer at last experiences the unveiling when the Truth is revealed to him.[221]

The first night of their hijra journey to Medina, the Prophet Muhammad ﷺ and Abū Bakr ؓ hid themselves in a cave on Mount Thawr on the outskirts of Mecca. Not long after their entry into the cave, suddenly a spider wove a large web across the opening and a dove nested in the ledge of rock beside the cave door. When the Meccans who were pursuing them approached the cave and witnessed the spider web and the nesting dove they assumed that such settled creatures could not have been disturbed by human beings in flight and so they left the cave and the Prophet sheltered under the protection of God's grace for the duration of their journey.

We journey, on and on in this journey of souls returning to their Creator.

---

[221] *The Speech of the Birds, Concerning Migration to the Real, Mantiqu't-Tair* by Faridu'd-Din Attar, presented in English by P.W. Avery, The Islamic Texts Society, Cambridge England, 1998, p. 59 and notes on pp. 464-465.

See *Sūrah An-Naml* (The Ants) 27:7-12.

Migrating Shorebirds

~ David Pitt-Brooke[222]

The front has passed during the night. A pale sun shows through flying cloud-wisps. Along the path, bushes are dripping and puddles have collected in the hollows among the roots. All is quiet, except for the songs of woodland birds.

Again, the tide is perfect, high and full. Water laps calmly on the shore. But nobody's here. The inlet seems vacant, empty, almost desolate.

I walk toward the spit. Nothing rises from the water's edge or from the grass. The rain has erased all tracks from the mud. Except for the odd feather or bit of down clinging to the wrack along the high-tide line there is no trace of the great flocks. They might almost have been, beginning and end, an illusion.

At the tip of the spit, I spot one solitary bird, a dowitcher. Perhaps there's something wrong with it; couldn't keep up and so was left behind. It flies off, calling, alone and forlorn.

I sit down and scan the inlet with binoculars. Far out across the water toward Browning Passage and Meares Island, a small flock of something semaphores its presence with a brief flash of white. The flock turns and vanishes into its surroundings. Otherwise the place is deserted.

I wait and watch until the tide starts to withdraw. The sun picks up strength. The air is warm. But nothing comes in. The birds are gone.

It's another instance of nature's flywheel moving relentlessly forward. Yesterday's flocks will be far to the north now. Some of the birds that were here two days ago may already have reached the Stikine River delta in Alaska. This is life in the fast lane. Shorebirds have long migrations and short breeding seasons. By mid-summer, less than two months from now, they'll be stopping here again, on their way back south. They haven't a moment to lose.

I understand that, but I miss them all the same. The sun is shining; there is promise of a beautiful day ahead. But life seems to have left this place. The excitement has gone elsewhere, following those birds. I

---

[222] Excerpted from *Chasing Clayoquot, A Wilderness Almanac* by David Pitt-Brooke, Raincoast Books, Vancouver, B.C., Canada, 2004, pp. 116-118.

imagine the flocks flying northward over a wild landscape of rugged mountains, dark forest, deep fjords. They are heading toward the danger and promise of an Arctic summer. I wish I could go. It's a bad case *of zugunruhe*, migration restlessness, cabin fever. I feel it every springtime and every autumn too.

Perhaps that's why shorebirds have such strong resonance, even for people with no particular interest in birds. They appeal to the nomad in all of us. They awaken some restless vestige of an earlier time—not all that long ago, in the great scheme of things—when human beings had not yet abandoned migration.

A Paradise of Birds

~ John Muir[223]

The Wisconsin oak openings were a summer paradise for song birds, and a fine place to get acquainted with them: for the trees stood wide apart, allowing one to see the happy homeseekers as they arrived in the spring, their mating, nest-building, the brooding and feeding of the young, and, after they were full-fledged and strong, to see all the families of the neighbourhood gathering and getting ready to leave in the autumn. Excepting the geese and ducks and pigeons, nearly all our summer birds arrived singly or in small draggled flocks, but when frost and falling leaves brought their winter homes to mind they assembled in large flocks on dead or leafless trees by the side of a meadow or field, perhaps to get acquainted and talk the thing over. Some species held regular daily meetings for several weeks before finally setting forth on their long southern journeys. Strange to say, we never saw them start. Some morning we would find them gone. Doubtless they migrated in the night time. Comparatively few species remained all winter: the nuthatch, chickadee,

---

[223] The following selection is excerpted from *The Eight Wilderness Discovery Books*, by *John Muir*, published jointly by The Mountaineers, Seattle, 1992, and Baton Wicks (UK), pp. 67-75.

owl, prairie chicken, quail and a few stragglers from the main flocks of ducks, jays, hawks and bluebirds. Only after the country was settled did either jays or bluebirds winter with us. The brave, frost-defying chickadees and nuthatches stayed all the year wholly independent of farms and man's food and affairs.

With the first hints of spring came the brave little bluebirds, darling singers as blue as the best sky, and of course we all loved them. Their rich, crispy warbling is perfectly delightful, soothing and cheering, sweet and whisperingly low, Nature's fine love touches, every note going straight home into one's heart. And withal they are hardy and brave, fearless fighters in defence of home. When we boys approached their knot-hole nests, the bold little fellows kept scolding and diving at us and tried to strike us in the face, and oftentimes we were afraid they would prick our eyes. But the boldness of the little housekeepers only made us love them the more.

None of the bird people of Wisconsin welcomed us more heartily than the common robin. Far from showing alarm at the coming of settlers into their native woods, they reared their young around our gardens as if they liked us, and how heartily we admired the beauty and fine manners of these graceful birds and their loud cheery song of Fear not, fear not, cheer up, cheer up. It was easy to love them for they reminded us of the robin redbreast of Scotland. Like the bluebirds they dared every danger in defence of home, and we often wondered that birds so gentle could be so bold and that sweet-voiced singers could so fiercely fight and scold. . . .

After the arrival of the thrushes came the bobolinks, gushing, gurgling, inexhaustible fountains of song, pouring forth floods of sweet notes over the broad Fox River meadows in wonderful variety and volume, crowded and mixed beyond description, as they hovered on quivering wings above their hidden nests in the grass. It seemed marvellous to us that birds so moderate in size could hold so much of this wonderful song stuff. Each one of them poured forth music enough for a whole flock, singing as if its whole body, feathers and all, were made up of music, flowing, glowing, bubbling melody interpenetrated here and there with small scintillating prickles and spicules. We never became so intimately acquainted with the bobolinks as with the thrushes, for they lived far out on the broad Fox River meadows, while the thrushes sang on the tree-tops around every home. The bobolinks were among the first of our great singers to leave us in the fall. . . .

But no singer of them all got further into our hearts than the little speckle-breasted song sparrow, one of the first to arrive and begin nest-building and singing. The richness, sweetness and pathos of this small darling's song as he sat on a low bush often brought tears to our eyes. . . .

The common grey goose, Canada honker, flying in regular harrow-shaped flocks, was one of the wildest and wariest of all the large birds that enlivened the spring and autumn. They seldom ventured to alight in our small lake, fearing, I suppose, that hunters might be concealed in the rushes, but on account of their fondness for the young leaves of winter wheat when they were a few inches high, they often alighted on our fields when passing on their way south, and occasionally even in our corn-fields when a snowstorm was blowing and they were hungry and wing-weary, with nearly an inch of snow on their backs. In such times of distress we used to pity them, even while trying to get a shot at them. They were exceedingly cautious and circumspect; usually flew several times round the adjacent thickets and fences to make sure that no enemy was near before settling down, and one always stood on guard, relieved from time to time, while the flock was feeding. Therefore there was no chance to creep up on them unobserved; you had to be well hidden before the flock arrived. . . .

It was a great memorable day when the first flock of passenger pigeons came to our farm, calling to mind the story we had read about them when we were at school in Scotland. Of all God's feathered people that sailed the Wisconsin sky, no other bird seemed to us so wonderful. The beautiful wanderers flew like the winds in flocks of millions from climate to climate in accord with the weather, finding their food—acorns, beechnuts, pine-nuts, cranberries, strawberries, huckleberries, juniper berries, hackberries, buckwheat, rice, wheat, oats, corn—in fields and forests thousands of miles apart. I have seen flocks streaming south in the autumn so large that they were flowing over from horizon to horizon in an almost continuous stream all day long, at the rate of forty or fifty miles an hour, like a mighty river in the sky, widening, contracting, descending like falls and cataracts, and rising suddenly here and there in huge ragged masses like high-plashing spray. How wonderful the distances they flew in a day—in a year—in a lifetime! They arrived in Wisconsin in the spring just after the sun had cleared away the snow, and alighted in the woods to feed on the fallen acorns that they had missed the previous autumn. A comparatively small flock swept thousands of acres perfectly clean of acorns in a few minutes, by moving straight ahead with a broad front. All got their share, for the rear constantly became the van by flying over the flock and alighting in front, the entire flock constantly changing from rear to front, revolving something like a wheel with a low buzzing wing roar that could be heard a long way off. In summer they feasted on wheat and oats and were easily approached as they rested on the trees along the sides of the field after a good full meal, displaying beautiful iridescent colours as they moved their necks backward and forward when we went very near them. Every shotgun was aimed at them and everybody feasted on pigeon pies, and not a few of the settlers feasted also on the beauty of the wonderful birds. The breast of the male is a fine rosy red, the lower part of the neck behind and along the sides changing from the red of the breast to gold, emerald green and rich crimson. The general colour of the upper parts is greyish blue, the under parts white. The extreme length of the bird is about seventeen inches; the finely modelled slender tail about eight inches, and extent of wings twenty-four inches. The females are scarcely less beautiful. "Oh, what bonnie, bonnie birds!" we exclaimed over the first that fell into our hands. "Oh, what colours! Look at their breasts, bonnie as roses." . . .

They seemed to require more than half of the continent for feeding-grounds, moving from one table to another, field to field, forest to forest, finding something ripe and wholesome all the year round. In going south in the fine Indian-summer weather they flew high and followed one another, though the head of the flock might be hundreds of miles in advance. But against head winds they took advantage of the inequalities of the ground, flying comparatively low. All followed the leader's ups and downs over hill and dale though far out of sight, never hesitating at any turn of the way, vertical or horizontal, that the leaders had taken, though the largest flocks stretched across several States, and belts of different kinds of weather.

There were no roosting or breeding-places near our farm, and I never saw any of them until long after the great flocks were exterminated.

I therefore quote, from Audubon's and Pokagon's vivid descriptions.

"Toward evening," Audubon says, "they depart for the roosting-place, which may be hundreds of miles distant. One on the banks of Green River, Kentucky, was over three miles wide and forty long.

"My first view of it," says the great naturalist, "was about a fortnight after it had been chosen by the birds, and I arrived there nearly two hours before sunset. Few pigeons were then to be seen, but a great many persons with horses and wagons and armed with guns, long poles, sulphur pots, pine pitch torches, etc., had already established encampments on the borders. Two farmers had driven upwards of three hundred hogs a distance of more than a hundred miles to be fattened on slaughtered pigeons. Here and there the people employed in plucking and salting what had already been secured were sitting in the midst of piles of birds. Dung several inches thick covered the ground. Many trees two feet in diameter were broken off at no great distance from the ground, and the branches of many of the tallest and largest had given way, as if the forest had been swept by a tornado.

"Not a pigeon had arrived at sundown. Suddenly a general cry arose—'Here they come!' The noise they made, though still distant, reminded me of a hard gale at sea passing through the rigging of a close-reefed ship. Thousands were soon knocked down by the pole-men. The birds continued to pour in. The fires were lighted and a magnificent as well as terrifying sight presented itself. The pigeons pouring in alighted everywhere, one above another, until solid masses were formed on the branches all around. Here and there the perches gave way with a crash, and falling destroyed hundreds beneath, forcing down the dense groups with which every stick was loaded; a scene of uproar and conflict. I found it useless to speak or even to shout to those persons nearest me. . . .

"Toward daylight the noise in some measure subsided; long before objects were distinguishable the pigeons began to move off in a direction quite different from that in which they had arrived the evening before, and at sunrise all that were able to fly had disappeared. The howling of the wolves now reached our ears, and the foxes, lynxes, cougars, bears, coons, opossums and polecats were seen sneaking off, while eagles and hawks of different species, accompanied by a crowd of vultures, came to supplant them and enjoy a share of the spoil.

"Then the authors of all this devastation began their entry amongst the dead, the dying and mangled. The pigeons were picked up and piled in heaps until each had as many as they could possibly dispose of, when the hogs were let loose to feed on the remainder.

"The breeding-places are selected with reference to abundance of food, and countless myriads resort to them. At this period the note of the pigeon is coo coo coo, like that of the domestic species but much shorter. They caress by billing, and during incubation the male supplies the female with food. As the young grow, the tyrant of creation appears to disturb the peaceful scene, armed with axes to chop down the squab-laden trees, and the abomination of desolation and destruction produced far surpasses even that of the roosting places."

Pokagon, an educated Indian writer, says: "I saw one nesting-place in Wisconsin one hundred miles long and from three to ten miles wide. Every tree, some of them quite low and scrubby, had from one to fifty nests on each. Some of the nests overflow from the oaks to the hemlock and pine woods. When the pigeon hunters attack the breeding-places they sometimes cut the timber from thousands of acres. Millions are caught in nets with salt or grain for bait, and schooners, sometimes loaded down with the birds, are taken to New York where they are sold for a cent apiece."

Note: Due to these practices, passenger pigeons are now extinct. (C.A.H.)

The Vulture and the Kite

~ Sa'di [224]

High in the clear air, two birds flew in the wind. One of the birds was a vulture. He hung in the air like a still, black flag.

The other bird was a kite. She soared and dipped and wheeled in the wind.

"What a marvelous day!" she cried. "Don't you think so, vulture, my friend?"

"Be still," snapped the vulture. "We superior birds prefer to hover in the air, not flutter about like moths. How else can you look at the land below?"

"But I can see what is below," answered the kite. "My eyes are as good as yours."

"That's nonsense!" sneered the vulture. "Tell me what you can see."

"I see the city," the kite said.

"I should hope so!" scoffed the vulture; "But I can see, lurking in the shadow of a house in one of the streets, a skinny dog. Can you?"

The kite tried to see it.

"Let's go closer," suggested the vulture. They flew down, wheeled and hovered, until the vulture hung still over a narrow street. There was the dog, its bright eyes looking up at them.

"You were right," said the kite.

"Of course I was."

The kite lifted away, soared high. The vulture, flapping slow black wings, followed.

"But if I look beyond the city," shrieked the kite, "I can see the distant hills, the streams, the trees, and a field where the grass moves like the sea."

"Ah yes," smiled the vulture, "but my keener sight can pick out—there!—a bright-eyed mouse. You don't believe me? Let me show you."

Again they swooped, and hung over the field. The mouse was still, terrified, but they detected it.

---

[224] Extracted from *The Discontented Dervishes* by Arthur Scholey, text © 2002, published by Watkins Publishing, London, pp. 139-142.

"I see it now."

"I should hope so," said the vulture. "We are almost on top of it!" He made as if to descend on it, but the kite screamed and flew upwards. The mouse scuttled. Annoyed, the vulture followed the kite.

"Beyond the fields," said the kite, "I can see a farm. And in the yard," she added quickly, "there is a small table. Can you see that, vulture?"

The vulture laughed in scorn. "Not only can I see the table, my half-blind friend, but I can see that on it there is a grain of wheat."

"I don't believe it."

The vulture sighed: "Come and see."

They flew over the farm, circled and sank down, hovering over the table.

"There now, what did I tell you?"

"You were right again," said the kite, "but now that we are closer, of course you can see that—"

"I can also show you," interrupted the vulture proudly, "that as well as having the best eyes of any bird, I can swoop and swirl like a kite, when the time comes. Watch me pluck up that grain of wheat."

The kite screamed in alarm, but the vulture swooped, landed on the table and caught up the grain of wheat. Suddenly—TWANG!—a wire writhed, tightened and caught hold.

"I'm caught, I'm caught!" screamed the vulture. "It was a trap!"

He tried to fly up, but the man laughed as he came out of the bush, pulling on the wire, pulling and catching hold, dodging the swirling of wings, twisting the legs expertly. The vulture suddenly found himself in a cage.

The kite fluttered helplessly above as the vulture was taken away.

"What is the use of having the keenest eyes of all the birds if you can't see a trap?" she thought sadly as she floated freely in the wind.

Freedom

~ Chuang-tzu[225]

In the Northern Deep there is a great fish, thousands of miles long. It turns into a giant bird whose back is thousands of miles in size. When it gets aroused and takes to flight, its wings are like clouds covering the sky.

When the ocean rolls, this bird sets off for the Southern Deep, which is the Pond of Heaven. A chronicler of unusual phenomena writes, "When the giant bird moves to the Southern Deep, it beats on the water for three thousand miles, whipping up a whirlwind and taking off on it, rising ninety thousand miles. It comes to rest six months after leaving."

Energy is movement, particulate matter, the breathing of living beings in concert: is the blue of the sky its real color, or is it so far-reaching as to be endless? This is how things seem to the vision of the giant bird when it looks down.

Now if water has not accumulated to sufficient depth, it does not have the power to carry a large boat. Pour a cup of water into a depression, and a mustard seed will be as a boat in it; but put the cup into the water, and it will stay put, because the water is too shallow for the size of the boat.

If the air layer is not thick enough, it does not have the power to support the wings of the giant bird; therefore the bird rises ninety thousand miles, so that the wind is below it. Then it rides on the wind, its back to the clear empyrean, with nothing to get in its way; now it makes for the south.

The locust and the pigeon ridicule the giant bird, saying, "We rise up quickly into flight and aim for the trees. At that, sometimes we don't make it and land on the ground. Why go ninety thousand miles up to head for the south?"

Those who go into the bush come back after three meals with their bellies still full. Those who are going a hundred miles need overnight provisions. Those who are traveling a thousand miles need three months'

---

[225] Excerpt from *The Essential Tao*, Translated and Presented by Thomas Cleary. Copyright ©1991 by Thomas Cleary. Reprinted by permission of HarperCollins Publishers, Inc., pp. 63-65.

supplies. So what do the locust and pigeon know? Small knowledge cannot reach great knowledge; those of little experience cannot comprehend those of great experience.

How do we know this is so? Morning mushrooms do not know the passing of days and nights, mayflies do not know the passing of spring and autumn. This is because they are short-lived.

In the south of Ch'u there is a tree for which spring was five hundred years and autumn five hundred years. In ancient times there was a great tree for which spring was eight thousand years and autumn was eight thousand years. And yet Grandfather P'eng [who is said to have lived for eight hundred years] is now noted for longevity. Are not ordinary people pitiful by comparison?

North of the desert there is a deep ocean, the Pond of Heaven. There is a fish in it that is thousands of miles wide and who knows how long. There is a bird there whose back is like an enormous mountain and whose wings are like clouds covering the sky. It grabs onto a whirlwind and rises ninety thousand miles, beyond the clouds, its back to the blue sky, and then makes for the south, going to the Southern Deep. Marsh quail ridicule it, saying, "Where is it going? We leap up no more than a few yards and fly around the reeds. This is as far as flight reaches; so where is that giant bird going?" This is the distinction between the small and the great.

So those whose knowledge is effective enough for one office, those whose conduct is compatible with one locality, those whose virtue is suitable for one ruler, and those who are sought for employment by one country look upon themselves in the same way as the marsh quail.

Thus the philosopher Jung of Sung laughed at them in derision; he was not encouraged even when everyone praised him, and he was not discouraged even when everyone denounced him. His determination of the division between inside and outside, his discernment of the boundary between glory and disgrace, only went this far. He was not occupied with the world, but even though he was thus, still he was not constructive.

Master Lieh rode on the wind, with serene expertise, returning after fifteen days. He was unconcerned with the acquisition of wealth, but though he avoided the need to walk, he still depended on something. If one can ride on the reality of heaven and earth, harnessing the expression of the six energies to travel through infinity, then what would one depend on?

> Therefore complete people have no self,
> spiritual people have no merit, saintly people have no name.

When the ancient king Yao wanted to abdicate in favor of Hsu Yu, he said, "Why keep a torch burning when the sun and moon are out? Why go on irrigating when the seasonal rains are falling? If you were established, the world would be orderly; and yet I am still in charge of it. I see myself lacking, and ask you to run the country."

Hsu Yu said, "You are governing the country, and the country is already orderly. If I were to take over for you, would I be doing it for the name? Names are guests of realities; should I be a guest? A wild bird nesting in the deep forest needs no more than a single branch; a wild animal drinking from a river takes no more than its fill. Go home. Majesty! I have no use for the country. Even if the cook is not managing the kitchen, a priest does not step over the sacrificial offerings to take over for him."

The Bee

~ Dr. Javad Nurbakhsh

The believer is like the bee, which consumes only what is pure and produces only what is pure.   ~ Prophet Muhammad ﷺ

Jami elaborates on this *hadith*: "The Prophet of God, that paragon of wisdom, declared that the highest of the faithful are like the honeybee in their righteousness. When the bee flies into the garden, it feeds on only the purest of substances. Likewise, the pious believers choose only the purest of sustenance in the world. They overlook faults and contemplate the art in things, partaking only of scented roses and sweet basil. As honey is emitted from the bee, only the nectar of praise pours forth from the tongues of the faithful."[226]

---

[226] Dr. Javad Nurbakhsh, *Traditions of the Prophet, Volume 2*, p. 69.

The bee is more expert in building than any craftsman among you humans. She builds her home from half-circles and makes her rooms with six equal sides; moreover, she does all this without tools—unlike you humans. The silkworm quickly spins a shelter for itself without study and without tools for building, weaving, or sewing. The spider weaves a web more expertly than any human weaver, tightening each thread as if it were a string of a violin or tent.

~ Ihkwan as-Safa' [227]

Writing the Sacred Into the Real
~ Alison Hawthorne Deming[228]

With the book I'd just finished, *The Edges of the Civilized World*, the question announced itself early in the writing, even though the answer can only be a process of unfolding: Can we restore faith in civilization as an expression of radical hope in the best of the collective human enterprise on Earth—those acts and accomplishments that honor beauty, wisdom, understanding, justice, inventiveness, love, and moral connection with others? In Hawai'i the question that began to form is this: How can I authentically speak about my experience of the sacred in nature when I do not feel connected spiritually or intellectually with a tradition, such as that of native Hawaiians, that grounds its beliefs in nature? . . .

★★★

Chuck [Burrows, a revered biology teacher and leader of the *Hui Lama* (hiking club)] convened the group into a circle where we stood and we introduced ourselves one at a time. The students said where they lived

[227] Excerpted from *The Animal's Lawsuit Against Humanity, A Modern Adaptation of an Ancient Animal Rights Tale*, Translated by Rabbi Anson Laytner and Rabbi Dan Bridge, Fons Vitae, Louisville, KY, 2005, p. 57.
[228] Alison Hawthorne Deming, *Writing the Sacred Into the Real*, edited by Scott Slovic. (Minneapolis: Milkweed Editions, 2001). Copyright © 2001 by Alison Hawthorne Deming. Reprinted with permission from Milkweed Editions, pp. 75, 81-83, 85-86, 87-91.

and what grade they were in. Steve [Montgomery, the visiting naturalist, who had invited me along] said, "I'm in grade fifty-one," and everyone laughed. Chuck asked Keawe to tell the special reason why he had joined us for the day. Then Chuck said we should listen to the sounds of the birds and winds when we entered the forest, and we would be with our ancestors. He asked Keawe to give us a chant, and the visceral music of it bound us. He asked him to tell us what it meant. Keawe said that he had asked permission for us to go into the forest and for us to go safely.

Steve led us on the way up the Poamoho Trail, and we followed in single file into the woods, stopping to learn things he knew along the way. Prehistoric banana tree. *Pinao,* the largest dragonfly in America (though I wondered later had I confused this in my notes with *Pinao ula,* the endemic red damsel-fly?). *Home* (welcome), orange berries, *Loulu,* the fan palm, the only palm native to Hawai'i. He pointed across the steep valley to the opposite ridge—the royal palm, which has no dispersal agent here so had to be planted, a native of the Florida Everglades. Then Steve ran on ahead, slipping and sliding in the mud, eager to get to the next fascination. He wore Japanese reef slippers—better than sneakers or hiking boots, he said, on rain-slicked jungle trails—and green combat pants with big pockets. The trail rose into the green folding cliffs, ridges bending and rippling into one another, rising to one side of us and falling to the other, and we hiked along the edges or over the tops of the cliffs, everything softened with lush foliage so that it was easy to forget the height and steepness always at our sides. When we approached a fallen rotting tree downslope of the trail, Steve stumbled willingly down through the scrub into the composting mulch. We learned that this was the characteristic behavior of the creature, the denser the scrub the more likely he'd slither and clamber and tuck his way into it, disappearing for pregnant minutes, then reemerging with a grin and a clear plastic pill bottle boasting his find. This time it was a tiny spider carrying a pearly white egg case on her back. He handed me the vial.

"You want to carry this for me?" And I nestled the treasure in my pack.

Back on the trail, he led us on. There were ferns clustered in the crotch of a tree—their name meaning "Woman who sits on the mountain." There was *aha kea,* in the coffee family, its yellowish wood the traditional material for the gunwales of canoes. When a boat builder uses another wood, he paints the gunwales yellow. There was *Clidemia* and more *Clidemia* (Koster's curse), the South American weed that wages chemical warfare with other plants by stopping them from germinating. In some places there was nothing else growing, though insects had been brought in to control it. In others, strawberry guava from Brazil spilled its fruit all over the trail. The Chinese leafhopper sucked sap from one hundred different kinds of plants, its saliva toxic to many of them. Researchers were looking for a wasp to attack the invader and restore the balance. There was the *olapa* tree (Chuck looked over my shoulder to help with the spelling of Hawaiian words); and the *akia* plant producing a neurotoxin used for catching fish, the weed thrown into a tidepool and fish gathered up with a scoop net; and *uluhe* ferns, spreading over the island for the past two and a half million years and covering the steep cliffsides, the first plant to grow after a landslide and called with affection the "forest Band-Aid."

The higher in altitude we climbed, the more dispersed became our group and the thinner the vegetation. The square-stemmed mintless mint and New Zealand tea and *uki* grass. The higher we got, the wetter and stonier the trail became.[229]

★★★

[Debbie] was quiet, staring at the knee of her wet jeans where a dopey bee staggered along. She set her palm beside it like a little boat, and the bee walked on board. She held it close to her face and admired it, then showed it closely to me.

"It doesn't belong up here," she said. "It's way too cold. I wish I had some way to take it down with us."

I remembered the plastic eyeglass case in my backpack and pulled it out. We popped the bee inside, and I tucked the case into my pack.

Debbie and I made the descent together, the others dispersed ahead or behind, and occasionally we'd intersect with some of them but seemed to keep ending up alone. We talked about work and marriage and mothering—our disappointments and our hopes. We helped each other

---

[229] Ibid., pp. 81-83.

over the gullies and savored guavas when our water ran out. Our legs were sore, muscles wasted and tense, our clothes and hair soaked; one or the other of us kept slipping and falling on slick mud or stone, and there was ridiculous joy in being so dirty and sweaty and exhausted together as we hiked farther from the stormy summit and deeper into sun-mottled forest. I might have preferred to hear more of the wind and birdsong in those last miles of wilderness, but our talking went on, and I gave myself to it.

We were within a quarter mile of the trailhead when she fell, though we didn't know where we were at the time. For miles we'd been encouraging each other, "We're almost there now." We were long past the most perilous passages of the trail—here was level ground, an easy curve, a wide pathway. A relaxed weedy cliff rose to our right, and to our left a steep fern-covered cliff descended out of sight. One minute she was walking a few feet ahead of me, and the next she was falling head first over the edge.[230]

★★★

I leaned over the edge to hear her whispering Hail Mary's between hyperventilating gasps. Below her the cliff fell another fifty feet or so, then met a seam where another cliff joined it, and the crease between the two ferny basaltic walls fell far below toward the tiny stream that laced through the distant valley floor.

"We'll get you up, don't worry," I said. "Try to breathe slowly. Try to hold on." And I looked around me for anything that would tell me what to do. And when I looked, I found a tree limb that had fallen in the trail, and I thought I could reach her with it, knowing she could not hold on long to wet rock and ferns. I lowered the limb to her.

"Brace as much of your weight as you can against the rock," I said, thinking, How can I hold her? What if I feel myself starting to fall? I kneeled on the trail, braced a knee against the slight mound of a protruding rock—surely not enough resistance to hold me, but it did, as I centered my body's gravity over the earth rather than the chasm.

For how long did we struggle there, reaching and grasping and

---

[230] Ibid., pp. 85-86.

praying and calling for help? Maybe twenty minutes. Maybe thirty. Maybe forever. I was fearless and I have no idea why. I thought calmly—after she'd said, I can't hold on anymore, after I'd felt the weight of her pulling me closer to falling, after I'd said, I'm not going to leave you, after we'd gotten her close enough to let the limb fall and grip each other's wrists, after we'd each said, Wait, I don't think I can hold on anymore, after we'd both called out, Dear Jesus help us—I thought calmly, What will I do if I feel myself going over? Will I let her go? And I thought calmly, Yes, I will let her go.

What horrifies me is the calmness with which I decided to let her life go out of my hands if saving her meant giving my own. But that was only thinking. I did not let her go. I was stronger than it was possible for me to be, and so was she. The thought of making the other choice gave me strength I did not know I had. At the last moment of our strength, her elbows now braced over the lip of the cliff, one of the ROTC boys came running, finally hearing our cries. He bristled with energy, leaned over the edge, grabbed her by the belt and heaved her body up onto the ground. She wept there for a while, lying on her stomach. I stroked her back, and then we walked down to the trailhead.

The others who had preceded us were standing around eating snacks and drinking sodas, wiping mud off their boots and putting on dry T-shirts, if they had them. Debbie tried to tell them what had happened, but no one seemed sufficiently impressed for her to feel they understood. . . .

But one of the Hawaiian kids heard her, a quiet boy who stood with us to listen and talk.

"Were there any animals around when this happened?" he asked.

"No, I don't think so," I said. Then I remembered the bee I still carried in my eyeglass case. Debbie and I stared at each other, as if we'd seen something invisible. She leaned over and pulled her jeans up over her calf to reveal her bee tattoo.

"Bees have always been very special to me," she said.

"That's amazing," I said, though I wasn't sure what I meant.

"Not really," the kid said. "That kind of thing happens all the time."

I knew then he was thinking that the bee was her 'aumakua—a fact as apparent to him as life-saving endorphins had been to me and the Holy Mother of Jesus had been to Debbie. Maybe it was not our belief that an animal or bug could give a person special protection, but it seemed as plausible as anything we could imagine. Maybe we didn't really believe that, but the bee was so integral a part to the pattern that was the day, we could not dismiss it, any more than we could dismiss the tree limb or the grip of our own hands. Meaning, like the sacred, is present if you look for it, but absent if you do not.

I dug the eyeglass case from my backpack and released the sleepy passenger. It wasn't until the next day when I woke up with my back and arms aching that I remembered the spider carrying her egg case, which I also had brought down from the mountain. I called Steve and asked him what to do with her, and he told me where to find the research lab on campus. I went there and handed the pill bottle over to a woman in a lab coat.

"I'm sorry it took so long for me to get her here. I hope she's okay," I said.

"Oh, she looks just fine," said the woman admiringly, and I handed over my charge.

I went to the library to research Hawaiian legends, to see if historical texture would add anything to my understanding of the remarkable events on Poamoho. I read some ancient stories, complex genealogies, and myths. But they did not help, because as rich as they were, they were not my story.

I'd been looking for a way to talk about the sacred that was authentically mine. What had I learned on that day? What was the ground note of its music? Bugs, I thought. Steve's more-than-twenty discoveries and my one apprenticeship to monarchs that had brought us together, the insects collaborating with scientists to restore balance within a besieged botanical system, Debbie's real and tattooed bees, and the spider carrying her egg case into the lab—all parts of the pattern that was the day, parts of the whole that is not perceivable because, as John Steinbeck wrote, "the pattern goes everywhere and is everything and cannot be encompassed by finite mind or by anything short of life—which it is." Bugs, I thought, on whose backs the world rides, unlike human beings who ride so heavily on Earth's back. Bugs, the smallest perceivable part of the biological whole. The world would be fine if people became extinct, but without bugs, the basic work they do of pollination, decomposition, stirring up the soil, and cleaning up everyone's mess with their fastidious appetites, Earth would become a barren dirty rock.

In my story I may not know how to define the sacred, but I have felt its presence in nature and in the coming-into-form that is language and art. I have felt it in the space inside the body and in the space between the stars. What holds the Creation together? Not emptiness. Without the health of the smallest among us, we could not exist.[231]

---

[231] Ibid., pp. 87-91.

CHAPTER FIFTEEN

CREATURES OF THE SEA

And the things on this earth
which He has multiplied in varying hues:
truly, in this is a sign
for those who celebrate the praises of God.
It is He Who has made the sea in service
that you may eat from it flesh that is fresh and tender
and that you may extract from it ornaments to wear;
and you see the ships that break across its waves
that you may seek of the bounty of God
and that you may be grateful.
[Sūrah An-Naḥl (The Bee) 16:13-14]

He is the Instructor of the two places of sunrise,
and the Instructor of the two places of sunset.
Then which of your Sustainer's blessings will you deny?
He has given freedom to the two great bodies of water
so that they might meet:
yet between them is a threshold which they cannot cross.
Then which of your Sustainer's blessings will you deny?
Out of these come pearls and coral.
Then which of your Sustainer's blessings will you deny?
And His are the ships sailing smoothly, lofty as mountains,
through the seas.
Then which of your Sustainer's blessings will you deny?
All that is on earth will perish;
but forever will abide the Face of your Sustainer,
Full of Majesty and Abundant Honor.
Then which of your Sustainer's blessings will you deny?
Every creature in the heavens and on earth depends on Him:
every day He manifests in wondrous new ways!
Then which of your Sustainer's blessings will you deny?
[Sūrah Ar-Raḥmān (The Most Gracious) 55:17-30]

It is God Who has made the sea in service to you
that ships may sail through it by His command
that you may seek His abundance and that you may be grateful.
And He has made in service to you as a gift from Him
all that is in the heavens and on earth:
witness, truly, in that are signs for those who reflect.
Tell those who have faith to forgive
those who do not consider the coming of the Days of God:
it is for Him to recompense each People
according to what they have earned.
If anyone does a righteous deed it is to his own benefit;
if he does harm it works against his own soul.
In the end you will all be brought back to your Sustainer.
[*Sūrah Al-Jāthiyah* (Kneeling Down) 45:12-15]

Mysteries of the Pacific

~ Thor Hyerdahl[232]

The sea contains many surprises for him who has his floor on a level with the surface and drifts along slowly and noiselessly. A sportsman who breaks his way through the woods may come back and say that no wild life is to be seen. Another may sit down on a stump and wait, and often rustlings and cracklings will begin and curious eyes peer out. So it is on the sea, too. We usually plow across it with roaring engines and piston strokes, with the water foaming round our bow. Then we come back and say that there is nothing to see far out on the ocean.

Not a day passed but we, as we sat floating on the surface of the sea, were visited by inquisitive guests which wriggled and waggled about us, and a few of them, such as dolphins and pilot fish, grew so familiar that they accompanied the raft across the sea and kept round us day and night.

---

[232] The following selection was excerpted from *Kon-Tiki, Across the Pacific by Raft* by Thor Heyerdahl, Translated by F. H. Lyon. Rand McNally & Co. Chicago, NY, and SF, pp. 117-121.

When night had fallen and the stars were twinkling in the dark tropical sky, a phosphorescence flashed around us in rivalry with the stars, and single glowing plankton resembled round live coals so vividly that we involuntarily drew in our bare legs when the glowing pellets were washed up round our feet at the raft's stern. When we caught them, we saw that they were little brightly shining species of shrimp. On such nights we were sometimes scared when two round shining eyes suddenly rose out of the sea right alongside the raft and glared at us with an unblinking hypnotic stare. The visitors were often big squids which came up and floated on the surface with their devilish green eyes shining in the dark like phosphorus. But sometimes the shining eyes were those of deep-water fish which came up only at night and lay staring, fascinated by the glimmer of light before them. Several times, when the sea was calm, the black water round the raft was suddenly full of round heads two or three feet in diameter, lying motionless and staring at us with great glowing eyes. On other nights balls of light three feet and more in diameter would be visible down in the water, flashing at irregular intervals like electric lights turned on for a moment.

We gradually grew accustomed to having these subterranean or submarine creatures under the floor, but nevertheless we were just as surprised every time a new species appeared. About two o'clock on a cloudy night, when the man at the helm had difficulty in distinguishing black water from black sky, he caught sight of a faint illumination down in the water which slowly took the shape of a large animal. It was impossible to say whether it was plankton shining on its body, or whether the animal itself had a phosphorescent surface, but the glimmer down in the black water gave the ghostly creature obscure, wavering outlines. Sometimes it was roundish, sometimes oval, or triangular, and suddenly it split into two parts which swam to and fro under the raft independently of each other. Finally there were three of these large shining phantoms wandering round in slow circles under us.

They were real monsters, for the visible parts alone were some five fathoms long, and we all quickly collected on deck and followed the ghost dance. It went on for hour after hour, following the course of the raft. Mysterious and noiseless, our shining companions kept a good way beneath the surface, mostly on the starboard side where the light was, but often they were right under the raft or appeared on the port side. The glimmer of light on their backs revealed that the beasts were bigger than elephants but they were not whales, for they never came up to breathe. Were they giant ray fish which changed shape when they turned over on their sides? They took no notice at all if we held the light right down on the surface to lure them up, so that we might see what kind of creatures they were. And, like all proper goblins and ghosts, they had sunk into the depths when the dawn began to break.

We never got a proper explanation of this nocturnal visit from the three shining monsters, unless the solution was afforded by another visit we received a day and a half later in the full midday sunshine. . . . I was having a refreshing plunge overboard at the bow, lying in the water but keeping a good lookout and hanging on to a rope end, when I caught sight of a thick brown fish, six feet long, which came swimming inquisitively toward me through the crystal-clear sea water. I hopped quickly up on to the edge of the raft and sat in the hot sun looking at the fish as it passed quietly, when I heard a wild war whoop from Knut, who was sitting aft behind the bamboo cabin. He bellowed "Shark!" till his voice cracked in a falsetto, and, as we had sharks swimming alongside the raft almost daily without creating such excitement, we all realized that this must be something extra-special and flocked astern to Knut's assistance.

Knut had been squatting there, washing his pants in the swell, and when he looked up for a moment he was staring straight into the biggest and ugliest face any of us had ever seen in the whole of our lives. It was the head of a veritable sea monster, so huge and so hideous that, if the Old Man of the Sea himself had come up, he could not have made such an impression on us. The head was broad and flat like a frog's, with two small eyes right at the sides, and a toadlike jaw which was four or five feet wide and had long fringes drooping from the corners of the mouth. Behind the head was an enormous body ending in a long thin tail with a pointed tail fin which stood straight up and showed that this sea monster was not any kind of whale. The body looked brownish under the water, but both head and body were thickly covered with small white spots.

The monster came quietly, lazily swimming after us from astern. It grinned like a bulldog and lashed gently with its tail. The large round dorsal fin projected clear of the water and sometimes the tail fin as well, and, when the creature was in the trough of the swell, the water flowed about the broad back as though washing round a submerged reef. In front of the broad jaws swam a whole crowd of zebra-striped pilot fish in fan formation, and large remora fish and other parasites sat firmly attached to the huge body and traveled with it through the water, so that the whole thing looked like a curious zoological collection crowded round something that resembled a floating deep-water reef. . . .

The monster was a whale shark, the largest shark and the largest fish known in the world today. It is exceedingly rare, but scattered specimens are observed here and there in the tropical oceans. The whale shark has an average length of fifty feet, and according to zoologists it weighs fifteen tons. It is said that large specimens can attain a length of sixty feet; one harpooned baby had a liver weighing six hundred pounds and a collection of three thousand teeth in each of its broad jaws.

Jonah and the Great Fish

~ Muhammad Asad

And, behold, Jonah was indeed one of Our message-bearers
when he fled like a runaway slave onto a laden ship.
And then they cast lots, and he was the one who lost;
[and they cast him into the sea,] whereupon the great fish swallowed him,
for he had been blameworthy. And had he not been of those who
[even in the deep darkness of their distress are able to] extol God's limitless glory,
he would indeed have remained in its belly
till the Day when all shall be raised from the dead:
but We caused him to be cast forth on a desert shore,
sick [at heart] as he was,
and caused a creeping plant to grow over him [out of the barren soil].
And [then] We sent him [once again] to [his people,]
a hundred thousand [souls] or more:
and [this time] they believed [in him]—

and so We allowed them to enjoy their life
during the time allotted to them.[233]
[*Sūrah As-Saffāt* (Those Ranged In Ranks) 37:139-147]

The story of Jonah's "great fish" is explicitly mentioned in the Qur'ān in three places: 68:48, 21:87-89, and 10:98, [in addition to this mention of the story in 37:139-147]. The legend of Jonah was and is so widely known that every reference to the allegory of "the great fish" is presumed to be self-explanatory. According to the Biblical account (which more or less agrees with the Qur'anic references to his story), Jonah was a prophet sent to the people of Nineveh, the capital of Assyria. At first his preaching was disregarded by his people, and he left them in anger. He abandoned the mission with which he had been entrusted by God (see *sūrah* 21, which gives the first part of Jonah's story), and thus, in the words of the Bible (The Book of Jonah, 1:3 and 10), committed the sin of "fleeing from the presence of the Lord." In its primary significance, the infinitive noun *ibāq* (derived from the verb *abaqa*) denotes "a slave's running-away from his master"; and Jonah is spoken of as having "fled like a runaway slave" because—although he was God's message-bearer—he abandoned his task under the stress of violent anger. The subsequent mention of "the laden ship" alludes to the central, allegorical part of Jonah's story. The ship ran into a storm and was about to founder; and the mariners "said everyone to his fellow, 'Come and let us cast lots, that we may know for whose cause this evil is upon us'." (The Book of Jonah 1:7)—a procedure to which Jonah agreed. "He cast lots [with the mariners], and was among the losers." According to the Biblical account (The Book of Jonah 1:10-15), Jonah told them that he had "fled from the presence of the Lord," and that it was because of this sin of his that they all were now in danger of drowning. "And he said unto them, 'Take me up, and cast me forth into the sea; so shall the sea be calm unto you: for I know that for my sake this tempest is upon you. . . .' So they took up Jonah, and cast him forth into the sea: and the sea ceased from her raging."

The inside of the fish that "swallowed" Jonah apparently symbolizes the deep darkness of spiritual distress of which *Sūrah Al-Anbiyā'* (The Prophets) 21:87 speaks. . . . Parenthetically, the story is meant to show

---

[233] Lit., "for a time": i.e., for the duration of their natural lives (Rāzī; also *Manār* XI, 483). ~ M.Asad

that, since *"man has been created weak"* [*Sūrah An-Nisā'* (Women) 4:28], even prophets are not immune against all the failings inherent in human nature. [Yet Jonah was able to remember his Sustainer and to repent of his behavior; this repentance carried him out of the darkness of the belly of the fish safely to the shore where God provided green plants] to shade and comfort him. Thus, rounding off the allegory of Jonah and the fish, the Qur'ān points out in the figurative manner so characteristic of its style that God, who can cause a plant to grow out of the most arid and barren soil, can equally well cause a heart lost in darkness to come back to light and spiritual life.

> *O humankind! there has come to you an admonition from your Sustainer*
> *and a healing for your hearts*
> *and for those who have faith, guidance and grace.*
> *Say: "In the abundance of God and in His grace,*
> *in that let them rejoice. . . ."*
> [*Sūrah Yūnus* (Jonah) 10:57-58]

Regenerating the Heart

~ Sarah Simpson[234]

Scarring prevents human hearts from repairing themselves, but a common aquarium dweller now appears to hold a secret remedy. Howard Hughes Medical Institute investigators Kenneth D. Poss, Lindsay G. Wilson and Mark T. Keating found that the zebrafish can naturally regenerate its own heart. Two months after the surgical removal of 20 percent of the hearts of adult fish, the vital organs had recovered their natural size and were beating properly. Under a microscope, the researchers could see that scar tissue clotted the wound initially, but proliferating muscle cells soon took over the healing process. Future exploration of the fish's regeneration-promoting genes—many of which are shared by humans—could lead to strategies for the scar-free repair of human hearts.

---

[234] The following selection was excerpted from "Regenerating the Heart," by Sarah Simpson. (The work appears in the December 13, 2002, *Science*.) Reprinted here from *The Scientific American*, February 2003, p. 24.

Where the Two Seas Meet

~ Muhammad Asad

*S*ūrah al-Kahf introduces an allegory meant to illustrate the fact that knowledge, and particularly spiritual knowledge, is inexhaustible, so that no human being—not even a prophet—can ever claim to possess answers to all the questions that perplex man throughout his life. . . .

The subsequent parable of Moses and his quest for knowledge (*Sūrah* 18: verses 60-82) has become, in the course of time, the nucleus of innumerable legends. . . . [There is] a Tradition on the authority of Ubayy ibn Ka'b (recorded in several versions by Bukhārī, Muslim, and Tirmidhī), according to which Moses was rebuked by God for having once asserted that he was the wisest of all men, and was subsequently told through revelation that a "servant of God" who lived at the "junction of the two seas" was far superior to him in wisdom. When Moses expressed his eagerness to find that man, God commanded him to "take a fish in a basket" and to go on and on until the fish would disappear: and its disappearance was to be a sign that the goal had been reached. There is no doubt that this Tradition is a kind of allegorical introduction to our Qur'anic parable. The "fish" mentioned in the latter as well as in the above-mentioned *ḥadīth* is an ancient religious symbol, possibly signifying divine knowledge or life eternal. As for the "junction of the two seas," which many of the early commentators endeavoured to "identify" in geographical terms (ranging from the meeting of the Red Sea and the Indian Ocean at the Bāb al-Mandab to that of the Mediterranean Sea and the Atlantic Ocean at the Straits of Gibraltar), Baydāwī offers, in his commentary on verse 60, a purely allegorical explanation: the "two seas" represent the two sources or streams of knowledge—the one obtainable through the observation and intellectual coordination of outward phenomena ('ilm aẓ-ẓāhir), and the other through intuitive, mystic insight ('ilm al-bāṭin)—the meeting of which is the real goal of Moses' quest.

> *And Lo! [In the course of his wanderings,] Moses said to his servant:*
> *"I shall not give up until I reach the junction of the two seas,*
> *even if I [have to] spend untold years [in my quest]!"*
> *But when they reached the junction between the two [seas],*
> *they forgot all about their fish,*

and it took its way into the sea and disappeared from sight.[235]
And after the two had walked some distance,
[Moses] said to his servant: "Bring us our mid-day meal;
we have indeed suffered hardship on this our journey!"
Said [the servant]: "Did you see?
When we betook ourselves to that rock for a rest, behold,
I forgot about the fish—and none but Satan made me thus forget it!
and it took its way into the sea! How strange!"
[Moses] exclaimed: "That [was the place] which we were seeking!"
And the two turned back, retracing their footsteps,
and found one of Our servants,
on whom We had bestowed grace from Ourselves
and unto whom We had imparted knowledge from Ourselves.
Moses said unto him: "May I follow you
on the understanding that you will impart to me
something of that consciousness of what is right
which has been imparted to you?"
[The other] answered: "Behold, you will never be able to have patience
with me—for how could you be patient
about something that you cannot comprehend
within the compass of [your] experience?"
Replied [Moses]: "You will find me patient, if God so wills. . . .
[Sūrah Al-Kahf, 18:60-69]

In the Tradition on the authority of Ubayy ibn Ka°b this mysterious sage
is spoken of as *Al-Khaḍir* or *Al-Khiḍr*, meaning "the Green One."
Apparently this is an epithet rather than a name, implying (according to
popular legend) that his wisdom was ever-fresh ("green") and
imperishable: a notion which bears out the assumption that we have here
an allegoric figure symbolizing the utmost depth of mystic insight
accessible to man.

[When he answers, " . . . how could you be patient about
something] that you do not encompass with [your] experience (*khubran*)":
according to Rāzī, [this is an allusion] to the fact that even a prophet like

---

[235] Their forgetting the symbolic "fish" is perhaps an allusion to man's frequently
forgetting that God is the ultimate source of all knowledge and life. ~ M. Asad

Moses did not fully comprehend the inner reality of things (*ḥaqā'iq al-ashyā' kamā hiya*); and, more generally, to man's lack of equanimity whenever he is faced with something that he has never yet experienced or cannot immediately comprehend. In the last analysis, the above verse implies—as is brought out fully in Moses' subsequent experiences—that appearance and reality do not always coincide; beyond that, it touches in a subtle manner upon the profound truth that man cannot really comprehend or even visualize anything that has no counterpart—at least in its component elements—in his own intellectual experience: and this is the reason for the Qur'anic use of metaphor and allegory with regard to "all that is beyond the reach of a created being's perception" (*al-ghayb*).

Raja Ampat
Recognizing the Treasures of the Sea
~ Djuna Ivereigh[236]

To protect Raja Ampat, scientists needed to first look more deeply to assess the islands' richness and rarity. That meant counting, cataloging and collecting. In 23 days the crew of fish and coral experts, botanists and socioeconomists circled 700 nautical miles, broke world-record species counts, interviewed local people, and felt, for the most part, that they'd barely scratched the surface. So it is with Rapid Ecological Assessment. It's like a mad dash at a salad bar with a woefully tiny plate.

Conservation scientists know they can't save everything. At the same time, they know that extinction rates are rising. So the scientists must home in on places suspected to be Earth's most bounteous and quickly take stock. Previous research trips to Raja Ampat had suggested that it was such a place. This trip was aimed at precisely determining Raja Ampat's ecological value as the first step to protecting it for years to come. . . .

---

[236] Nature Conservancy, Vol. 53, No 3, Fall 2003. 4245 N. Fairfax Drive, Suite 100, Arlington, VA 22203. nature.org. Excerpts from pp. 26-30 of "In the Bull's Eye of Biodiversity" by Djuna Ivereigh.

Indeed, these researchers, led by Nature Conservancy senior marine scientist Rod Salm and including a dozen other scientists from Indonesia and around the globe, felt an especially strong sense of urgency. . . .

Still, Salm calls this place "the heart of the heart of marine biodiversity." . . .

The *Pindito*, a 130 foot wooden ketch, served as the expedition's lab, transport and home away from home. Swiss dive guide Edi Frommenwiler had built the boat 12 years earlier in Indonesian Borneo. . . . By 8 a.m., skiffs raced off in all directions, and the *Pindito* was left in peace.

Sunset saw another flurry of activity, as teams reconvened. Emre Turak, a reef ecologist, scrutinized corals under his hand lens while Jemmy Souhoka of the Indonesian National Research Institute cleaned samples in fizzing vats of bleach. Wayne Takeuchi of Harvard University's Arnold Arboretum and Johannes Mogea of the Bogor Herbarium on Java pressed plants between layers of *The Papua Post*. And Gerry Allen, an ichthyologist at Western Australian Museum, glanced up from his freshly pickled cardinalfish to announce "*Apogon ocellicaudus.*"

On this expedition, all stereotypes of staid, soft-spoken scientists were blown, well, out of the water: Not a day went by without researchers exclaiming their amazement: "Unreal!" "Far out!" "Unlike anything I've ever seen." . . .

"Looks like a great place for saltwater crocs," said Salm, and his interest was more than academic. Frommenwiler pulled the skiff alongside an outrigger canoe, from which a family of Papuans hunted sea cucumbers. "*Ada buaya disini?*" he asked.

"*Begini,*" said the father, holding his hands about 10 inches apart. The divers shrugged and wiggled further into wet suits.

"*Kepalanya,*" continued the fisherman.

"The *heads* are 10 inches," Frommenwiler translated.

"*Lebar begini.*"

"Ten inches *wide.*"

Allen and Turak figured that the crocs, in their entirety, were longer than our skiff, while Frommenwiler worked out that they *mostly* lived farther in the bay. The divers were undaunted.

Underwater at Kofiau Island, there were corals like trees and mushrooms, brains and Bubble Wrap. Purple, yellow, pink, green and every color in between. Feather stars embroidering sea fans. Soft corals plucking at plankton with flowery, tentacled "hands." And fish! Shimmering swarms of fusiliers, squirrelfish conversing in clicks, spotted eels gaping, and lionfish, frogfish and woebegons, who look as sad as their name suggests. There were giant blue clams, cuttlefish flashing psychedelic hues, glass shrimp prancing, sea snakes snaking and green turtles frolicking. But as soon as the divers hit the water, they went to work.

Gerry Allen's wet suit was barely soaked through before he'd scribbled *"Heni. acuminatus"* on his dive slate. Sinking slowly through a swirling school of neon-colored anthias, he spotted bannerfish and soldierfish and noted those, too. . . .

Throughout 50 dives on the Raja Ampat expedition. Allen tallied 896 reef-fish species, including 101 newly known to Raja Ampat and four newly known to Indonesia. Adding these to his observations from preliminary surveys and a 2001 expedition with Conservation International, he now lists 1,071 different reef fish for the islands and predicts that 1,149 species will eventually be found. "As far as the Raja Ampat's comparing to other areas—this is the Holy Grail," Allen said back on the *Pindito*. "This is the richest place for fishes that I've ever been."

After decades surveying Indonesian waters—the most biodiverse seas on Earth—Allen sees a "bull's-eye of biodiversity" coming into focus. He sees Raja Ampat as an ichthyological crossroads, hosting fish from Papua New Guinea and the Solomons to the east, Palau and the Philippines to the north and south, and Maluku and the rest of Indonesia to the west and south.

Within the Raja Ampat bull's-eye, the expedition pinpointed an even finer hot spot. "No other area of the Coral Triangle surveyed to date has greater diversity than Kofiau," said Allen. Around this little far-flung island, he averaged 228 species in each of six dives and broke his all-time single-dive fish count: 284 species.

While Allen scribbled away, Emre Turak and Jemmy Souhoka of the coral crew collected mysterious *Montipora* corals. Hard-coral taxonomy is defined largely by skeletal structures, so coral researchers often collect samples to get positive IDs. But despite Turak's 12 years of experience and Souhoka's local knowledge of Indonesian reefs, some 35 Raja Ampat corals defied identification during the expedition. Turak is convinced that at least 13 are new to science.

The coral team positively identified 487 species of reef-building hard corals. Adding that to the results from the Conservation International survey brings the Raja Ampat total to 535 species . . . and counting. By comparison, the Gulf of Mexico and the Caribbean host just 58 reef-building hard-coral species. Like Allen, Turak found "the highest per site species diversity" on average at Kofiau.

A model scientist, Turak doles out enthusiasm judiciously. Before confirming that, yes, Raja Ampat is the richest place for corals he's ever seen, Turak refers to his clipboard. When pressed, he'll hazard that Raja Ampat harbors more than 75 percent of the planet's reef-building corals. But that's known *Scleractinian* corals, he insists. Any way you slice it, the figure will knock more excitable biologists right off their seats.

While Turak and Souhoka moved methodically over the Kofiau reef, Salm sprinted off on a broader survey of his surroundings. On a dive slate, he recorded indicators of habitat health and wealth: coral coverage, reef impacts, sightings of turtles and sharks. (He was disappointed to record just three lonely sharks in three weeks diving. Throughout Asia, top reef predators are now most commonly found in bowls of shark's fin soup.)

Salm was keen to see how Raja Ampat might fit into a new global strategy to save coral reefs. A man of fiftysomething with the energy of two 25-year-olds, Salm is set on "transforming coral reef conservation." He leads a Conservancy program known by that name, aiming to save reefs that prove resistant and resilient to coral bleaching and other worldwide threats. Salm theorizes that conservationists may be able to protect a great many reefs by focusing on corals that are resistant to bleaching or that are resilient enough to bounce back after bleaching and other damage. He found strong evidence of both in Raja Ampat.

Like Allen, Salm sees Raja Ampat as an important biological crossroads. The islands are spread east to west across north and south-flowing currents, including those of the coral-rich Banda-Flores Seas. As such, they are well-positioned to pocket and pump coral larvae to other reefs, he explains. Resistant, resilient and regionally replenishing, Salm believes that Raja Ampat reefs should be the centerpiece of a new network of marine reserves. Kofiau island would perhaps be the center of this centerpiece. There, he happened upon a particularly awesome sight: a coral dome as big as the cab of a Mack truck. Measuring the giant dome in body lengths, he figured the colony was 22 feet and pushing 700 years old. "Imagine what this magnificent coral has 'seen' throughout the centuries," he mused.

CHAPTER SIXTEEN

CREATURES OF THE LAND

And cattle He has created for you:
from them you derive warmth and numerous benefits
and of them you eat.
And you have a sense of pride and beauty in them
as you drive them home in the evening
and as you lead them forth to pasture in the morning.
And they carry your heavy loads
to lands that you could not reach
except with great hardship to yourselves:
truly, your Sustainer is indeed Infinitely Compassionate, Most Merciful.
And He creates horses and mules and asses for you to ride,
as well as for beauty;
He will yet create things of which you have no knowledge.
[*Sūrah An-Naḥl* (The Bee) 16:5-8]

And also in cattle you will find an instructive sign.
From what is within their bodies between excretions and blood
We produce for you pure milk, pleasing to those who drink it.
And from the fruit of the date-palm and the vine
you obtain nourishing food and drink:
witness, in this, also, is a sign for those who are wise.
[*Sūrah An-Naḥl* (The Bee) 16:66-67]

To David We gave Solomon, what an excellent servant!
He always turned to Us!
See how there were brought before him at nightfall
chargers of the highest breeding, and swift of foot.
And he said, "Truly, I love the love of the Good
because of remembrance of my Sustainer."
[*Sūrah ṣād* 38:30-32]

308

The Horse
~ Imrio'ul Qais (d.64BH/560CE)[237]

Often I've been off with the morn,
The birds yet asleep in their nests,
My horse short-haired, outstripping the wild game,
> huge-bodied, charging, fleet-feeting,
> head-foremost, headlong, all together,
the match of a rugged boulder hurled from on high by the torrent.
A chestnut-horse, sliding the saddle-felt from his back's thwart,
> Just as a smooth pebble slides off the rain cascading.
Fiery he is, for all his leanness, and when his ardour boils on him,
> How he roars—a bubbling cauldron isn't it! . . .
The lightweight lad slips landward from his smooth back,
> He flings off the burnous of the hard, heavy rider;
Very swift he is, like the toy spinner a boy will whirl,
> Playing it with his nimble hands by the knotted thread.
His flanks are the flanks of a fawn, his legs like an ostrich's;
The springy trot of the wolf he has, the fox's gallop;
Sturdy his body-look from behind, and he bars his leg's gap
> with full tail, not askew, reaching almost to the ground;
His back, as he stands beside the tent,
> seems the pounding-slab of a bride's perfumes
> or the smooth stone a colocynth's broken on.

The Art of Horsemanship
~ Charles Upton

Horsemanship is a spiritual art, because to train a horse correctly, so that animal and rider respond as one, is also to train one's *nafs*—not by grossly dominating it, but by teaching it to follow, willingly, the human spirit that rules it." And [*it is He who creates*] *horses and mules and asses for you to ride, as well as for beauty; and He will yet create things of which you have no knowledge* [16:8]. This passage may indicate, among other things, the

---

[237] Excerpted from *Xenel Diary* AH 1405/AD 1985, January-February.

transformation, through perfect submission to God, of the commanding self or headstrong ego into the self-at-peace. It may also refer to the body which will be ours after the Resurrection. The human-headed horse named *Buraq,* which, according to legend, the Prophet rode on his *miraj,* is a symbol of the self-at-peace.

King of the Wind

~ Marguerite Henry[238]

The new moon hung over Agba's shoulder as he ran to get the mare. She was standing patiently in a corner of her stall, her head lowered, her tail tucked in. Placing a hand on her neck, Agba led her out into the night, past endless stalls and under endless archways to her new quarters. She walked slowly, heavily.

At the door of the new stall a tremor of fear shook her. She made a feeble attempt to go back, but Agba held her firmly, humming to hide his own nameless fears.

She entered the stall. She tried the soft bed with her feet. She went to the manger. Her nostrils widened to snuff the dried grasses, but she did not eat. She put her lips to the water cask, but did not drink. At last she tucked her hooves underneath her and with a groan lay down. Her head nodded. She steadied it in the straw. Then her breathing, too, steadied.

As Agba stood on watch, his mind was a mill wheel, turning, turning, turning. He trembled, remembering the time he and the mare had come upon a gazelle, and he had ridden the mare alongside the gazelle, and she had outrun the wild thing. Agba could still feel the wind singing in his ears.

By closing his eyes, he brought back the whole day. On the way home they had passed a wizened old storyteller in the streets, who, when Agba came near, motioned him close. The old man placed his hand on the mare's head. Then, in a voice that was no more than a whisper, he

---

[238] *King of the Wind,* Marguerite Henry, Scholastic Book Services New York, 1968. Copyright Rand McNally & Co. 1948, pp. 24-29.

had said, "When Allah created the horse, he said to the wind, 'I will that a creature proceed from thee. Condense thyself.' And the wind condensed itself, and the result was the horse."

The words danced in Agba's head as he watched the sleeping mare. *I will that a creature proceed from thee. Condense thyself! I will that a creature proceed from thee. Condense thyself!* He told the words over and over in his mind, until suddenly the stable walls faded away and Agba was riding the South Wind. And there was nothing to stop him. No palace walls. No trees. Nor hedges. Nor rivers. Only white clouds to ride through, and a blue vaulted archway, and the wind for a mount.

With a sigh he sank down in the straw. His head dropped.

A Foal Is Born

The boy's dreams spun themselves out until there was nothing left of them. He slept a deep sleep. The candle in the lanthorn sputtered and died. The new moon rode higher and higher. Bats and nighthawks, flying noiselessly in the velvet night, went about their business, swooping insects out of the air. With the gray light of morning they vanished, giving way to the jangling chorus of the crows.

Agba woke. The stable walls had closed in again. And there was the mare lying on her side as before. But her head was raised now, and she was drying off a newborn foal! Her tongue strokes filled the silence of the stall, licking, licking, licking.

The boy watched in fear that if he took his eyes away the whole scene might vanish into the mist of the morning. Oh, how tiny the foal was! And so wet there was no telling what its color would he. But its eyes were open. And they were full of curiosity.

Agba's body quivered with the wonder of the little fellow's birth. He had seen newborn foals before, but none so small and finely made. In the distance he could hear the softly padding feet of the horseboys. He could hear the wild boar grunting and coughing in his hole behind the stables. He wondered if the boar really did keep evil spirits from entering into the horses.

Afraid to move, he watched the mare clumsily get to her feet. He watched her nudge the young thing with her nose.

The foal tried to get up. He thrust out his fore-feet, but they splayed and he seemed to get all tangled up with himself. He tried again and again. For one breathless instant he was on his feet. Then his legs buckled and he fell in a little heap. Agba reached a hand toward him, but the mare came between. She pushed the little one with her nose. She pushed him with her tongue. She nickered to him. He was trying again. He was standing up. How spindly he was! And his ribs showed. And he had hollows above his eyes, just like his dam.

"I could carry him in my arms," thought Agba. "He is not much bigger than a goat, and he has long whiskers like a goat. Long and silky. And his tail is curly. And he is all of one color. Except—except . . ." Suddenly the boy's heart missed a beat. On the off hind heel there was a white spot. It was no bigger than an almond, but it was there! The white spot—the emblem of swiftness!

Agba leaped to his feet. He wanted to climb the tower of the mosque. He wanted to blow on the trumpet. He wanted to cry to the four winds of heaven: "A foal is born! And he will be swift as the wind of the desert, for on his hind heel is a white spot. A white spot. A white . . ."

Just then a shaft of early sunlight pierced the window of the stable and found the colt. It flamed his coat into red-gold. It made a sun halo around his head.

Agba was full of fear. He opened his mouth, but no sound escaped. Maybe this was all a dream. Maybe the foal was not real. The golden coat. The crown of sun rays. Maybe he was a golden horse belonging to the chariot of the sun!

"I'll capture him with a name," the boy thought quickly. And he named the young thing Sham, which is the Arabic word for sun.

No sooner had Agba fastened a name on him than the little creature seemed to take on a new strength. He took a few steps. He found his mother's milk. He began to nurse, making soft sucking noises.

Agba knew he should be reporting to Signor Achmet. He knew he should be standing in line for his measure of corn. But he could not bear to break the spell. He listened to the colt suckling, to the mare munching the dried grasses. He smelled their warm bodies. A stable was a *good* place to be born.

Camels

~ A'sha b. Qays[239]

Daily I raced fast red-grey camels across the distance between al-Nujayr and Sarkhada.

O you enquiring where she has gone, she has an appointment with the people of Yathrib.

And if you enquire about me, then (know that) there are many kind-hearted ones who ask about A'sha enquiring where he went.

My mount stretches her swift legs and draws them back, carefully turning out her hooves, not splaying them.

Sprightly she is, even in noonday heat, when you would imagine even the afternoon chameleon bending its neck.

I swore I'd not assuage her fatigue nor her sore feet until she reached Muḥammad.

When she should kneel at Ibn Hashim's door, only then would [she] rest and receive, through his munificence, some generosity. . . .

---

[239] Ibn Kathīr, *The Life of the Prophet Muḥammad*, Volume II, p. 52.

"Ibn Hisham stated, "Khallād b. Qurra b. Khālid al-Sudusī, and other sheikhs of Bakr b. Wā'il told me, from certain scholars, that A'shā b. Qays b. Tha'laba b.'Ukāba b. Sa'b b. 'Alī b. Bakr b. Wā'il went to see the Messenger of God 緣 intending to accept Islam." These are a portion of the verses he spoke in praise of the Messenger of God.

Qaswā'

The Prophet's camel, Qaswā', was a very sensitive creature. It was this she-camel that the Prophet purchased from Abu Bakr when they made their journey of emigration from Mecca to Medina. Upon arriving at last in Medina, it became evident to the Prophet that it was she who would choose where he was to settle. From Ibn Kathīr,[240] we have the following account:

> Ibn Ishaq stated, "When Friday came the Messenger of God ﷺ was there among the Banū Sālim b.'Awf; he prayed that day in the mosque in the Rānūnā' valley, this being the first Friday he prayed in Medina.
>
> "'Itbān b. Mālik and 'Abbās b. 'Ubāda b. Nadla came to him there along with some men of the Banū Salim and told him, 'O Messenger of God, stay here among us enjoying our protection and our wealth.' He replied, referring to his camel, 'Give her free passage; for she is being guided.' And they cleared a path for her.
>
> "She proceeded and got as far as the homes of the Banū Bayāda, where he was met by Ziyād b. Labīd and Farwa b. 'Amr, along with other men of the Banū Bayāda. They asked him, 'O Messenger of God, come and join us and share our protection and our wealth.'
>
> "He replied, 'Make way before her, she has received a command.' And they cleared a path for her.
>
> "She went on again and passed by the homes of the Banū Sā'ida where she was blocked by Sa'd b. 'Ubāda and al-Mundhir b. 'Amr along with some men of the Banū Sā'īda. They said, 'O Messenger of God, come to us and have our protection. "Make way before her,' he replied, 'she has received a command.' And they did so.
>
> "On she went until she was opposite the home of Banū al-Hārith b. al-Khazraj. There her way was blocked by Sa'd b. al-Rabī', Khārija b. Zayd and 'Abd Allāh b. Rawāha, along with men of Banū al-Hārith b. al-Khazraj. They called out, 'Messenger of

---

[240] Ibn Kathīr, *The Life of the Prophet Muhammad*, Volume II, pp. 179-180.

314

God, come to us; we have many to protect you.' But he replied as before.

"She proceeded further, as far as the homes of the Banū ʿAdī b. al-Najjār, to whom he was related. The closest of these was the mother of ʿAbd al-Muṭṭalib, Sālma, daughter of ʿAmr, being one of their women. There were Salīṭ b. Qays and Abū Salīṭ, Usayra b. Abū Khārija and some men of the Banū ʿAdī b. al-Najjār. They told him, 'O Messenger of God, join your own relatives and enjoy our wealth and protection.' 'Make way before her,' he replied, 'she has received a command.' And they did so.

"She went further, up to the homes of the Banū Mālik b. al-Najjār, where she knelt down before what is today his mosque. At that time it was a drying shed for dates owned by two orphan youths of the Banū Mālik b. al-Najjār, Sahl and Suhayl by name, sons of ʿAmr. They were under the protection of Muʿādh b. ʿAfrāʾ." . . .

"Whenever he passed by the home of one of the *anṣār* they would invite him inside, but he would say, 'Leave her alone; she has received a command. I will only stay where God decides.'

"When she arrived at the house of Abū Ayyūb she knelt before the door and he dismounted. He entered that house and stayed there until his mosque and its apartments were built."

Ibn Isḥāq stated, "When the camel of the Messenger of God ﷺ first knelt he did not dismount and she got up and went a little further, while the Messenger of God left its rein free without his control. She then turned around and came back to where she had knelt and did so there again. She then shook herself, and sank to the ground stretching out fully. The Messenger of God ﷺ then dismounted.

"Abū Ayyūb Khālid b. Zayd then picked up his bags and took them into the house. The Messenger of God ﷺ stayed there with him.

Come into Animal Presence

~ Denise Levertov[241]

Come into animal presence
No man is so guileless as
the serpent. The lonely white
rabbit on the roof is a star
twitching its ears in the rain.
The llama intricately
folding its hind legs to be seated
not disdains but mildly
disregards human approval.
What joy when the insouciant
armadillo glances at us and doesn't
quicken his trotting
across the track into the palm brush.
What is this joy? That no animal
falters, but knows what it must do?
That the snake has no blemish,
that the rabbit inspects his strange surroundings
in white star-silence? The llama
rests in dignity, the armadillo
has some intention to pursue in the palm-forest.
Those who were sacred have remained so,
holiness does not dissolve, it is a presence
of bronze, only the sight that saw it
faltered and turned from it.
An old joy returns in holy presence.

Owen and Mzee

~ C.A.H. with Peter Greste

The wolf shall dwell with the lamb,
and the leopard shall lie down with the kid, . . .
[The Bible, Isaiah, 11:6]

Once upon a time there was a hippo and a tortoise. . . .

On December 26, 2004, a tsunamai struck the coast of Banda Aceh, Indonesia. Inestimable damage occurred and hundreds of lives were lost. Twelve hours later, resulting waves suddenly hit the distant coast of Kenya near the town of Malinda.

At that moment, a family of hippos who had been swept downriver by an earlier storm were swimming by the mouth of the river. The huge waves sent them out to sea. As everyone struggled to rescue endangered fishermen, the family of hippos was forgotten.

The next day, someone noticed that only one baby hippo remained, stranded on the fragile coral reef. Hippo rescue efforts immediately began. After many hours and much struggling, the small hippo, dubbed "Owen" after the soccer player who finally managed to wrestle him onto the boat, was on his way to safety. But where to take him? Most baby hippos remain under the watchful care of their mothers for four years. Yet trying to find a foster mother for Owen would be difficult, because the oldest male of a pod (hippo family unit) would probably not accept an outsider. At last a home was found for Owen at Haller Park in Mombasa.

Strangely, when he was first unloaded, his eye caught that of Mzee, a 130-year-old Aldabran tortoise. He immediately sidled up to this formerly rather unsociable tortoise, the oldest resident of the Park, who himself had been brought there from near Madagascar, probably rescued from pirates. Unphased, Mzee accepted him. The two then became inseparable, wandering everywhere together—swimming, sunning, strolling. People around the world have been amazed that such unrelated species might become such fast friends.

Perhaps that is what makes the story of Owen and Mzee so powerful, the fact that it is so unexpected. After all, every animal behavior expert we have spoken to is at a loss to explain it. Herpetologists tell us that reptiles are purely creatures of instinct that could never respond to a mammal, however affectionate they may be. Yet Mzee [whose name in Swahili means "wise old man"] seems undeniably happy to have Owen around. Behavioralists say that Owen will eventually grow to understand that the old tortoise is not of his kind, and go his own way. Yet every time I go out to take photographs, he seems as bonded as ever to his old friend.

Owen and Mzee have come together only because of the unusual circumstances of Owen's separation from his family, his transfer to Haller Park, and the fact that they now share a big space to live in. But it seems to be a powerful sign that all of us—hippos and tortoises included—need the support of family and friends; and that it doesn't matter if we can't be near our blood-kin.

Then again, perhaps it doesn't matter what Owen and Mzee are thinking. Perhaps it is enough that we humans are able to learn something simply from watching them.

~ Peter Greste, photographer[242]

---

[242] Isabella Hatkoff, Graig Hatkoff, and Dr. Paula Kahumbu, with photographs by Peter Greste, *Owen and Mzee, The True Story of a Remarkable Friendship*, copyright © 2005 Turtle Pond Publications.

The Faces of Deer

~ Mary Oliver[243]

When for too long I don't go
　deep enough
into the woods to see them,
　they begin to
enter my dreams. Yes, there
　they all are, in the
pinewoods of my inner life.
　I want to live a life
full of modesty and praise.
　Each hoof of each
animal makes the sign of a
　heart as it touches
then lifts away from the ground.
　Unless you
believe that heaven is very near,
　how will you
find it? Their eyes are pools
　in which one
would be content on any
　summer afternoon,
to swim away through the
　door of the world.
Then, love and its blessings.
　Then: heaven.

---

[243] Mary Oliver, *New and Selected Poems*, Volume 2, Beacon Press, Boston, MA, copyright © 2005 Mary Oliver, p. 33.

CHAPTER SEVENTEEN

THE HUMAN UMMAH[244]

And I have created the invisible beings and human beings
only that they may worship Me.
No sustenance do I require of them
nor do I require that they should feed Me.
For God is the Giver of All Sustenance,
the Lord of All Power, the Eternally Steadfast.
[*Sūrah Adh-Dhāriyāt* (The Dust-Scattering Winds) 51:56-58]

Thus, He begins the creation of man out of clay;
then He causes him to be begotten out of the essence of a humble fluid;
and then He forms him in accordance with what he is meant to be,
and breathes into him of His spirit:[245]
and He endows you with hearing, and sight,
and feelings as well as minds:[246] *how seldom are you grateful!*
[*Sūrah As-Sajdah* (Prostration) 32:7-9]

He has created the heavens and the earth in accordance with Truth
and has shaped you and made your shapes beautiful;
and with Him is your journey's end.
He knows what is in the heavens and on earth;
He knows what you conceal and what you reveal:
yes, God knows well the secrets of hearts.
[*Sūrah At-Taghābun* (Loss And Gain) 64:3-4]

---

[244] As with each species or grouping of creation, within the Qur'anic context, humanity is also spoken of as an *ummah*, a "community."

[245] God's "breathing of His spirit into man" is a metaphor for the divine gift of life and consciousness, or of a "soul" (which is one of the meanings of the term *rūḥ*). Consequently, "the soul of every human being is of the spirit of God" (Rāzī). ~ M. Asad

[246] Lit., "hearts" (*af'idah*), which in classical Arabic is a metonym for both "feelings" and "minds"; hence my composite rendering of this term. ~ M. Asad

By the fig and the olive,
and Mount Sinai,
and this city of security,[247]
truly, We have created human beings in the best proportion.
Then We reduce them to the lowest of the low
except those who have faith and act rightly:
for they shall have an unceasing reward.
Then what after this can cause you to turn from this Way?
Is God not the wisest of judges?
[*Sūrah At-Tīn* (The Fig) 95:1-8]

The Originator of the heavens and the earth—
He has made for you pairs from among yourselves
and pairs among cattle:
by this means He multiplies you; there is nothing whatever like Him
and He is the All-Hearing, the All-Seeing.
To Him belong the keys of the heavens and the earth;
He grants abundant sustenance
or bestows it in meager measure to whom He wills:
for He knows well all things.
The same clear Path has He established for you
as that which He enjoined on Noah,
that which We have sent by inspiration to you,
and that which We designated for Abraham, Moses, and Jesus:
that you should steadfastly uphold the Faith
and make no divisions within it.
To those who worship other things than God,
the way to which you call them may appear difficult.
God draws to Himself those who are willing
and guides to Himself everyone who turns to Him.
[*Sūrah Ash-Shūrā* (Consultation) 42:11-13]

---

[247] The "fig" and the "olive" symbolize, in this context, the *lands* in which these trees predominate: i.e., the countries bordering on the eastern part of the Mediterranean, especially Palestine and Syria. As it was in these lands that most of the Abrahamic prophets mentioned in the Qur'ān lived and preached, these two species of tree may be taken as metonyms for the *religious teachings* voiced by the long line of those God-inspired men. ~ M. Asad

Among the signs of God is this: that He created you from dust,
and then, see how you become human beings ranging far and wide!
And among His Signs is this: that He created for you mates
from among yourselves that you may dwell in tranquillity with them,
and He engenders love and compassion between you;
truly in that are signs for those who reflect.
And among His signs is the creation of the heavens and the earth
and the variations in your languages and your colors:
truly in that are signs for those who know.
[*Sūrah Ar-Rūm* (The Byzantines) 30:20-22]

O humankind! We created you all out of a male and a female,
and made you into nations and tribes
that you might come to know each other.
Truly, the most highly regarded of you in the sight of God
is the one who does the most good.
And God is All-knowing and is Well-Aware of all things.
[*Sūrah Al-Ḥujurāt* (The Private Apartments) 49:13]

It was We Who created the human being
and We know what his inmost self whispers within him,
for We are nearer to him than his jugular vein.
Whenever the two demands of his nature come face to face,
contending from the right and the left,
not a word does he utter but there is a watcher with him, ever-present.
And the twilight of death will bring truth before his eyes:
[*Sūrah Qāf* 50:16-19]

Is he not acquainted with what is in the books of Moses
and of Abraham who was true to his trust?
Namely that no bearer of burdens can bear the burden of another;
that the human being can have nothing but that for which he strives;

322

that in time his striving will become apparent;
and then he will be recompensed with the most complete recompense;
that to your Sustainer is the final Goal;
that it is He alone who causes your laughter and your tears;
that it is He Who grants death and life;
that He created in pairs, male and female,
from a drop of sperm as it is poured forth;
and that with Him rests another coming to life;
that it is He Who gives wealth and contentment;
and that it is He alone Who sustains the brightest star.[248]
[*Sūrah An-Najm* (The Unfolding) 53:36-49]

Has there not been over the human being a long span of time
when he was nothing—not even mentioned?
Truly, We created the human being
from a drop of mingled sperm in order to test him.
So We gave him hearing and sight, We showed him the Way:
it is up to him whether he is grateful or ungrateful.
[*Sūrah Al-Insān* (Man) 76:1-3]

I call to witness this land
in which you are free to dwell,
and the bond between parent and child:
truly, We have created the human being to labor and struggle.
Does he think that no one has power over him?
He may boast: "I have spent abundant wealth!"
Does he think that no one sees him?
Haven't We made a pair of eyes for him?
And a tongue and a pair of lips?
And shown him the two ways?
But he has not quickened along the path that is steep.
And what will explain to you what the steep path is?—

---

[248] Sirius, of the constellation Canis Major, the brightest star in the heavens. This phrase might also be understood as, "it is God alone who sustains the brightest of the saints, those who shine with His Light." ~ M. Asad

the freeing of one who is enslaved,
or the giving of food in time of need
to the orphan with claims of relationship,
or to the helpless, lowly one in the dust,
and being of those who have faith and encourage patience,
and who encourage deeds of kindness and compassion.
These are the companions of the right hand.
[*Sūrah Al-Balad* (The Land) 90:2-18]

In the Name of God, the Infinitely Compassionate and Most Merciful
Recite! In the name of your Sustainer Who created,
created the human being out of a connecting cell:
Recite! And your Sustainer is the Most Generous,
the One Who taught by the pen,
taught humankind what it did not know.
No, but humankind goes beyond all bounds
when it considers itself self-sufficient.
In truth, to their Sustainer all will return.
[*Sūrah Al-ʿAlaq* (The Germ-cell) 96:1-8]

Bow down in adoration and draw near!
[*Sūrah Al-ʿAlaq* (The Germ-cell) 96:19]

The Trust

~ Charles Upton

*T*he Qur'an mentions something called *"the Trust"* which God offered . . . unto the heavens and the earth and the hills, but they shrank from bearing it and were afraid of it. And man assumed it [33:72]. What exactly is this *"Trust"*?

The Trust is our ability, which is also our duty, to see the forms of the world around us, both natural and man-made, as signs of the Creator. The angels can witness God's presence without having to deal with the many distractions our five human senses confront us with. The animals are immersed in the world of the senses; they have no way of standing apart

324

from it. Only we human beings have the power to sense God's presence and submit to His will, while at the same time living in, and dealing with, a material world. In other words, humanity is the bridge or *barzakh* (isthmus) between God and the created universe. We are God's *khalifa* on earth, his delegated representative. And because we are *khalifa,* we have a privileged relationship to knowledge. The animals are fixed, by God's will, in their basic views of reality; we call this "instinct." Humanity alone is capable of growing in knowledge by moving from view to view.

This ability to change and enhance our view of reality is the reason why humanity has been able to develop art, culture, science and technology. But if this ability remains separate from our capacity to sense the presence of God—which is also our God-given duty, since it is part of the Trust—then it becomes destructive. We end up using our uniquely human ability to manipulate the environment in the service of desires which are still basically on an animal level. This is appropriate for animals, of course, since they don't possess civilization and advanced technology. But if dogs or pigs, for example, had access to nuclear weapons, this would definitely not be a desirable state of affairs. Our ability to fulfill our desires has grown over the centuries; our ability to *change what we desire,* or *sacrifice a given desire entirely,* apparently has not. Rationality helps us to satisfy our desires, but faith gives us the power to change or sacrifice them. And faith is the basis of the Trust. If we do not fulfill this Trust, then we are not yet, or no longer, fully human; rather we are animals without the protection of a single unchanging pattern of perception, chaotic animals who are always shifting from pattern to pattern without being able to control ourselves, who are addicted to "trying things out" and so end up destroying much of the world we might have loved.

Part of the Trust is the human capacity to know the names of things, their inner essences. *And He imparted unto Adam the names of all things* [2:31] This is a kind of knowledge even the angels do not possess: *He brought them within the ken of the angels and said: "Declare unto me the names of these [things] . . ." They replied, . . . "No knowledge have we save that which Thou hast imparted unto us. . . ." Said He, "O Adam convey unto them the names of these [things]"* [2:31-33]. It is because God taught Adam all the names, names which even the angels did not know, that it is often said that the human form, alone in all creation, is capable of reflecting all the Names of God; it is precisely this which makes us so destructive when we fail to live up to this form, or when we betray it.

To name something is to distinguish it from its background, to see it as a separate entity. When God taught Adam all the names, He gave the human race the unequalled ability to discriminate between things, largely through the gift of human language. Yet God is not many; He is One. His Names are not separate entities; they are names of Him alone. The forms of the universe are not separate "gods" which exist in their own right, but signs of the One God. This means that our heightened ability to tell the difference between things is a two-edged sword. If we practice discrimination while remembering God, then we are fulfilling the Trust. But if we forget God in our desire to analyze, dissect and control the world around us, then we have become idolaters. . . .

One of the arts of appreciating nature is developing our knowledge of the names and characteristics of things; the other, companion art is knowing how to keep quiet and pay attention, both within and without. Speech is knowledge of the many; silence is knowledge of the One. Only if we forget, for a while, what we already know, will we be able to learn something we don't yet know. (And it is exactly the same in relation to God: we can know *about* Him through His Names, but we cannot know God Himself in His Essence; and yet—if we are silent enough and vigilant enough—God Himself may make His presence known to us.)

Longing for the Divine

~ Aisha Rafea[249]

The Holy Qur'an asserts that the human soul is created to long to know the Divine and to seek to live according to His Law. That longing is part of its primordial nature that the Holy Qur'an terms as *fitra*. The human soul acquired that quality in the moment Allah breathed into Adam of His Spirit. And it is that quality of human nature that qualified the offspring of Adam to long for devotion to the Divine. When the human soul lives in

---

[249] Aisha Rafea, excerpted from "The Soul's Longing" *Women of Sufism, A Hidden Treasure*, by Camille Helminski, p. 212.

accordance with its own primordial nature or *fitra*, it fulfills its own longing, and a human life becomes a language of spirit. There is no wonder then that humankind, at all times, and in different cultures and civilizations has witnessed the existence of human souls who have been looking for an ultimate goal of existence and have never been satisfied with the objectives of the physical realm. Their whole life has been a language of spirit.

Poetic Spirit

~ Matsuo Basho[250]

Within this temporal body composed of [hundreds of] bones and nine holes there resides a spirit which, for lack of an adequate name, I think of as windblown. Like delicate drapery, it may be torn away and blown off by the least breeze. It brought me to writing poetry many years ago, initially for . . . gratification, but eventually as a way of life. True, frustration and rejection were almost enough to bring this spirit to silence, and sometimes pride brought it to the brink of vanity. From the writing of the very first line, it has found no contentment as it was torn by one doubt after another. This windblown spirit considered the security of courtly life at one point; at another, it considered risking a display of its ignorance by becoming a scholar. But its passion for poetry would not permit either. Since it knows no other way than the way of poetry, it has clung to it tenaciously.

Saigyo in poetry, Sogo in linked verse, Sesshu in painting, Rikyu in the tea ceremony—the spirit that moves them is one spirit. Achieving artistic excellence, each holds one attribute in common: each remains attuned to nature throughout the four seasons. Whatever is seen by such a heart and mind is a flower, whatever is dreamed is a moon. Only a barbarian mind could fail to see the flower; only an animal mind could fail to dream a moon. The first task for each artist is to overcome the barbarian or animal heart and mind, to become one with nature.

---

[250] Matsuo Basho, *Narrow Road to the Interior and Other Writings*, pp. 55-56.

Mouthfuls of food are the gift of every tree bearing fruit;
but the gift of a throat is from God alone.
He bestows a throat on the body and the spirit;
He gives an appropriate throat to every part of you.

~ Jalaluddin Rumi [Mathnawi III, 17-18][251]

Ask

~ Scott Russell Sanders[252]

In the Book of Job, the beleaguered man cries out that all creatures, himself included, rest in the hand of God:

But ask the beasts, and they will teach you;
The birds of the air, and they will tell you;
Or the plants of the earth, and they will teach you;
And the fish of the sea will declare you.

The key word here is *ask*. What the birds and beasts and countryside teach us depends on the questions we pose. A person wielding a fifty-ton digger in search of coal will learn quite different lessons from one who wields a pair of binoculars in search of warblers. Job assumed that anybody who listened to the creation would hear the whisper of the creator. But generally we hear what our ears have been prepared for, and if we do not go seeking divinity we are not likely to find it. In the long run and in a blunt manner, nature has its own say: species that poison or exhaust their habitat die out. But in the short run, nature does not declare how we should approach it; that lesson we learn from culture.

---

[251] Translated by Camille and Kabir Helminski, *Jewels of Remembrance*, p. 2.

[252] Excerpted from *The Sacred Earth, Writers on Nature and Spirit*, edited by John Gardner, p. 131.

Tokens of Mystery

~ Wendell Berry[253]

The significance—and ultimately the quality—of the work we do is determined by our understanding of the story in which we are taking part.

If we think of ourselves as merely biological creatures, whose story is determined by genetics or environment or history or economics or technology, then, however pleasant or painful the part we play, it cannot matter much. Its significance is that of mere self-concern. "It is a tale / Told by an idiot, full of sound and fury, / Signifying nothing," as Macbeth says when he has "supp'd full with horrors" and is "aweary of the sun."

If we think of ourselves as lofty souls trapped temporarily in lowly bodies in a dispirited, desperate, unlovable world that we must despise for Heaven's sake, then what have we done for this question of significance? If we divide reality into two parts, spiritual and material, and hold (as the Bible does *not* hold) that only the spiritual is good or desirable, then our relation to the material Creation becomes arbitrary, having only the quantitative or mercenary value that we have, in fact and for this reason, assigned to it. Thus, we become the judges and inevitably the destroyers of a world we did not make and that we are bidden to understand as a divine gift. It is impossible to see how good work might be accomplished by people who think that our life in this world either signifies nothing or has only a negative significance.

If, on the other hand, we believe that we are living souls, God's dust and God's breath, acting our parts among other creatures all made of the same dust and breath as ourselves; and if we understand that we are free, within the obvious limits of mortal human life, to do evil or good to ourselves and to the other creatures—then all our acts have a supreme significance.

---

[253] Excerpted from "Sex, Freedom, and Community" by Wendell Berry. *The Sacred Earth, Writers on Nature and Spirit*, edited by Jason Gardner, pp. 136-137.

Spacious Soul

~ St. Teresa of Avila[254]

Turn your eyes towards the center, which is the room or royal chamber where the King stays, and think of how a palmetto has many leaves surrounding and covering the tasty part that can be eaten. So here, surrounding this center room are many other rooms; and the same holds true for those above. The things of the soul must always be considered as plentiful, spacious, large; to do so is not an exaggeration. The soul is capable of much more than we imagine, and the sun that is in this royal chamber shines in all parts. It is very important for any soul that practices prayer, whether little or much, not to hold itself back and stay in one corner. Let it walk through these dwelling places which are above, down below, and to the sides, since God has given it such dignity.

---

[254] *Teresa of Avila, Mystical Writings* by Tessa Bielecki, The Crossroad Publishing Co., 1997, NY, NY, p. 41.

Consciousness

~ Peter Russell[255]

Nothing in Western science predicts that any living creature should be conscious. It is easier to explain how hydrogen evolved into other elements, how they combined to form molecules and then simple living cells, and how these evolved into complex beings such as ourselves, than it is to explain why we should ever have a single inner experience.

Scientists are in the strange position of being confronted daily by the indisputable fact of their own consciousness, yet with no way of explaining it.

~ Christian de Quincey

. . . a nature found within all creatures but not restricted to them; outside all creatures, but not excluded from them.

~ *The Cloud of Unknowing*

What is consciousness? The word is not easy to define, partly because we use it to cover a variety of meanings. We might say an awake person has consciousness, whereas someone who is asleep does not. Or, someone could be awake, but so absorbed in their thoughts that they have little consciousness of the world around them. We speak of having a political, social, or ecological consciousness. And we may say that human beings have consciousness while other creatures do not, meaning that humans think and are self-aware.

The way I shall be using the word *consciousness* is not in reference to a particular state of consciousness, or a particular way of thinking, but to the faculty of consciousness—the capacity for inner experience, whatever the nature or degree of the experience.

For every psychological term in English there are four in Greek and forty in Sanskrit.   ~ A. K. Coomaraswamy

The faculty of consciousness can be likened to the light from a film projector. The projector shines light onto a screen, modifying the light so

---

[255] Excerpted from *From Science to God* by Peter Russell. Used with permission from New World Library, Novato, CA 94949, pp. 26, 31, 32. www.newworldlibrary.com

as to produce any one of an infinity of images. These images are like the perceptions, sensations, dreams, memories, thoughts, and feelings that we experience—what I call the "forms of consciousness." The light itself, without which no images would be possible, corresponds to the faculty of consciousness.

We know all the images on the screen are composed of this light, but we are not usually aware of the light itself; our attention is caught up in the images that appear and the stories they tell. In much the same way, we know we are conscious, but we are usually aware only of the many different perceptions, thoughts, and feelings that appear in the mind. We are seldom aware of consciousness itself.

The Rising Dawn

~ Henry David Thoreau, *Walden*

Morning is when I am awake and there is a dawn in me. Moral reform is the effort to throw off sleep. Why is it that men give so poor an account of their day if they have not been slumbering? They are not such poor calculators. If they had not been overcome with drowsiness, they would have performed something. The millions are awake enough for physical labor; but only one in a million is awake enough for effective intellectual exertion, only one in a hundred millions to a poetic or divine life. To be awake is to be alive. I have never yet met a man who was quite awake. How could I have looked him in the face?

We must learn to reawaken and keep ourselves awake, not by mechanical aids, but by an infinite expectation of the dawn, which does not forsake us in our soundest sleep. I know of no more encouraging fact than the unquestionable ability of man to elevate his life by a conscious endeavor. It is something to be able to paint a particular picture, or to carve a statue, and so to make a few objects beautiful; but it is far more glorious to carve and paint the very atmosphere and medium through which we look, which morally we can do. To affect the quality of the day, that is the highest of arts. Every man is tasked to make his life, even in its details, worthy of the contemplation of his most elevated and critical hour.

The Marvel of Creation

~ Michael Lerner [256]

Everything that has ever happened in the history of the universe is the prelude to each of our lives. Everything that has happened from the beginning of time has become the platform from which we launch our lives.

We are the heirs of the long evolution of Spirit. Each of us is the latest unfolding of the event of Creation. Our bodies are composed of the material that was shaped in the Big Bang. And so, too, our spirit. The loving goodness of the universe breathes us and breathes through us, giving us life and consciousness, and the capacity to recognize and love others.

Each stage in the development of the universe incorporates and transcends that which went before. It has been so from the earliest stages in the formation of galaxies, to the emergence of solar time for our particular planet, through the geological development of the Earth and the emergence of biological reality, until we ultimately emerge into human time, or history. Each stage of history, in turn, makes further developments possible, which finally bring us to the present moment.

That evolving reality has been understood through much of recorded history as an integrated and mutually interacting web of body, mind, soul, and spirit. When we faced problems in our human reality, we can often understand those problems as dysfunctions in the way these different levels of reality interacted with each other.

Recognizing One's Place in the Unity of All Being

Jewish tradition relates the story of a rabbi who sought to understand his place in the universe. To keep a balance between too much grandiosity and too much self-diminution, he had two notes, one for each of his two pants pockets. One note read: "For me the world was created." The other note read; "I am nothing more than dust and ashes." The task of the rabbi is our task: to integrate these two messages and keep them in appropriate balance.

---

[256] Excerpted from *Spirit Matters* by Michael Lerner published by Walsch Books, an imprint of Hampton Roads Publishing Company, Inc. (www.hrpub.com), Charlottesville, VA. Copyright © 2000 by Michael Lerner, pp. 42-48.

"For me the world was created." The grandeur of creation comes to full expression in the creation of human beings. Complexly magnificent, able to be conscious of ourselves, able to transcend that which is and to move toward what *ought to be,* human beings were "created in the image of God" and reflect the universe's greatest outpouring of love and generosity.

But also, "nothing more than dust and ashes." We are part of the totality of all that is, and we are ever arrogant when we see ourselves as somehow better than everything else, as having the right to use everything else for our own ends. We are here on the planet for a brief moment, and for much of that time we are deeply enmeshed in foolish schemes to perpetuate ourselves for eternity, imagining that if we amass enough power or control we can somehow live forever.

Emancipatory Spirituality offers a different kind of immortality, not a promise that our own individual personalities with their specific sets of memories and experiences will last forever, but the immortality of being part and parcel of the totality of all being. To appreciate this second kind of immortality, we need to reach a fuller awareness of our place in the universe and our identity as manifestations of the totality of all that is.

We are what Ken Wilber calls "holons," entities who are simultaneously separate beings, seeking to maintain our own individual existence, and parts of something much bigger than ourselves. In the contemporary world, it's easy to understand the consciousness of ourselves as separate beings, but it's very hard to develop a sense of ourselves as part of the Unity of All Being.

The Western intellectual tradition tends to encourage us to see the world as a collection of individual things, separated from each other, and then tries to figure out how they might interact. Much of our language contributes to this sense of separateness because it was developed to break up nature and our visual field into objects that could be used or shaped by human action.

But this isn't the only possible human goal. There's another way of thinking, one that stresses the fundamental interconnectedness of all being, one that starts with the premise of totality and moves from there. To understand the world from the standpoint of its fundamental unity, we need to transcend the language that was created to serve a different and narrower purpose. It's difficult for words to capture our intuition or perception of "the totality of all with all."

I sometimes think of our individual consciousness as a liver cell in a complex body. The liver cell understands what it can take in given the limited consciousness a liver cell can have. It has some inkling of connection to other liver cells, and probably some notion of a larger consciousness of the entire body. But it can't imagine a larger interconnected reality with a consciousness of the totality that is filled with love and pours out its generosity to all of its parts.

When a liver cell gets out of balance with the rest of the body we get a destructive expansiveness in which certain cells start to crowd out neighboring cells. We call that condition cancer. Cancer is the perfect analogy for individual egos that lose their sense of balance and begin to expand themselves at the expense of others.

In some spiritual traditions, the solution to this problem is to obliterate the individual ego. The ego itself is seen as the big problem, so the solution is to overcome it.

Emancipatory Spirituality, however, does not seek to obliterate the ego, but to put it in balance with the rest of the universe. In our society, we are in great need of this kind of rebalancing. Our society is full of people who go around saying "I am a self-made man or woman. I did it myself and therefore I deserve more money or power or recognition than anyone else." Many people say that because they were spiritually wounded, because they have been deprived of recognition and love, or because they never had the experience of being in a supportive community. It never occurs to them that the science and technology, the phone lines and the paved streets, the automobiles and airplanes that they use, even the conceptual distinctions and the language they draw upon were not built by them but by others. Instead, they need to puff themselves up to defend against their feeling of aloneness and their certainty that they cannot count on others. Said often enough, the myth of the self-made individual starts to take on the dimension of common sense in contemporary capitalist societies.

But look a little closer. Emancipatory Spirituality teaches that every one of us is standing on the platform of thousands of previous generations of human beings. We inherited the wisdom, the language, the categories, and the work of the past.

***

Even as I write this, I have to remember that the food on my table, shelter over my head, the computer in front of me, and the language and categories I use are the products of a planetary economy and tens of thousands of years of human effort. That economy has been made possible by all of humanity's previous experiments with forming larger and more inclusive cooperative enterprises. You and I are the beneficiaries of the goodness of tens of millions of human beings who struggled to get information, who developed techniques, tools, systems, words, and institutions. It was out of their love for each other and for the future of the human race that we can now live in peace, ease, dignity, security, affection, and harmony.

Here is one spiritual exercise that each of us needs to try every day. Take anything in your life—a musical instrument, a computer, a car, a piece of fruit that sits in your home but was grown far away, a television, a phone line, a book. Now try to imagine all the steps that needed to happen between the moment that human beings began to evolve and the moment you were able to have this thing in your life. If you ask what knowledge those who brought this object into your life had to have, what those who developed that knowledge had to learn from previous people who developed their knowledge, you will quickly be overwhelmed by the amount of cooperation through thousands of years that made all the things that populate your daily life possible. Try this exercise with a different object or aspect of your life every day and you'll soon see how much each of us is a beneficiary of the goodness and cooperation of past generations.

And that's what the universe is—a vast system of cooperation. Though many contemporary social institutions teach us to see others as enemies or potential rivals for scarce resources, the truth is that we live in a world in which the basic principle is one of cooperation.

My Hawaiian friend Morty Breyer taught me to recognize this in our own bodies. In his words: "My lungs with their system of bellows, branching, and oxygen-exchange membranes; my circulatory system with its tubes, valves, and pumps; my nervous system with its wiring; my digestive system with its juices and absorption linings; my sensory systems with their lenses, keying sites, and tympani membranes; my movement systems with their structural members, hinges, and rigging tendons; all of these and much more do not occur anywhere in the internal structures of any of my cells, nor in the life of any cell that preceded it. The beautifully cooperative actions of all of these systems with their common goal of preserving and empowering me, their organizational creation, developed over a long period of the evolution of animal life with the ultimate desire to cooperate on a vast scale. And we human beings have similarly built human technologies and cooperative organizing strategies just like the cells built within us."

Or think of DNA and the way, when damaged, it reorganizes itself. The individual parts work together to reveal the astonishing interconnectedness of Spirit.

What makes this cooperation possible is the force of love. Each of us was a product of the love of the universe pulsating through our parents. Though many of us think about how our parents were not as loving as we needed them to be, the fact that we are alive at all is testimony to the interaction between their loving and the loving manifested in social institutions that made it possible for children to be fed, housed, clothed, and protected.

The Possibilities Created by the Legacy of Love

On the platform of embodied love we have received from the universe we can create our world afresh. We are poised to take the next step in the evolution of human consciousness. To do that, we have to be aware of all that has gone before.

Human beings were never truly isolated or thrown into the world alone. That existential picture, described by the German philosopher Heidegger, is a further elaboration of the philosophers of early capitalism like Hobbes and Leibniz, who saw human beings as isolated nomads who forged contracts to enter into community only to avoid the war of all against all. Ironically, this war of all against all may be a good picture of what it's like to live in our contemporary "looking out for number one" society. It was seldom true of human life throughout most of our history.

Much of human history has been the history of smaller groups beginning to see common interests and ties to larger groups, first as clans, then as tribes, then as peoples, then as nations.

The next stage of human history requires that we take the next step in the evolution of consciousness and begin to see ourselves as one—as deeply connected, sharing one planet.

The idea of our fundamental interconnection with each other and with nature was already articulated in the Bible when its Prophets warned that without a society based on justice, peace, love, and caring, the whole world will face ecological catastrophe. From the Bible's perspective, we commit a global sin by allowing injustice and lack of love toward the stranger and our neighbor to persist. And its message is clear: You cannot act immorally without global consequences.

The next stage in the evolution of our spiritual consciousness will be facilitated when we internalize the awareness that you and I are deeply linked to the other six billion human beings who share this planet. But more than that—we are interdependent with all the other creatures who are traveling with us on spaceship Earth, and beyond that, with all life throughout the universe.

Here I think that the human race has a lot to learn from Biblically based religions. The central message of the Jewish Torah, the Christian Bible, and the Muslim Koran is that we were: born from God's love and the love that permeates the universe, and that we have every reason to see each other as created in the image of God, as embodiments of God, and to treat each other as such.

When I talk of God, I am talking about YHVH (mistranslated in the King James version as Jehovah, but actually four letters that Jews never pronounce precisely because they do not signify a specific being, but a world process, a God-ing, or, as David Cooper put it in the title of his book, *God Is a Verb*. YHVH comes from the root HVH, the Hebrew word for "the present tense" and the Y, which indicates the future. What the word really means is "the transformation of the present into that which can and should be in the future." In this sense, God is the Power of Healing and Transformation in the universe—and the Voice of the Future calling us to become who we need to become.

The word "God" has accumulated so much authoritarian and Patriarchal baggage that many people find it impossible to believe in the God they were taught about as children. Part of my reason for using the word Spirit throughout this book has been to avoid those associations. But if we think of God as the totality of all that is, was, and ever will be, as seen from the perspective of its evolution toward higher levels of consciousness and higher levels of loving connection, then many people who do not believe in God can still come to see the universe from this Spirit-oriented perspective.

Looking at the world in this way, we can each understand ourselves as one of the billions of ways Spirit has chosen to pour its love into existence. We are at once a manifestation of all the love of the universe, and an opportunity for the universe to manifest greater loving, cooperation, and harmony. This is what the angels meant in the Psalm when they said, "What is Man that thou shouldst think of him or the son of man that thou shouldst take account of him? But you have made man just a little lower than the angels." And yet, we are also, as the Psalmist proclaims, ". . . like a passing shadow, like a dream that vanishes."

While we are here on Earth, we have an incredible opportunity to recognize and rejoice in the Unity of All Being, to stand in awe and wonder at the glory of all that is, and to bring forward as much consciousness, love, solidarity, creativity, sensitivity, and goodness as we possibly can.

Developing and refining this kind of consciousness is a central element in what it means to develop an inner life. And this is one of the central aspects of spiritual practice.

Remembering God

~ Gai Eaton[257]

When the earth is shaken by a mighty shaking,
and the earth yields up her burdens,
and man cries out 'What ails her?' —
On that Day she will tell her tales,
as thy Lord will have inspired her.
On that Day mankind will issue, separately,
to be shown their deeds.
Whosoever has done an atom's weight of
good will see it then,
and whosoever has done an atom's weight of ill will see it then.

[*Sūrah Az-Zalzalah* (The Earthquake) 99:1-8]

Reinforcing the implications of this short *Surah*, the Prophet is reported to have said that, when the Last Day dawns, the earth herself will bear witness to everything that man has done. It might be said that we leave our fingerprints upon all that we touch, and they remain in place long after we have gone on our way. We forget so much of the past but the past is still there and cannot be wiped out, unless God—under His Name "the Effacer" (*al-ʿAfū*) —chooses to erase it from our record. But how can this earth, upon which we walk so carelessly, be said to bear witness against us? The Quranic answer is that God will inspire it to reveal its secrets, but still one asks: how could this be? There are several possible answers to the question, but I will suggest only one. Among the divine Names revealed in the Quran is *al-Ḥayy*, the "Ever-Living" or, quite simply, "Life". Since the Creator lends His attributes to everything that He creates, there can be nothing in existence that does not possess a kind of life, even if we do not understand in what sense to take this. Like all the other rigid distinctions which apply in this world, that between the animate and the inanimate is provisional, not absolute.

---

[257] Excerpted from *Remembering God, Reflections on Islam* by Gai Eaton, The Islamic Texts Society, Cambridge, England, 2000, "The Earth's Complaint" pp. 39 –52.

This brings me, once again, to the problem of terminology and the way in which words change their meaning. The word "psychic" has come to refer to fortune-tellers, spooks and things that go bump in the night. Yet, when it takes a suffix and becomes "psychology," we know at once that we are dealing, not with magic but with the science of the soul as practised by scientists who do not believe in the soul. The realm of the psyche, the "subtle realm" as it is sometimes called is not open to sense-perception but that does not mean that it is supernatural. It is the unseen face of the natural world. For Muslims it is also the realm of the *jinn*, those mysterious beings who form communities, as we do, and are equally capable of virtue or vice. The whole of nature has an unseen face, a "subtle" aspect of which we are generally unaware, although we speak sometimes of the "spirit" of a place without realising that this "spirit" is just as real as the place in its physical presence. It is upon this hidden side of the natural world that we leave our ineradicable imprint.

There are no hiding places. We are, as the Quran reminds us in many different ways, surrounded by a host of witnesses, ranging from God Himself and His angels to the earth we tread. We can have no secrets from them. I have wondered sometimes if this is why the Arabs tend to be secretive. Knowing that they are observed from every side, from above and from below, they treasure the only privacy they have, placing a discrete veil between themselves and their fellow men and women. In contrast, people in the West today eagerly confess all, not only to their friends but also on television and in the press. Believing themselves alone, self-enclosed and unobserved, they feel the need for self-exposure as a way of escaping from their isolation.

The spoor which we leave behind us on the earth is, however, only one side of the relationship we have with everything around us, a relationship of reciprocity. We are not insulated but, as it were, porous. We soak up elements from whatever we see, hear or touch, absorbing them into our substance. When we treat the natural world as an object to be exploited and conquered, we are damaging ourselves. The environmentalists are, no doubt, correct when they predict that our abuse of the earth will have disastrous consequences for humanity as a whole, but that should be the least of our worries. The consequences are on many different levels; the higher the level, the more deadly they are likely

341

to be. The Quran commands: "Work not confusion in the earth after the fair ordering thereof." When it says also that the earth and everything in it is created for our use, this does not imply a transfer of ownership; it is a trust delegated to us, and we are answerable to the "Owner of all things" for our stewardship. The Muslim is reminded again and again, both in the Quran and in the recorded sayings of the Prophet, that greed and wastefulness are among the major sins. We may use what is made so readily available to us for our sustenance, but that is all, and even that little is no more than theft if we have abandoned our human function and opted out of the universal prayer which carries the whole of creation back towards its source.

The Muslim is assured that the whole earth is a mosque for him. The walled buildings to which he is summoned for prayer are simply a convenience. The fields, the forests and the desert are equally fitting as places of prayer and therefore demand the same respect that is accorded to a conventional mosque. The link with heaven can be established anywhere and everywhere (*Wheresoever you turn, there is the Face of God*). One of the essential features of Islam is expressed in the Arabic word ādāb, which means "manners," "courtesy" or "correct behaviour," and it goes hand-in-hand with the dignity which the Muslim is required to demonstrate under all circumstances. God's Viceregent on earth is, after all, no mean figure, whether he is in robes or in rags. To show good manners, not only to our fellows but also towards everything that God has created, is a part of faith, for everything bears the imprint of His hand. The man or woman who stands, bows and prostrates in the midst of nature is a member of a universal congregation, joining in a universal prayer. "*All that is in the heavens and the earth glorifies God,*" says the Quran.

This is such a constant theme in the Quranic revelation that one can only be astonished by the fact that so many Muslims—unless they are Sufis—ignore it. *Have you not seen that all who are in the heavens and the earth glorify God, and the birds in their flight? Indeed He knows the worship and the praise of each, and God is aware of what they do.* Moreover, He "*disdains not to coin the similitude even of a gnat.*" How much greater the similitude of a lion or a swan, a mountain or a tree. Again, *See! In the creation of the heavens and the earth, and the difference of night and day . . . and the water which God sends down from the sky, thereby reviving the earth after its death, and dispersing all kinds of animals therein, and the ordering of the winds, and the clouds obedient between heaven and earth: (in these) are signs for people who have sense.* Whatsoever He has created in the earth *of different colours* conveys a message to us. So: *Look therefore upon the imprints of God's mercy.* They are everywhere.

The earth's beauties—its "ornaments"—are, the Quran tells us, a *reminder to mankind*, a reminder to those who are disposed to remember their origin and their end. For such as these, the natural world sparkles with light, but it would be dark if unperceived by man as the central being in creation, that is to say the link between what is above and what is below. Here again there is reciprocity. This world is not some chance agglomeration of material atoms, unrelated to our innermost being. It gives and it receives. We receive and we give. There is intercourse and mutuality; the objective world and human subjectivity might be compared to two circles which intersect rather than float, separate and divided, quite independent of each other. This is already implicit in the Islamic principle of *tawḥīd,* the unbroken unity of all that exists. It is implicit also in the word "cosmos" (as opposed to "universe," a neutral term that implies nothing). The cosmos is, by definition, an ordered whole, organised and harmonious, in which the parts are interdependent. As such it has meaning and, as the English word "cosmetics" suggests, it is beautiful.

But to perceive, evenly dimly, the "signs of God" around us—those signs to which the Quran refers repeatedly—requires a child's eye preserved in maturity. The Prophet is said to have prayed: "Lord, increase me in marvelling!" This is how a child sees the world, fresh from the hand of God and full of marvels but, with the passage of the years and the passing anxieties which time imposes, the vision fades; yet, in the words of the Quran, *It is not the eyes that grow blind, but the hearts within the breasts that grow blind.* Imbued with faith, the heart may still regain its sight, its insight. After the Call to Prayer, when Muslims have assembled in tightly packed ranks behind their Imam, their prayer leader, they are required to spend a few moments divesting themselves of the day's cares and all those urgent matters which had seized their attention, turning to face their Creator and address Him. It sometimes happens that the Imam turns to advise them: "Pray as if this is your last prayer!" So it will be for those fated to die before the next prayer is called, but one might equally say: "Pray as if this is your first prayer!" Every time we turn to God is a new beginning, a rebirth, and so it should be when we look with awakened hearts upon the world around us.

In doing so we have to remember that nothing is what it seems, or rather nothing is only what it seems. As with the verses of the Quran (the same Arabic word is used both for these verses and for the "signs" in nature), there is a literal meaning and, at the same time, a deeper meaning. The verses are sacred, and so are the "signs." It is here that we come to one of the most dangerous symptoms of alienation; the loss of the sense of the sacred in the modern world, a loss—a deprivation—which affects the Muslim *ummah* as it does the West. The Quran condemns those who separate that which God has joined, and the fragmentation which we see today is an obvious example of this severing of connections. The French critic of our technological civilization, Jacques Ellul, has pointed out that, in the past, man's deepest experience of the sacred was his immediate contact with the natural world. It is almost impossible fully to comprehend religion as such—or the great myths that bore witness to the unity of the cosmos—when nature has become remote and wholly "other." As Ellul says, the sense of the sacred withers when it is no longer rejuvenated by experience. The city dweller's awareness dries up for lack of support in his new experience with the artificial world of urban technology.

The loss of harmony between man and his natural environment is but an aspect of the loss of harmony between man and his Creator. Those who turn their backs on their Creator and forget Him can no longer feel at home in creation. They assume the role of bacteria which ultimately destroy the body they have invaded. "God's Viceregent on earth" is then no longer the custodian of nature and, having lost his function, he is a stranger who cannot recognise the landmarks or conform to the customs of this place; alienated—in the literal sense of "having become an alien"— he can see it only as raw material to be exploited. He may find riches and comfort in exploitation, but not happiness. He can never hope to sing with the Persian poet, Saʿdī:

> I am joyous with the cosmos,
> For the cosmos receives its joy from Him;

I love the world,

For the world belongs to Him.

We are, according to the Quran, "the poor" in relation to God, needy from the moment of birth till the end of our lives, and another of His Quranic Names is *al-Kāfī*, the Satisfier of all needs." The source of this hunger, inherent in our substance as human beings, is the need for Him, however it may be disguised or sidetracked by worldly desires. Since He is the only ultimate satisfier of desire it follows that, when we turn our backs and walk away, we will be perpetually unsatisfied and, still seeking to assuage our hungers, exceed all bounds. Until the development of technology this may have harmed only the perpetrator, but it did little harm to the earth. Our range has now been extended immeasurably, and we have become the great destroyers. One of the Buddhist hells is inhabited by huge creatures who were once men and women, ravaged by greed, but now their mouths are no bigger than a pin head. Surrounded by a feast of nourishment, they can take in only the tiniest crumbs.

Today, whether we are Muslims or Christians, we seem to have lost the key to the language of "signs," God's language. It has become both incomprehensible and irrelevant. This is particularly dangerous for the Muslim for whom the Quran must eventually become a partially closed book if the constant references to the natural world as a tissue of "signs" no longer coincide with his experience or touch his heart. That world, when seen through the window of a motor car or from a height of 30,000 feet, has nothing to say to us, even if it presents a pretty picture. Moreover, since everything has to be spelled out nowadays, it is typical of the modern mindset to ask: what exactly do these "signs" mean? If they could be expressed in words they would be redundant. They touch us at a deeper level than articulate speech, but this is already so with the Quran which, when it is recited to those who have no knowledge of Arabic, still moves their hearts though they understand nothing in terms of human language. So God has at His disposal two languages, the one composed of words and the other of "signs," although it could also be said that, in practice, He has three means of communication, the third being our personal destinies. These too contain messages for us if we are prepared to understand, and even the most arid sceptic, when struck down by bitter

345

misfortune, asks: "Why? Why me?" He is not supposed to believe that life has any meaning, but he believes none the less, or rather he knows in his heart what his mind denies.

To speak of the natural world is to speak of beauty. Since "God is beautiful" (according to a *ḥadīth*), beauty must in some sense be universally present as He is everywhere present. The common saying that "Beauty is in the eye of the beholder" is one of those half-truths which can either enlighten or deceive us according to our disposition. A particular individual or a particular culture will find the sacred in places where it is hidden from others who, in their turn, will discover it elsewhere. The same applies to the perception of what is beautiful. This does not make it any less real, any less objective. But saying that "God is beautiful, He loves beauty" is a statement about the nature of Reality, and it indicates something very important. Just as good and evil are on different levels—the former closer to the Real than the latter—so beauty and ugliness belong to different orders. Ugliness is not one of a pair, like hot and cold, black and white. It represents the spoiling of beauty, the unmaking of what has been well made. It might be compared to a stain on the fabric and belongs to that class of things which, the Quran tells us, last for but a short while and are then extinguished. This is why the Muslim, when he encounters things that are ugly or unseemly, tends to look away, not because he wishes to deny their existence but because not everything that exists is worth his attention. There is a story of Jesus in the Islamic tradition which makes this point. He was walking with his disciples when they passed a dead dog. "How it stinks!" said his companions. Jesus replied: "How white its teeth are!"

What is the beauty of nature if not an act of adoration, in that it reflects the divine Beauty? "Do you not see," asks the Quran, "that everything in the heavens and all that is in the earth pays adoration to God, as do the sun and the noon and the stars, the hills and the trees and the beasts. . . ?" There is a Turkish story of a spiritual teacher who sent his pupils to gather flowers for the house. All but one returned with the finest blooms they could find. One, however, was gone for a long time and, when he returned, held in his hand only a single, faded bloom. "When I went out to pick the flowers," he said, "I found them all singing the praises of their Creator and I dared not interrupt them. Finally I saw one that had finished her song, and this is the one that I have brought you." It would be a mistake to regard this little story as a poetic fancy. The blood that courses through our bodies may lend itself to poetry and to myth, but the fact remains that it has a very important practical function. When the Quran speaks of this perpetual and universal adoration it is doing neither more nor less than telling us what happens, the down-to-earth reality of the situation. Our subjective awareness—or unawareness—cannot alter the facts.

If there is nothing in existence that is only and exclusively what it seems to be, then everything has its own particular significance. I can imagine someone saying: "This is too much! Women's rights, animal rights, even plant rights, and now you talk about the rights of sticks and stones! Where will it end?" It has no end. That is the only possible answer. We did not make the world, we do not own it. You cannot, the Quran reminds us, create even a fly. This vast picture-book, filled with the "signs" of God, is what it is. Appearances, as we are so often told, are deceptive and, if we float only on the surface of our world, then we are indeed deceived. There is always more to it than that, then more and then still more, until you have plumbed the depths and found—behind the "seventy-thousand veils of light and darkness"—the Face of God. The modern age is frequently condemned for its "materialism." Perhaps it is not materialistic enough, that is to say it no longer seeks, beyond the shifting surface of material objects—these clouds that constantly form and re-form—what it is that they both veil and reveal.

Two further Names by which God has defined Himself in the Quran are *al-Muḥīṭ*; the "All-Embracing" or the "All-Surrounding" and *al-Ẓāhir*, which means "the Outward." It follows that, ultimately and behind all the appearances, He is our "environment" and there is no other. But that is an intellectual statement which might seem to rob the things we see and touch of their due measure of reality. While we are in this life, situated midst the "veils," they are the only reality we know, reflecting after their fashion the greater realities which remain hidden, too bright for our perception. It is their meaning rather than their material structure that should be our prime concern. The mechanism of a clock may be of practical interest, but the purpose of the clock is to tell the time.

The very sounds of nature may add to this universe of meaning, this flood of communication between Creator and creation. I remember a certain Sheikh who was about to deliver his sermon when the thunder sounded, rolling on and on. He fell silent and kept silent even after the heavens had spoken. What could he have added? But we must be very patient and very attentive to catch, through hearing as through sight, that note of universal praise. When the Muslim is at prayer in the early hours of the day or in the act of remembering God, bird song, the ocean's roar or the drumming of rain do not disturb him, on the contrary they contribute to his remembrance. But the noise of cars or machinery introduces into the harmony of his worship a discord against which he is obliged to struggle.

Prayer and contemplation, supported by a cosmic environment which, in a sense, cries out to be seen, heard and understood are central to the religious life. But there is also involvement, for which we are still situated at a distance from the natural world. There are children in Europe and America who are not even aware of the fact that the packaged meat on supermarket shelves is the flesh of living creatures or that the vegetables from which every grain of earth has been washed once grew in open fields and took their time to grow. The patience of the agriculturist is unimaginable to an increasingly impatient generation. Their needs are satisfied in relation to the moving hands of a clock, not by the seasons or by the discipline imposed by the weather. They are "out of touch," and this phrase can have a profound significance. It represents remoteness, separation and—once again—alienation. In towns and cities the stars are blotted out by street lighting, their brightness hidden and their message dimmed. Here too, it is not only contemplation but also involvement that has been lost. "*He it is,*" says the Quran, "*who has set for you the stars that you may guide your course by them amidst the darkness of the land and the sea.*" We no longer need them. They can be left to the specialists who talk in terms of light years and have nothing to offer that would help us on our way through the darkness that has penetrated within our breasts and within our minds.

This, of course, is "progress," and it is certainly convenience, although one of the ironies of the situation is that our contemporaries in the West, freed from the labour once required of them in their encounter with the natural world and their dependence upon it, now have to work harder than ever as ciphers in the industrial or bureaucratic machine to afford the lifestyle to which they have a "right." This work offers no spiritual nourishment. It is not expected to do so. It provides no contact with reality on any level and no involvement with the "signs" that point our way and remind us of who we are. An almost superhuman effort would be required for us to remember that we are God's "Viceregents," responsible for our province just as the farmer is responsible for his stock and his crops. We keep the wheels turning, but they turn to no purpose except to keep the speeding train on tracks which lead nowhere. Eventually it will hit the buffers, the invisible limits which frame our worldly existence.

The Muslim tries to live within the limits of the *Sharīʿah*, the road or path which leads safely to the watering place and so, beyond all limits, to Paradise and the ultimate satisfaction of all needs. Being human, we are free to wander from the road. The rest of creation does not have this freedom. In terms of the Islamic perspective, the animals and the plants, the mountains and the oceans have, each of them, their own *Sharīʿah*. They are bound inescapably to the function decreed for them. They cannot be other than they are meant to be and there is, in this, a lesson for mankind. Our environment obeys God and encourages us to do the same. The rocks and the rivers are subject to the "laws of nature," the animals follow their "instincts"; this is but one way of describing the divine Decree which governs their existence. They cannot sin, they cannot break bounds, and this exposes the absurdity of the remark frequently addressed to vicious criminals by a learned Judge: "You are no better than an animal!" As human creatures we can be better than the animals or worse than them; we cannot, however, exist on their level since we are not subject to the laws which direct and enclose their lives. "there is not an animal on earth," says the Quran, "nor a bird flying on two wings but they are communities like you" (or "in your likeness"), and the verse ends: "And unto their Lord they will be gathered." It is not open to us to join one or other of their communities but we can, if we depart from the *Sharīʿah* laid down for us, become not only subhuman but subanimal.

There is great confusion in the Western mind concerning the animal species. Hardly a day passes that one does not hear someone say: "After all, we're only animals." This is not an opinion but an ideological statement regarding the origin and status of the human being. It proclaims an unquestioning adherence to the Darwinian theory and often sounds like a political slogan. The curious thing is that its implications are ignored. At least for the time being—although this may change—men and women are treated quite differently from animals. It does not occur to us to bring a pig to court, as sometimes happened in the Middle Ages, and charge it with a crime. The owner of an animal that is mortally sick is blamed for not having it "put down"; the same person will be tried for murder if he or she "puts down" a terminally ill patient. Most people believe that we are neither more nor less than clever primates (or so they are told), but they are horrified if human beings are treated as if they were apes.

It seems to me that there is also confusion, although of a different kind, in the Muslim mind. No religion lays greater stress on the good treatment of animals than does Islam, yet Muslims have in general a bad reputation in this regard (as did Christians until very recently). If we represent a religion—any traditional religion—as a circle or a sphere, then it is likely that its adherents will absorb and practice only a segment of the whole. They will also emphasise this segment, as though to fill the empty space, so that they are blinded to all that they have ignored. Their religion, one might say, is too big for them. You cannot pour the ocean into a pint pot. The fact that people of the same faith may choose different segments for their exclusive attention is one of the reasons for conflicts within the religion, not least within the Islamic *ummah*.

The good Muslim's life is lived in imitation of the Prophet's example, followed as faithfully as circumstances permit. It is in this example, the acts and the sayings of God's Messenger, that we find the most uncompromising references to animal welfare. If they are taken seriously—and how can the Muslim not take them seriously?—they have very grave implications for all who fall short in their care for the animals in their charge. Not only are there the famous stories of the woman sent to hell for shutting up a cat till it died of hunger and of the prostitute forgiven all her sins because she gave water to a dog that was dying of thirst, but there are also a number of small incidents in the record which emphasise the same principle. When the Prophet saw a donkey that had been branded on the face he cried out: "God curse the one who branded it." A man who was about to slaughter a goat for food was severely reproached for allowing the animal to see him sharpening his knife. A prophet of earlier times was scolded by God Himself for burning an ants nest because an ant had stung him—*You have destroyed a community that glorified Me*—and there is, according to another saying, a reward in Paradise for whoever shows kindness to a creature possessed of "a living heart." The law books instruct us as to what to do if we find a poisonous snake in our garden. It is to be warned to leave. If it returns a second time, it is to be warned again, but if it makes a third visit it may be killed.

The Quran tells us: "Your Lord inspired the bee, saying: Choose dwellings in the hills and in the trees and in what is built; then eat all manner of fruit and follow humbly the ways of your Lord made smooth"; in other words, follow your *Sharīʿah*, for that is your path and your destiny. This again brings out the Islamic view that each of the diverse non-human "communities" has a particular relationship with its Lord, but the Lord is one; ours as well as theirs. The relationships differ and so the paths differ, but the goal is the same. It is the harmonious interaction of all the components of the cosmos, both animate and inanimate, which reflects in countless different ways the unity of the Real. The killing of an animal except for food, and then only the permitted minimum, and even the unnecessary cutting down of a tree or uprooting of a plant goes, as it were, against the grain. It exceeds, from motives of greed, the bounds laid down for humankind. There is no place here, no excuse, for the luxuries of modern civilization.

Were it not for the divine Mercy, scattered like rain throughout creation, and God's readiness to forgive all sins (except the association of other deities with the One) if they are followed by sincere repentance, we would be in a bad way, but what matters most is to keep these principles always in mind, and that is possible only if we observe what might aptly be called the Prime Directive of Islam: the constant "remembrance of God." All that we need to know and all that

351

we are required to do is encompassed in this remembrance; it is the shield against temptation and the spur to keep us on the "straight path" made smooth for us. In choosing to follow it, we are in step with the animals, the plants and the earth itself which, then and only then, has no cause for complaint.

III. Caring
for God's Creation

CHAPTER EIGHTEEN

INTRODUCTION:
RECOGNIZING THE SACRED

Have you not turned your vision towards your Sustainer?
See how He lengthens the shadow!
If He willed He could make it stand still!
But We have made the sun its guide,
and then We draw it in towards Ourselves—
a contraction by easy stages.
And He it is Who makes the night as a robe for you,
and sleep as repose, and makes every day a resurrection.
And He it is Who sends the winds as heralds of glad tidings
preceding His Mercy.
And We send down purifying water from the sky
that with it We may give life to a dead land
and assuage the thirst of things We have created—
cattle and people in great numbers.
And We have distributed it among them
so that they may celebrate Our praises—
but most people are reluctant to be anything but ungrateful.
[*Sūrah Al-Furqān* (The Standard Of True And False) 25:45-50]

And [Jesus] said to his disciples, "Therefore I say to you, take no thought
for your life, what you shall eat;
neither for the body, what you shall wear.
The life is more than meat, and the body is more than clothing.
Consider the ravens for they neither sow nor reap
neither do they have storehouses nor barn, and God feeds them:
how much better are you than the birds?
And which of you by thinking can add one cubit to his stature?
If you can't do this which is least, why do you think about the rest?
Consider the lilies of the field how they grow:

they do not toil, neither do they spin, and yet I say to you
that Solomon in all his glory was not arrayed like one of these.
If then God so clothes the grass, which is today in the field
and tomorrow is cast into the oven,
how much more will he clothe you, O you of little faith?
And seek not what you shall eat, or what you shall drink,
neither be of doubtful mind,
For all these things do the nations of the world seek after:
your Father knows that you have need of these things.
But rather seek the kingdom of God,
and all these things shall be added to you.
Fear not, little flock, for it is your Father's good pleasure
to give you the kingdom.
Sell what you have and give alms;
Provide yourselves with bags which will not grow old,
a treasure in the heavens which does not fail,
where no thief approaches, neither moth corrupts.
For where your treasure is, there will your heart be also.
[The Bible, St. Luke 12:22-34]

Where the Wasteland Ends

~ Michael A. Cremo and Mukunda Goswami[258]

"The desacralized world is doomed to become an obstacle inviting conquest, a mere object. Like the animal or the slave who is understood to have no soul, it becomes a thing of subhuman status to be worked, used up, and exploited." ~ Theodore Roszak

Among those calling for a spiritual solution to our planet's environmental crisis are, interestingly enough, some of the world's leading

---

[258] Michael A. Cremo and Mukunda Goswami, "Divine Nature," excerpted from *Science, Nature and the Environment*, The Bhaktivedanta Book Trust, LA, CA. 1995.

scientists. At the Global Forum of Spiritual and Parliamentary Leaders, held in Moscow in January 1990, thirty-two scientists signed a document titled "Preserving and Cherishing the Earth: An Appeal for Joint Commitment in Science and Religion."

The signers included astronomer Carl Sagan, nuclear winter theorist Paul J. Crutzen, physicist Freeman J. Dyson, paleontologist Stephen J. Gould, environmental scientist Roger Revelle, and former Massachusetts Institute of Technology (MIT) president Jerome Wiesner.

"We are close to committing—many would argue we are already committing—what in religious language is sometimes called Crimes against Creation," said the scientists. They therefore issued an urgent "appeal to the world religious community to commit, in word and deed, and as boldly as is required, to preserve the environment of the earth."

"The environmental crisis requires radical changes not only in public policy," said the scientists, "but also in individual behavior. The historical record makes clear that religious teaching, example, and leadership are powerfully able to influence personal conduct and commitment."

"As scientists, many of us have had profound experiences of awe and reverence before the universe," added the signers. "We understand that what is regarded as sacred is more likely to be treated with care and respect. Our planetary home should be so regarded. Efforts to safeguard and cherish the environment need to be infused with a vision of the sacred."

Sacred Science and the Environmental Crisis: An Islamic Perspective

~ Seyyed Hossein Nasr[259]

"O Lord, show us things as they really are." (*Ḥadith* of the Prophet)

It is . . . essential for those who speak for religion and the world of the Spirit, to collaborate and apply that inner unity and harmony which binds them together to the terrestrial realm and the question of saving the planet from a humanity in rebellion against both heaven and earth. The person who speaks for the life of the Spirit today cannot remain indifferent to the destruction of that primordial cathedral which is virgin nature nor maintain silence concerning the harm that man does to himself as an immortal being by absolutising the "kingdom of man" and as a consequence brutalising and destroying everything else in the name of the earthly welfare of members of that kingdom.

Islam certainly has its share of responsibility in drawing the attention of its own adherents as well as the world at large to the spiritual significance of nature and the necessity to live in peace and harmony with the rest of Allah's creation. The Islamic tradition is particularly rich in preserving to this day its sacred sciences, a sapiential knowledge combined with a love of the natural environment, a metaphysics of nature which unveils her role as the grand book in which the symbols of the world of Divine Majesty and Beauty are engraved. It also possesses a system of ethics, rooted in the revelation and bound to the Divine Law, which concerns the responsibilities and duties of man towards the non-human realms of the created order. It is incumbent upon Muslims to resuscitate both of these dimensions of their tradition in a contemporary language which can awaken and lead men and women to a greater awareness of the spiritual significance of the natural world and the dire consequences of its destruction.

---

[259] Excerpted from (pp. 134-136) of "Sacred Science and the Environmental Crisis: An Islamic Perspective" by Seyyed Hossein Nasr, pp. 118-137 of *Islam and the Environment*, Edited by Harfiyah Abdel Haleem, Ta-Ha Publishers Ltd., London, England, 1998. Reprinted by permission of Ta-Ha Publishers Ltd.

It is also the duty of those who speak for traditional Islam to carry out a dialogue with followers of other religions on an issue which concerns men and women everywhere. By sharing the wisdom of their tradition with others, they can contribute a great deal not only to the Islamic world itself as it struggles with the consequences of the environmental crisis, but to the whole of humanity. As the sun shines upon all men and women from east to west and the night stars reveal their mysterious beauty to those with eyes to see whether they behold them in Japan, India, Arabia or America, so does the wisdom concerning nature and the compassionate care for nature as taught by various religions belong to human beings wherever they might be, as long as they are blessed with the gift of appreciation of the beauty of the rose and the song of the nightingale. The Qur'an asserts that *to Allah belong the East and the West* [2:115]. This statement possesses many levels of meaning, one of which is that where the sun rises and where it sets, where forests cover the land and where sand dunes rove over empty spaces, where majestic mountains touch the void of heaven and where deep blue waters reflect the Divine Infinitude, all belong to Allah and are hence interrelated. The destruction of one part of creation affects other parts in ways that the science of today has not been able to fathom. In such an interdependent natural environment in which all human beings live, it is for men and women everywhere to unite, not in an agnostic humanism which kills the divine in them,[260] and so veils the reflection of the divine in nature, but in awareness of the one God, Allah, who manifests His power in different ways in the vast and complex ocean of humanity.

To rediscover the divine and its reflection in oneself, is the first essential step. To see the reflection of the divine in the world of nature is its natural consequence. Man cannot save the natural environment except by rediscovering the nexus between the Supreme Artisan and nature, His creation, and becoming once again aware of the sacred quality of His works. And man cannot gain such an awareness of the sacred aspect of nature without discovering the sacred within himself and ultimately the

---

[260] The part of them which is described as the breath of Allah, breathed into the first man at his creation. (S.H.N.)

Sacred as such. The solution of the environmental crisis cannot come but from the cure of the spiritual malaise of modern man and the rediscovery of Allah's attributes; and Allah, being compassionate, always gives to those open and receptive of His life-giving bounty. The bounties of nature and Allah's generosity to man are there, proofs of this reality, for despite all that man has done to destroy nature, it is still alive and reflects on its own ontological level the love and compassion, the wisdom and the power which belong ultimately to the realm of Allah.

And We have spread the earth out wide;
set upon it firm and immovable mountains;
and produced upon it all kinds of things in balance.
And We have provided there means of subsistence for you
and for those whose provision does not depend on you.
And there is not a thing but its storehouses are with Us;
but We only send it down in appropriate measures.
[*Sūrah* 15:19-21]

Measuring

~ Fazlur Rahman[261]

The most fundamental disparity between God and His creation is that, whereas God is infinite and absolute, every creature is finite. All things have potentialities, but no amount of potentiality may allow what is finite to transcend its finitude and pass into infinity. This is what the Qur'an means when it says that everything except God is "measured out" (*qadar* or *qadr, taqdir*, etc.), and is hence *dependent upon* God, and that whenever a creature claims complete self-sufficiency or independence (*istiqhad', istikbar*), it thus claims infinitude and a share in divinity (*shirk*). When God creates anything, He places within it its powers or laws of behavior, called

---

[261] Fazlur Rahman, *Major Themes of the Qur'an,* Bibliotheca Islamica, Chicago, IL, 1980, pp. 67-68.

in the Qur'an a "guidance," "command," or "measure" whereby it fits into the rest of the universe: *He gave everything its creation and then guided [it]* [20:50]; *He who created [things] and [created them] well, and who measured* [them] *out and thus guided [them]* [87:2-3]; *Lo, to Him belong both creation and commanding* [7:54]; and, *Indeed, We have created everything with a measure* [54:49; cf.15:21]. If things should break their laws and violate their measure, there would be not an ordered universe, but chaos. The Qur'an speaks frequently of the perfect order in the universe as proof not only of God's existence but also of His unity [21:22; cf. also the moving passage at 27:60-64].

It should be noted that this "measuring" has a strong holistic bias in terms of patterns, dispositions, and trends. Nor is the resulting total performance conceived of in terms of particular events and acts. It is, therefore, *not* a theory of predetermination, although it does mean a kind of "holistic determinism." This is clear from the references where "measured" does not mean "predetermined" but "finite" or "limited." The following passage must be understood in the same light:

> *And the sun moves [along its course] to its resting place—*
> *that is the measuring [or determination] of the All-Mighty, the All-Knowing.*
> *And for the moon We have appointed certain stations,*
> *until it returns like an old curved stick.*
> *It is not for the sun to overtake the moon, nor for the night to overstrip the day,*
> *each coursing in its own orbit.*
> [*Sūrah Yā Sīn* (O Thou Human Being) 36:38-40]

This *qadar* or "measure" also operates at the holistic level in the sphere of human moral actions, which by definition are free. Judgment in history, for instance, concerns the total performance of a people; in the Last Judgment, it is primarily the total performance of individuals that comes under review. The difference between nature and man is that in the case of man the particular moral actions take place by free choice.

Nature is in fact so well-knit and works with such regularity that it is the prime miracle of God, cited untiringly in the Qur'an. No being short of God could have built this vast and stable edifice:

> *He who created seven heavens one on top of another—*
> *you shall not find in the creation of the Merciful any dislocation.*
> *Look again—do you see any gap?*

Look again and again—your sight will return to you frustrated
[in the attempt to find any discontinuity or irregularity] and fatigued.

[Sūrah Al-Mulk (Dominion) 67:3-4]

And you see the mountains and think them solid
[and stationary] but they are fleeting like clouds—
the creation of God who has well-completed
[the creation of] everything.

[Sūrah An-Naml (The Ants) 27:88]

References to phenomena like the regularity of the day following the night and the night following the day, the rainy season when the earth is quickened following the dry season when it had been parched and dead, are strewn through the pages of the Qur'an.

This gigantic machine, the universe, with all its causal processes, is the prime "sign" (*ayah*) or proof of its Maker. Who else but an infinitely powerful, merciful, and purposeful Being could have brought into existence something with dimensions so vast and an order and design so complex and minute? Yet, man, the Qur'an complains recurrently, is ordinarily apt to "forget" God so long as "natural" causes work for him; it is only when natural causes fail him that he "discovers" God.

Recognizing the Sacred Earth

~ Thomas Berry[262]

Suddenly we awaken to the devastation that has resulted from the entire modern process. A thousand pages would be needed to recount what has happened. It can best be summarized by the title of Rachel Carson's book, *Silent Spring*, a title taken from Keats: "The sedge is withered from the lake / and no birds sing." The book itself is dedicated to Albert Schweitzer, who tells us: "Man has lost the capacity to foresee and to forestall. He will end by destroying the earth."

---

[262] Excerpted from *Creative Energy: Bearing Witness for the Earth* by Thomas Berry. Copyright © 1988 by Thomas Berry. Reprinted by permission of Sierra Club Books.

This is a bitter moment, not simply for the human, but for the earth itself.[263]

★★★

Our legal system fosters a sense of the human as having rights over the rights of natural beings. Our commerce, industry, and economics are based on the devastation of the earth. Disengagement from such basic life commitments requires a certain daring.

In order to get a sense of just how difficult it is to change basic commitments, we might recall the story of the *Titanic* on her maiden voyage. Abundant evidence indicated that icebergs were ahead. Nevertheless, the course was set, and no one wished to alter the direction. Confidence in the survival capacities of the ship was unbounded, and there were already a multitude of other concerns related to carrying out the simply normal routine of the voyage. I relate the story of the *Titanic* here as a kind of parable, since even in dire situations we often do not have the energy required to alter our way of acting on the scale that is required. For us there is still time to change course, to move away from our plundering economy to a more sustainable ecological economy.

We cannot obliterate the continuities of history. Nor can we move into the future without guidance from the more valid elements of our existing cultural forms, yet we must reach far back into the genetic foundations of our cultural formation for a healing and a restructuring at the most basic level. This is particularly true now, since the anthropogenic shock that is overwhelming the earth is of an order of magnitude beyond anything previously known in human historical or cultural development. As we have indicated, only those geological and biological changes of the past that have taken hundreds of millions of years for their accomplishment can be referred to as having any comparable order of magnitude.

The new cultural coding that we need must emerge from the source of all such codings, from revelatory vision that comes to us in those special psychic moments, or conditions, that we describe as "dream." We are, of course, using this term not only as regards the psychic processes that take place when we are physically asleep, but also to indicate an intuitive,

---

[263] Ibid., p. 59.

nonrational process that occurs when we awaken to the numinous powers ever present in the phenomenal world about us, powers that possess us in our high creative moments; Poets and artists continually invoke these spirit powers, which function less through words than through symbolic forms.

In moments of confusion such as the present, we are not left simply to our own rational contrivances. We are supported by the ultimate powers of the universe as they make themselves present to us through the spontaneities within our own beings. We need only become sensitized to these spontaneities, not with a naive simplicity, but with critical appreciation. . . .[264]

What I am proposing here is that these prior archetypal forms that guided the course of human affairs are no longer sufficient. Our genetic coding, through the ecological movement and through the bioregional vision, is providing us with a new archetypal world. The universe is revealing itself to us in a special manner just now. Also the planet Earth and the life communities of the earth are speaking to us through the deepest elements of our nature, through our genetic coding.

In relation to the earth, we have been autistic for centuries. Only now have we begun to listen with some attention and with a willingness to respond to the earth's demands that we cease our industrial assault, that we abandon our inner rage against the conditions of our earthly existence, that we renew our human participation in the grand liturgy of the universe.[265]

> Say: "Behold, my prayer, and [all] my acts of worship,
> and my living and my dying are for God [alone],
> the Sustainer of all the worlds.
> [Sūrah Al-Anʿām (Cattle) 6:162]

---

[264] Ibid., pp. 70-72.
[265] Ibid., p. 78.

CHAPTER NINETEEN

WORKING TOWARDS SUSTAINABILITY

Don't you see that God has made in service to you
all that is in the heavens and on earth
and has made His bounties flow to you
in abundant measure, seen and unseen?
[*Sūrah Luqmān* 31:20]

For it is He who has brought into being gardens—
both the cultivated ones and those growing wild—
and the date-palm, and fields bearing all manner of produce,
and the olive, and the pomegranate:
all resembling one another and yet so different!
Eat of their fruit when it ripens,
and contribute appropriate portions on harvest day.
And do not be wasteful:
truly, He does not love those who are wasteful!
[*Sūrah Al-Anᶜām* (Cattle) 6:141]

The parable of the life of this world is as the rain
which We send down from the skies—
absorbed by the earth, it encourages plants to spring forth
which provide nourishment for humans and animals;
until the earth is adorned with its golden ornaments and is enhanced,
so that those who dwell on it may think they have gained mastery over it;
but by night or by day, Our command reaches it,
and We make it become like a clear-cut field
as if only the day before it had not flourished!
And so We explain the signs in detail for those who reflect.
but God invites to the Abode of Peace;
He guides those that will to a way that is straight.

364

To those who do good is a good recompense, even more!
No darkness nor shame will veil their faces!
They are companions of the Garden; there will they dwell!
[*Sūrah Yūnus* (Jonah) 10:24-26]

Do not allow to be corrupted that which God has made.
That is the true way,
but most people do not understand.
Turn in repentance to Him and remain conscious of Him:
[*Sūrah Ar-Rūm* (The Byzantines) 30:30-31]

Call to your Sustainer humbly, and in the secrecy of your hearts.
Truly, He does not love those who go beyond the bounds
of what is right.
And so, do not spread corruption on earth
after it has been so well ordered.
And call to Him with awe and longing:
truly, God's grace is very near those who do good.
[*Sūrah Al-Aᶜrāf* (The Faculty Of Discernment) 7:55-56]

Consider the sun and its splendor,
and the moon as she follows.
Consider the day as it reveals this world,
and the night as it conceals it.
Consider the scope of the heavens
and its wondrous structure;
consider the earth and its broad expanse.
Consider the soul and the order and proportion given to it,
and its enlightenment as to that which is wrong and right:
truly, the one who purifies it shall reach a happy state
and the one who corrupts it shall truly be lost!
[*Sūrah Ash-Shams* (The Sun) 91:1-10]

365

And unto [the people of] Madyan [We sent] their brother Shuᶜayb.[266] *He said:*
"O my people! Worship God alone:
you have no deity other than Him.
Clear evidence has now come to you from Your Sustainer.
Give therefore, full measure and weight [in all your dealings],
and do not deprive people of what is rightfully theirs;
and do not spread corruption on earth after it has been so well ordered:
[all] this is for your own good, if you would but have faith."
[*Sūrah Al-Aᶜrāf* (The Faculty Of Discernment) 7:85]

The Prophet said, "Charity is incumbent upon every Muslim."

The people asked him, "O Prophet of God, what about one who has nothing to give?"

The Prophet said, "Then one works with one's own hands to support oneself and to give to others."

They asked, "And if one cannot find work?"

The Prophet said, "Then one should be good and refrain from evil; for that in fact is charity for the one who does so."[267]

Widening the Circle of Compassion

~ Albert Einstein

A human being is a part of a whole, called by us a universe, a part limited in time and space. He experiences himself, his thoughts and feelings as something separated from the rest . . . a kind of optical delusion of his consciousness. This delusion is a kind of prison for us, restricting us

---

[266] Shuᶜayb is said to be identical with Jethro, the father-in-law of Moses, also called in the Bible *Reu-el* (Exodus II:18), meaning "Faithful to God." The region of Madyan—the Midian of the Bible—extended from the present-day Gulf of Aqabah westwards deep into the Sinai Peninsula and to the mountains of Moab east of the Dead Sea. ~ M. Asad

[267] *The Wisdom of the Prophet, Sayings of Muhammad, Selections from the Hadith,* Translated by Thomas Cleary, Shambhala Publications, Inc., Boston, Massachusetts, copyright by Thomas Cleary 1994, p. 14.

to our personal desires and to affection for a few persons nearest to us. Our task must be to free ourselves from this prison by widening our circle of compassion to embrace all living creatures and the whole of nature in its beauty.

What's the use of a fine house if you haven't got a tolerable planet to put it on?

~ Henry David Thoreau

Where the quality of life goes down for the environment, the quality of life goes down for humans.

~ George Holland

We've begun destroying the things we need for the things that we want.

~ Julia Butterfly Hill

The frog does not drink up the pond in which it lives.

~ Native American Proverb

Let us permit nature to have her way, she understands her business better than we do.

~ Michel Eyquem de Montaigne

Man should not destroy what he cannot create.

~ Dr. Ruth Kiew

The destiny of humans cannot be separated from the destiny of earth.

~ Thomas Berry

Only in the last moment in history has the delusion arisen that people can flourish apart from the rest of the living world.

~ E.O. Wilson

A field that has rested gives a bountiful crop.

~ Ovid

We are praying, many of the medicine people, the spiritual leaders, the elders, are praying for the world. We are praying that mankind does wake up and think about the future, for we haven't just inherited this earth from our ancestors, but we are borrowing it from our unborn children.

~ Joseph Chasing Horse[268]

Threads of a Whole Cloth

~ Charles Upton

Our soul needs a sense of place. We often experience soul in nature because the direct experience of the sun, trees, grass, flowers, and the earth is so nourishing to our soul. . . . When I am truly present in nature I feel a sense of awe and reverence from just witnessing the beauty of it all. . . . Thomas Moore advocates a "soul-ecology" where we respect the soul in nature that is based on a "felt relationship." He argues that the root meaning of ecology is seeing the Earth as "home." We are moved to take care of earth as we would our own home when we feel a deep affection for it.

Moore goes on to suggest that the problem of what he refers to as our homelessness is rooted in our abstraction from the earth. Because we have lost the felt relationship to the Earth most human beings have become inwardly homeless on the planet. The Zuni Indians of New Mexico see their home as a "particular place and the entire world."

Earth education demands that things and events be looked at within larger patterns and relationships. David Orr (1994) suggests that many of our personal and societal problems stem from seeing the world in a fragmented and disconnected way. Building freeways, shopping malls, parking lots at a non-stop pace without consideration of the real need and impact on ecology is a product of the compartmentalized way of seeing and behaving.

These things are threads of a whole cloth. The fact that we see them

---

[268] Joseph Chasing Horse, "White Buffalo Calf Woman" www.kstrom.net/:sk/arvol/buffpipe.html. Accessed 6/04.

as disconnected events or fail to see them at all is, I believe, evidence of a considerable failure that we have yet to acknowledge as an educational failure. It is a failure to educate people to think broadly, to perceive systems and patterns and to live as whole persons.

John Ralston Saul in his 1995 Massey Lectures, *The Unconscious Civilization,* points out the failure to make important connections in our society. In one ecological example, he states:

> The world-wide depletion of fish stocks is a recent example. The number of fish caught between 1950 and 1989 multiplied by five. The fishing fleet went from 585,000 boats in 1970 to 1.2 million boats in 1990 and on to 3.5 million today. No one thought about the long or even the medium-term maintenance of stocks; not the fishermen, not the boat builders, not the fish wholesalers, who found new uses for their product, including fertilizer and chicken feed; not the financiers. It wasn't their job. Their job was to worry about their own interests. (p. 135)

As we awaken to the Earth and its processes, we free ourselves from this modern blindness and start to look at life interdependently. We then can see the effects of industrialization in the air we breathe and the water we drink, not to mention the harm to the ozone layer and the ongoing process of global warming. A strictly rationalist approach to life denies this broader perspective. A soulful approach not only enables but demands such a perspective because soul is immersed in connections.

Being Caretakers

~ Leyla Knight[269]

In Saudi Arabia, where I grew up, girls aren't allowed to play outside. My stepfather would take all 12 children to his tribal lands—you can

---

[269] Leyla Knight, Marketing and Communications Assistant, The Nature Conservancy, Arizona. Muslim: Excerpted from "Portraits of Faith," Interviews by Susan Enfield Esrey, Laura Fisher Kaiser, Danielle Furlich, and Meaghan O'Neil. Edited by Laura Fisher Kaiser. Nature Conservancy, Spring 2003 issue, p. 28.

imagine how much my mother appreciated getting eight girls out of the house—and the desert is where I developed a love for nature and being outside.

This was in the 1980s. I noticed that some natural places were becoming cement and asphalt. It didn't feel right to me. I remember one city on the Red Sea where most of the beaches were cemented right up to the water. That was considered progress. It was heartbreaking.

I think my faith and work at the Conservancy really agree with each other. According to the Koran, we're supposed to be caretakers. There's a lot of emphasis on what will benefit the culture as a whole. We're saving land and water that everyone needs, not just humans but animals also. It just seems to fit.

Responsibility

~ Tenzin Gyatso, the Dalai Lama[270]

Essentially, nature's elements have secret ways of adapting. When something is damaged, another element helps out and improves the situation through some kind of evolution. This is nature's way of adjustment. But then, human intervention creates certain changes which do not give nature and its elements time to cope. So the main troublemaker, the major cause of imbalance, is we human beings ourselves. Therefore, the responsibility should be borne by us. We must find some way to restrain our destructive habits. We cause these problems mainly with our modern economy. With different kinds of factories and chemicals, we have a strong negative impact on the balance of nature. The next question is, if that is the case, whether we have to stop all

---

[270] Excerpted from "A Tibetan Buddhist Perspective on Spirit in Nature" from *Seeing God Everywhere, Essays on Nature and the Sacred.* Edited by Barry McDonald, Copyright 2003 World Wisdom, Inc., pp. 21-23, from a talk delivered at the Symposium on Spirit and Nature held at Middlebury College in Middlebury, Vermont in 1990.

factories, all chemicals. Of course, we cannot do that. While there are negative side effects there are also tremendous benefits. True science and technology bring humanity a lot of benefit.

So what to do? We must use our human intelligence. And in some cases, we must have more patience. We must cultivate more contentment. And we must handle new progress and development in a proper way, keeping the side effects to a minimum. At the same time, we must take care of the earth and its basic elements in a more balanced way, no matter how expensive the cost. I think that's the only way. . . .

Based on a practical ethic of caring for our home, grounded in our understanding of interdependence, what kind of measures can we take to correct these imbalances in nature? Generally speaking, crises emerge as a consequence of certain causes or conditions. Principal among them is ignorance of the real situation. In order to overcome that, the most effective means is to develop knowledge and understanding. . . .

In some cases, we might be able to overcome ignorance, understand reality, and reach the situation where everyone knows what is going on. But still we do not act to prevent disaster. Such a lack of will to act—in spite of having the knowledge and understanding—stems, I think, either from negligence (becoming totally oblivious to the crisis) or from discouragement (the feeling that "I have no ability, I simply cannot do anything").

I firmly believe that the most important factor is our attitude and human motivation. Genuine human love, human kindness, and human affection. This is the key thing. That will help us to develop human determination also. Genuine love or compassion is not a feeling of lofty pity, sympathy tinged with contempt toward the other, looking down on them; it is not like that. True love or compassion is actually a special sense of responsibility. A strong sense of care and concern for the happiness of the other, that is genuine love. Such true love automatically becomes a sense of responsibility.

Sustainability

~ Shams Helminski

In our culture we like definitions, facts, cause and effect scenarios provided by experts, yet in order to achieve sustainability we need to focus more on the development of stronger individual responsibility. We may never be able to accurately define where the boundary to sustainability lies; although we are a clever species, to assume that we could identify that boundary and modify our behavior just enough to reach it seems egotistical. If we value the quality of life, the difficult truth is that we need to pull well back from any boundary. What scientists label *the web of life* is too complex for us to fully understand.

Very few choices that we make do not have an environmental impact, and even more importantly, the consequences are seldom simple. As Rachel Carson said, "The question is whether any civilization can wage relentless war on life without destroying itself, and without losing the right to be called civilized."[271] The "relentless war" that Carson alludes to is comprised of the innumerable negative ways in which we impact our environment every day.

Rachel Carson's *Silent Spring* primarily describes the use of DDT and the associated dangers. It is a book of nearly three hundred pages that highlights the negative impact of one human created chemical. According to the United Nations Environmental Program "the number of chemicals coming onto the market has dramatically increased with an estimated 80,000 introduced over the last half century."[272] If a book were written about the effects of each of these new chemicals we would have in hand around two hundred and forty million pages. Of course, this is an extrapolation; many chemicals are probably analogues in the environmental sense. However, since we influence the environment in numerous other ways than the production and use of chemicals, to catalogue our

---

[271] Rachel Carson, *Silent Spring*, Houghton Mifflin Company, NY, NY, 1994, p. 99.

[272] United Nations Environmental Programme, 20002, *UNEP News Relase 2002/04*, http://www.unep.org/Documents/Default.asp?DocumentID=233&ArticleID=2 997 accessed 3.22.02

total impact could prove to be an infinite task. If we were to follow a strictly analytical model, an immense effort would be needed to end this "war." The time and energy required to scrutinize all the issues might keep us from moving towards change.

Let's look at a simple example: suppose you have an older sports utility vehicle. On the average trip this car burns one gallon of gas every twelve miles. Perhaps this level of consumption makes you feel guilty, so you look at the alternatives. You decide to buy a new car that gets forty or more miles per gallon. You feel good about all the gas you are going to save, but then, what will you do with the old car? If you sell it to another person, it will still be driven. Maybe you decide to send it to the junkyard. There it will be disassembled and some of the metal would be recycled. However, to recycle the metal takes energy and creates pollution in the process. Then you would still have to purchase a new car, but, of course, automakers do not just snap their fingers and make a car out of thin air. They all have factories that construct these vehicles, and how much of the metal, glass, rubber, and plastic that go into these new cars do you suppose comes from recycling? Now you have to consider all the environmental consequences of building this new car. Are you willing to take the time to research all these questions and figure out which solution is most environmentally friendly? Perhaps, but this is only one seemingly simple problem. For each person the answer might be different. Factors change and the answer to the equation changes as well. Nobody wants to go through this thought process for every decision they must make in their lives.

Instead, we could simply use less and require less. Perhaps rather than looking for a new car, you might drive the one you have less often. Maybe you could drive more slowly or more carefully and reduce the potential for accidents. Maybe you could maintain your car more meticulously. The longer it lasts, the fewer resources you use. We do not need to rely upon experts to provide us with complicated information for every choice in life. The benefits realized by simply mitigating our influence on the environment accrue exponentially. Not only can we minimize our reliance upon experts for personal decisions, we can also then decrease the need for extensive management of our impact.

The world is already overpopulated. It appears that we have outstripped the planet and must pay the price. You are now asking how we can correct the course of history. We need to increase our ability and willingness to share our resources more equitably, reduce population, and consume less. The reality of this is not so easy:

Walk up to someone on the street and tell them that they should buy much less and have fewer kids. They may tell you that you are mad, that the economy will crash, and life will not be as fulfilling. At the very least that person will ask you to justify your request.

Everyone wants hard facts, and more evidence. Look at global warming for a moment. The consensus in the scientific community is that global warming exists. They agree that humans are causing the current increase in global mean temperature. Do we listen? Not too closely: there have been no dramatic changes in societal patterns of consumption. Society wants to wait for the scientists to research the problem even more. We want to know the exact consequences. What are the exact risks we face? Are they significant enough for us to bother changing our lifestyles? Look at any ecological problem. We are not willing to change behavior until we are convinced that we face impending doom. Rachel Carson wrote about the harm that widespread spraying of DDT causes. Only when faced with a terrifying tale of death and destruction could we be inspired to change the status quo, curtailing the widespread use of DDT. Passionately, she had alerted us to a time that could come when, poisoned by pesticides, "The birds would no longer sing."

There is a chance that we will be able to correct our course, but to do this will require a paradigm shift. We need to encourage each other towards a more proactive approach to life based on the recognition of our interdependence, the essential value of a healthy environment, and better regulation of our desires.

If we were to pull back our desires and needs, and shrink our level of consumption, especially in the heavily developed countries, we might live in a world that is less negatively impacted by our species. Making this fundamental decision does not involve complex calculations or cost benefit analyses. The less we encroach upon nature, the less we need to help her achieve some measure of equilibrium.

Rachel Carson gave prophetic advice, "Critically important facts have been overlooked in designing the modern insect control programs. The first is that the really effective control of insects is that applied by nature, not by man."[273] George Perkins Marsh placed great faith in the natural environment's ability to self-regulate. "Nature, left undisturbed, so fashions her territory as to give it almost unchanging permanence of form, outline, and proportion."[274]

We now believe that nature is characterized by a sort of dynamic stasis. If nature is allowed to regain this state there is less danger that we will cause further damage by trying to manage things without full understanding. There is a balance to be found, and a broader understanding of our place in the world can help to develop our real human potential.

How can you buy or sell the sky, the warmth of the land? If we do not own the freshness of the air and the sparkle of the water, how can you buy them?

~ Suquamish Chief

What happens if we begin from the premise not that we know reality because we are separate from it (traditional objectivity), but that we can know the world because we are connected with it?

~ Katherine N. Hayles, 1995:48[275]

---

[273] Ibid., p. 247.

[274] Stephen C. Trombulak, *So Great a Vision: The Conservation Writings of George Perkins Marsh*, Middlebury College Press, 2001, p. 129.

[275] Sarah Whatmore, *Hybrid Geographies*, Sage Publications, Inc., Thousand Oaks, CA, 2002, p.1.

Property is one of, if not the primary currency of ongoing conversations between Law and Geography. This should come as no surprise given their shared complicity in the cartographies of governance, commerce, and science and the recalibration of a litany of "exterior" and/or "prior" space-times within the coordinates of modernity's compelling embrace, whether those associated with the age of empire or, today, with the rubric of global environmental management. . . . For example, the spatial codification of "real" property as a grid-like surface finitely divisible into mutually exclusive estates is both unimaginable and impracticable if we substitute the socio-materialities of land for those of air or water.

~ Sarah Whatmore[276]

Through exclusively social contracts, we have abandoned the bond that connects us to the world. . . . What language do the things of the world speak that we might come to an understanding of them contractually? . . . In fact, the Earth speaks to us in terms of forces, bonds and interactions . . . each of the partners in symbiosis thus owes . . . life to the other; on pain of death.

~ Michel Serres[277]

---

[276] Ibid., p. 79.
[277] Ibid., p. 146, quote from Michel Serres, 1995:39.

How do We Care?

~ Juliette de Bairacli Levy[278]

There are laws for protection of the trees and florae. Never uproot over-large numbers of any species, nor take too much of the seeds of any species. Their survival is essential to man and animal, bird and insect, for their food and medicine, and their beauty for the pleasure and comfort of the soul.

Do not harm the beasts, birds, or insects unless they are a direct danger to the life of man or to the animals that man has domesticated. Do not kill any creature for mere sport, but only for food requirements (and never in greed for food or as a dealer in food, kill any species to extinction).

A prayer of Saint Basil, Bishop of Caesarea, the Holy land, 326 A.D., although over sixteen hundred years old, is apt on this matter of regard for animals. (It may persuade travelers to leave their guns at home.)

> O God enlarge within us the sense of fellowship with all living things, our brothers the animals—to whom thou hast given the Earth as their homes in common with us. We remember with shame that in the past we have exercised the high dominion of man with ruthless cruelty so that the voice of the Earth, which should have gone up to Thee in song, has been a groan of suffering. May we realize that they live, not for us alone, but for themselves and for Thee, and that they too love the sweetness of life. . . . [279]

Never before have times been so *dreadful* for them. The meat industry (as it is called) is now in full production; even China has recently joined the other countries that treat their cattle, for instance, as if they were as lifeless and as unfeeling as sacks stuffed with rubbish. Worldwide, cattle are now commonly confined in cells of concrete. Their food is brought to them, and often it is blood-soaked sawdust from slaughter-house floors, "rich in protein," as its vendors claim. But cattle are God-made as vegetarians; if they eat filth, it is because they are forced by

---

[278] Juliette de Bairacli Levy, *Traveler's Joy,* pp. 207-208, 226-228.
[279] Ibid., pp. 207-208.

hunger. "The Friendly Cow," in Robert Louis Stevenson's poem of that name, "who wanders here and there," is almost no more! I have worked with cows, and they have loving hearts and noble minds. (Cows have escaped from slaughterhouses and found their long way back to their home farm.)

Flocks of sheep, so well known as being praised by Christ, are also being subjected to cruel indoor confinement, glibly called "intensive farming."

A warning from the Bible (Joel, Chapter I, Verse 18):

"How do the beasts groan! the herds of cattle are perplexed because they have no pasture; yea, the flocks of sheep are made desolate."

Furthermore, terrible! the tiny bee is being exploited, robbed by big, greedy, mad Man! In that holy, very wise, ancient book of the Hebrews, the Talmud, it says of bees "that of all the creatures that God created, the bee pleased him most."

Honey is extremely valuable; many times it is referred to in the Bible. We read of a "land flowing with milk and honey," meaning a land of great wealth. In the book of Emanuel, it says, "Eat honey, my son, it is good for thy bones." . . .

Modern man now takes almost all the honey from the hives, and replaces it with the basest of the sweeteners, a coarse root sugar derived from the common sugar beet. Man knows that much white sugar is bad for human health, yet he now compels the bees to live on this instead of their wonderful honey.

It is quite recent, but now common, that the royal jelly which the bees make to feed the best of their larvae is taken away to be used as a human medicine. Even the pollen, gathered with such toil by the bees, is taken from them in quantity, brushed off by implements at the entry to their hive. Now the bees of the world are very sick, and the reason for their decline is truly pathetic. Bees are ill because they are now very afraid, afraid of starvation for their hives, robbed of the vital bee foods by human so-called "beekeepers," who should rightly be named bee-robbers, plunderers.

The only way to end this cruel exploitation of animals, poultry and bees is for the public to refuse to buy produce rooted in cruelty. In any case, the flesh, eggs and honey from creatures under long-term stress must make extremely unhealthy eating. I take great care as to what I buy as I travel.

Be like a bee; anything he eats is clean, anything he drops is sweet and any branch he sits upon does not break.

~ Hazrat Ali bin Abi Talib ﷺ[280]

Exposing the True Nature of Chocolate
~ Michael Lipske [281]

If past statistics are any measure, Americans may eat more than three billion pounds of chocolate this year. . . . more than 60 million chocolate bunnies will go on sale in this country for Easter, and millions more chocolate candies will roll off the assembly lines in time for Mother's Day. None of them, it turns out, could be made or sold without a little help from Mother Nature. "A tiny fly no bigger than the head of a pin is responsible for the world's supply of chocolate," says Allen Young, a leading cacao expert and curator of zoology at the Milwaukee Public Museum.

Every piece of chocolate we eat starts out as seeds found within football-shaped green, yellow, or red pods that grow from cacao trees. *Theo-broma cacao,* the source of cocoa and chocolate, is a native of Central and South American rain forests. Cacao was, in fact, the name for the tree used by ancient Mayans who cultivated the plant and concocted beverages of foaming chocolate more than 1,000 years before the first European explorers arrived in the New World.

In pollination studies conducted during the past decade in Costa Rica, Young has discovered that midges—tiny flies that live in dense, Neotropical rain forests—are crucial to the perpetuation of cacao trees.

---

[280] Maxims of Ali; translated by Al-Halal from *Nahj-ul-Balagha*; Sh.Muhammad Ashraf, Lahore, Pakistan, p. 436.

[281] The Following selection is excerpted from *National Wildlife,* magazine of the National Wildlife Federation, April/May 2003 issue. (www.nwf.org), pp. 18,19, by Michael Lipske. For more information about both chocolate and pollinators, including links for buying environmentally sound products, see www.nwf.org/chocolate.

That's because the flies are the only creatures that can work their way into the small, convoluted flowers the trees grow. Without the pollination functions the midges perform, the seed-pods would not become fertilized. And without the seeds, chocolate would become an endangered product. "As rain forests are cleared, we are losing the pollinators that live in them, and that could have dire consequences," notes NWF (National Wildlife Federation) senior biologist Gabriela Chavarria, a pollinator expert.

Today, cacao is cultivated in equatorial countries worldwide, frequently in open plantations rather than beneath a forest canopy, as it was originally grown. As a result, cacao farming in many areas has created a host of environmental problems. Roughly a third of the world crop is lost every year due to plant pests and diseases. Growers in Asia have fought back with fungicides, pesticides and herbicides, resulting in "a tremendous loss of biodiversity and contaminated waters and soils," says Joe Whinney, founder of Organic Commodity Project, Inc. (OCP), a Massachusetts-based buyer and seller of organic cocoa. In West Africa, vast areas of rain forest have been replaced by cacao plantations, as well as coffee and other tree crops. Ultimately, much of the land ends up as pasture. "It's a terrible cycle that is not slowing down," says Whinney.

He and some other experts believe, however, that the cycle can be broken. Grown wisely, cacao—more than most other crops—has the potential to help preserve tropical forests and biodiversity while providing a living for small-scale farmers.

Like shade-grown coffee, cacao grown in the traditional manner under a sheltering canopy of taller rain forest trees provides winter habitat for dozens of bird species that migrate between the United States and Latin America. In 1994, scientists in Brazil even discovered a previously unknown species of ovenbird, dubbed the pink-legged graveteiro, on shade-grown cacao farms in the state of Bahia. The natural forest that the pink-legged graveteiro evolved in "is extremely close to being wiped out," says Bret Whitney, an American ornithologist who has studied the species. Without cacao, he adds, the bird "would be extinct."

Most of the world's cacao is still grown on small farms and many of America's large chocolate companies have come to understand that with cacao production, small can definitely be beautiful. The World Cocoa Foundation, established by the chocolate companies in 2000, has declared its mission to be "improving the standard of living of cocoa farmers around the world by providing training on low-cost methods to produce quality cocoa in a sustainable, environmentally friendly manner."

"The industry now definitely gets it," says Whinney, who has allied his company with the World Cocoa Foundation. For evidence, Whinney points to "one tiny piece" of what he believes could be cacao's "hopeful environmental future."

It's a project being conducted by the Cocoa Research Institute of Ghana with help from the World Cocoa Foundation. Seeds from the neem tree (a native Indian species with documented natural pesticide properties) are collected, dried, crushed and mixed with water. This neem slurry is then sprayed on cacao trees to kill capsid beetles, a serious cacao pest in West Africa. The natural pesticide apparently causes no harm to pollinators and other beneficial insects. Ideally, the project will enable Ghanian farmers to harvest more cacao pods from their trees, thus increasing their income and reducing their need to clear more forest.

Many cacao growers have long been frustrated by the fact that only one to three percent of the hundreds of flowers on a cacao tree bear fruit. In the plantations, says Young "you tend to have this discrepancy between flower production and fruit set. We think the whole dynamic of pollination is disrupted in a plantation habitat."

If that's bad news for plantation operators, it's yet another argument for growing cacao on farms tucked in and around natural rain forests rather than clearing the forests to make room for agriculture. "We have a project now in Costa Rica looking at what kind of canopy cover provides the best pollination in cacao trees," says Young. Supported by the U.S. Department of Agriculture, the long-term study will examine the role of cacao farms in maintaining biodiversity. "We think cacao is a good candidate for a model of saving biodiversity while providing small farmers with a diversified revenue stream." The scientist explains that farmer income could flow not just from cacao but also from fruit trees and even selective timber cutting.

It seems too good to be true: Save rain forests and satisfy candy cravings. But as Young says, "Cacao has a lot going for it."

But for their cries,
The herons would be lost
Amidst the morning snow.

~ Chiyo-Ni [282]

---

[282] From *The Moon in the Pines, Zen Haiku selected and translated by Jonathon Clements*, *published by* Frances Lincoln, Ltd, © 2000. Reproduced by permission of Frances Lincoln Ltd., 4 Torriano Avenue, London NW5 2RZ. Distributed in the USA by Publishers Group West and in Canada by Raincoast Books. p. 13.

CHAPTER TWENTY

HONORING DIVERSITY

O humankind! We created you all out of a male and a female,
and made you into nations and tribes
that you might come to know each other.
Truly, the most highly regarded of you in the sight of God
is the one who does the most good.
And God is All-Knowing and is Well-Aware of all things.
[*Sūrah Al-Ḥujurāt* (The Private Apartments) 49:13]

The Messenger, and the faithful with him,
have faith in what has been revealed to him by his Sustainer;
they all have faith in God, and His angels,
and His revelations, and His messengers,
making no distinction between any of His messengers;
and they say; "We have heard and we pay heed.
Grant us Your forgiveness, O our Sustainer,
for with You is all journey's end!"
[*Sūrah Al-Baqarah* (The Cow) 2:285]

There is not an animal on earth,
nor a bird that flies on its wings,
but they are communities like you.
[*Sūrah Al-Anʿām* (Cattle) 6:38]

A Sign for them is the earth that is dead;
We give it life and produce grain from it
of which you eat.
And We produce there orchards with date-palms and vines
and We cause springs to gush forth from within it,
that they may enjoy the fruits there.
It was not their hands that made this;
will they not then give thanks?

Limitless in His glory is God Who created in pairs
all things that the earth produces
as well as their own humankind
as well as things of which they have no knowledge.
[*Sūrah Yā Sīn* (O Thou Human Being) 36:33-36]

More and more as we come closer and closer in touch with nature and its teachings are we able to see the Divine and are therefore fitted to interpret correctly the various languages spoken by all forms of nature about us.

~ George Washington Carver

Nature is an endless combination and repetition of a very few laws. She hums the old well known air through innumerable variations.

~ Ralph Waldo Emerson

We are not separated from the rest of the animal kingdom by an unbridgeable chasm. Rather, we are simply a part of the intricate tapestry of life.

~ Jane Goodall

To see the earth as it truly is, small and blue in that eternal silence where it floats, is to see riders on the earth together, brothers on that bright liveliness in the eternal cold—brothers who know now they are truly brothers.

~ Archibald McLeish

The Prophet related, "While a man was walking, he became extremely thirsty, so he went down into a well and drank from it. Then he came out, only to find a panting dog eating moist earth in its thirst. The man said, 'The same thing happened to this creature as happened to me.' So he filled his shoe, climbed out holding it in his teeth, and thus gave the dog water to drink. Then God thanked the man and forgave him."

People asked, "O Messenger of God, are we rewarded for our treatment of animals?"

The Prophet said, "There is a reward for your treatment of every living thing." [283]

Our beloved Prophet 	ﷺ says in a *ḥadith* reported by Abu Hurayrah, "There are ninety-nine names that are Allah's alone. Whoever learns, understands and enumerates (*iḥsā*) them enters Paradise and achieves eternal salvation."

This *ḥadith* does not mean that Allah has only ninety-nine names. There are infinite others which He has revealed to His choice creation. If someone says, "So-and-so has one thousand dollars that he has reserved to give to others," does it mean that the person does not have any more money?

The ones who know say that Allah has three thousand names: one thousand He has revealed to His angels; one thousand He has revealed to His prophets; three hundred are in the *zabūr*—the psalms of David; three hundred are in the Torah; three hundred are in the Gospel; 99 are in the Holy Qur'an. One, the name of His Essence, He has kept for Himself and hidden in the Qur'an.

The beautiful names of Allah are proof of the existence and oneness of Allah. O you who are burdened and troubled with the weight and suffering of the material world, may Allah make His beautiful names a soothing balm for your wounded hearts. Learn, understand, recite Allah's beautiful names. Seek traces of Allah's attributes in the skies above, on the earth below, and in what is beautiful in your being. You will find blessings in it to the extent of your sincerity. With the permission of Allah, the doubter will find security, the ignorant will find wisdom, the denier will confirm. The stingy will become generous, the tyrants will bow their heads, the fire in the hearts of the envious will be extinguished. [284]

---

[283] *The Wisdom of the Prophet, Sayings of Muhammad, Selections from the Hadith,* Translated by Thomas Cleary, Shambhala Publications, Inc., Boston, Massachusetts, copyright by Thomas Cleary 1994, p. 28.

[284] Sheikh Tosun Bayrak al-Jerrahi al-Halveti, *The Most Beautiful Names.* Threshold Books, VT, 1985, p. 3.

The Music of Diversity

~ Boethius[285]

The music of the universe is especially to be studied in the combining of the elements and the variety of the seasons which are observed in the heavens. How indeed could the swift mechanism of the sky move silently in its course? And although this sound does not reach our ears . . . , the extremely rapid motion of such great bodies could not be altogether without sound, especially since the courses of the stars are joined together by such mutual adaptation that nothing more equally compacted or united could be imagined. For some are borne higher and others lower, and all are revolved with a just impulse. . . .

Now unless a certain harmony united the differences and contrary powers of the four elements, how could they form a single body and mechanism? But all this diversity produces the variety of seasons and fruits, and thereby makes the year a unity. Wherefore if you could imagine any one of the factors which produce such a variety removed, all would perish, nor, so to speak, would they retain a vestige of consonance. And just as there is a measure of sound in low strings lest the lowness descend to inaudibility, and a measure of tenseness in high strings lest they be broken by the thinness of the sound, being too tense, and all is congruous and fitting, so we perceive that in the music of the universe nothing can be excessive and destroy some other part by its own excess, but each part brings its own contribution or aids others to bring theirs. For what winter binds, spring releases, summer heats, autumn ripens; and the seasons in turn bring forth their own fruits or help the others to bring forth theirs.

---

[285] Boethius, excerpt from *De Institutione Musica,* as excerpted in *The Education of the Heart,* edited by Thomas Moore. *Readings and Sources for Care of the Soul, Soul Mates, and the Re-enchantment of Everyday Life,* HarperPerrenial, 1997, pp. 61-62.

Divine Radiance

~ Hildegard von Bingen[286]

All living creatures are, so to speak, sparks from the radiation of God's brilliance, and these sparks emerge from God like rays of the sun." [Hildegard] asks a necessary question: "How would God be known as life if not through the fact that the realm of the living, which glorifies and praises God also emerges from God? On this account God has established the living, burning sparks as a sign of the brilliance of the divine renown." The fiery firmament is a footstool to the throne of God and all creatures are sparks from this fire. We sparks come from God. "But if God did not give off these sparks, how would the divine flame become visible? And how would God be known as the Eternal One if no brilliance emerged from God? For no creature exists that lacks a radiance—be it greenness or seed, buds or beauty. Otherwise it would not be a creature at all.

Bearing Witness for the Earth

~ Thomas Berry[287]

Saint John tells us that in the beginning all things took on their shape through the word. The word was seen as psychic and personal. This was the numinous reality through which all things were made and without which was made nothing that has been made. The word, the self-spoken word, by its own spontaneities brought forth the universe and established itself as the ultimate form of reality and of value. This is in accord with Lao Tzu, the Chinese sage, who tells us that the human models itself on the earth, earth models itself on heaven, heaven models itself on tao, tao models itself on its own spontaneity.

This spontaneity as the guiding force of the universe can be thought of as the mysterious impulse whereby the primordial fireball flared forth in

---

[286] Hildegard von Bingen, excerpted from *Illuminations of Hildegard of Bingen* by Matthew Fox, Bear & Company, Santa Fe, New Mexico, 1985, pp. 47-48.

[287] Excerpted from *Creative Energy, Bearing Witness for the Earth* by Thomas Berry, Copyright © Thomas Berry, 1988. Reprinted by permission of Sierra Club Books, pp. 47-54.

387

its enormous energy, a fireball that contained in itself all that would ever emerge into being, a fireball that was the present in its primordial form, as the present is the fireball in its explicated form. What enabled the formless energies to emerge into such a fantastic variety of expression in shape, color, scent, feeling, thought, and imagination?

As with any aesthetic work, we attribute it especially to the imaginative capacities of the artist, for only out of imaginative power does any grand creative work take shape. Since imagination functions most freely in dream vision, we tend to associate creativity also with dream experience. The dream comes about precisely through the uninhibited spontaneities of which we are speaking. In this context we might say: In the beginning was the dream. Through the dream all things were made, and without the dream nothing was made that has been made.

While all things share in this dream, as humans we share in this dream in a special manner. This is the entrancement, the magic of the world about us, its mystery, its ineffable quality. What primordial source could, with no model for guidance, imagine such a fantastic world as that in which we live—the shape of the orchid, the coloring of the fish in the sea, the winds and the rain, the variety of sounds that flow over the earth, the resonant croaking of the bullfrogs, the songs of the crickets, and the pure joy of the predawn singing of the mockingbird?

Experience of such a resplendent world activated the creative imagination of Mozart in *The Magic Flute,* of Dante in his *Divine Comedy,* and gave to Shakespeare that range of sensitivity, understanding, and emotion that found expression in his plays. All of these derive from the visionary power that is experienced most profoundly when we are immersed in the depths of our own being and of the cosmic order itself in the dream-world that unfolds within us in our sleep, or in those visionary moments that seize upon us in our waking hours. There we discover the Platonic forms, the dreams of Brahman, the Hermetic mysteries, the divine ideas of Thomas Aquinas, the infinite worlds of Giordano Bruno, the world soul of the Cambridge Platonists, the self-organizing universe of Ilya Prigogine, the archetypal world of C.G. Jung.

Each of these is enormously attractive, having a certain inner coherence and revealing some aspect of the universe and of the planet

Earth that is fascinating to the human mind. They can be understood as facets of a mystery too vast for human comprehension, a mystery with such power that even a fragment of its grandeur can evoke the great human cultural enterprises. In this context we have shaped our languages and lifestyles, our poetry and music, our religious scriptures, our political ideals, our humanistic literature, our life-sustaining economies. Of special importance is the grand sequence of rituals whereby we insert ourselves into the ever-renewing sequence of springtime renewals in nature.

The excitement of life and the sustaining of psychic vigor are evoked by our participation in this magnificent process. Even before we give expression to any intellectual statement about the natural world, we stand in awe at the stars splashed in such prodigal display across the heavens, at the earth in its shaping of the seas and the continents, at the great hydrological cycles that lift such vast quantities of water up from the seas and rain them down over the land to nourish the meadows and the forests and to refresh the animals as the waters flow down through the valleys and back again to the seas. We marvel, too, at the millionfold sequence of living forms, from the plankton in the sea and the bacteria in the soil to the larger lifeforms that swim through the oceans and grow up from the soil and move over the land.

Much could be said, too, about the human as that being in whom this grand diversity of the universe celebrates itself in conscious self-awareness. While we emerge into being from within the earth process and enable the universe to come to itself in a special mode of psychic intimacy, it is evident that we have also a special power over the universe in its earthly expression. Therein lies the dramatic issue that is being played out in these centuries of human time that succeed to the ages of geological and biological time. From our vantage point we can sketch out the great story of the universe from its beginning until now. We can recognize the earth as a privileged planet and see the whole as evolving out of some cosmic imaginative process. Any significant thought or speech about the universe finds its expression through such imaginative powers. Even our scientific terms have a highly mythic content—such words as *energy, life, matter, form, universe, gravitation, evolution.* Even such terms as *atom, nucleus, electron, molecule, cell, organism.* Each of these terms spills over into metaphor and mystery as soon as it is taken seriously.

389

As regards the origin and shaping forces in the universe, the geneticist Theodosius Dobzhansky considers that the universe in its emergence is neither determined nor random, but creative. This word *creative* is among the most mysterious words in any language.

Continuing Creation

~ David James Duncan

In researching my latest novel, I read of a contemporary band of natives, down in South America's Colombia, who spoke to me on my river of the same name:

Colombia's Makuna tribe are a Neolithic people—grass-and-tree-bark clothing; handmade hunting and fishing tools. That makes me nervous in searching for cultural models, since I don't believe we'll be surrendering what technology has given us anytime soon. I do believe, however, that compassion will, of necessity, become the basis of every technological decision we make. And the Makuna live in a way that dissolves the Industrial World's usual compassionless split between nature and culture, between product and conscience, between animals and people, between deadly daily work and life-loving daily beliefs.

The Makuna maintain that humans, animals, plants, all of nature, are part of a great oneness. Our ancestors, they say, were magical fish who came ashore along the rivers and turned two-legged. As these first land beings began to conduct their lives, and to sing about it, everything in the world began to be created from their songs: hills and forests; animal and bird people; insect and fish people.

But—the twist I love—*this creation process is ongoing.* The making of the world is no past-tense event. . . . The world, say the Makuna, is still being created: our words, actions, and songs still determine the nature of the hills and forests, and still help create, sustain, or destroy the animal, fish, and bird people.

We share a spiritual essence, the Makuna say, with the swimming, flying, and four-legged peoples. They live in communities, just as we do, with their own chiefs (picture a bull elk) and shamans (picture an old coyote, a raven, a great horned owl). They have dance houses and birth houses, songs and rites, and material possessions, just as we do. (We think easily of feathers and fur in this context, but remember, too, the nests and dens, and the carefully defended territories; remember the salmon's virtual ownership of the herring, the seal's of the salmon, the trout's of the Mayfly, the osprey's of the trout.) Fish, according to the Makuna, even have ceremonial paints and ritual ornaments, which they don, as we do, for certain crucial occasions. (Consider the endangered coho, justly named "silver" during its life in the ocean, but donning greens and crimson for the sex-driven return to its birth house.)

I'll cut to the chase: according to the Makuna, our essential oneness with other species is not just a source of vague mystical pleasure, or of cool, ripped-off Indian images for hip writers and artists. Our oneness is the source of an enormous obligation. We depend on fish, animal and bird people to eat and live. In return, the fish, animal, and bird people depend on us to spiritually enact, daily, the hidden oneness of all life. Anytime humans eat, anytime we gather, anytime we make merry or celebrate in our world, we have a dire obligation to offer "spirit food" to the winged, fish, and animal people, that they may celebrate in their worlds. And if we fail to make such offerings—if we do not spiritually share with the other species—they quickly die. So say Makuna.[288]

★★★

"In the Beginning," say the very first lines of the Bible, *"God created the heavens and the earth. And the earth was without form, and void; and darkness was upon the face of the deep. And the Spirit of God moved upon the face of the water."* The best way I know to begin to grasp the seriousness and scope of the Northwest's salmon crisis is to sit down in a quiet place and try to imagine the mysterious movement, across waters of pre-creation, of the spirit of God. Imagine a quickening that pierces the Pacific—the entire ocean suddenly invested with being, suddenly restless, inhaling and exhaling the moon-coaxed breaths called tides. Limn this vast being with glaciers in the north, volcanic fissures in its depths. Imbue it

---

[288] From *My Story as Told by Water*, by David James Duncan. Copyright © 2001 by David James Duncan. Reprinted by permission of Sierra Club Books, pp. 104-105.

with the same blue, gray, and green surfaces and glass-smooth-to-mountainous textures as the Pacific; same molten-to-frozen temperature ranges; same unknowable, 36,000-foot depths; same power to produce wonder, terror, beauty, death, and life.[289]

★★★

Trees and mountains are holy. Rain and rivers are holy. Salmon are holy. For this reason I will fight with all my might to keep them alive.[290]

And it is God Who has created all animals out of water,
and He has willed that among them
are some that crawl on their bellies,
and some that walk on two legs,
and some that walk on four.
God creates what He wills:
for, truly, God has the power to will anything.
Indeed, from on high
We have bestowed messages clearly showing the truth;
but God guides to a straight way only the one who wills to be guided.
[*Sūrah An-Nūr* (The Light) 24:45-46]

Leave the Wetlands to Beaver

As beavers reclaim their rightful places in our environment,
experts help us adjust to our industrious new neighbors.

~ Christie Aschwanden[291]

Some people are born certain of their purpose in life. For Sherrie Tippie, it took a special event to illuminate her calling. One evening in 1985, Tippie sat watching the local news on television when she saw a report about a beaver that was cutting down trees at a golf course in Aurora,

---

[289] Ibid., p. 185.
[290] Ibid., p. 107.
[291] Christie Aschwanden, "Leave the Wetlands to Beaver," National Wildlife, October/November 2002 issue, pp. 32, 34–36. Reprinted by permission of C.A.

Colorado. Tippie, a resident of nearby Denver, was horrified to learn that the beaver's misdeeds had earned him a death sentence.

"I thought, there's gotta be someplace to relocate that poor beaver," she recalls. She got on the phone and didn't hang up until she'd found the problem beaver a new home. Even though Tippie was a hairdresser with no prior experience in relocating wild animals, "I found a home for him," she notes. Sherrie Tippie had found her niche.

In the 17 years since then, Tippie has made a career of helping people solve their beaver problems. She preaches coexistence first, but when that isn't possible, she traps the amphibious creatures and transports them to happier homes. "We capture the complete family and relocate all of them," she says. Since she started her business, dubbed Wildlife 2000, Tippie has relocated about 500 beavers all over Colorado. Each spring and summer brings a flood of calls to Tippie's hotline.

"People think beaver populations are exploding when they're really just reclaiming their natural territory," says biologist Sharon Brown, director of Beavers: Wetlands and Wildlife, an educational group based in Dolgeville, New York. Brown estimates that beavers today number 6 million to 12 million in the United States—a remarkable comeback after being extinguished from much of the country by overtrapping.

With adults weighing a hefty 40 to 70 pounds, beavers own the title of North America's largest rodent. They spend about a quarter of their lives in the water where their broad, scaly tails act like rudders, helping them maneuver gracefully through the water. To stay warm in winter's icy waters, the creatures bundle up in an extra layer of fat. Voracious vegetarians, beavers devour as much as five pounds of tree bark, leaves and stems per day. Though beavers' back feet are webbed, their front paws are dexterous, a trait that makes them superior builders.

Only humans can rival beavers' ability to alter their environment, says Marilyn Irwin, a ranger at Colorado's Rocky Mountain National Park, where beavers are one of the top attractions. Beavers build fortified homes along streams using only sticks, logs, mud and river debris. Underwater entrances to these lodges keep predators out.

To extend their safety zone, beavers construct elaborate dams from mud, stones, branches and logs. The resulting ponds and channels provide them with safe passage to food sources. Fast and diligent workers, beavers often topple multiple trees in one night to supply their construction projects.

The sound and current created by running water acts as an alarm to alert the beavers to a breech in their dam. When leaks occur, beavers mobilize quickly to fortify their dike. Many a farmer has spent an afternoon breaking down a beaver dam, only to return the next day to find it standing again as if nothing had ever happened, says Irwin.

It's that sort of diligence that gets beavers in trouble with people. With beaver populations on the rebound, conflicts with humans have skyrocketed, and more people are making a living solving these conflicts. Since founding their company, Beaver Solutions, Massachusetts residents Mike and Ruth Callahan have fixed more than 200 beaver problems without removing the creatures. "We get a lot of calls from homeowners who have flooded basements and we also do a lot of work for the highway departments," says Mike Callahan.

Recently the Callahans got a call from town officials in Billerica, Massachusetts. Beavers had overrun the town, and their dams were washing out roads and flooding basements. Locals were spending thousands of dollars to keep culverts clear, but the beavers flooded them again as fast as they could be cleared. "Politicians were really tired of people complaining and no one had any answers," Mike Callahan says. So the town hired the Callahans to find solutions.

Plugged up culverts and flooding were Billerica's biggest complaints. Both problems arise from beavers' desire to keep their ponds at a constant level. The solution is finding a water depth that will keep both humans and beavers happy, says Mike Callahan. Once this depth is found, the next step is developing a way to maintain it that won't trigger the beaver's dam-break alarm.

When beavers hear water draining from a culvert, they respond by stopping the leak. The Callahans prevent beavers from plugging these drains by tricking them with a specially designed fence that keeps beavers beyond earshot of the culvert's flow. To prevent beaver dams from causing unwanted flooding, they install flow devices that allow water to drain without beavers sensing a leak in the dam. In Billerica, these so-called "beaver-deceiver" devices are keeping both humans and beavers happy without leaving either species homeless.

Biologists say there's more at stake here than just saving a few individual animals. "We've lost more than half our wetlands in this country, and the beavers are returning the land back to its natural state," says Brown. A National Academy of Sciences report issued last year concluded that man-made wetlands are not doing a good job of duplicating the functions of natural wetlands.

"Beavers are ecosystem engineers, they create habitat diversity in the watershed," says Joel Snodgrass, a biologist at Towson University in Towson, Maryland. His research shows that beavers greatly increase the diversity of fish in headwater streams. "When you add beaver ponds to streams the overall diversity increases," says Snodgrass. "Vascular plant diversity is fairly low in streams, but the flooding from dams kills trees and you get very lush wetland areas with lots of plants."

"Beavers can help us manage our water resources," says Brown. "They slow the flow of water, and this provides flood control downstream. Beaver ponds clean the water by collecting silt and breaking down pollutants." In 1997 ecological economist Robert Costanza at the University of Maryland and his colleagues published a scientific paper estimating that natural wetlands provide goods and services valued at just under $8,000 per acre annually. "That means that in New York alone, where there are approximately 20,000 beaver colonies, beavers provide almost $2.5 billion worth of benefits each year," says Brown.

People are starting to appreciate beavers' work. As a result, finding new homes for the critters is surprisingly easy, Tippie says. Buck Ingersoll and Donald Downs were among the first to request beavers from Tippie. Three streams run through Twelve Mile Ranch, located in Colorado's South Park, which Ingersoll and Downs jointly own with several of their friends. The ranch's approximately 1,000 acres stretch across a backdrop of jagged mountains, and beavers have made their homes on the ranch for ages. When a mysterious disease suddenly killed off the ranch's beavers, the men grew worried. "We depend on those beavers for our water," says Ingersoll. With the beavers gone, the dams they'd built all washed away, and "our fishing went down the drain too," says Downs.

Downs realized they needed to get beavers back on the ranch, the question was: How? Eventually the men called Tippie, and she agreed to bring Twelve Mile Ranch her next batch of beavers. "I was expecting her to show up in a station wagon with some cages in the back, but Sherrie pulled up in a Ford Pinto with a beaver on her lap and a 50-pound beaver in the back," recalls Downs. Tippie stepped out of the car with a rotund beaver in her arms, and gave it a gentle belly rub before setting it loose. "It was the damnedest thing I'd ever seen," says Ingersoll.

With the beavers in place, the dams were soon back in operation. The fishing holes returned and the area flourished. Today more than 50 beaver dams stand on the ranch. The resulting ponds create habitat for four species of trout: brook, rainbow, brown and cutthroat. And fish aren't the only creatures that appreciate the beavers' handiwork. "We get a lot of ducks and birds around the beaver ponds," says Downs. During the summer, neighboring ranchers run their cattle on the ranch, and the cows thrive on the ranch's copious watering holes.

Beavers are in high demand these days, says Tippie. "I've had outfitters call me and request beavers so they can increase their fish stocks. I had a rancher who wanted beavers to control soil erosion," she says. Recently a developer asked Tippie to relocate beavers to a new development so residents would have a place to fish.

"I've always thought there's no such thing as nuisance wildlife, only uninformed and irresponsible humans," says Tippie.

Do You Know?

What soil series are you standing on?
When was the last time a fire burned in your area?
Name five native edible plants in your region and their seasons of availability.
From what direction do winter storms generally come in your region?
Where does your garbage go?
How long is the growing season where you live?
Name five grasses in your area. Are any of them native?
Name five resident and five migratory birds in your area.
What primary geological event or processes influenced the land form where you live?

What species have become extinct in your area?
What are the major plant associations in your region?

~ *Co-Evolution Quarterly*[292]

Looking at Birds through Creative Eyes

~ Doug Stewart [293]

David Sibley's innovative books on species identification and behavior have become must-reading for many American birders; what's behind his passion for the feathered world?

"Hear that tinkling sound?" asks David Sibley.

Not really, but now that he mentions it, a faint, high-pitched trill is just audible over the rustle of wind-riffled pines and the soft whoosh of traffic farther away. Standing in a grove of red oak and white pine beside a pond near his home in Concord, Massachusetts, Sibley purses his lips and makes a harsh, scolding noise. He's imitating a wren or chickadee that's seen an owl. Aroused by the disturbance, small dark birds that have been hidden in the woods down by the water now flit into the nearby branches in twos and threes. "Dark-eyed juncos," he says quietly.

For the 41-year-old author and illustrator of the explosive best-seller, *The Sibley Guide to Birds*, such identification is second nature. David Sibley's brain is stuffed with a phenomenal compendium of avian information. Even before the birds darted into view, he knew that exactly three and a half feathers on their tails would be white. And that when flushed they might sing *tsititit tit* but never *tzew tzew titititititi tsidip*—that would be the yellow-eyed junco. Now, less than a minute after he started calling, the trees around him are filled with a dozen or more chittering birds.

---

[292] *Co-Evolution Quarterly* 32 [Winter 1981—82]: 1.

[293] Doug Stewart, "Looking at Birds Through Creative Eyes" *National Wildlife,* Magazine of the National Wildlife Federation, Reston, VA, April-May 2003, pp. 30-36.

Somehow the spectacle of David Sibley standing in the woods surrounded by excited birds seems perfectly apt. A college dropout and self-taught artist, Sibley spent 15 years watching and sketching birds from Alaska to the Dry Tortugas, then cloistered himself for six more to write the text and paint the 6,600 watercolors for the book. It was a mammoth and risky undertaking—a life's work that has been compared to Samuel Johnson's 18th-century English dictionary, though Sibley was just 39 when he finished. . . .

Sibley explains that he has always been fascinated by birds. In his tiny home studio, he works at a slanted drafting board resting on an old oak desk. Annotated sketches and well-thumbed field guides lie on surfaces here and there. Vying for his attention, a birdfeeder stands outside the window.

"It's a very poetic thing to see a bird fly overhead and disappear into the distance," he says. "And flight gives birds the power to turn up in unexpected places. You never know what you're going to see, even when you look out the window. Birds come and go at will. It makes anyplace you go bird-watching exciting, whether it's a city park or your backyard."

To the nonbirder, bird-watching may seem like a strange way to interact with nature: blurting out species names as you spot them, often competing with the person next to you to do so first. Sibley, for his part, is interested in much more than assigning a name to the birds he sees—his goal, after all, is to paint them in loving detail, from covert to auricular. Still, he defends bird identification as the heart of bird-watching. He chose to open *Birding Basics* with a line from Jim Wright and Jerry Barrack's book *In the Presence of Nature:* "A rose by any other name may smell as sweet, but without a name it is simply a flower." Sibley elaborates: "The first thing you learn about a bird is its name, then you attach other information, like what it eats, what time of year it appears, what habitat it prefers and so on. It all follows from learning its name."

Like Roger Tory Peterson's classic bird field guide, first published in 1934, Sibley conceived, wrote and illustrated his first book by himself. He admires Peterson's (as a boy, Sibley pored over it under his covers at night), but in his own field guide he wanted more pictures, more plumages, more birds in flight, more songs and calls. Of the book he produced, he says, "This is the field guide I always wished I had in my own library."

His thoroughness is astonishing. His book has an average of eight full-color paintings for each species. Hawks and eagles are shown in flight from different angles, gulls in their first, second and third winter plumages, storm-petrels soaring, flapping, landing, swimming, even "foot-pattering" on the water when feeding. His notes on bird sounds include songs, warning cries, flight and display calls, and the begging cries of nestlings.

In his paintings, Sibley sought to show what's distinctive about each bird without exaggerating their markings. "I tried to simplify my illustrations just enough to eliminate extraneous details, like individual feathers, while keeping the important details. What I tried to show is what you actually see at a distance through binoculars."

Sibley has probably spent years of his life looking contentedly through binoculars. Many, if not most, people who spot a bird, of course, are hard-pressed to find it in the field guide they're holding before the creature flies away. Trying to draw in detail a bird perched briefly on a distant branch, not just copying its photograph (or visiting an aviary), would seem to be infinitely harder. Sibley explains that each illustration he makes is really a composite of many hours of observations spread over many years.

"My notebooks are filled with partial sketches of where I saw a bird just long enough to notice one particular thing about it," he says. "But if you spend a lot of time birding, sooner or later you bump into an individual bird that you can watch for three hours." Yes, he insists, he'll see things in hour three he didn't notice in hour two. "With each sketch I get to know the bird that much better." Sibley is obviously a patient fellow.

He finds the hardest part of embodying a bird on paper to be simply getting its outline right. If the outline is off, nothing will fit—he compares it to starting out a map with a distorted outline of the United States and winding up with misshapen states. From his sketches and notes, he creates a pencil sketch that he scales up using an opaque projector. He traces the projected image at the size he wants, usually three times the published size. Then he gets out his paints.

With its 810 species of bird life, *The Sibley Guide* weighs more than two pounds and fits more comfortably in a backpack or bookshelf than in even a very large coat pocket. . . . In his introduction, Sibley offers readers a few basic rules for getting started. Rule number one: *"Look at the bird. Don't fumble with a book . . . watch what the bird does, watch it fly away, and only then try to find it in your book."* He also recommends sketching what you see as a way to hone your skills as an observer.

He himself has been drawing birds since he was five and planning his own field guide since he was twelve. By then, he already knew hundreds of bird calls. His father, Fred Sibley, not surprisingly, is an ornithologist who was manager of bird collections at Yale's Peabody Museum of Natural History before retiring. His mother, Peggy, is a retired librarian. David recalls his father taking him and his older brother out bird-watching when he was in grade school. "Pretty quickly, it got so we wanted to go birding more often than he could take us," he says. "We'd nag him to go."

Intending to study ornithology himself, Sibley enrolled at Cornell University, but classrooms and lectures didn't hold his attention the way a live bird could. He dropped out after less than a year. His parents were mostly understanding, urging only that he "do something." And he did. He worked from time to time at the Cape May Bird Observatory in New Jersey, doing short-term jobs, and later led birding tours.

For the most part, however, he watched birds on his own. His low income for much of the 1980s was just enough to support a nomadic lifestyle. "For about eight years, I was living mostly in a camper-van," he says. He was in heaven. "I was getting to do virtually everything I wanted to do: hanging out in the mountains in Arizona and on the coast of California and the Florida Keys, just watching and sketching birds."

In the early 1990s, he settled down. He married biologist and fellow birder Joan Walsh; they now have two boys, ages 5 and 8. ("They have some interest in birds," he says, "but they're more interested in things they can catch, like salamanders and fish.") With his wanderlust satisfied, Sibley began planning his field guide in earnest. . . . A multi-year publishing advance allowed him to concentrate on turning his vast knowledge of birds into paintings and text.

Earlier, Sibley had toyed with the idea of supporting himself purely as a painter, selling his original gouaches to collectors. But he was always drawn back to the technical challenge of bird identification—illustrating precisely how to tell a perching northern flicker from its near twin, the gilded flicker, for example. To Sibley, the beauty of nature is in the details.

"As you get to know more about birds, you see how all the little bits of information fit together," he says. "It's like a giant web of details out there that form larger patterns. There's a beauty to this rhythm, this organized complexity of the lives of birds."

For all his success, Sibley regrets that his book work has cut into his birding time. Someday he hopes to travel to the central Aleutian Islands off Alaska, where a breeding colony of whiskered auklets lives. "That's the only North American breeding species I've never seen," he says. This may involve hitching a ride in a cargo plane from the military base on Adak Island, but if he can swing it, he'll go. "I'm sure I'll get there."

And if he does, it won't be just so he can make a better whiskered-auklet drawing. "I once drove from Georgia to Nova Scotia to see a Eurasian kestrel," he says a little sheepishly. "The Eurasian kestrel's not in my book. I just wanted to see it."

The kingdom of heaven is like a grain of mustard seed,
which a man took, and sowed in his field;
Which indeed is the least of all seeds:
but when it is grown, it is the greatest among herbs,
and becomes a tree,
so that the birds of the air come and lodge in its branches.
[The Bible, Matthew 13:31-32]

Monocultures of the Mind

~ Vandana Shiva[294]

Diversity is characteristic of nature and the basis of ecological stability. Diverse ecosystems give rise to diverse life forms, and to diverse cultures. The co-evolution of cultures, life forms and habitats has conserved the biological diversity on this planet. Cultural diversity and biological diversity go hand in hand.

Communities everywhere in the world have developed knowledge and found ways to derive livelihoods from the bounties of nature's diversity, in wild and domesticated forms. Hunting and gathering communities use thousands of plants and animals for food, medicine and shelter. Pastoral, peasant, and fishing communities have also evolved knowledge and skills to derive sustainable livelihoods from the living diversity on the land and in rivers, lakes, and seas. The deep and sophisticated ecological knowledge of biodiversity has given rise to cultural rules for conservation reflected in notions of sacredness and taboos.

Today, however, the diversity of ecosystems, life forms and ways of life of different communities is under threat of extinction. Habitats have been enclosed or destroyed, diversity has been eroded and livelihoods deriving from biodiversity are threatened.[295]

★★★

"Social" Forestry and the "Miracle" Tree

Social forestry projects are a good example of single-species, single commodity production plantations, based on reductionist models which divorce forestry from agriculture, and water management and seeds from markets.

A case study of World Bank-sponsored social forestry in Kolar district of Karnataka[296] is an illustration of reductionism and maldevelop-

---

[294] Vandana Shiva, *Monocultures of the Mind*, Zed Books and Third World Network, 2000 (228 Macalister Road, 10400 Penang, Malaysia). By permission of Zed Books Ltd., pp. 29-31, 36, 42, 45, 47-49, 56-58, 64.

[295] Ibid., p. 64.

[296] Shiva, V. Bandyopadhyay, J. and Sharatchandra, H.C. 1981, *The Social Ecological and Economic Impact of Social Forestry in Kolar*, IIM, Bangalore.

ment in forestry being extended to farmland. Decentred agro-forestry, based on multiple species and private and common tree-stands, has been India's age-old strategy for maintaining farm productivity in arid and semi-arid zones. The honge, tamarind, jackfruit and mango, the jola, gobli, kagli and bamboo traditionally provided food and fodder, fertilizer and pesticide, fuel and small timber. The backyard of each rural home was a nursery, and each peasant a silviculturalist. The invisible, decentred agro-forestry model was significant because the humblest of species and the smallest of people could participate in it, and with space for the small, everyone was involved in protecting and planting.

The reductionist mind took over tree-planting with "social forestry." Plans were made in national and international capitals by people who could not know the purpose of the honge and the neem, and saw them as weeds. The experts decided that indigenous knowledge was worthless and "unscientific," and proceeded to destroy the diversity of indigenous species by replacing them with row after row of eucalyptus seedlings in polythene bags, in government nurseries. Nature's locally available seeds were laid waste; people's locally available knowledge and energies were laid waste. With imported seeds and expertise came the import of loans and debt and the export of wood, soils, and people. Trees, as a living resource, maintaining the life of the soil and water and of local people, were replaced by trees whose dead wood went straight to a pulp factory hundreds of miles away. The smallest farm became a supplier of raw material to industry and ceased to be a supplier of food to local people. Local work, linking the trees to the crops, disappeared and was replaced by the work of brokers and middlemen who bought the eucalyptus trees on behalf of industry. Industrialists, foresters and bureaucrats loved the eucalyptus because it grows straight and is excellent pulp wood, unlike the honge which shelters the soil with its profuse branches and dense canopy and whose real worth is as a living tree on a farm.

The honge could be nature's idea of the perfect tree for arid Karnataka. It has rapid growth of precisely those parts of the tree, the leaves and small branches, which go back to the earth, enriching and protecting it, conserving its moisture and fertility. The eucalyptus, on the other hand, when perceived ecologically, is unproductive, even negative, because this perception assesses the "growth" and "productivity" of trees in relation to the water cycle and its conservation, in relation to soil fertility and in relation to human needs for food and food production. The eucalyptus has destroyed the water cycle in arid regions due to its high water demand and its failure to produce humus, which is nature's mechanism for conserving water.

Most indigenous species have a much higher biological productivity than the eucalyptus, when one considers water yields and water conservation. The non-woody biomass of trees has never been assessed by forest measurements and quantification within the reductionist paradigm, yet it is this very biomass that functions in conserving water and building soils. It is little wonder that Garhwal women call a tree 'dali' or branch, because they see the productivity of the tree in terms of its non-woody biomass which functions critically in hydrological and nutrient cycles within the forest, and through green fertilizer and fodder in cropland.

The most powerful argument in favour of the expansion of Eucalyptus is that it is faster growing than all indigenous alternatives. This is quite clearly untrue for ecozones where Eucalyptus has had no productivity due to pest damage. It is also not true for zones with poor soils and poor water endowment, as the reports on yields make evident.[297]

★★★

An important biomass output of trees that is never assessed by foresters who look for timber and wood is the yield of seeds and fruits. Fruit trees such as jack, jaman, mango, tamarind, etc., have been important components of indigenous forms of social forestry as practised over centuries in India. After a brief gestation period, fruit trees yield annual harvests of edible biomass on a sustainable and renewable basis.

Tamarind trees [can] yield fruits for over two centuries. Other trees, such as neem, pongamia and sal, provide annual harvest of seeds which yield valuable non-edible oils. These diverse yields of biomass provide important sources of livelihood for millions of tribes or rural people. The coconut, for example, besides providing fruits and oil, provides leaves used in thatching huts and supports the large coir industry in the country. Since social forestry programmes in their present form have been based on

---

[297] *Monocultures of the Mind*, Vandana Shiva, op.cit., pp. 29-31.

only the knowledge of foresters who have been trained only to look for the woody biomass in the tree, these important high yielding species of other forms of biomass have been totally ignored in these programmes. Two species on which ancient farm forestry systems in arid zones have laid special stress are pongamia and tamarind. Both these trees are multi-dimensional producers of firewood, fertiliser, fodder, fruit, and oil seed. More significantly, components of the crown biomass that are harvested from fruit and fodder trees leave the living tree standing to perform its essential ecological functions in soil and water conservation. In contrast, the biomass of the Eucalyptus is useful only after the tree is felled.[298]

★★★

In a country like India, crops have traditionally been bred and cultivated to produce not just food for man but fodder for animals, and organic fertiliser for soils. According to A. K. Yegna Narayan Aiyer, a leading authority on agriculture, "as an important fodder for cattle and in fact as the sole fodder in many tracts, the quantity of straw obtainable per acre is important in this country. Some varieties which are good yielders of grains suffer from the drawback of being low in respect to straw."

The destruction of diversity in agriculture has also been a source of non-sustainability. The "miracle" varieties displaced the traditionally grown crops and through the erosion of diversity, the new seeds became a mechanism for introducing and fostering pests. Indigenous varieties, or "land races," are resistant to locally occurring pests and diseases. Even if certain diseases occur, some of the strains may be susceptible, while others will have the resistance to survive. Crop rotations also help in pest control. Since many pests are specific in particular plants, planting crops in different seasons and different years causes large reductions in pest populations. On the other hand, planting the same crop over large areas year after year encourages pest build-ups. Cropping systems based on diversity thus have a built-in protection. . . .

Sustainable agriculture is based on the recycling of soil nutrients. This involves returning to the soil part of the nutrients that come from the soil, either directly as organic fertilizer, or indirectly through the manure from farm animals. Maintenance of the nutrient cycle, and through it the

---

[298] Ibid., p. 36.

fertility of the soil, is based on this inviolable law of return, which is a timeless, essential element of sustainable agriculture. . . . Technologies cannot substitute for nature and work outside nature's ecological processes without destroying the very basis of production.[299]

★★★

Gandhi's spinning wheel is a challenge to notions of progress and obsolescence that arise from absolutism and false universalism in concepts of science and technology development. . . . Parochial notions of productivity, perceived as universal, rob people of control over their means of reproducing life and rob nature of her capacity to regenerate diversity. . . . Ecological erosion and destruction of livelihoods are linked to one another.

The conservation of livelihoods, along with the conservation of resources, has been a special concern for us in India. It was the basis of our freedom movement and the struggle against colonialism.

Mahatma Gandhi had recognised that poverty and under-development in India was rooted in the destruction of jobs linked to our rich textile industry. The regeneration of livelihoods was central to the process of regaining independence. Gandhi categorically stated that what is good for one nation situated in one condition is not necessarily good for another differently situated. One man's food is often another man's poison. Mechanisation is good when hands are too few for the work intended to be accomplished. But according to Gandhi, it is an evil where there are more hands than required for the work, as is the case in India (Pyarelal 1959).

The spinning wheel became for Gandhi and India a symbol of a technology that conserves resources, people's livelihoods and people's control over their livelihoods. In contrast to the imperialism of the British textile industry, which had destroyed India's industrial base, the "charkha" was decentred and labour generating, not labour displacing. It needed people's hands and minds, instead of treating them as surplus, or as mere inputs into an industrial process.

Displacement of diversity and displacement of people's sources of sustenance both arise from a view of development and growth based on

---

[299] Ibid., p. 56-58.

uniformity created through centralised control. . . . As the spinning wheel was rendered backward and obsolete by the industrialisation of the manufacture of textiles, farmers' seeds are being rendered obsolete and valueless by technological change associated with the industrialisation of seed production.

The indigenous varieties or landraces in agriculture have evolved through millenia of natural and human selection. . . . The destruction of diversity and the creation of uniformity simultaneously involves the destruction of stability and the creation of vulnerability. Local knowledge, on the other hand, focuses on multiple use of diversity. Rice (for instance) is not just grain, it provides straw for thatching and mat-making, fodder for livestock, bran for fish ponds, husk for fuel. Local varieties of crops are selected to satisfy these multiple uses. . . .

Local knowledge systems have evolved tall varieties of rice and wheat to satisfy multiple needs. They have evolved sweet Cassava varieties whose leaves are palatable as fresh greens. However, all dominant research on cassava has focused on breeding new varieties for tuber yields, with leaves which are unpalatable.

Ironically, breeding for a reduction in usefulness has been viewed as important in agriculture, because uses outside those that serve the market are not perceived and taken into account. . . .

Angus Wright has observed: "One way in which agricultural research went wrong was precisely in saying and allowing it to be said that some miracle was being produced. . . . Historically, science and technology made their first advances by rejecting the idea of miracles in the natural world. Perhaps it would be best to return to that position."[300]

---

[300] Ibid., pp. 47-49.

Animals in Islam

~ Al-Hafiz B.A. Masri[301]

The *Qur'an Majeed* (*The Holy Quran*) states that man has dominion over animals: *He [God] it is Who made you vicegerents on earth*. [*Qur'an* 35:39], but makes clear that this responsibility is not unconditional and states what happens to those who misuse their freedom of choice and fail to conform to the conditions that limit this responsibility: *then We reduce him [to the status of] the lowest of the low.* [*Qur'an* 95:4, 5] . . . *they are those whom Allah has rejected and whom He has condemned . . . because they served evil* [*Qur'an* 5:63]. . . .*they have hearts wherewith they fail to comprehend, and eyes wherewith they fail to see, and ears wherewith they fail to hear. . . . Such [humans] are far astray from the right path* [*Qur'an* 7:179].

There are . . . people who take the concept of man's dominion over animals as a licentious freedom to break all the established moral rules designed to protect animal rights. The Imam Hazrat Ali has this to say about [those who misuse their authority over the weak]: "A savage and ferocious beast is better than a wicked and tyrant ruler." (*Maxims*, see Ref. No. 4, pp. 203, 381).

Again, the *Qur'an Majeed* urges in remonstrance: *And be not like those who say, "we have heard," while they do not hearken. Verily, the vilest of all creatures, in the sight of Allah, are those deaf and dumb ones who do not use their rationality* [*Qur'an* 8:21, 22].

---

[301] This selection is excerpted from *Animals in Islam*, written by Al-Hafiz B.A. Masri, as quoted on the website of Concern for Helping Animals in Israel, (CHAI) www.chai-online.org. Reprinted by permission from CHAI.

The sources quoted in this book are the *Qur'an Majeed (The Holy Qur'an)*, the first source of Islamic law (*Shari'ah*); Hadith or Tradition, the second source; and *Ijtihad*, inference by analogy, the third source. Together, these three sources make up Islamic case law or "Juristic Rules" that are the guidelines to be followed for any legal question. Many issues relating to animals, such as vivisection, factory farming, and animal rights did not exist 14 centuries ago and therefore, no specific laws were passed about them. To decide on issues developed in recent times, Islamic Jurisprudence (*fiqh*) has left it to Muslim Jurists (*fuqaha'a*) to use their judgement by inference and analogy, based on the three above-mentioned sources. ~ A. B. A. Masri (also all notes of article)

Animals Are Our Teachers

Muslims have often been advised by their mentors to learn lessons from some species of animal. For example, the Imam Hazrat Ali gives this piece of advice: "Be like a bee; anything he eats is clean, anything he drops is sweet and any branch he sits upon does not break." (*Maxims* of Ali; translated by Al-Halal from *Nahj-ul-Balagha* (in Arabic); Sh. Muhammad Ashraf, Lahore, Pakistan; p. 436. The Imam, Hazrat Ali bin Abi Talib was the son-in-law of the Holy Prophet Muḥammad 變, and the fourth Caliph (644-656 A.C. = 23-24 A.H.)

Animals Are Members of Communities and the Family of God

The Holy Prophet Muḥammad 變 puts it in these words: "All creatures are like a family (*Ayal*) of God: and he loves the most those who are the most beneficent to His family. (Narrated by Anas. *Mishkat al-Masabih*, 3:1392; quoted from Bukhari.)

The *Qur'an Majeed* says: *There is not an animal on earth, nor a bird that flies on its wings, but they are communities like you. . .* [*Qur'an* 6:38].

The Holy Prophet 變 used to say: "Whoever is kind to the creatures of God, is kind to himself." (*Wisdom of Prophet Mohammad* 變; Muhammad Amin; The Lion Press, Lahore, Pakistan; 1945).

According to the learned commentators of the *Qur'an Majeed* . . . animals all live a life, individual and social, like members of a human commune. In other words, they are like communities in their own right and not in relation to the human species or its values. These details have been mentioned to emphasize the point that even those species which are generally considered as insignificant or even dangerous deserve to be treated as communities; that their intrinsic and [less] perceptible values should be recognized, irrespective of their usefulness or their apparent harmfulness.

The significant point to note is that, physically, man has been put in the same bracket as all other species. The following *hadith* leaves no ambiguity in the sense in which the *Qur'an Majeed* uses the word "community." Abu Huraira reported the Prophet 變 as telling of an incident that happened to another prophet in the past. This prophet was stung by an ant and, in anger, he ordered the whole of the ants' nest to be burned. At this, God reprimanded this prophet in these words: "because one ant stung you, you have burned a whole community which glorified Me" (Bukhari and Muslim).

409

The Islamic law (*Shari'ah*) concerning the rights of animals is very elaborate and explicit. In the case of the ants' nest, the following Juristic Rule would apply: Any damage or a damaging retaliation for a damage is forbidden. (*La zarara wa la zirar*).

Human / Animal Communication

There are numerous legends about the Muslim saints and other holy men who could talk to animals. However, for lack of authentication, they are taken generally as mere fables. There is one statement in the *Qur'an Majeed*, though, which proves that man had acquired the lore of speech with animals as early as the time of King Solomon. Perhaps in those days human civilization was more in tune with nature than it is today. The Qur'anic verse runs like this: *And Solomon was David's heir, and he said: "O ye people! We have been taught the speech of birds . . ."* [*Qur'an* 27:16].

The *Qur'an Majeed* tells us that God actually communicates with animals, as the following verse shows: *And your Lord revealed to the bee, saying: make hives in the mountains and in the trees, and in (human) habitations* [*Qur'an* 16:68].

The *Qur'an Majeed* uses the same Arabic word "Wahi" for God's revelation to all His Prophets, including the Holy Prophet Muḥammad ﷺ, as it has been used in the case of the bee . . . it proves the basic fact that animals have a sufficient degree of psychic endowment to understand and follow God's messages—a faculty which is higher than instinct and intuition.

Animals Have Consciousness

Many passages from the *Qur'an Majeed* and *Aḥadith* (traditions of the Prophet) state that all animals are endowed with spirit and mind and . . . there is ample evidence in the *Qur'an Majeed* to suggest that animals' consciousness of spirit and mind is of a degree higher than mere instinct and intuition. We are told in the *Qur'an Majeed* that animals have a cognizance of their Creator and, hence, they pay their obeisance to Him by adoration and worship: *Seest thou not that it is Allah Whose praises are celebrated by all beings in the heavens and on earth, and by the birds with extended wings? Each one knows its prayer and psalm, And Allah is aware of what they do* [*Qur'an* 24:41].

It is worth noting the statement that "*each one knows its prayer and psalm.*" The execution of a voluntary act, performed consciously and intentionally, requires a faculty higher than that of instinct and intuition. Lest some people should doubt that animals could have such a faculty, the following verse points out that it is human ignorance that prevents them from understanding this phenomenon: *The seven heavens and the earth and all things therein declare His glory. There is not a thing but celebrates His adoration; and yet ye mankind! ye understand not how do they declare His glory . . .* [*Qur'an* 17:44].

The following verse tells us how all the elements of nature and all the animal kingdom function in harmony with God's laws; it is only some humans who infringe and, thus, bring affliction on themselves. The *Qur'an Majeed* dwells on this theme repeatedly to emphasize the point that man should bring himself into harmony with nature, according to the laws of God—as all other creation does: *Seest thou not that unto Allah payeth adoration all things that are in the heavens and on earth—the sun, the moon, the stars, the mountains, the trees, the animals, and a large number among mankind? However, there are many (humans) who do not and deserve chastisement . . .* [*Qur'an* 22:18].

A Dutch team of scientists has found scientific evidence of mental suffering in animals. They have discovered that, like the human brain, an animal's brain too releases a substance called "endorphin," to cope with emotional distress and pain caused by frustration or conflict. This substance is 100 times more powerful than morphine.[302]

Animals and Humans Must Share Natural Resources

Once it has been established that each species of animal is a "community" like the human community, it stands to reason that each and every creature on earth has, as its birth-right, a share in all the natural resources. In other words, each animal is a tenant-in-common on this Planet with human species.

But "Man has always been in competition with animals for food, and the problem has been aggravated in the current world situation, especially

---

[302] This was reported in the newsletter of Compassion in World Farming Agscene, August 1985, 20 Lavant Street, Petersfield, Hants, England. ~ A. B. A. Masri

because of modern agrarian mismanagement." The *Qur'an Majeed* has tried to allay this fear of man by reassuring him that God is not only the Creator but also the Sustainer and the Nourisher of all that He creates. However, the *Qur'an Majeed* lays down the condition that human beings, like all other creatures, shall have to work for their food, and that their share would be proportionate to their labor: *And that man shall have nothing, but what he strives for* [53:39].

The *Qur'an Majeed* repeatedly emphasizes that food and other resources of nature are there to be shared equitably with other creatures. Below are just a few of numerous such verses: *Then let man look at his food: how We pour out water in showers, then turn up the earth into furrow-slices and cause cereals to grow therein—grapes and green fodder; olive-trees and palm-trees; and luxuriant orchards, fruits and grasses . . . as Provision for you as well as for your cattle* [*Qur'an* 80:24-32].

Again, in the following verses, the bounties of nature are enumerated with the accent on animals' share in all of them. Everything was created for human AND non-human animals: *And He it is Who sends the winds, as glad tidings heralding His mercy. And We send down pure water from the clouds, that We may give life thereby, by watering the parched earth, and slake the thirst of those We have created—both the animals and the human beings in multitude* [*Qur'an* 25-48,49].

And do they not see that We meander water to a barren land and sprout forth from it crops, whereof their cattle as well as they themselves eat? Will they take no notice of it? [*Qur'an* 32:27].

We [God] brought forth from it [the earth] its waters and its pastures, and established the mountains firm—as a source of provision for you and for your animals [*Qur'an* 79:31-33].

There is no doubt that the message includes all animals, not just domestic livestock, in whose welfare we have a vested interest: *There is no moving creature on earth, but Allah provides for its sustenance . . .* [*Qur'an* 11:6]

And the earth: He [God] has assigned to all living creatures [*Qur'an* 55:10].

The essence of Islamic teachings on "Animal Rights" is that depriving animals of their fair share in the resources of nature is so serious a sin in the eyes of God that it is punishable by punitive retribution: The *Qur'an Majeed* describes how the people of Thamud demanded that the

Prophet Saleh ﷺ show them some sign to prove he was a prophet of
God. (The tribe of Thamud were the descendants of Noah. They have
also been mentioned in the Ptolemaic records of Alexander's astronomer
of the 2nd century A.C.)

At the time of this incident, the tribe was experiencing a dearth of
food and water and was, therefore, neglecting its livestock. It was revealed
to Prophet Saleh ﷺ to single out a she-camel as a symbol and ask his
people to give her her fair share of water and fodder. The people of
Thamud promised to do that but, later, killed the camel. As a retribution,
the tribe was annihilated. This incident has been mentioned in the *Qur'an
Majeed* many times in different contexts [*Qur'an* 7:73, 11:64, 26:155, 156;
54:27-31].

Is Animal Suffering Fate (Allah's Will) or the Fault of Humans?

Many people misunderstand the real sense of the doctrine of "pre-
destination," or "fate" (*qaza wa qadr* or *qismat*). The literal meaning of
"pre-destination," in the Islamic sense, is: "pre-fixing the fate of someone
or something," in the sense of determining the capacity, capability,
endowment, function and other faculties. The *Qur'an Majeed* uses the
Arabic word "taqdir," meaning "destiny," even for the decreed orbits of
the planetary motions; for inorganic substances; as well as for animated
creatures, including human beings. Within those pre-fixed limitations,
however, conditions could be changed for the better, suffering could be
avoided or lessened by human effort and skill.

Experimentation on Animals

Scientific and pharmaceutical experiments on animals are being done
to find cures for diseases, most of which are self-induced by our own
disorderly lifestyle. All human problems—physical, mental or spiritual—
are of our own creation and our wounds self-inflicted. By no stretch of
imagination can we blame animals for any of our troubles and make them
suffer for it. All this (experiments), and much more, is being done to
satisfy human needs, most of which are non-essential, fanciful, wasteful
and for which alternative, humane products are easily available. To kill
animals to satisfy the human thirst for non-essentials is a contradiction in
terms within the Islamic tradition. Let us hope a day will dawn when the

413

great religious teachings may at last begin to bear fruit; when we shall see the start of a new era, when man accords to animals the respect and status they have long deserved and for so long have been denied.

Vivisection did not exist at the time of the Holy Prophet Muhammad 鑗 and therefore, was not specifically cited in the law (*Shari'ah*). Guidance on such issues comes from analogy and inference (*Ijtihad*). One of the main excuses for all kinds of cruelties to animals is selfish interest or human needs. Let us see how the Juristic Rules define "needs" and "interests" and judge these cases according to those definitions. The basic Juristic Rule (*qaidatul-fiqhiyah*) that would apply to pecuniary experiments is: "One's interest or need does not annul other's right" (*al-idtiraru la yabtil haqqal-ghair*).

Needs are classified in three categories: necessities (*al-Masalih ad-darurfyan*) without which life could not be sustained; needs required for comfort and easement from pain or any kind of distress, or for improving the quality of life (*al-Masalih-al-haiya*); and luxuries (*al-Masalih at tahsiniyah*) desirable for enjoyment or self-indulgence.

Some rules that can be applied to these needs to determine whether experiments on animals would be allowed: What allures to the forbidden, is itself forbidden (*ma'ad'a ela al-harame, fahuwaharamun*). This rule implies that material gains, including food, obtained by wrongful acts, such as unnecessary experiments on animals, become unlawful (*haram*).

"No damage can be put right by a similar or a greater damage" (*ad-dararu la yuzalu be mislehi au be dararin akbaro minho*). When we damage our health and other interests by our own follies, we have no right to make the animals pay for it by inflicting similar or greater damage on them, such as by doing unnecessary experiments to find remedies for our self-induced ailments.

Resort to alternatives, when the original becomes undesirable. (*Iza ta'zuro al-aslu, yusaru ila-l-badle*). This rule places a great moral responsibility on experimenters and medical students to find alternatives.

The basic point to understand about using animals in science is that the same moral, ethical and legal codes should apply to the treatment of animals as are being applied to humans. According to Islam, all life is sacrosanct and has a right of protection and preservation.

The Holy Prophet Muhammad 鑗 laid so much emphasis on this

point that he declared: "There is no man who kills [even] a sparrow or anything smaller, without its deserving it, but God will question him about it."[303]

He who takes pity [even] on a sparrow and spares its life, Allah will be merciful on him on the Day of Judgement.[304]

Like all other laws of Islam, its laws on the treatment of animals have been left open to exceptions and are based on the criterion: "Actions shall be judged according to intention" (al-A'amalo binniyah). . . . If the life of an animal can be saved only by the amputation of a part of its body, it will be a meritorious act in the eyes of God to do so.

There is no doubt that the Islamic prohibition against the cutting or injuring of live animals, especially when it results in pain and suffering, does apply to modern vivisection in science. We are able to support this interpretation of the Islamic teachings by referring not only to the above-quoted representative Traditions (Aḥadith), but also to the Qur'an Majeed. In the verses quoted below, the principle is expressed that any interference with the body of a live animal which causes pain or disfigurement is contrary to the Islamic precepts. These verses were revealed in condemnation of the pagan superstitious custom that she-camels, ewes or nanny goats which had brought forth a certain number of young in a certain order should have their ears slit, be let loose, and dedicated to idols. Such customs were declared by the Qur'an Majeed as devilish acts, in these words: *It was not Allah who instituted the practice of a slit-ear-she-camel, or a she-camel let loose for free pasture, or a nanny-goat let loose . . . [Qur'an 5:103]. Allah cursed him [Satan] for having said: "I shall entice a number of your servants, and lead them astray, and I shall arouse in them vain desires; and I shall instruct them to slit the ears of cattle; and most certainly, I shall bid them—so that they will corrupt Allah's creation." Indeed! He who chooses the Devil rather than Allah as his patron, ruins himself manifestly. [Qur'an 4:118, 119].*

---

[303] Narrated by Ibn 'Omar and by Abdallah bin Al-As. An-Nasai, 7:206,239, Beirut. Also recorded by Musnad al-Jami—Ad-Darimi; Delhi, 1337. Also, *Mishkat al-Masabih;* English translation by James Robson, in four volumes; Sh. Muhammad Ashraf, Lahore, Pakistan; 1963 (hereafter referred to as "Robson").
[304] Narrated by Abu Umama. Transmitted by Al-Tabarani.

Fur and Other Uses of Animals

There is a large-scale carnage of fur-bearing animals . . . to satisfy human needs, most of which are non-essential, fanciful, wasteful and for which alternative, humane products are easily available. . . . The excuse that such things are essential for human needs is no longer valid. Modern technology has produced all these things in synthetic materials and they are easily available all over the world, in some cases at a cheaper price.

Some Juristic Rules that apply are: "That which was made permissible for a reason, becomes unpermissible by the absence of that reason" (*ma jaza le uzrin, batala be zawalehi*), and "All false excuses leading to damage should be repudiated" (*Sadduz-zarae al-mua'ddiyate ela-l-fasad*). These rules leave no excuse for the Muslims to remain complacent about the current killing of animals in their millions for their furs, tusks, oil, and various other commodities.

The Qur'an Majeed does mention animals as a source of warm clothing [Qur'an 16:5], but modern-day clothing made of synthetic fibers is just as warm as clothing made from animal skins and makes clothing from animal skins unnecessary. The Qur'an refers only to the skins and furs of domesticated cattle which either die their natural death or are slaughtered for food. Today, millions of wild animals are killed commercially just for their furs and skins, while their carcasses are left to rot. Fourteen centuries ago Islam realized the absurdity of this wasteful and cruel practice and passed laws to stop it in the following *Ahadith*:

The Holy Prophet Muḥammad ﷺ prohibited the use of skins of wild animals.[305]

The Holy Prophet Muḥammad ﷺ forbade the skins of wild animals being used as floor-coverings, (id).

The Holy Prophet ﷺ said: "Do not ride on saddles made of silk or leopard skins."[306]

---

[305] Narrated by Abu Malik on the authority of his father. Abu Dawud and Tirmidhi as recorded in *Garden of the Righteous—Riyad as-Salihin* of Imam Nawawi; translated by M.Z. Kahn; Curzon Press, London, 1975; [hereafter referred to as Riyad]; Hadith No. 815, p. 160.

[306] Narrated by Mu'awiah. Abu Dawud; (see *Riyad*, Ref. No. 28); Hadith No. 814, p. 160.

Animal Fights

All kinds of animal fights are strictly forbidden in Islam. Out of the numerous such injunctions, one would suffice here: God's Messenger ﷺ forbade inciting animals to fight each other.[307]

Like camel-humps, fat-tails of sheep and target-animals (*mujaththema*), the meat of animals who die as a result of fights is also declared in Islam as unlawful to eat (haram). For example, the Spaniards hold fiestas on special occasions to eat the bull killed by a matador.

Factory Farming

Our Holy Prophet's ﷺ overwhelming concern for animal rights and their general welfare would certainly have condemned (*La'ana*) those who practice such methods (factory farming), in the same way as he condemned similar other cruelties in his days. He would have declared that there is no grace or blessing (*Barakah*)—neither in the consumption of such food nor in the profits from such trades.

Vegetarianism

There is no suggestion in the *Qur'an Majeed* or in any other of the Islamic sources that eating meat is good for physical or spiritual health. Islam's approach in this matter is neutral; it has left the choice to the individual, but those who opt to eat meat are urged in the *Qur'an Majeed* to eat in moderation [*Qur'an* 7:31; 5:87 and other verses]. Furthermore, there are elaborate and stringent laws governing the overall treatment of animals used for food—their rearing and breeding; the pre-slaughter; and handling during and after slaughter.

The Holy Prophet ﷺ has placed the killing of animals without a justifiable reason as one of the major sins:

Avoid ye the seven obnoxious things: polytheism; magic; the killing of breathing beings! Which God has forbidden except for rightful reason.[308]

---

[307] Narrated by Abdullah bin Abbas. Bukhari, Muslim, Tirmidhi and Abu al-Darda; recorded in *Riyad* (Ref. No. 28); Hadith No. 1606; p. 271. Also "Robson" (Ref. No. 15), p. 876.

[308] Narrated by Abu Huraira. *Sahih Mulim—Kitab-ul-Imam* (Ref. No. 46); Chapt. XXXIX, Vol.1; p. 52. Bukhari, 4:23. Also *Awn*, (Ref. No. 32); Hadith No.

The Arabic word for "breathing beings" is "nafs." Until recently it used to be taken as meaning "human beings" only. All the Arabic dictionaries give the meaning of "nafs" as "ruh" (soul), and since they are breathing creatures, there seems to be no reason why the Qur'anic verses No. 6:151, 152 and others should not comprehend all "breathing beings," i.e., all species of animals. These verses should be read in conjunction with other verses of the *Qur'an Majeed* and numerous *Ahadith* which speak of the sanctity of life as a whole, declare animals as possessing soul (*zi ruhin*) and place animals physically on a par with human beings.

The baneful [sinful] things are: polytheism; disobedience to parents; the killing of breathing beings without a valid reason. (id. Narrated by Abdullah Ibn 'Amr.)

Slaughter of Animals Used for Food

Meat-eating is neither encouraged nor even recommended by Islam:

"Say [O Muhammad!] I find not in what has been revealed to me any food [meat] forbidden to those who wish to eat it, unless it be dead meat, or blood that pours forth, or the flesh of swine—for it is unclean [rijs]—or the sacriligious [fisq] meat which has been slaughtered in anybody's name other than that of Allah. It is significant to note that these laws have been laid down for those *"who wish to eat it"* (*ta'imin yat'amohu*). Eating meat is not required.

While Islam permits eating meat, it gives instructions to ensure humane slaughter, with as little pain to the victim as possible:

God's Messenger 鑠 was reported as saying: "Allah Who is Blessed and Exalted has prescribed benevolence toward everything [and has ordained that everything be done in a good way]; so, when you must kill a living being, do it in the best manner and, when you slaughter an animal, you should [use the best method and] sharpen your knife so as to cause the animal as little pain as possible.[309] The Messenger of Allah was heard forbidding to keep waiting a quadruped or any other animal for slaughter.[310]

2857.

[309] Narrated by Shaddad bin Aus. *Muslim*; Vol. 2, Chapter 11; Section on "Slaying"; 10:739, verse 151. Also "Robson" (Ref. No. 15); p. 872. Also recorded in *Riyad*. (Ref. No. 28); Hadith No. 643; p. 131.

[310] Bukhari. Also *Muslim*; Vol. 2, Chapter 11; Section on "Slaying"; 10:739;

The Prophet 🕌 forbade all living creatures to be slaughtered while tied up and bound.[311]

The Holy Prophet 🕌 said to a man who was sharpening his knife in the presence of the animal: 'Do you intend inflicting death on the animal twice—once by sharpening the knife within its sight, and once by cutting its throat?'[312]

Hazrat Imam Ali says: "Do not slaughter sheep in the presence of other sheep, or any animal in the presence of other animals."[313]

Hazrat 'Omar once saw a man denying a sheep, which he was going to slaughter, a satiating measure of water to drink. He gave the man a beating with his lash and told him: "Go, water it properly at the time of its death, you knave!"[314]

If animals have been subjected to cruelties in their breeding, transport, slaughter, or in their general welfare, meat from them is considered impure and unlawful to eat (haram). The flesh of animals killed by cruel methods (al-muthiah) is carrion (al-mujaththamah). Even if these animals have been slaughtered in the strictest Islamic manner, if cruelties were inflicted on them otherwise, their flesh is still forbidden (haram) food:

Oh, ye messengers! Eat of the good things (tayyibat) and do righteous deeds. Surely, I know what you do [Qur'an 23:51].

Oh believers! Eat what We have provided for you of lawful and good things, and give thanks for Allah's favour, if it is He whom you serve [Qur'an 2:172; 16:114].

The word "tayyib," translated as "good," "pure," "wholesome," etc., means pure both in the physical and the moral sense.

The main counsel of Islam in the slaughter of animals for food is to do it in the least painful manner. All the Islamic laws on the treatment of animals, including the method of slaughter, are based in all conscience on "the spirit" of compassion, fellow-feeling, and benevolence:

---

verse 152. Also "Robson" (Ref. No. 15), p. 872.

[311] Ibid., (Ref. No. 46); Hadith No. 4817; p. 1079.

[312] Al-Furu Min-al-Kafi Lil-Kulini; 6:230.

[313] Ibid., (for Hazrat Ali see Ref. No. 4).

[314] Reported by Ibn Sirin about Hazrat 'Omar and recorded in Badae al-Sande; 6:2811.

"Allah, Who is Blessed and Exalted, has prescribed benevolence toward everything and has ordained that everything be done in the right way; so when you must kill a living being, do it in the proper way—when you slaughter an animal, use the best method and sharpen your knife so as to cause as little pain as possible."[315]

Failure to stun animals before slaughter causes them pain and suffering. Muslims should give serious thought to whether this is cruelty (al-muthiah]. If so, then surely the meat from them is unlawful (haram), or at least, undesirable to eat (makruh). Al-Azhar University in Cairo appointed a special committee to decide whether the meat of animals slaughtered after stunning was lawful. The committee consisted of representatives of the four acknowledged Schools of Thought in Islam, i.e., Shafii, Hanafi, Maliki and Hanbali. The unanimous verdict (fatwa) of the committee was: "Muslim countries, by approving the modern method of slaughtering, have no religious objection in their way. This is lawful as long as the new means are 'shar' (ahadd) and clean and do 'cause bleeding' (museelah al-damm). If new means of slaughtering are more quick and sharp, their employment is a more desirable thing. It comes under the saying of the Prophet 鸞, 'God has ordered us to be kind to everything.' "[316]

To crown all verdicts (fatawa), here is the "Recommendation" of a preeminent Muslim organization of this century—The Muslim World League (Rabitat al-Alam al-Islami). It was founded in Makkah al-Mukarramah in 1962 A.C. (1382 A.H.) with 55 Muslim theologians (Ulama'a), scientists and leaders on its Constituent Council from all over the world. MWL is a member of the United Nations, UNESCO and UNICEF. In January 1986 it held a joint meeting with the World Health Organization (WHO) and made the following "recommendation" about pre-slaughter stunning (No 3:1. WHO-EM/FOS/1-E, p. 8):

Pre-slaughter stunning by electric shock, if proven to lessen the animal's suffering, is lawful, provided that it is carried out with the

---

[315] The Sahih Muslim, 2:156. Also Al-Taaj fi Jaami al-Usool, Vol. 3, p. 110, Cairo Edition. Also Al-Faruo min-al-Kafi, p. 2, and others.
[316] Inna'l-laha Kataba-'l-ihsan 'ala kulle Shay'in. The History of Azhar, Cairo; 1964; pp. 361-363.

weakest electric current that directly renders the animal unconscious, and that it neither leads to the animal's death nor renders its meat harmful to the consumer.

As of 1989, in the following countries, Muslims were NOT exempt from stunning: Norway, Sweden, Denmark, Switzerland, Australia and New Zealand. The following countries allow only partial exemption to Muslims under special conditions and regulations: Belgium, Germany, Netherlands, Italy, Spain, Finland and Canada.

Providing for Animals Used to Carry Heavy Loads

Animals in the service of man should be used only when necessary and their comfort should not be neglected.

The Prophet ﷺ once passed by a lean camel whose belly had shrunk to its back. "Fear God," he said to the owner of the camel, "in these dumb animals and ride them only when they are fit to be ridden, and let them go free when it is meet that they should rest."

About taking care of animals while traveling, the Holy Prophet ﷺ used to give the following advice:

"When you journey through a verdant land, [go slow to] let your camels graze. When you pass through an arid area, quicken your pace (lest hunger should enfeeble the animals). Do not pitch your tents for the night on the beaten tracks, for they are the pathways of nocturnal creatures."[317]

Saying daily prayers (salat) is one of the five most important obligations of the Muslim religion. In the following hadith, one of his companions tells us that the Holy Prophet ﷺ and his fellow travelers used to delay even saying their prayers until they had first given their riding and pack animals fodder and had attended to their needs:

"When we stopped at a halt, we did not say our prayers until we had taken the burdens off our camels' backs and attended to their needs."[318]

---

[317] Narrated by Abu Huraira. *Sahih Muslim—Kitab-ul-Imam* (Ref. No. 53); Vol. Ill; Chapter DCCVII; Hadith No. 4724; pp. 1062, 1063.
[318] Narrated by Anas. Awn (Ref. No. 32); 7:223; Hadith aNo. 5234. Also 'Guillaume' (Ref. No. 57); pp. 106, 107.

Hazrat Imam Ali's general advice about pack animals is: "be kind to pack animals; do not hurt them; and do not load them more than their ability to bear."[319]

Cruelty to Animals

According to the spirit and overall teachings of Islam, causing unavoidable pain and suffering to the defenseless and innocent creatures of God is not justifiable under any circumstances. Islam wants us to think and act in the positive terms of accepting all species as communities like us in their own right and not to sit in judgement on them according to our human norms and values.

Prevention of physical cruelty is not enough; mental cruelty is equally important. In the following incident, a bird's emotional distress has been treated as seriously as a physical injury:

We were on a journey with the Apostle of God ﷺ, and he left us for a while. During his absence, we saw a bird called hummara with its two young and took the young ones. The mother bird was circling above us in the air, beating its wings in grief, when the Prophet came back and said: "who has hurt the feelings of this bird by taking its young? Return them to her."[320]

It is reported by the same authority that: "a man once robbed some eggs from the nest of a bird. The Prophet ﷺ had them restored to the nest."[321]

The Holy Prophet ﷺ has even tried the "Punishment and Reward" approach in the following *Ahadith*:

The Islamic concern about cruelty to animals is so great that it has declared the infliction of any unnecessary and avoidable pain "even to a sparrow or any creature smaller than that" as a sin for which the culprit would be answerable to God on the Day of Judgement.

The Prophet ﷺ told his companions of a woman who would be

---

[319] Maxims (Ref. No. 4).

[320] Narrated by Abdul Rahman bin Abdullah bin Mas'ud. Muslim. Also Awn (Ref. No. 32) Hadith No. 2658. Also "Guillaume" (Ref. No. 57); p. 106.

[321] Ibid.

sent to Hell for having locked up a cat; not feeding it, nor even releasing it so that it could feed herself."[322]

Islam's concern for animals goes beyond the prevention of physical cruelty or even condescending kindness to them, which is a negative proposition. It enjoins on the human species, as the principal primates of the animated world, to take over the responsibility of all creatures in the spirit of a positive philosophy of life and to be their active protectors.

The Prophet ﷺ was asked if acts of charity even to the animals were rewarded by God. He replied: "Yes, there is a reward for acts of charity to every beast alive."[323]

Mishkat Al-Masabih concluded from "Bukhari" and "Muslim" to the effect that: "A good deed done to a beast is as good as doing good to a human being; while an act of cruelty to a beast is as bad as an act of cruelty to human beings" and that: "Kindness to animals was promised by rewards in Life Hereafter."[324]

The Prophet ﷺ told his companions of a serf who was blessed by Allah for saving the life of a dog by giving it water to drink and quenching its thirst.[325]

To catch birds and imprison them in cages without any special purpose is considered abominable.

No advantages and no urgency of human needs would justify the

---

[322] Narrated by Abdullah bin 'Omar. Bukhari, 4:337; recorded in Riyad (Ref. No. 28), Hadith No. 1605; p. 271. Also *Muslim*, Vol. 4, Hadith No. 2242. English translation by Abdul Hamid Siddiqi; Sh. Muhammad Ashraf, Lahore, Pakistan; 1976; Vol. 4, Hadith No. 5570; p. 1215. (According to the English translation, this Hadith was also narrated by the Abu Huraira and by Naqi who had heard it from Abdullah); Hadith No. 5573; p. 1215.) This Hadith has been recorded by almost all the authentic books of hadith, as the Re. No. 53 will show.

[323] Narrated by Abu Huraira, Bukhari, 3:322. Also *Muslim*, Vol. 4; Hadith No. 2244. Also Awn (Ref. No. 32), 7:222, Hadith No. 2533. Also *Mishkat al-Masabih*. Book 6; Chapter 6.

[324] *Mishkat al-Masabih*; Book 6; Chapter 7, 8:178.

[325] Narrated by Abu Huraira. *Muslim*, Vol. 4, Hadith No. 2244. Also Bukhari, 3:322. Also Awn (Ref. No. 32); Hadith No. 2533, and others.

kind of calculated violence which is being done these days against animals, especially through international trade of livestock and meat. One of the sayings of the Holy Prophet Muḥammad ﷺ tells us: "If you must kill, kill without torture." (*la taqtolu bi'l-idha'i*). While pronouncing this dictum, he did not name any animal as an exception—not even any noxious or venomous creature, such as scorpions and snakes.

Luckily, on this theme, we have quite a few of the Holy Prophet's ﷺ sayings. During the pre-Islamic period, certain pagan superstitions and polytheistic practices involving acts of torture and general cruelties to animals used to be common in Arabia. All such practices were condemned and stopped by Islam. The following few sayings of the Holy Prophet ﷺ will serve as an example:

> Jabir told that God's Messenger ﷺ forbade striking the face or branding on the face of animals . . . . The same companion of the Holy Prophet ﷺ reported him as saying, when an ass which had been branded in its face passed him by: "God curse the one who branded it."[326]

This *hadith* is concerned with causing pain to the animal on the sensitive parts of its body, as well as with the disfigurement of its appearance.

When the Holy Prophet ﷺ migrated to Medina from Mecca in 622 A.C., people there used to cut off camels' humps and the fat tails of sheep. The Prophet ﷺ ordered this barbaric practice to be stopped. The temptation for the people to perform this sort of vivisection on the animals was that the juicy humps and fatty tails could be eaten while the animal remained alive for future use. To remove this avidity, he declared: "whatever is cut off an animal while it is still alive, is carrion and is unlawful (*haram*) to eat."[327]

To make sure that no injury was inflicted on the animal while there

---

[326] Narrated by Jabir bin Abdullah. Muslim, Vol.3, Hadith No. 2116. Also *Awn al-Ma'bud Sharh Abu Dawud* (hereafter referred to as *Awn*); 7:232, hadith No. 2547. Also *The Lawful and Unlawful in Islam* (in Arabic); Yusuf el-Kardawi; *Mektebe Vahba*, Cairo; 1977; p. 293. Also "Robson" (Ref. No. 15); p. 872.

[327] Narrated by Abu Waqid al-Laithi. Tirmidhi; Hadith No. 1480, Chapt. One Al-At'imah. Also "Robson" (Ref. No.15), p. 872.

was even a flicker of life in it, it was forbidden by the Holy Prophet 鱉 to molest the carcass in any way, such as: by breaking its neck, skinning, or slicing off any of its parts, until the body is dead cold. One of his sayings on this theme is: "Do not deal hastily with a 'being' before it is stone dead."[328]

Hazrat 'Omar ibn al-Khattab used to instruct repeatedly: "Give time to the slaughtered being" till it is dead cold.[329]

Many other Muslim authorities have also given juristic opinions (*fatawa*) to the effect that, after slaughter, time should be given for the rigor mortis to set in before cutting up the carcass.[330]

Another malpractice in Arabia in those days, which caused pain and discomfort to the animals, was stopped by the Holy Prophet 鱉 in these words: "Do not store milk in the udders of animals. . . ."[331]

Not only physical but also emotional care of animals was so much emphasized by the Holy Prophet 鱉 that he once reprimanded his wife, A'ishah, for treating a camel a bit offhandedly. Hazrat A'ishah herself narrates: "I was riding a restive camel and turned it rather roughly. The Prophet 鱉 said to me: 'It behooves you to treat the animals gently.'"[332]

The Holy Prophet 鱉 himself was once reprimanded by God for neglecting his horse, as the following *hadith* tells us: "The Prophet 鱉 was seen wiping the face of his horse with his gown (*jullabiyah*). When asked why he was doing that, he replied: 'Last night I had a reprimand from Allah regarding my horse for having neglected him.' "[333]

The following *hadith* forbids the disfiguration of the body of an animal:

---

[328] *Kitab al-Muqni*, 3:542. Also Al-Muhalla, 7:457; Ibn Hazm.

[329] Al-Muhalla, 7:457; Ibn Hazm. Hazrat 'Omar ibn al-Khattab was the second Caliph (634-644 A.C.=1222 A.H.).

[330] *Kitab al-Nil wa Shifa'al-Alil*, 4:460.

[331] Muslim and Bukhari. Also *Holy Traditions*; 1st Edition; Vol. 1; Muhammad Manzur Ilahi; Ripon Press, Lahore, Paistan; 1932; p. 149.

[332] Narrated by A'ishah. *Muslim*, Vol. 4, Hadith No. 2593. Also *Awn*, 7:155, Hadith No. 2461; (Ref. No. 32).

[333] Narrated by Yahya bin Said. "Malik bin Anas al-Asbhahi". Also *Al-Muwatta*, (in English); Divan Press, Norwich, England; 1982; p. 205.

The Prophet ﷺ said: "Do not clip the forelock of a horse, for a decency is attached to its forelock; nor its mane, for it protects it; nor its tail, for it is its fly-flap."[334]

The incidents of the Holy Prophet Muhammad's ﷺ personal grooming of his horse; his wife A'isha's rough handling of her camel; the Holy Prophet's ﷺ prohibition of cutting forelocks, the mane or tail; the condemnation of striking and branding on the face or ears—all these and many other such *Ahadith* show that this great man, Muhammad ﷺ, had realized even fourteen centuries ago that animals have a sense of adornment and sensitivity.

Animal Sacrifice

It is not their flesh, nor their blood, that reaches Allah; it is your righteousness [piety and spiritual volition] that reaches Him. . . . Their flesh will never reach Allah, nor yet their blood, but your devotion will reach Him [Qur'an 22:37].

The main purpose of allowing Muslims to continue with animal sacrifices was to turn this tradition into an institution of charity. All the verses of the *Qur'an Majeed* which deal with the subject wind up with the proviso that the meat be fed to the poor, the needy, those who are too modest to beg, as well as the mendicants—those who beg openly [*Qur'an*, 2:196; 22:28; 33-37].

In some cases, the offerers of the sacrifice are allowed to consume a portion of the meat themselves, while in others the whole of the carcass is to be given in charity. Sacrifice is meant to be an act of worship and thanksgiving to solicit the approbation of God neither in the sense of atonement nor in the sense of transposing one's sins onto a scapegoat; but it is meant to be an act of benevolence (*ihsan*) to fulfill a social obligation. After reading the Qur'anic version of sacrifice, there remains no doubt in one's mind that any sacrifice that is allowed to go to waste is a sinful as well as a criminal violation of the Islamic law (*shariah*). Verses 22:36 and 37 make this proviso abundantly clear.

The Qur'anic injunctions are so exacting on the point of not taking

---

[334] Narrated by 'Utbah ibn Farqad Abu Abdillah al-Sulami. Abu Dawud. Also Awn, 7:216, 217, Hadith No. 2525 (Ref. No. 32).

the life of an animal without a justifiable cause (*be-ghair-e-haqqin*) that wasting meat, even by offering it to deities and gods, is called a devilish act.

During the early period of Islam the traditional offerings of animals made some sense. Meat was then an important ingredient of human diet and not even a scrap of it was wasted. Today we have made their killing an empty ritual and forgotten the intent.

A learned Muslim scholar, Sheikh Farid Wagdi, says in his Wagdi Encyclopaedia's "Article on Sacrifice" that there might come a day when Muslims shall have to substitute the rite of animal sacrifice with other methods of giving alms.

The Importance of Respecting the Balance of Nature

"Those who take undue advantage of other species break the Divine Law of equilibrium in nature—and nature never forgives." The *Qur'an Majeed* dwells on this theme recurrently, such as:

Allah has not created all this without truth (ḥaqq) [Qur'an 10:5] for it is He who created everything and ordained it with due potential (taqdir) [Qur'an 25:2] not to allow any change to corrupt what Allah has created [Qur'an 30:30]. Then a warning is given to those people who are guilty of infraction, in these words: "Do they not know how many We have annihilated before them—those whom We had established on earth as more powerful than We have established you . . ." [Qur'an 6:6].

The Importance of Conserving Nature

[Even when the world is coming to an end] on Doomsday, if any one has a palm-shoot in hand, he should plant it.[335]

Blood Sports

There are many *Aḥadith* forbidding blood sports and the use of animals as targets, some of which are as follows:

The Prophet 鬱 condemned those people who take up anything alive as a mere sport.[336]

---

[335] *Musnad* of Ahmad, 5:440 and 3:184 (hereafter referred to as *Musnad*).
[336] Narrated by Abdullah bin 'Omar. Muslim, Vol. 3, Hadith No. 1958.

The Prophet 🕮 forbade blood sports.[337]

The Prophet said: "Do not set up living creatures as a target."[338]

Ibn 'Umar happened to pass by a party of men who had tied a hen and were shooting arrows at it. When they saw Ibn 'Umar coming, they scampered off. Ibn 'Umar angrily remarked: "Who has done this? Verily! Allah's Messenger 🕮 has invoked a curse upon one who does this kind of thing."[339]

The Prophet 🕮 passed by some children who were shooting arrows at a ram. He told them off, saying: "Do not maim the poor beast."[340]

The fact that these *Ahadith* repeat the same sayings of the Holy Prophet 🕮 in slightly varying wordings shows that he took the matter very seriously and repeated them again and again on different occasions in the presence of different people. Another significant point to note in this respect is that, to stop the use of animals as targets or in blood sport, the Holy Prophet 🕮 did the same as he did in the case of camel-humps and sheep-tails, quoted above. He declared their meat as *mujaththema* and unlawful (*haram*) for consumption, according to the following *hadith*:

God's Messenger 🕮 forbade eating a *mujaththema* (carrion) of a bird or animal set up and shot at as a target for shooting.[341]

Military Research, Including Wound Labs

One might also appeal to the Islamic law (*Shari'ah*) to oppose using animals in military research in general and in the so-called wound laboratories in particular. The above-quoted *Ahadith*, as well as the Juristic Rules, would seem to support the view that our wars are our own problems and that we have no right to make the animals suffer for them.

---

[337] Narrated by Abdullah Ibn Abbas. *Awn*, (Ref. No. 32); 8:15, Hadith No. 2603. Also "Robson"; p. 876 (Ref. No. 15).

[338] Narrated by Abdullah bin Abbas. *Muslim* Vol. 3, Hadith No. 1957. Also "Robson"; p. 872 (Ref. No. 15).

[339] Ibid. Narrated by Said bin Jubair.

[340] Narrated by Abdallah bin Ja'far. An-Nasai, 7:238.

[341] Narrated by Waqid al-Laithi. Abu al-Darda. Tirmidhi, Hadith No. 1473, Chapt. "Al-At'imah." Also "Robson" (Ref. No.15); p. 874.

Preservation

~ C.A.H.

And [always] does He give you something
out of what you may be asking of Him;
and should you try to count God's blessings,
you could never compute them.
Behold, man is indeed most persistent in wrongdoing,
stubbornly ungrateful!
And [remember the time] when Abraham spoke:[342]
"O my Sustainer! Make this land secure,
and preserve me and my children from ever worshipping idols[343]
for, truly, O my Sustainer, these have led many people astray!
[*Sūrah Ibrāhīm* (Abraham) 14:34-36]

O my Sustainer! bestow wisdom on me and join me with the righteous;
grant me the ability to convey the truth to those who will come after me;
make me one of the inheritors of the Garden of Bliss.
[*Sūrah Ash-Shuᶜarāʾ* (The Poets) 26:83-85]

Such beauties and admirable creatures God created in this universe, such

---

[342] The whole of this passage represents a parenthetic reminder, in the form of Abraham's prayer, of the only way to righteousness, in the deepest sense of the word, open to man: namely, a recognition of God's existence, oneness, and uniqueness and, hence, a rejection of all belief in "other powers" supposedly co-existent with Him. . . . This prayer implies a realization of, and gratitude for, God's infinite bounty. ~ M. Asad

[343] The term "idols" (*asnām*, sing. *sanam*) does not apply exclusively to actual, concrete representations of false "deities": for *shirk*—that is, an attribution of divine powers or qualities to anyone or anything beside God—may consist also, as Rāzī points out, in a worshipful devotion to all manner of "causative agencies and outward means to an end"—an obvious allusion to wealth, power, luck, people's favour or disfavour, and so forth—"whereas genuine faith in the oneness and uniqueness of God (*at-tawḥīd al-maḥḍ*) consists in divesting oneself of all inner attachment to [such] causative agencies and in being convinced that there exists no real directing power apart from God." ~ M.Asad

abundance. Yet due to the expansion of increasing human population and our ungrateful and thoughtless actions, the further development of technologies for mining the earth's resources, and the sometimes irresponsible production of goods for the use of the human population, many of the habitats of the creatures of this earth have been damaged or destroyed. The beauty and abundance still manifest within the remaining preserved areas can remind us to awaken to the abundant generosity of the Source of Being and our responsibility to maintain and protect the vitality of the environment of this earth as a whole. The continued appropriate maintenance of such preserves remains a challenge, but their existence and further protection, as well as wise changes in our human habits in relation to the whole environment and its creatures appears essential to the preservation of the diversity of creation here as well as the actual breathing and well-being of humankind. Often it is a delicate balance we must seek to maintain and improve. Can we consider not just the need of this moment, but prepare for the needs of our children, our children's children, our future generations, and theirs?

Lake Manyara National Park

Though some time ago the hunting of their ivory tusks was prohibited in most areas, elephants continue to be the target of aggression, both directly for their ivory and indirectly through the diminishment of their safe havens. Lake Manyara National Park is one of those remaining safe havens, though with decreasing resources and overpopulation they—as well as many of their fellow creatures, including humans—are severely challenged. God willing, these majestic creatures, known for their strength and their loyalty, may endure and we may recognize and learn to better care for them, their fellow wild creatures, and for each other.

> Stretching for 50 km along the base of the rusty-gold 600-metre high Rift Valley escarpment, Lake Manyara is a scenic gem, with a setting extolled by Ernest Hemingway as "the loveliest I had seen in Africa."
> . . .
> From the entrance gate, the road winds through an expanse of lush jungle-like groundwater forest where hundred-strong baboon troops lounge nonchalantly along the roadside, blue monkeys scamper nimbly between the ancient mahogany trees, dainty

bushbuck tread warily through the shadows, and outsized forest hornbills honk cacaphonously in the high canopy.

Contrasting with the intimacy of the forest is the grassy floodplain and its expansive views eastward, across the alkaline lake, to the jagged blue volcanic peaks that rise from the endless Maasai Steppes. Large buffalo, wildebeest and zebra herds congregate on these grassy plains, as do giraffes—some so dark in coloration that they appear to be black from a distance.

Inland of the floodplain, a narrow belt of acacia woodland is the favored haunt of Manyara's legendary tree-climbing lions and impressively husked elephants. Squadrons of banded mongoose dart between the acacias, while the diminuitive Kirk's dik-dik forages in their shade.[344]

★★★

As usual, the elephants paid no attention to our Land Rover and we watched them until the sun dropped behind the cliffs, their shadows vanished and the word was given—no doubt by the senior matriarch—to seek the night-time safety of the dark ravines. In their orderly fashion they formed into a file, two or three abreast, calves by their mother's flanks, older children in her footsteps or not far from them, . . . Their manners were impeccable. . . .

They passed so close that we could see each eyelash clearly, and the wrinkles on their heads, the scars and old slits in their ears and the blood-vessels under the skin, like the veins of a leaf, by which each individual elephant can be identified. Despite their indifference to our presence one was aware of their awareness, and knew that any sudden move or noise on our part would cause the whole group, numbering thirty or forty, to raise their trunks, break into a loping trot and be away and gone. . . .

Another day is over, those big-bellies filled with tasty fruit, with bark and branches, grass and seedpods, herbs and leaves, such a variety to choose from and to relish; mud-baths have been taken, children suckled, a drowsy siesta in the shade enjoyed, sunrise to

---

[344] Lake Manyara National Park, http://www.tanzaniaparks.com/manyara.htm accessed 12/26/2005.

sunset passed without alarums and excursions. May it so continue until the little calf we saw getting in the way of her elders, rolling under their bellies with her legs in the air, grows to be a matriarch with her grandchildren and great grand-children around her. May she live to lay her bones in peace when old age comes. May hunters with guns and poisoned arrows, may accident and mishap, may starvation as the woodlands shrink and wither, pass her by.[345]

★★★

The largest of the creatures of the sea are also challenged in their existence, but find safe haven in parks to the north like Glacier Bay National Park. Here species threatened with extinction have been able to survive and continue to lend inspiration.

In wildness is the preservation of the world.

~ Henry David Thoreau

---

[345] Elspeth Huxley and Hugo van Lawick, *Last Days in Eden*, The Amaryllis Press, NY, NY, 1984, pp. 166-167.

Whale Dreams

~ Kim Heacox[346]

All night long whales swam into our dreams. Every time I turned over I heard them spouting, splashing, and feeding on the bounty of summer. Early in the pale light of morning I awoke to catch Melanie in her sleeping bag next to me, her eyes wide with wonder as a massive humpback blew again. WHOOSH! It was probably a hundred yards from our tent, swimming near shore at high tide, but it sounded so close as to be in the tent with us. We smiled at one another and drifted back to our dreams, vaguely aware that a sleep so ancient and deep was attainable only in a wild place.

We had made camp in a motorless cove in Glacier Bay National Park and skipped dinner that first night. Our kayaks, Red Windancer and Boysenberry Raven, were hauled up the beach and tied to alders. Our food was in bear-resistant canisters 200 yards down the beach. Too tired to eat on our first night out, we had fallen asleep from the sheer fatigue of our daily lives. Why, we wondered, were we always so busy? Always in such a hurry? Back home we "hopped" into the shower, "jumped" into our car, and "ran" to the store. Our watches weren't strapped to us; we were strapped to them. We ate quick microwave meals that left us feeling full, but empty. We gave hours to our e-mail and the Internet as if the computer might one day grant us happiness.

We needed to rest, to get off the information superhighway and embrace the open terrain of mystery. We needed a place to slow down and get to know each other again; to find our laughter and our smiles.

For ten days Glacier Bay did that. It healed us with blue ice prisms and magical hours that refracted our lives and made us see the simple, important things. "It's always like this out here," Melanie said. "Why don't we do this more often?"

---

[346] "Whale Dreams" The Gift of Alaska's National Parks by Kim Heacox, pp. 43-47 Wilderness, The Wilderness Society 2002-2003 (www.wilderness.org) See also *An American Idea: The Making of the National Parks*, about 400 years of [the] changing land ethic, and *Caribou Crossing*, a novel about the Arctic National Wildlife Refuge.

Every time we go into the wilds of Alaska—for more than 20 years now—we find ourselves whole again. Not just Melanie and me but a growing tide of over-civilized people from across America and around the world who find the national parks of Alaska are a window into the first day of creation. These places give people a new faith in themselves and in each other, and perhaps just as important, a new faith in the possibility that the human race might get it right this time. Having shaped so many American landscapes over three centuries, in Alaska we have a few that still shape us

Taken together, the national parks of Alaska offer the full scale and scope of the state. In Gates of the Arctic National Park, home to wild rivers and the majestic Brooks Range, I remember rafting down the North Fork of the Koyukuk where explorer Robert Marshall traveled in the summer of 1929. It was mid-August and the mountain slopes pulsed with crimson bearberry leaves and birds winging their way south. In Wrangell-St. Elias, I hiked high ridges and camped above glaciers that spilled into rock-ribbed bowls full of ice. In Katmai's Valley of Ten Thousand Smokes, I found bear tracks in rain-soaked volcanic ash that seemed to say: "No place is too remote for me." In Kobuk Valley, the far northwestern corner of the state, I watched caribou swim the Kobuk River at Onion Portage, a bend in the river where Eskimos have hunted for at least 14,000 years. In Lake Clark National Park, a short plane ride from Anchorage, I've enjoyed dozens of remote hiking and boating opportunities. In Kenai Fjords, also relatively accessible, I opened the tent flap to find a mountain goat staring at me, And in Denali, the Yellowstone of Alaska with its bears, caribou, moose, Dall sheep, wolves and mountains, I found my life enriched in ways that still warm me on the coldest of nights.

Yes, the threats to these places are serious; they always will be. "Nothing dollarable is safe," said John Muir. But a dedicated and growing corps of people work daily to protect these parks, and an increasing percentage of those guardians are Alaskans who realize that the gift of living where they do magnifies as the rest of the world sinks under concrete and the tread of human feet.

"These parks in Alaska were done right," says The Wilderness Society's Don Barry, a Wisconsin native who has fallen in love with the

49th state. "They were created with careful attention to ecological boundaries and whole watersheds. Now the challenge is to keep them intact and have the wisdom to avoid the worst aspects of industrial tourism—the crowds, signs, curio shops, parking lots and crass commercialism that plague so many national parks elsewhere in the country." For a long time a mantra among national conservation organizations has been to save Alaska from Alaskans. . . . But that's changing. The people of Seward who marched in protest against the creation of Kenai Fjords National Park now support it. Park superintendents and chief rangers serve on school boards. Maintenance employees coach baseball and volunteer for local fire departments and emergency response teams. Friendships form and ideologies merge, or at least the edges soften. People discover that they have a lot in common. National parks attract tourists, and tourists, for better or worse, bring dollars.

Increasingly Alaskans are sensing that they cannot survive without a pristine environment. Tourism brings 1.2 million visitors to the state every year and has surpassed fishing to become the second-largest industry (behind oil). In Alaska six times more jobs rely on a healthy ecosystem than on oil and gas. In a recent poll by the Alaska Conservation Foundation, 92 percent of the respondents (Alaskans) said a healthy environment is necessary for a strong economy; 71 percent considered themselves conservationists. This is a tectonic shift from the Don't-lock-it-up-Don't-tread-on-me majority that defined Alaska through the rancorous 1970s. . . . John Quinley, a 14-year veteran in public affairs in the National Park Service's Alaska Regional Office, says, "The demographics have changed. Alaska is a young state composed of young people. For many Alaskans today, the parks have always been here. They feel no threat from them. In fact, they feel fortunate to have them nearby." . . .

"This is a critical time," says Eleanor Huffines, The Wilderness Society's regional director for Alaska. "The National Park Service is embarking on a series of back-country management plans that will determine the future of millions of acres of Alaska's most spectacular natural resources. . . ."

Quinley adds, "This last couple years has been busy with new visitor centers and hotels in and near the parks. Visitation has increased dramatically in the front country and in the backcountry. Snow machines are more powerful and dependable and take people into more remote country. Four hundred businesses are now licensed to operate in Alaska's national parks, from mega-corporations to little single-plane air taxis."

All this activity underlines a fundamental challenge: How to allow for the most enjoyment of the parks and maximize economic opportunities for Alaskans without degrading these natural treasures. The Park Service's mission is to protect our parks so that they can be handed down, undiminished, to future generations. The pressure to give in to the forces of industrial tourism will continue to mount. . . .

There are many victories. Thirty years ago the Park Service made news in Alaska by closing Denali (then Mount McKinley) National Park to private vehicle traffic in lieu of a bus system. It was criticized as too restrictive. But it worked. It reduced traffic and kept wildlife along the road. Thousands of visitors see magic in that park every day of every summer, and most people endorse the transportation system.

Denali is a ship in a bottle. To get inside you must pass through the narrow neck; you must stand in line in a visitor center to get a campground, vehicle and/or backcountry permit. But once inside you find what Melanie and I have found: peace and quiet. You find a prism, a diamond among the jewels.

Glacier Bay is the same. Only so many cruise ships, tour boats, and private vessels are allowed into the bay each day. This leaves room for the whales.

That night as I climbed back into my sleeping bag, I heard spouting over still water and remembered Thomas Merton, from *Raids on the Unspeakable*, "Here in the wilderness," he wrote, "I have learned to sleep again."

Then I closed my eyes and dreamed.

Awakenings

~ Paul Gorman[347]

In the fall of 1986, at the direction of World Wildlife Fund president Prince Philip, the organization convened its 25th anniversary in Assisi to affirm what Prince Philip called the "spiritual and religious dimensions of conservation." The four-day event had emblematic highpoints. Thousands of activists from both hemispheres, carrying paintings of endangered species, walked 15 miles a day over the Umbrian countryside toward Assisi, spent nights in village piazzas and called themselves "green pilgrims."

In the Sacro Convento of the 13th-century Basilica of San Francesco, scientists briefed senior religious leaders from five faith traditions.

"This amount of soil has been eroded away through deforestation in several years," said John Hanks, a WWF researcher, indicating 1 foot of depth. "How long do you think it took to build up?"

"Five years," guessed a Muslim. "Ten," ventured a Christian. "Twenty," said a Jew, smiling at the Christian.

"One thousand!" trumped the Dalai Lama's mischievous abbot.

Much smiling.

"Six thousand," answered the scientist. Much sobriety.

On the last day, in the Basilica—as if inside a jewel with Giotto's frescoes lit by television lights—we tied Hindu bands of fellowship to one another's wrists and observed liturgies from each tradition. Afterward, from the Basilica's tower, the religious leaders read solemn declarations of commitment to "cherish and care for creation." They passed these covenants of five faiths to pilgrims who took them home to five continents.

To the delight of all. Prince Philip bid a traditional farewell to a Maori warrior by rubbing noses. "I believe today, in this famous shrine of St. Francis, the patron saint of ecology, a new and powerful bond has been affirmed between the forces of religion and conservation," he said as

---

[347] Paul Gorman (National Religious Partnership for the Environment), "Awakenings, Spiritual Perspectives on Conservation" Nature Conservancy Magazine, Spring 2003 pp. 22-23.

he concluded the historic convocation. "Neither can ever quite be the same again."

In the 15 years since, I've observed in reflecting on this broad encounter a constellation of awakenings rather than the fixed course of a single pilgrimage. We glimpse that diversity in the wonderful testimonies that accompany this essay.

For some, the inquiry is more immediately religious: an Arkansas synagogue's celebration of Tu B'Shevat, the Jewish new year of trees, with children seeding native grasses; a visit to a Kenyan grandmother's rural homestead, "with . . . insects chirping and smelling the breeze . . . what God is all about"; a Nature Conservancy land purchase understood as an act of redemption.

Others, perhaps unaffiliated with any religion, evoke spirituality in their experiences of awe and insight in observing nature: humility in a sudden encounter with a fisher [wildcat]; reverence in the Hawaiian "hana kupono" protocol on entering a forest; comfort of grief in the Everglades.

These are deep stirrings of the human heart. But the integration of private vision into programmatic public life also requires human reason and initiative for the common good.

For the organized Judeo-Christian religious communities in America, this has called for theological inquiry and social teaching. Faith groups have sent educational resources to tens of thousands of congregations, addressing perennial questions: human place and purpose in the greater web of life, dominion and stewardship, the rights of other creatures, private property and the claims of the commons, prudence and precaution, environmental justice, intergenerational equity.

Collaborative initiatives embody this deeper inquiry. For example, in 1995, evangelical Christians met with House Republicans—allies on most other issues—to argue against rolling back the Endangered Species Act. They pointed out that in Genesis, after the flood, God established "the covenant which I make between me and you and every living creature that is with you for perpetual generations." All life, future as well as present, has intrinsic moral value.

When the Jewish community has addressed conservation, it has set forth a vision of the intrinsic ethical connection between people and land:

"The Lord hath a controversy with the inhabitants of the land. Because there is no truth, nor knowledge of God, nor mercy . . . therefore shall the Land mourn, and all that dwelleth therein shall languish. . . ." In biblical ecology, the condition of our habitat reflects the health of our character. Fruition is assured in the soil of neighborly love.

In a pastoral letter on the Columbia River, the Catholic bishops of the Pacific Northwest portray a sacred commons in the river and its tributaries, arteries of transformative, living water. "The watershed is the common home and habitat of God's creatures, a source of human livelihood, and a setting for human community. The commons belongs to everyone. . . . Seen through eyes alive with faith, [the watershed] can be a revelation of God's presence, an occasion of grace and blessing . . . [that] requires us to enter into a gradual process of conversion and change."

These religious perspectives move millions and are essential as ancient faith traditions engage New World historical challenges. The teachings come first. And though many may not follow them, there is growing recognition that they invite more universal moral vision and values for an environmentalism thus far shaped primarily by science and law.

Meanwhile, spiritual and moral perspectives—however respected as inner callings—have generated some hesitancy as they have surfaced more explicitly in organized environmentalism. Here, after all, sound science has necessarily come first. Struggles are usually about policy. Laws have to be passed.

Moreover, religion is seen as volatile, spirituality as vague; morality can be "moralistic." Why get into it, or how?

One response, skillfully modest, has been simply to create safe space for conversation. At retreats of senior staff members from national organizations, participants are asked to bring "sacred objects" and reflections on their deeper meaning. Bark from "a family tree." A picture of two sons and word of a toxic dump being planned nearby. Water from a polluted river where baptisms can no longer take place. A piece of the Berlin Wall. A memory: "A photo forever in my mind's eye: after two days alone in the California desert, I turn the corner of a canyon and suddenly see . . . dozens of people, limping, or with crutches, wheelchairs and helpers, slowly climbing to the top of a ridge for the view."

When asked what's important, what comes forward here are values: home, family, stewardship, peace, healing and restoration. When this inquiry has been authentic and sustained, organizations report that it has revitalized mission, refreshed message and renewed long-term purpose, especially in a challenging political climate.

The Wilderness Society now integrates the perspectives of a mature land ethic—"sustaining the community of life"—into all of its land management trainings. The Trust for Public Land, then, speaks of how it is "endeavoring to translate the soul of the land into the soul of the culture." The Nature Conservancy recognizes that it is saving the landscapes "of our hearts, our souls, our very being" and that these places sustain and enhance our lives spiritually.

Nor is this entirely novel. The conservation movement was born in such vision. Its own prophet, Aldo Leopold, warns against an arid conservation, "which defines no right or wrong, assigns no obligation, calls for no sacrifice, implies no change in the philosophy of values." His call to inner transformation is no less uncompromising: "Nothing can be done without creating a new kind of people."

Each year, at the Feast of St. Francis at New York's Cathedral of St. John the Divine, there is a "procession of creation" through the nave, under a dome tall enough to enclose the Statue of Liberty, and then to the altar in the crossing, within sight of the high altar—which is flanked by two bronze menorahs, two Shinto vases and a pedestal from the stand on which the Magna Carta was signed.

The cathedral's 2-ton bronze doors, opened again only on Easter morning, let in city light, a view of a nursing home across the street and an elephant, a llama, a camel, an eagle, a python, a pony, a very big dog, a turtle, a sparrow, a tarantula, a flask of two trillion algae, a rain forest orchid, a meteorite, and—this is New York City, after all— a rat with a garland and a cockroach in a bowl on a purple liturgical pillow.

What will be the reaction, organizers always wonder, as the procession comes into view: stampede, flashbulb, cheers? More than a few tears and a great silence, year after year.

Why are the doors closed in the first place? Fear of what's outside, fear of others, fear of life?

What are those tears? Of loss, longing, joy, shame, reconciliation?

440

What is the silence? Readiness to pause, draw on our deepest spiritual and moral resources, and ask once again what it must really mean to be here and to be human? Readiness to wake up?

In the Name of God,
the Infinitely Compassionate and Most Merciful
Consider time . . .
Truly, human beings are in loss
except those who have faith and do righteous deeds
and encourage each other in the Truth,
and encourage each other in patient perseverance.
[*Sūrah l-ᶜAṣr* (The Flight Of Time) 103:1-3]

Behold, as for those who attain to faith and do righteous deeds—
truly, We do not fail to requite any who persevere in doing good:
theirs shall be gardens of perpetual bliss
through which running waters flow.
[*Sūrah Al-Kahf* (The Cave) 18:30-31]

CHAPTER TWENTY-ONE

HUMILITY

It is God Who has made for you the earth as a resting place
and the sky as a canopy
and has given you shapes and made your shapes beautiful
and has provided for you sustenance of pure and good things—
such is God, your Sustainer.
So Glory to God, the Sustainer of all the Worlds!
He is the Ever-Living: there is no god but He.
Call upon Him, offering Him sincere devotion.
Praise be to God, Sustainer of all the Worlds!
[*Sūrah Ghāfir* (Forgiving) 40:64-65]

Blessed is He Who made constellations in the skies
and placed there a lamp and a moon giving light;
And it is He Who made the night and the day to follow each other,
for such as have the will to celebrate His praises
or to show their gratitude.
And the servants of the Infinitely Compassionate One
are those who walk on the earth in humility
and when the ignorant address them they say, "Peace!"—
those who spend the night in adoration of their Sustainer
in prostration and standing straight.
[*Sūrah Al-Furqān* (The Standard Of True And False) 25:61-64]

The black crow that I always despised.
And yet, against the snowy dawn . . .
~ Basho[348]

---

[348] Jonathan Clements, *The Moon in the Pines, Zen Haiku*. London: Frances Lincoln, Ltd., 2000, p. 19.

If you know wilderness in the way that you know love, you would be unwilling to let it go.

~ Terry Tempest Williams

The ruin or the blank that we see when we look at nature, is in our own eye. The axis of vision is not coincident with the axis of things, and so they appear not transparent but opaque. The reason why the world lacks unity, and lies broken and in heaps, is because man is disunited with himself. He cannot be a naturalist until he satisfies all the demands of the spirit. Love is as much its demand as perception. Indeed, neither can be perfect without the other. In the uttermost meaning of the words, thought is devout, and devotion is thought. Deep calls unto deep. But in actual life, the marriage is not celebrated. There are innocent men who worship God after the tradition of their fathers, but their sense of duty has not yet extended to the use of all their faculties. And there are patient naturalists, but they freeze their subject under the wintry light of the understanding. Is not prayer also a study of truth, a sally of the soul into the unfound infinite? No man ever prayed heartily without learning something.

~ Ralph Waldo Emerson

Let Me Walk in Beauty
~ Chief Yellow Lark (Lakota American Indian)[349]

Oh Great Spirit,
Whose voice I hear in the winds
And whose breath gives life to all the world, hear me:
I am small and weak.
I need your strength and wisdom.

[349] *Prayers for Peace*, 2002 Graphis, Inc. 307 Fifth Ave., NY, NY 10016 p. 83.

Let me walk in beauty and make my eyes
Ever behold the red and purple sunset.
Make my hands respect the things you have made
And my ears sharp to hear your voice.
Make me wise so that I may understand
The things you have taught my people.
Let me learn the lessons you have hidden
In every leaf and rock. . . .
I seek strength, not to be superior to my brother,
But to fight my greatest enemy—myself.
Make me always ready to come to you
With clean hands and straight eyes,
So that when life fades, as the dying sunset,
my spirit will come to you
without shame.

The Prophet 🌿 himself was ready to learn from his companions about the natural world. When he discovered that palm trees no longer produced dates due to his advice not to germinate them, he told his companions to do as they did before.

~ Rafea [350]

The Prophet honored all of nature, encouraged by the words of the Qur'an. Even a cat's comfort was more important to him than his own. Once when he was sitting, a cat fell asleep near him upon the edge of his cloak. When he needed to rise, rather than disturb the cat, he cut the fabric off around the cat, leaving her resting peacefully.

~ C.A.H.

---

[350] Rafea, Ali, Aliaa, and Asihs. *Islam from Adam to Muhammad and Beyond.* Sadek Publishing Cairo, p. 140.

The Latin word for "earth" or "soil" is *humus,* from which we get our word "humility." Trees, rocks, and animals cannot consciously humble themselves, nor do they need to; their *islam* is part of their nature. Only Man can bow consciously, because his is the Trust.

God, in His own nature, is rich in all things. *God was in no need of them. And God is All-Sufficient* [64:6]. We, on the other hand, are poor in all but Him. *O men, you are the ones who have need of God* [35:15]. The essence of nature, the essence of all manifest existence, is poverty. It possesses nothing of its own. It's like a mirror reflecting the many faces of the One.

~ Charles Upton

Moments of Recognition
~ Barry Lopez[351]

One summer evening I was camped in the western Brooks Range of Alaska with a friend. From the ridge where we had pitched our tent we looked out over tens of square miles of rolling tundra along the southern edge of the calving grounds of the Western Arctic caribou herd. During those days we observed not only caribou and wolves, which we'd come to study, but wolverine and red fox, ground squirrels, delicate-legged whimbrels and aggressive Jaegers, all in the unfoldings of their obscure lives. One night we watched in awe as a young grizzly bear tried repeatedly to force its way past a yearling wolf standing guard alone before a den of young pups. The bear eventually gave up and went on its way. We watched snowy owls and rough-legged hawks hunt and caribou drift like smoke through the valley.

---

[351] This selection is excerpted from Barry Lopez, "Arctic Dreams: Imagination and Desire in a Northern Landscape." *This Sacred Earth, Religion, Nature, Environment,* Edited by Roger S. Gottlieb, pp. 21-22. Reprinted by permission of Sterling Lord Literistic, Inc. Copyright © 1986 by Barry Holstun Lopez.

On the evening I am thinking about—it was breezy there on Ilingnorak Ridge, and cold; but the late-night sun, small as a kite in the northern sky, poured forth an energy that burned against my cheekbones—it was on that evening that I went on a walk for the first time among the tundra birds. They all build their nests on the ground, so their vulnerability is extreme. I gazed down at a single horned lark no bigger than my fist. She stared back resolute as iron. As I approached, golden plovers abandoned their nests in hysterical ploys, artfully feigning a broken wing to distract me from the woven grass cups that couched their pale, darkly speckled eggs. Their eggs glowed with a soft, pure light, like the window light in a Vermeer painting. I marveled at this intense and concentrated beauty on the vast table of the plain. I walked on to find Lapland longspurs as still on their nests as stones, their dark eyes gleaming. At the nest of two snowy owls I stopped. These are more formidable animals than plovers. I stood motionless. The wild glare in their eyes receded. One owl settled back slowly over its three eggs, with an aura of primitive alertness. The other watched me, and immediately sought a bond with my eyes if I started to move.

I took to bowing on these evening walks. I would bow slightly with my hands in my pockets, toward the birds and the evidence of life in their nests—because of their fecundity, unexpected in this remote region, and because of the serene arctic light that came down over the land like breath, like breathing.

I remember the wild, dedicated lives of the birds that night and also the abandon with which a small herd of caribou crossed the Kokolik River to the northwest, the incident of only a few moments. They pranced through like wild mares, kicking up sheets of water across the evening sun and shaking it off on the far side like huge dogs, a bloom of spray that glittered in the air around them like grains of mica.

I remember the press of light against my face. The explosive skitter of calves among grazing caribou. And the warm intensity of the eggs beneath these resolute birds. Until then, perhaps because the sun was shining in the very middle of the night, so out of tune with my own customary perception, I had never known how benign sunlight could be. How forgiving. How run through with compassion in a land that bore so eloquently the evidence of centuries of winter. . . .

446

Whatever evaluation we finally make of a stretch of land, however, no matter how profound or accurate, we will find it inadequate. The land retains an identity of its own, still deeper and more subtle than we can know. Our obligation toward it then becomes simple: to approach with an uncalculating mind, with an attitude of regard. To try to sense the range and variety of its expression—its weather and colors and animals. To intend from the beginning to preserve some of the mystery within it as a kind of wisdom to be experienced, not questioned. And to be alert for its openings, for that moment when something sacred reveals itself within the mundane, and you know the land knows you are there. . . .

In the face of a rational, scientific approach to the land, which is more widely sanctioned, esoteric insights and speculations are frequently overshadowed, and what is lost is profound. The land is like poetry: it is inexplicably coherent, it is transcendent in its meaning, and it has the power to elevate a consideration of human life.

Opening the Heart

~ John P. Milton[352]

The natural fusion of relaxation and presence cultivates a spontaneous flow of universal life energy (*qi*). When you surrender into this life energy, you may experience it as open-hearted joy—even bliss. . . .

A good way to begin cultivating the radiance of the open heart is through the practice of simple appreciation. Take a few minutes or more each day to go to that special place in nature where you feel whole and unaffectedly centered. Enter this sacred space with the intention to experience all life from a deeper, richer perspective. As you begin to connect with the plants, animals, earth, and sky, give gentle appreciation from your heart for the gift of each being you encounter.

---

[352] This section is excerpted from the *Sky Above, Earth Below*, Study Guide by John P. Milton, Sounds True/Boulder, CO. 1999, www.soundstrue.com Excerpted from pp. 15-16, 20, 33-35.

If you initially feel a little awkward doing these things, relax and connect first with something that spontaneously inspires you. Perhaps it is a blue flower, shaped as a perfect mandala; or it may be the searing cry of an eagle passing overhead; or perhaps the puffy, white swirl of a flowing cloud. As your appreciation deepens, you may be amazed to discover the natural reverence you hold for all nature. Wherever your perceptions touch, simply allow your gratitude and loving appreciation to flow naturally to each being.

Now sit for a few moments and allow your perceptions to rest gently in themselves. Let the experiences of sight, sound, taste, smell, and touch each open into natural communion with everything perceived. Instead of viewing plants, stones, or a brook as separate from yourself, let each sense bring you into the experience of union with whatever you are perceiving. Perhaps you smell a flower lifting its head before you; you feel its leaves brush softly against your hand, and you hear the wind move through its petals. Experience that flower as one with you: one view, one sound, one touch, one smell, one taste. Realize the continuum of that unique, mysterious union: the union that is flower and you. There is no separation, no division—you are simply resting in the perceptual oneness of sight, sound, touch, taste, and smell. This unified awareness experiences the natural, heartfelt communion of inner and outer nature.

Once your body feels centered, move your focus to the air moving in and out of your nostrils. Breathing in, gratefully acknowledge the gift of oxygen freely offered to you by the trees and grasses. On the out-breath, feel your breath dissolve out into all of nature. Return to it your own gift of carbon dioxide: food for all the plants that need it. Experience your breathing as a direct exchange with the wild.

★★★

Each time you realize you are tense, practice relaxation. Take a deep breath into the tension. Remember how it felt to be totally relaxed in the wild, and ask nature to assist you. Allow your body to remember and return to that state.

Remember, too, that energy follows thought. Visualize the energy of relaxation washing over you as you talk to a difficult customer, client, boss, or stressed employee. Once you are relaxed, you can be totally nondistracted and present with them. This energy creates an environment that can potentially engender a spiritually transforming experience for yourself, the other, or both of you.

Tonglen is another practice that lends itself well to spontaneous expression: When you witness suffering, open your heart and breathe it in. Allow happiness to arise from its bottomless well and to radiate out with each exhalation, liberating the suffering of all living beings around you. Where appropriate, teach these practices to others so that they can join in also.

The more you practice these spiritual processes, the more natural they become. They also provide a model for others in your community to support healing relationships among people and with nature everywhere. The healing and revitalization of the Earth and all the beings living within and upon it truly begins only when we heal our own relationships. Healing ourselves helps heal all our relations.

As you walk lightly on the Earth, you may want to do something in your own community to bring awareness of how to cultivate spirit in nature, or to help revitalize the Earth there. There are many others around the world with the same vision. Contact groups already formed and work together to create harmonious community. Learn about your home bioregion. Find out what ecologically sustainable technologies (such as solar and wind power) are available and practical where you live.

Do you know what is produced locally in the way of food, clothing, water, fuel, etc.? What must be imported? Where does it come from? How stable is the economy in your area? What are your dependencies on other regions, and how are their goods transported to you? What do you need to do or learn to be able to live more simply, more connected to Gaia (Mother Earth)? Start where you are and cultivate a deeper relationship with your home. That is the most important thing any of us can do.

Here are some ways you can begin making these crucial connections.

• Plant vegetables, flowers, and trees. Local nurseries will be able to advise you on selection and care. . . .

• Universities and colleges often sponsor agricultural extension programs. If there is one in your area, use it to get tips on natural pest and weed control for your garden. (You will also find information at your public library and on the Internet.)

• Call the [local] water department and ask where your water comes from. Buy a map of your region and trace the path of the water from its reservoir to your faucet. Learn where the water treatment plant is, and find out what chemicals are added to the water you use. . . .

• Become a bird-watcher. Learn to recognize the songs of all of the birds in your area. . . .

These are only initial suggestions. There are literally countless ways you can tend to the Earth while simultaneously cultivating your own relationship with the natural world. As you engage in these environmental transformations, carry the essence of spiritual warriorship with you. No matter what the challenge, remain relaxed, be present, and radiate an open heart. Return to [your] Source.

Being Balance

~ Ali, Aliaa, and Aisha Rafea[353]

While it is true that faith is a private matter between an individual and God, that relationship is reflected in man's behavior and ethics. A balanced life starts on the individual level, when man recognizes her/his place in the universe and becomes aware of the continuation of life, so that s/he resists the tendancy to give absolute values to false goals. In doing so, s/he will be just to her/himself. In this respect, a balanced life means that a person can make every moment on earth fruitful by relating her/his deeds in this life to the harvest that awaits her/him in the hereafter. Her/his endeavors would be directed toward purifying her/his intentions, in order to be honest and sincere in acquiring spiritual, rather than material, rewards. To awaken to this reality reduces man's vanity and increases her/his readiness to move forward on the ladder of spiritual development. That awareness means that s/he is continuously attempting to restore and retain balance.

---

[353] Rafea, Ali, Aliaa, and Aisha. *Islam from Adam to Muhammad and Beyond*. Sadek publishing, Cairo. p. 169.

Because human beings live on earth, their relation with the natural world should also be balanced. That balance is only achieved when humans realize the unity of life, that they are a part of the whole, a reflection of it. Man's body is but part of the natural world and s/he should respect it and fulfill its needs without indulging in desires. When s/he attempts to fulfill those needs, s/he encounters nature. Approaching nature with respect and appreciation guarantees bounty for all. For when human beings are careful not to take more than they require and not to destroy a plant, shoot birds for pleasure, and pollute the environment, Mother Nature prospers and continues to give.

There is no Muslim who plants a tree, or sows a field, and man, birds or beasts eat from them, but it is charity for him.

~ The Prophet Muḥammad ﷺ[354]

The Man Who Planted Trees
~ Jean Giono [355]

For a human character to reveal truly exceptional qualities, one must have the good fortune to be able to observe its performance over many years. If this performance is devoid of all egoism, if its guiding motive is unparalleled generosity, if it is absolutely certain that there is no thought of recompense and that, in addition, it has left its visible mark upon the earth, then there can be no mistake.

About forty years ago I was taking a long trip on foot over mountain heights quite unknown to tourists in that ancient region where the Alps

---

[354] As quoted in *The Wisdom of Muhammad*, by Allama Sir Abdullah Al-Mamun Al-Suhrawardy, Citadel Press and Kensington Publishing Corp., NY, NY 2001, p. 52.

[355] This selection written by Jean Giono is excerpted from *Sharing Nature with Children II* by Joseph Cornell, Dawn Publications, Nevada City, CA5959 1989. pp. 143-153. Reprinted with permission from Dawn Publications.

thrust down into Provence. All this, at the time I embarked upon my long walk through these deserted regions, was barren and colorless land. Nothing grew there but wild lavender.

I was crossing the area at its widest point, and after three days' walking found myself in the midst of unparalleled desolation. I camped near the vestiges of an abandoned village. I had run out of water the day before, and had to find some. These clustered houses, although in ruins, like an old wasps' nest, suggested that there must once have been a spring or well here. There was, indeed, a spring, but it was dry. The five or six houses, roofless, gnawed by wind and rain, the tiny chapel with its crumbling steeple, stood about like the houses and chapels in living villages, but all life had vanished.

It was a fine June day, brilliant with sunlight, but over this unsheltered land, high in the sky, the wind blew with unendurable ferocity. It growled over the carcasses of the houses like a lion disturbed at its meal. I had to move my camp.

After five hours' walking I had still not found water, and there was nothing to give me any hope of finding any. All about me was the same dryness, the same coarse grasses. I thought I glimpsed in the distance a small black silhouette, upright, and took it for the trunk of a solitary tree. In any case I started towards it. It was a shepherd. Thirty sheep were lying about him on the baking earth.

He gave me a drink from his watergourd and, a little later, took me to his cottage in a fold of the plain. He drew his water—excellent water—from a very deep natural well above which he had constructed a primitive winch.

The man spoke little. This is the way of those who live alone, but one felt that he was sure of himself, and confident in his assurance. That was unexpected in this barren country. He lived, not in a cabin, but in a real house built of stone that bore plain evidence of how his own efforts had reclaimed the ruin he had found there on his arrival. His roof was strong and sound. The wind on its tiles made the sound of the sea upon its shores.

The place was in order, the dishes washed, the floor swept, his rifle oiled; his soup was boiling over the fire. I noticed then that he was cleanly shaved, that all his buttons were firmly sewed on, that his clothing had been mended with the meticulous care that makes the mending invisible. He shared his soup with me and afterwards, when I offered my tobacco pouch, he told me that he did not smoke. His dog, as silent as himself, was friendly without being servile.

It was understood from the first that I should spend the night there; the nearest village was still more than a day and a half away. And besides I was perfectly familiar with the nature of the rare villages in that region. There were four or five of them scattered well apart from each other on these mountain slopes, among white oak thickets, at the extreme end of the wagon roads. They were inhabited by charcoal-burners, and the living was bad. Families, crowded together in a climate that is excessively harsh both in winter and in summer, found no escape from the unceasing conflict of personalities. Irrational ambition reached inordinate proportions in the continual desire for escape. The men took their wagonloads of charcoal to the town, then returned.

The soundest characters broke under the perpetual grind. The women nursed their grievances. There was rivalry in everything, over the price of charcoal as over a pew in the church. And over all there was the wind, also ceaseless, to rasp upon the nerves. There were epidemics of suicide and frequent cases of insanity, usually homicidal.

The shepherd went to fetch a small sack and poured out a heap of acorns on the table. He began to inspect them, one by one, with great concentration, separating the good from the bad. I smoked my pipe. I did offer to help him. He told me that it was his job. And in fact, seeing the care he devoted to the task, I did not insist. That was the whole of our conversation. When he had set aside a large enough pile of good acorns he counted them out by tens, meanwhile eliminating the small ones or those which were slightly cracked, for now he examined them more closely. When he had thus selected one hundred perfect acorns he stopped and he went to bed.

There was peace in being with this man. The next day I asked if I might rest here for a day. He found it quite natural—or, to be more exact, he gave me the impression that nothing could startle him. The rest was not absolutely necessary, but I was interested and wished to know more about him. He opened the pen and led his flocks to pasture. Before leaving, he plunged his sack of carefully selected and counted acorns into a pail of water. I noticed that he carried for a stick an iron rod as thick as my thumb and about a yard and a half long. Resting myself by walking, I followed a path parallel to his. His pasture was in a valley. He left the little flock in the charge of the dog and climbed towards where I stood. I was afraid that he was about to rebuke me for my indiscretion, but it was not that at all: this was the way he was going, and he invited me to go along if I had nothing better to do. He climbed to the top of the ridge about a hundred yards away.

There he began thrusting his iron rod into the earth, making a hole in which he planted an acorn; then he refilled the hole. He was planting oak trees. I asked him if the land belonged to him. He answered no. Did he know whose it was? He did not. He supposed it was community property, or perhaps belonged to people who cared nothing about it. He was not interested in finding out whose it was. He planted his hundred acorns with the greatest care. After the midday meal he resumed his planting. I suppose I must have been fairly insistent in my questioning, for he answered me. For three years he had been planting trees in this wilderness. He had planted 100,000. Of these, 20,000 had sprouted. Of the 20,000 he still expected to lose about half to rodents or to the unpredictable designs of Providence. There remained 10,000 oak trees to grow where nothing had grown before.

That was when I began to wonder about the age of this man. He was obviously over fifty. Fifty-five, he told me. His name was Elzéard Bouffier. He had once had a farm in the lowlands. There he had had his life. He had lost his only son, then his wife. He had withdrawn into this solitude, where his pleasure was to live leisurely with his lambs and his dog. It was his opinion that this land was dying for want of trees. He added that, having no very pressing business of his own, he had resolved to remedy this state of affairs.

Since I was at that time, in spite of my youth, leading a solitary life, I understood how to deal gently with solitary spirits. But my very youth forced me to consider the future in relation to myself and to a certain quest for happiness. I told him that in thirty years his 10,000 oaks would be magnificent. He answered quite simply that if God granted him life, in thirty years he would have planted so many more that these 10,000 would be like a drop of water in the ocean.

Besides, he was now studying the reproduction of beech trees and had a nursery of seedlings grown from beechnuts near his cottage. The seedlings, which he protected from his sheep with a wire fence, were very beautiful. He was also considering birches for the valleys where, he told me, there was a certain amount of moisture a few yards below the surface of the soil.

The next day we parted.

The following year came the War of 1914, in which I was involved for the next five years. An infantryman hardly had time for reflecting upon trees. To tell the truth, the thing itself had made no impression upon me; I had considered it as a hobby, a stamp collection, and forgotten it.

The war over, I found myself possessed of a tiny demobilization bonus and a huge desire to breathe fresh air for a while. It was with no other objective that I again took the road to the barren lands.

The countryside had not changed. However, beyond the deserted village I glimpsed in the distance a sort of greyish mist that covered the mountaintops like a carpet. Since the day before, I had begun to think again of the shepherd tree-planter. "Ten thousand oaks," I reflected, "really take up quite a bit of space." I had seen too many men die during those five years not to imagine easily that Elzéard Bouffier was dead, especially since, at twenty, one regards men of fifty as old men with nothing left to do but die. He was not dead. As a matter of fact he was extremely spry. He had changed jobs. Now he had only four sheep but, instead, a hundred beehives. He had got rid of the sheep because they threatened his young trees. For, he told me (and I saw for myself), the war had disturbed him not at all. He had imperturbably continued to plant.

The oaks of 1910 were then ten years old and taller than either of us. It was an impressive spectacle. I was literally speechless and, as he did not talk, we spent the whole day walking in silence through his forest. In three sections, it measured eleven kilometres in length and three kilometres at its greatest width. When you remembered that all this had sprung from the hands and the soul of this one man, without technical resources, you understood that men could be as effectual as God in realms other than that of destruction.

He had pursued his plan, and beech trees as high as my shoulder, spreading out as far as the eye could reach, confirmed it. He showed me handsome clumps of birch planted five years before—that is, in 1915, when I had been fighting at Verdun. He had set them out in all the valleys where he had guessed—and rightly—that there was moisture almost at the surface of the ground. They were as delicate as young girls, and very well established.

Creation seemed to come about in a sort of chain reaction. He did not worry about it; he was determinedly pursuing his task in all its simplicity; but as we went back towards the village I saw water flowing in brooks that had been dry since the memory of man. This was the most impressive result of chain reaction that I had seen. These dry streams had once, long ago, run with water. Some of the dreary villages I mentioned before had been built on the sites of ancient Roman settlements, traces of which still remained; and archaeologists, exploring there, had found fishhooks where, in the twentieth century, cisterns were needed to assure a small supply of water.

The wind, too, scattered seeds. As the water reappeared, so there reappeared willows, rushes, meadows, gardens, flowers, and a certain purpose in being alive. But the transformation took place so gradually that it became part of the pattern without causing any astonishment. Hunters, climbing into the wilderness in pursuit of hares or wild boar, had of course noticed the sudden growth of little trees, but had attributed it to some caprice of the earth. That is why no one meddled with Elzéard Bouffier's work. If he had been detected he would have had opposition. He was undetectable. Who in the villages or in the administration could have dreamed of such perseverance in a magnificent generosity?

To have anything like a precise idea of this exceptional character one must not forget that he worked in total solitude: so total that, towards the end of his life, he lost the habit of speech. Or perhaps it was that he saw no need for it.

In 1933 he received a visit from a forest ranger who notified him of an order against lighting fires out of doors for fear of endangering the growth of this *natural* forest. It was the first time, the man told him naively, that he had ever heard of a forest growing of its own accord. At that time Bouffier was about to plant beeches at a spot some twelve kilometres from his cottage. In order to avoid travelling back and forth—

for he was then seventy-five—he planned to build a stone cabin right at the plantation. The next year he did so.

In 1935 a whole delegation came from the Government to examine the "natural forest." There was a high official from the Forest Service, a Deputy, technicians. There was a great deal of ineffectual talk. It was decided that something must be done and, fortunately, nothing was done except the only helpful thing: the whole forest was placed under the protection of the State, and charcoal burning prohibited. For it was impossible not to be captivated by the beauty of those young trees in the fullness of health, and they cast their spell over the Deputy himself.

A friend of mine was among the forestry officers of the delegation. To him I explained the mystery. One day the following week we went together to see Elzéard Bouffier. We found him hard at work, some ten kilometres from the spot where the inspection had taken place.

This forester was not my friend for nothing. He was aware of values. He knew how to keep silent. I delivered the eggs I had brought as a present. We shared our lunch among the three of us and spent several hours in wordless contemplation of the countryside.

In the direction from which we had come the slopes were covered with trees twenty to twenty-five feet tall. I remembered how the land had looked in 1913: a desert. . . . Peaceful, regular toil, the vigorous mountain air, frugality and, above all, serenity in the spirit had endowed this old man with awe-inspiring health. He was one of God's athletes. I wondered how many more acres he was going to cover with trees.

Before leaving my friend simply made a brief suggestion about certain species of trees that the soil here seemed particularly suited for. He did not force the point. "For the very good reason," he told me later, "that Bouffier knows more about it than I do." At the end of an hour's walking—having turned it over in his mind—he added, "He knows a lot more about it than anybody. He's discovered a wonderful way to be happy!"

It was thanks to this officer that not only the forest but also the happiness of the man was protected. He delegated three rangers to the task, and so terrorized them that they remained proof against all the bottles of wine the charcoal-burners could offer.

The only serious danger to the work occurred during the War of 1939. As cars were being run on gazogenes (wood-burning generators), there was never enough wood. Cutting was started among the oaks of 1910, but the area was so far from any railway that the enterprise turned out to be financially unsound. It was abandoned. The shepherd had seen nothing of it. He was thirty kilometres away, peacefully continuing his work, ignoring the war of 1939 as he had ignored that of 1914.

I saw Elzéard Bouffier for the last time in June of 1945. He was then eighty-seven. I had started back along the route through the wastelands; but now, in spite of the disorder in which the war had left the country, there was a bus running between the Durance Valley and the mountain. I attributed the fact that I no longer recognized the scenes of my earlier journeys to this relatively speedy transportation. It took the name of a village to convince me that I was actually in that region that had been all ruins and desolation.

The bus put me down at Vergons. In 1913 this hamlet of ten or twelve houses had three inhabitants. They had been savage creatures, hating one another, living by trapping game, little removed, physically and morally, from the conditions of prehistoric man. All about them nettles were feeding upon the remains of abandoned houses. Their condition had been beyond hope. For them, nothing but to await death— a situation which rarely predisposes to virtue.

Everything was changed. Even the air. Instead of the harsh dry winds that used to attack me, a gentle breeze was blowing, laden with scents. A sound like water came from the mountains; it was the wind in the forest; most amazing of all, I heard the actual sound of water falling into a pool. I saw that a fountain had been built, that it flowed freely and—what touched me most—that someone had planted a linden beside it, a linden that must have been four years old, already in full leaf, the incontestable symbol of resurrection.

Besides, Vergons bore evidence of labor at the sort of undertaking for which hope is required. Hope, then, had returned. Ruins had been cleared away, dilapidated walls torn down and five houses restored. Now there were twenty-eight inhabitants, four of them young married couples. The new houses, freshly plastered, were surrounded by gardens where vegetables and flowers grew in orderly confusion, cabbages and roses, leeks and snapdragons, celery and anemones. It was now a village where one would like to live.

From that point I went on foot. The war just finished had not allowed the full blooming of life, but Lazarus was out of the tomb. On the lower slopes of the mountain I saw little fields of barley and rye; deep in that narrow valley the meadows were turning green.

It has taken only the eight years since then for the whole countryside to glow with health and prosperity. On the site of the ruins I had seen in 1913 now stand neat farms, cleanly plastered, testifying to a happy and comfortable life. The old streams, fed by the rains and snows that the forest conserves, are flowing again. Their waters have been channelled. On each farm, in groves of maples, fountain pools overflow on to carpets of fresh mint. Little by little the villages have been rebuilt. People from the plains, where land is costly, have settled here, bringing youth, motion, the spirit of adventure. Along the roads you meet hearty men and women, boys and girls who understand laughter and have recovered a taste for picnics. Counting the former population, unrecognisable now that they live in comfort, more than 10,000 people owe their happiness to Elzéard Bouffier.

When I reflect that one man, armed only with his own physical and moral resources, was able to cause this land of Canaan to spring from the wasteland, I am convinced that, in spite of everything, humanity is admirable. But when I compute the unfailing greatness of spirit and the tenacity of benevolence that it must have taken to achieve this result, I am taken with an immense respect for that old and unlearned peasant who was able to complete a work worthy of God.

Elzéard Bouffier died peacefully in 1947 at the hospice in Banon.

Even if you know the world will end tomorrow, plant a tree.

~ The Prophet Muḥammad ﷺ

CHAPTER TWENTY-TWO

WONDER

Look around you!—
In the creation of the heavens and the earth,
in the alternation of night and day;
in the sailing of ships through the ocean
for the profit of humankind;
in the waters which God sends down from the skies
and the life which the One gives by means of it
to an earth that is dead;
in the living creatures of all kinds which multiply there;
in the change of the winds
and the clouds that follow, between sky and earth;
truly, these are signs for people who reflect.
[Sūrah *Al-Baqarah* (The Cow) 2:164]

Don't they look at the sky above them?
How We have made it and adorned it
and how there are no flaws in it?
And the earth—We have spread it wide
and firmly established mountains on it
and caused it to bring forth every kind of beautiful growth,
so offering an insight and a reminder
to every human being who willingly turns to God.
And We send down from the sky rain charged with blessing
and with it cause gardens to grow, and fields of grain,
and tall palm-trees with their thickly-clustered dates,
as sustenance for human beings;
and by all this We bring dead land to life:
even so will be the Resurrection.
[Sūrah *Qāf* 50:6–11]

By the Peonies

~ Czeslaw Milosz[356]

The peonies bloom white and pink.
And inside each, as in a fragrant bowl,
A swarm of tiny beetles have their conversation,
For the flower is given to them as their home.

Mother stands by the peony bed,
Reaches for one bloom, opens its petals,
And looks for a long time into peony lands,
Where one short instant equals a whole year.

Then lets the flower go. And what she thinks
She repeats aloud to the children and herself.
The wind sways the green leaves gently
And speckles of light flick across their faces.

There is something obscure which is complete
before heaven and earth arose;
tranquil, quiet, standing alone without change,
moving around without peril.
It could be the Mother of everything.
I don't know its name, and call it Tao.

~ Tao Te Ching [357]

---

[356] "By the Peonies," from *The Collected Poems 1931-1987* by Czeslaw Milosz, copyright © 1988 by Czeslaw Milosz Royalties, Inc. Reprinted by permission of HarperCollins Publishers.

[357] *Tao Te Ching*, XXV. Excerpted from *Seeing God Everywhere, Essays on Nature and the Sacred.* Edited by Barry McDonald, Copyright 2003 World Wisdom, Inc., p. 33. Reprinted by permission of World Wisdom, Inc.

Civilization no longer needs to open up wilderness; it needs wilderness to open up the still largely unexplored human mind.

~ David Rains Wallace

Earth's crammed with heaven
and every common bush afire with God.

~ Elizabeth Barrett-Browning

Renewing Wonder
~ David James Duncan[358]

My earliest conception of the meaning of the word wonder was a feeling that would come over me as a little kid, when I'd picture the shepherds on the night hills above Bethlehem. Even when those shepherds were made of illuminated plastic, standing around in Christmas dioramas on my neighbors' lawns, their slack-jawed expressions of wonder appealed to me. Years later, having become literate enough to read, I learned that those shepherds were also "sore afraid." But—a personal prejudice—I didn't believe in their afraidness. I believed the star in the east smote them with wonder, and that once wonder smites you, you're smitten by wonder alone. Fear can't penetrate till wonder subsides.

Wonder is my second favorite condition to be in, after love, and I sometimes wonder whether there's a difference; maybe love is just wonder aimed at a beloved.

Wonder is like grace, in that it's not a condition we grasp; it grasps us.

Wonder is not an obligatory element in the search for truth. We can seek truth without wonder's assistance. But seek is all we'll do; there will be no finding. Unless wonder descends, unlocks us, turns us as slack-jawed as plastic shepherds, truth is unable to enter. Wonder may be the aura of truth, the halo of it. Or something even closer. Wonder may be the caress of truth, touching our very skin.

---

[358] From *My Story as Told by Water*, by David James Duncan. Copyright © 2001 by David James Duncan. Reprinted by permission of Sierra Club Books, pp. 88-89.

Philosophically speaking, wonder is crucial to the discovery of knowledge, yet has everything to do with ignorance. By this I mean that only an admission of our ignorance can open us to fresh knowings. Wonder is the experience of that admission: wonder is unknowing, experienced as pleasure.

Punctuationally speaking, wonder is a period at the end of a statement we've long taken for granted, suddenly looking up and seeing the sinuous curve of a tall black hat on its head, and realizing it was a question mark all along.

As a facial expression, wonder is the letter O our eyes and mouths make when the state itself descends. O: God's middle initial. O: because wonder Opens us.

Wonder is anything taken for granted—the old neighborhood, old job, old life, old spouse—suddenly filling with mystery. Wonder is anything closed, suddenly opening: anything at all opening—which, alas, includes Pandora's Box, and brings me to the dark side of the thing—Grateful as I am for this condition, wonder has—like everything on Earth—a dark side. Heartbreak, grief, and suffering rend openings in us through which the dark kind of wonder pours. I have so far found it impossible to feel spontaneously grateful for these violent openings. But when, after struggle, I've been able to turn a corner and at least accept the opening, the dark form of wonder has invariably helped me endure the heartbreak, the suffering, the grief.

Wonder is not curiosity. Wonder is to curiosity what ecstasy is to mere pleasure. Wonder is not astonishment, either. Astonishment is too brief. The only limit to the duration of wonder is the limit of our ability to remain open.

I believe some people live in a state of constant wonder. I believe they're the best people on Earth. I believe it is wonder, even more than fidelity, that keeps marriages alive. I believe it's wonder, even more than courage, that conquers fear of death. I believe it is wonder, not D.A.R.E. bumper stickers, that keeps kids off drugs. I believe, speaking of bumper stickers, that it's wonder, even more than me, who I want to "HUG MY KIDS YET TODAY," because wonder can keep on hugging them, long after I'm gone.

I would love to live
Like a river flows,
Carried by the surprise
Of its own unfolding.

~ John O'Donohue[359]

Morning

~ Emily Dickinson

Will there really be a morning?
Is there such a thing as day?
Could I see it from the mountains,
If I was as tall as they?

Has it feet like water lilies?
Has it feathers like a bird?
Does it come from famous places
Of which I have never heard?

Oh, some scholar! Oh some sailor!
Oh, some wise men from the skies!
Please to tell this little pilgrim
Where the place called morning lies.

---

[359] "Fluent" from *Conamara Blues* by John O'Donohue, published by Doubleday. Reprinted by permission of the Random House Group Ltd.

Cleansing the Doors of Perception

~ Charles Upton

To learn how to see nature as a carpet woven of symbols or signs of God, you must, in a sense, become profoundly naive—guileless, sincere and simple-minded. You must learn, again, to trust your direct experience of things, like you did when you were a child. Symbolic consciousness reminds us how to see the world as it actually appears, and how to let that appearance instruct us. It was not without purpose that God placed us in a world of mountains and plains and forests and deserts and oceans, with the sun, moon, and stars above us, with winds and clouds and rain, the day following the night and the night the day. It was not without purpose that he gave us the kind of bodies we have, and the kind of senses that allow us to perceive the world around us in exactly the way He has willed us to perceive it.

In order to really see the natural world as a living symbol of its Creator, we must "cleanse the doors of perception." But we also need to sense how, as we contemplate the universe, we are also *being contemplated;* as we sit quietly, watching the natural world, Someone Else is watching us. In the words of Muḥammad, peace and blessings be upon him:

"Pray to God as if you saw Him: because even if you don't see Him, He sees you."

Winter Paradise

~ Kathleen Raine[360]

Now I am old and free from time
How spacious life,
Unbeginning unending sky where the wind blows
The ever-moving clouds and clouds of starlings on the wing.
Chaffinch and apple-leaf across my garden lawn,
Winter paradise
With its own birds and daisies
And all the near and far that eye can see.

Each blade of grass signed with the mystery
Across whose face unchanging everchanging pass
Summer and winter, day and night.
Great countenance of the unknown known
You have looked upon me all my days.
More loved than lover's face,
More merciful than the heart, more wise
Than spoken word, unspoken theme
Simple as earth in whom we live and move.

---

[360] "Winter Paradise," from *Selected Poems* of Kathleen Raine, Lindisfarne Press (RR4, Box 94 A-1, Hudson, New York 12554), 1988.

Renewing Soul

~ William Wordsworth

Knowing that Nature never did betray
The heart that loved her; 'tis her privilege,
Through all the years of this our life, to lead
From joy to joy:
for she can so inform
The mind that is within us, so impress
With quietness and beauty, and so feed
With lofty thoughts, that neither evil tongues,
Rash judgements, nor the sneers of selfish men,
Nor greetings where no kindness is, nor all
The dreary intercourse of daily life,
Shall e'er prevail against us, or disturb
Our cheerful faith that all which we behold
is full of blessings.[361]

[As Alain de Botton observes:] "Looking back on Wordsworth's early poems, Coleridge would assert that their genius had been to:

> give the charm of novelty to things of every day, and to excite a feeling analogous to the supernatural, by awakening the mind's attention from the lethargy of custom, and directing it to the loveliness and wonders of the world before us; an inexhaustible treasure, but for which, in consequence of the film of familiarity and selfish solicitude we have eyes, yet see not, ears that heard not, and hearts that neither feel nor understand.

"Nature's "loveliness" might in turn, according to Wordsworth, encourage us to locate the good in ourselves. Two people standing on the edge of a rock overlooking a stream and a grand wooded valley might transform their relationship not just with nature but, as significantly, with each other.

---

[361] William Wordsworth, excerpted from "Lines Written a Few Miles above Tintern Abbey."

"There are concerns that seem indecent when one is in the company of a cliff; others to which cliffs naturally lend their assistance, their majesty encouraging the steady and high-minded in ourselves, their size teaching us to respect with good grace and an awed humility all that surpasses us. It is of course still possible to feel envy for a colleague before a mighty cataract. It is just, if the Wordsworthian message is to be believed, a little more unlikely. Wordsworth argued that, through a life spent in nature, his character had been shaped to resist competition, envy and anxiety—and so he celebrated,

> . . . that first I looked
> At Man through objects that were great or fair;
> First communed with him by their help. And thus
> Was founded a sure safeguard and defence
> Against the weight of meanness, selfish cares,
> Coarse manners, vulgar passions, that beat in
> On all sides from the ordinary world
> In which we traffic." [362]

> Sweet is the lore which Nature brings;
> Our meddling intellect
> Mis-shapes the beauteous forms of things
> We murder to dissect.
>
> Enough of science and of art:
> Close up these barren leaves;
> Come forth, and bring with you a heart
> That watches and receives.
>
> ~ William Wordsworth

---

[362] Alain de Botton, *The Art of Travel,* op.cit., pp. 148, 150.

Heaven's River

~ Issa[363]

A lovely thing to see:
Through the paper window's hole,
The Galaxy.

Ocean Views

~ Rachel Carson[364]

One stormy autumn night when my nephew Roger was about twenty months old I wrapped him in a blanket and carried him down to the beach in the rainy darkness. Out there, just at the edge of where-we-couldn't-see, big waves were thundering in, dimly seen white shapes that boomed and shouted and threw great handfuls of froth at us. Together we laughed for pure joy—he a baby meeting for the first time the wild tumult of Oceanus, I with the salt of half a lifetime of sea love in me. But I think we felt the same spine-tingling response to the vast, roaring ocean and the wild night around us.

A night or two later the storm had blown itself out and I took Roger again to the beach, this time to carry him along the water's edge, piercing the darkness with the yellow cone of our flashlight. Although there was no rain the night was again noisy with breaking waves and the insistent wind. It was clearly a time and place where great and elemental things prevailed.

Our adventure on this particular night had to do with life, for we were searching for ghost crabs, those sand-colored, fleet-legged beings

[363] Issa, "Heaven's River," from *An Introduction to Haiku* by Harold G. Henderson. Copyright ©1958 by Harold G. Henderson.
[364] "Ocean Views" was excerpted from Pages 8-10, 42-43, and 88-89 from *The Sense of Wonder* by Rachel Carson. Copyright © 1956 by Rachel L. Carson. Copyright © renewed 1984 by Roger Christie. Reprinted by permission of HarperCollins Publishers, Inc. and Frances Collin.

which Roger had sometimes glimpsed briefly on the beaches in daytime. But the crabs are chiefly nocturnal, and when not roaming the night beaches they dig little pits near the surf line where they hide, seemingly watching and waiting for what the sea may bring them. For me the sight of these small living creatures, solitary and fragile against the brute force of the sea, had moving philosophic overtones, and I do not pretend that Roger and I reacted with similar emotions. But it was good to see his infant acceptance of a world of elemental things, fearing neither the song of the wind nor the darkness nor the roaring surf, entering with baby excitement into the search for a "ghos."

It was hardly a conventional way to entertain one so young, I suppose, but now, with Roger a little past his fourth birthday, we are continuing that sharing of adventures in the world of nature that we began in his babyhood, and I think the results are good. The sharing includes nature in storm as well as calm, by night as well as day, and is based on having fun together rather than on teaching. . . .

A child's world is fresh and new and beautiful, full of wonder and excitement. It is our misfortune that for most of us that clear-eyed vision, that true instinct for what is beautiful and awe-inspiring, is dimmed and even lost before we reach adulthood. If I had influence with the good fairy who is supposed to preside over the christening of all children I should ask that her gift to each child in the world be a sense of wonder so indestructible that it would last throughout life, as an unfailing antidote against the boredom and disenchantments of later years, the sterile preoccupation with things that are artificial, the alienation from the sources of our strength. . . .

What is the value of preserving and strengthening this sense of awe and wonder, this recognition of something beyond the boundaries of human existence? Is the exploration of the natural world just a pleasant way to pass the golden hours of childhood or is there something deeper?

I am sure there is something much deeper, something lasting and significant. Those who dwell, as scientists or laymen, among the beauties and mysteries of the earth are never alone or weary of life. Whatever the vexations or concerns of their personal lives, their thoughts can find paths that lead to inner contentment and to renewed excitement in living. Those who contemplate the beauty of the earth find reserves of strength that will endure as long as life lasts. There is symbolic as well as actual beauty in the migration of the birds, the ebb and flow of the tides, the folded bud ready for the spring. There is something infinitely healing in the repeated refrains of nature—the assurance that dawn comes after night, and spring after the winter.

I like to remember the distinguished Swedish oceanographer, Otto Pettersson, who died a few years ago at the age of ninety-three, in full possession of his keen mental powers. His son, also world-famous in oceanography, has related in a recent book how intensely his father enjoyed every new experience, every new discovery concerning the world about him.

"He was an incurable romantic," the son wrote, "intensely in love with life and with the mysteries of the cosmos." When he realized he had not much longer to enjoy the earthly scene, Otto Pettersson said to his son: "What will sustain me in my last moments is an infinite curiosity as to what is to follow."

Open a window towards God
and begin to delight yourself
by gazing upon Him through the opening.
The business of love is to make this window in the heart,
for the breast is illumined by the beauty of the Beloved.
Gaze incessantly on the face of the Beloved.
Listen, this is in your power, my friend.

~ Jalaluddin Rumi[365]

---

[365] Jalaluddin Rumi, *Mathnawi* IV, 3095-3097 translated by Camille and Kabir Helminski, *Jewels of Remembrance*, Threshold Books.

CHAPTER TWENTY-THREE

AWE

There is no god but He.
Everything is perishing except His Face.
To Him belongs the Command,
and to Him will you all return.
[*Sūrah Al-Qaṣaṣ* (The Story) 28:88]

Glorify the name of your Sustainer Most High
Who has created and further given order and proportion;
Who has determined the order, and gives guidance;
and Who brings forth the fertile pasture
and then reduces it to darkened stubble.
We shall teach you to remember
so that you shall not forget, except as God wills:
for truly, He knows what is manifest and all that is hidden.
And We will make easy for you the path towards true ease.
So remind in case the reminder may benefit the hearer.
It will be kept in mind by those who stand in awe of God.
[*Sūrah Al-Aʿlā* (The All-highest) 87:1-10]

All that is on earth will perish;
but forever will abide the Face of your Sustainer,
Full of Majesty and Abundant Honor.
Then which of your Sustainer's blessings will you deny?
Every creature in the heavens and on earth depends on Him:
every day He manifests in wondrous new ways!
Then which of your Sustainer's blessings will you deny?
[*Sūrah Ar-Raḥmān* (The Most Gracious) 55:26-30]

O God, show me things as they really are.

~ Ḥadith of the Prophet Muhamamd

I come to my solitary woodland walk as the homesick go home. I thus dispose of the superfluous and see things as they really are, grand and beautiful.

~ Henry David Thoreau

In wildness I sense the miracle of life, and behind it our scientific accomplishments fade to trivia.

~ Charles A. Lindbergh

Every part of the earth is sacred, every shining pine needle,
every sandy shore, every light mist in the dark forest,
every clearing, and every winged creature is sacred to my people.
We are part of the earth and it is part of us.
The fragrant flowers are our sisters,
the deer and mighty eagle are our brothers;
the rocky peak, the fertile meadows,
all things are connected
like the blood that unites a family.

~ Chief Seattle

Modes of Divine Presence
~ Thomas Berry[366]

We should be clear about what happens when we destroy the living forms of this planet. The first consequence is that we destroy modes of divine presence. If we have a wonderful sense of the divine, it is because we live amid such awesome magnificence. If we have refinement of emotion and sensitivity, it is because of the delicacy, the fragrance, and indescribable beauty of song and music and rhythmic movement in the

---

[366] "The Dream of the Earth," excerpted from *The Sacred Earth, Writers on Nature and Spirit*, Edited by Jason Gardner, p. 121.

world about us. If we grow in our life vigor, it is because the earthly community challenges us, forces us to struggle to survive, but in the end reveals itself as a benign providence. But however benign, it must provide that absorbing drama of existence whereby we can experience the thrill of being alive in a fascinating and unending sequence of adventures.

If we have powers of imagination, these are activated by the magic display of color and sound, of form and movement, such as we observe in the clouds of the sky, the trees and bushes and flowers, the waters and the wind, the singing birds, and the movement of the great blue whale through the sea. If we have words with which to speak and think and commune, words for the inner experience of the divine, words for the intimacies of life, if we have words for telling stories to our children, words with which we can sing, it is again because of the impressions we have received from the variety of beings about us.

You Are the Moon

~ Swampy Cree[367]

All the warm nights
sleep in moonlight

Keep letting it
go into you

Do this
all your life

Do this
you will shine outward
in old age

The moon will think
you are
the moon

---

[367] "The Wishing Bone Cycle," Swampy Cree, gathered and translated by Howard A. Norman, copyright 1972 by Howard Norman. Ross-Erikson Publishing, as reprinted in *Changing Light* by J. Ruth Gendler, p. 30.

The Lote Tree

~ Ibn Kathīr[368]

Muḥammad ﷺ rose one heaven to another on the ladder until he passed over the seventh heaven. Whenever he reached a heaven its favoured attendants and the most important angels and prophets therein would meet him.

He made reference to major persons from among the *mursalin,* the messengers of God, like Adam in the nearest heaven, John and Jesus in the second, Idrīs in the fourth, Moses in the sixth, and Abraham in the seventh, leaning his back against the *bayt al-ma'mur,* the "eternal abode," that is entered each day by 70,000 angels who worship therein in prayer and circumambulation, and they do not return there again until Judgement Day.

He then ascended above their ranks and reached a level where the squeaking of pens could be heard. There the *sidrat al-muntaha,* the "lote tree at the boundary," stood high before the Messenger of God ﷺ; its leaves were like the ears of an elephant, its fruit like summits of Mt. Hidjr, and covered all about by great deeds and many splendid colours, with angels perching upon it as numerous as starlings on a tree. And there was a canopy of gold, bathed in the light of our Lord, All-Glorious is He.

That which God said to the rose,
and caused it to laugh in full-blown beauty,
He said to my heart,
and made it a hundred times more beautiful.

~ Jalaluddin Rumi[369]

---

[368] Ibn Kathīr, *The Life of the Prophet Muḥammad,* Volume II, p. 66.
[369] *Mathnawi* III, 4129 excerpted from *Jewels of Remembrance,* op. cit., p. 43.

Lost in the wilderness between
true awareness and the senses,

I suddenly woke inside myself
like a lotus opening
in waterweeds.

~ Lalla[370]

The Peace of Wild Things

~ Wendell Berry[371]

When despair for the world grows in me
And I wake in the night at the least sound
in fear of what my life and my children's lives may be,
I go and lie down where the wood drake
Rests in his beauty on the water, and the great heron feeds.
I come into the peace of wild things
Who do not tax their lives with forethought
Of grief. I come into the presence of still water.
And I feel above me the day-blind stars
Waiting with their light. For a time
I rest in the grace of the world, and am free.

---

[370] Lalla, *Lalla, Naked Song*, translations by Coleman Barks, Maypop Books, Athens, Georgia, 1992, p. 77. Reprinted by permission of Coleman Barks.
[371] Wendell Berry, "The Peace of Wild Things," from *The Selected Poems of Wendell Berry*, copyright by Wendell Berry 1998. Reprinted by permission of the author.

The most beautiful thing we can experience is the mysterious. It is the source of all true art and all science. He to whom this emotion is a stranger, who can no longer pause to wonder and stand rapt in awe, is as good as dead: his eyes are closed.

~ Albert Einstein

Some nights, stay up till dawn,
As the moon sometimes does for the sun.
Be a full bucket pulled up the dark way
Of a well, then lifted out into the light.

~ Jalaluddin Rumi[372]

Felicity

~ Kathleen Raine[373]

Plotinus wrote of "felicity" as the goal and natural term of all life, and attributed it not only to man and animals but to plants also. Beatitude—felicity—is not an accident of being and consciousness: it is our very nature to seek, and to attain, joy; and it is for the arts to hold before us images of our eternal nature, through which we may awaken to, and grow towards, that reality which is our humanity itself.

This view of reality Blake defended in its darkest hour, at the end of the rationalist eighteenth century and the beginning of the materialist nineteenth. Few heeded him or understood him when he said, "all that I see is vision" and "to me this world is one continued vision of

---

[372] John Moyne and Coleman Barks, *Unseen Rain, Quatrains of Rumi.* Threshold Books, Putney, VT, 1986, p. 11.
[373] Excerpted from *Seeing God Everywhere: Essays on Nature and the Sacred.* Ed. Barry McDonald, World Wisdom Books, 2003, pp. 174-175. This paper was originally written for the 1985 Conference of the Center for Spiritual Studies, whose theme was The Underlying Unity, "The Underlying Order: Nature and the Imagination" by Kathleen Raine.

imagination." That is the sort of thing unpractical poets and painters do say! But Blake was in earnest and spoke as a metaphysician sure of his ground when he wrote of the living sun:

> "What," it will be Questioned, "When the Sun rises, do you not see A round disk of Fire somewhat like a Guinea?" O no, no, I see an Innumerable company of the Heavenly host crying, "Holy, Holy, Holy Is the Lord God Almighty." I question not my Corporeal or Vegetative Eye any more than I would Question a Window concerning A Sight. I look thro' it and not with it.[374]

Plato had used the same words about looking "through not with" the eye. And what else, after all, could that innumerable multitude of beings proclaim, being themselves not objects in a lifeless mechanism, but an epiphany of life which not only has, but is, being, consciousness and bliss? The real, therefore, is ultimately—and this again has been understood by all traditions—not an object but a Person. A "Person" in this sense not by a human act of personification of something in its innate reality neither living nor conscious; but rather human "persons" are a manifestation in multitude of the single Person of Being itself, from which consciousness and meaning are inseparable, these being innate qualities of life itself as such. Not "life" as a property of matter, but life as experienced. "Everything that lives is holy" summarizes Blake's total vision of reality—not holy because we choose to think it so, but intrinsically so. The "holy" is, again, a reality that cannot be defined but can be experienced as the ultimate knowledge of consciousness. It cannot be measured, but neither can it be denied, if by knowledge we mean what is experienced. Within the scope of human experience there are degrees of knowledge and value, self-authenticating, of which those who have reached the farthest regions tell us, the vision of the holy, and the beatitude of that vision is the highest term. And therefore Blake's stars and grains of sand can say no other than "Holy, Holy, Holy."

---

[374] Geoffrey Langdon Keynes, ed., "A Vision of the Last Judgment" from *The Complete Writings of William Blake* (London, Oxford University Press, 1966), p. 617.

To see a World in a Grain of Sand
And Heaven in a Wild Flower,
Hold Infinity in the palm of your hand
And Eternity in an hour.[2375]

That is not poetic fancy: it is profoundest knowledge.

How deeply we are all immersed in the world of duality is clear in the bewilderment we must all share through our Western conditioning in the matter of "inner" and "outer." Blake was very clear in his understanding that the externalization of nature is a tragic consequence of what he called the "wrenching apart" of the apparently external world from the unity of the wholeness of being. This has created an unhealed wound in the soul of modern Western man, leaving nature soulless and lifeless, and the inner world abstracted from the natural universe, its proper home. In the *unus mundus* the very terms "inner" and "outer" are not applicable at all. Both soul and nature have suffered; nature by being banished, in Blake's words, "outside existence" in "a soul-shuddering vacuum," natural space. At the same time the soul can no longer inhabit nature, and the "afterlife" is situated—again in Blake's words—"in an allegoric abode where existence has never come." But, for the universal spiritual teaching, mind is not in space, but space in mind. "Nothing," as it is said in the *Hermetica,* "is more capacious than the incorporeal."

Those things that nature denied to human sight,
she revealed to the eyes of the soul.

~ Ovid (43 BC-AD 17)

---

[375] Ibid., p. 431, "Auguries of Innocence."

i thank You God for most this amazing

~ e. e. cummings

i thank You God for most this amazing
day: for the leaping greenly spirits of trees
and a blue true dream of sky; and for everything
which is natural which is infinite which is yes

(i who have died am alive again today,
and this is the sun's birthday; this is the birth
day of life and of love and wings: and of the gay
great happening illimitably earth)

how should tasting touching hearing seeing
breathing any—lifted from the no
of all nothing—human merely being
doubt unimaginable You?

(now the ears of my ears awake and
now the eyes of my eyes are opened)

I walk across a green lawn of cropped grass to the creek, stoop, and splash cold water in my face. The filtered light, reflecting off the ripples in the spring creek, creates a sparkling dance of diamond glints, while beneath the water long strands of moss, moving slowly in the current, wave in emerald banners. Water in the desert is an incongruity always to be celebrated, and a cold spring percolating out of hardpan and gathering into a crystal stream supporting a surrounding oasis of green grass is a wonder worthy of worship. The only thing I can find wrong with this place is that soon we must leave it.

~ Rick Ridgeway[376]

---

[376] Rick Ridgeway, *The Big Open, On Foot Across Tibet's Chang Tang,* National Geographic Society, Washington, D.C., 2004.

God is the friend of silence.
See how nature—trees, flowers, grass—grows in silence;
see the stars, the moon and the sun, how they move in silence.
We need silence to be able to touch souls.

~ Mother Teresa

The Morning Glory

I break my fast
Amidst the morning glory.

~ Basho

Like the morning glory
How fleeting is my life
Today . . . and then . . .?

~ Moritake[377]

---

[377] From *The Moon in the Pines, Zen Haiku* selected and translated by Jonathon Clements, *published by* Frances Lincoln, Ltd, © 2000. Reproduced by permission of Frances Lincoln Ltd., 4 Torriano Avenue, London NW5 2RZ. Distributed in the USA by Publishers Group West and in Canada by Raincoast Books, pp. 15 and 16.

And your Sustainer knows
all that their hearts conceal and all that they reveal.
And He is God: there is no god but He.
To him be praise at the first and at the last:
for His is the Command, and to Him shall you return.
Say: "Do you see? If God were to make the night
perpetual over you
until the Day of Reckoning, what god is there other than God
who can give you enlightenment?
Will you not then pay attention?"
Say: "Do you see? If God were to make the Day
perpetual over you
until the Day of Reckoning, what god is there other than God
who can give you a night in which you can rest?
Then will you not see?"
It is out of His Mercy that He has made for you night and day—
that you may rest within it, and that you may seek His Grace,
and so that you might be grateful.

[*Sūrah Al-Qaṣaṣ* (The Story) 28:69-73]

Love, You have created us with thirsty hearts,
You have bound us to the Source of Splendor.
For You my thorns have blossomed, my atoms embraced the worlds.
Contemplating in my leaping atoms the universe
Makes my days stagger and sob with wonder! . . .
Joseph, I beg you, see in your pit the crown and the kingdom!
A thorn that has not blossomed cannot illumine the field;
How can a being made of water and clay find life
If Divine Breath does not Itself kindle it?
Clap your hands, clap your hands again, and know each sound
Has its origin in self-surrender!
Be silent! Spring is here! The rose is dancing with its thorn.
Beauties have come from the Invisible to call you home.

~ Jalaluddin Rumi

482

O my God, fill me with awe of You in my inner being and outer form. Let me be truthful in contentment and in anger. Give me modesty in poverty and wealth. Give me ever-lasting ease. Let my peace of mind be uninterrupted. Make me content with your judgement. Grant me goodness after death. Give me the pleasure of gazing upon Your Face. Make me long to meet you. Do not let affliction harm me and do not let my trials misguide me.

~ Prayer of the Prophet Muḥammad ﷺ

Wherever you turn, there is the Face of God.

[*Sūrah Al-Baqarah* 2:115]

BIBLIOGRAPHY

David Abram, *The Spell of the Sensuous*. NY, NY: Pantheon Books, 1996.

Jesse Ackerman, *Australia from a Woman's Point of View*. London, England: Cassell and Company, Ltd., 1913.

Leila Ahmad, *A Border Passage*. NY, NY: Penguin Books, Penguin Putnam, Inc., 1999.

Dr. Assad Ali, *Happiness without Death*, translated by Camille Adams Helminski, Kabir Helminski, and Dr. Ibrahim Al-Shihabi. Putney, VT: Threshold Books, 1991.

Tsultirm Allione, *Women of Wisdom*. NY, NY: Routledge & Kegan Paul, Inc. 1984.

Muhammad Asad, *The Message of the Qur'an*. Bristol, England: The Book Foundation, 2003.

The Road to Mecca. Louisville, KY: The Book Foundation and Fons Vitae, 2004.

Faridud-Din Attar, *The Speech of the Birds*, Presented by Peter Avery. Cambridge, England: The Islamic Texts Society, 1998.

Christie Aschwanden, "Leave the Wetlands to Beaver," Reston, VA: National Wildlife, magazine of the National Wildlife Federation, October/November issue, 2002.

Coleman Barks, translator of *Lalla, Naked Song*. Athens, GA: Maypop Books, 1992.

Anne Bancroft, *The Pocket Buddha*. Boston, MA. Shambhala Publications, Inc., 2001.

John D. Barrow, *The Artful Universe, "A Handful of Dust: the Earth Below."* Oxford, England: Oxford University Press, 1995.

Lincoln Barnett, *The Treasure of Our Tongue*, Knopf, New York, NY 1962

Matsuo Basho, *Narrow Road to the Interior and Other Writings*. Translated from the Japanese by Sam Hamill, Boston, MA: Shambhala Publications Inc.

Shaykh Tosun Bayrak al-Jerrahi al-Halveti, *The Most Beautiful Names*. Putney, VT: Threshold Books, 1985.

Lawrence Blair with Lorne Blair, *Ring of Fire*. NY, NY: Bantam Books, 1988.

Thomas Berry, *Creative Energy: Bearing Witness for the Earth*. San Francisco, CA: Sierra Club Books, 1988.

Wendell Berry, *The Selected Poems of Wendell Berry*, NY, NY: Counterpoint, 1998.

Tessa Bieleki, *Teresa of Avila*. NY, NY: The Crossroad Publishing Co., 1997.

Lawrence Blair with Lorne Blair, *Ring of Fire, Exploring the Last Remote Places of the Earth*. NY, NY: Bantam Books, 1988.

Robert Bly, *Selected Poems of Rainer Maria Rilke*. NY, NY: HarperCollins, 1981.

Rachel Carson, *The Sense of Wonder*. Reprinted in *This Sacred Earth*, NY, NY: HarperCollins Publishers, Inc., 1984.

Jonathan Clements, *The Moon in the Pines, Zen Haiku*. London, England: Frances Lincoln, Ltd., 2000.

Thomas Cleary, *The Essential Tao*, NY, NY: HarperCollins Publishers, Inc. 1991.

Michael A. Cremo and Mukunda Goswami, "Divine Nature," excerpted from *Science, Nature and the Environment*. LA, CA: The Bhaktivedanta Book Trust, 1995.

Juliette de Bairacli Levy, *Traveler's Joy*, Woodstock, VT: Ash Tree Publishing, 1994.

Alain de Botton, *The Art of Travel*. London: Penguin Books Ltd., 2002.

Alison Hawthorne Deming, *Writing the Sacred into the Real*. Minneapolis, MN: Milkweed Editions, 2001.

Michael J. Denton, *Nature's Destiny, How the Laws of Biology Reveal Purpose in the Universe*. New York. London: The Free Press.

Annie Dillard, *Teaching a Stone to Talk*. NY,NY: Harper Perennial, 1982.

David James Duncan, *My Story as Told by Water*. San Francisco, CA: Sierra Club Books, 2001.

Gai Eaton, *Remembering God*. Cambridge England: Islamic Texts Society.

Ralph Waldo Emerson, *Essays*.

Masaru Emoto, *The Hidden Messages of Water*. Hillsboro, Oregon: Beyond Words Publishing, 2004.

Kate Farrell, *Art and Nature, An Illustrated Anthology of Nature Poetry*. Boston, Massachusetts: The Metropolitan Museum of Art, A Bullfinch Press Book/Little, Brown and Company, 1992.

Brian J. Ford, *Sensitive Souls, Senses and Communication in Plants, Animals, and Microbes*. London, England: Time Warner Book Group UK.

Ruth Gendler, *Changing Light, The Eternal Cycle of Night and Day*. NY, NY: HarperCollins, 1991.

Jason Gardner, Editor, *The Sacred Earth, Writers on Nature and Spirit*. Novato, California: New World Library.

Jean Giono, "The Man Who Planted Hope and Grew Trees." *Sharing Nature with Children II*, by Joseph Cornell, Nevada City, CA: Dawn Publications, 1989.

Sam Gon III, Sudaryanto, Juana Londono, and Leyla Knight. "Portraits of Faith", Interviews by Susan Enfield Esrey, Laura Fisher Kaiser, Danielle Furlich, and Meaghan O'Neil. Edited by Laura Fisher Kaiser. Arlington, VA: Nature Conservancy, Spring 2003 issue. Paul Gorman, "Awakenings, Spiritual Perspectives on Conservation" Nature Conservancy Magazine, Arlington, VA. Spring 2003.

Paul Gorman, "Awakenings, Spiritual Perspectives on Conservation" Nature Conservancy Magazine, Spring, 2003. Arlington, VA: The Nature Conservancy, 2003.

Roger S. Gottlieb, editor, *This Sacred Earth*. "From Arctic Dreams: Imagination and Desire in a Northern Landscape" by Barry Lopez. NY, NY: Routledge, 1986.

Brian Greene, *The Elegant Universe*. NY, NY: WW. Norton & Company, Inc., 1999.

Shaykh Fadhlalla Haeri, *Heart of Qur'an and Perfect Mizan. Surat Ya Sin. With Tafsir on Surat al-Fatihah* by Khwaja Abdullah Ansari. Zahra Publications.

M.A.S. Abdel Haleem, "Water in the Qur'an," from *Islam and the Environment*, edited by Harfiyah Abdel Haleem, London, England: TaHa Publishers Ltd., 1998.

Sue Halpern, *Four Wings and a Prayer*. NY, NY: Vintage Books, 2002.

Thich Nhat Hanh, *No Death, No Fear, Comforting Wisdom for Life*. NY, NY: Riverhead Books, 2002.

Isabella Hatkoff, Craig Hatkoff, and Dr. Paula Kahumbu with photographs by Peter Greste, *Owen and Mzee*. Turtle Pond Publications, LLC, 2005.

Kim Heacox, "Whale Dreams." "Wilderness," magazine of The Wilderness Society, Washington, D.C. 2002.

Padma Hejmadi, *Room to Fly, a Transcultural Memoir,* Berkeley, CA: University of California Press, 1999.

Camille Helminski, *The Light of Dawn, A Daybook of Verses from the Holy Qur'an.* Boston, MA: Shambhala Publications, 2003.

Camille and Kabir Helminski, *Jewels of Remembrance, A Daybook of Spiritual Guidance Containing 365 Selections from the Wisdom of Mevlana Jalaluddin Rumi,* Boston, MA: Shambhala Publications, Inc. 2000.

Marguerite Henry, *King of the Wind.* NY, NY: Rand McNally and Co. 1948.

Thor Heyerdahl, *Kon-Tiki, Across the Pacific by Raft,* translated by F. H. Lyon. NY, NY: Rand McNally & Co.

Elspeth Huxley, *The Flame Trees of Thika: Memories of an African Childhood.* London, England: Penguin, 1962.

Elspeth Huxley & Hugo van Lawick, *Last Days in Eden.* NY, NY: The Amaryllis Press, Inc., 1984.

Ibn Kathir, *The Life of the Prophet Muhammad, Volume II.* Reading, UK: Garnet Publishing Ltd., 1998.

Djuna Ivereigh, "In the Bull's Eye of Biodiversity." Arlington, VA: Nature Conservancy magazine, Vol. 53, No 3, Fall 2003.

George Johnson, *Miss Leavitt's Stars.* NY,NY: Atlas Books, W.W. Norton & Company, 2005.

Debra Katz, *Wild Flower Plant Spirits.* Soudorgues, France: The Petite Bergerie Press, 2005.

Nacer Khēmir, compiler, *The Wisdom of Islam.* NY, NY: Abbeville Publishing Group, 1996.

Etienne Klein and Marc Lachieze-Rey, *The Quest for Unity, The Adventure of Physics.* Translated by Axel Reisinger. Oxford, England: Oxford University Press. 1999.

Mark Kurlansky, *Salt, A World History.* NY, NY: Penguin Putnam, Inc., 2002.

Rabbi Anson Laytner and Rabbi Dan Bridge, *The Animal's Lawsuit Against Humanity.* Louisville, KY: Fons Vitae, 2005.

Kevin Lax, "Protecting Taipei's Trees." Excerpted from "Discover Taipei," January-February 2003. Department of Information, Taipei City Government.

Michael Lerner, *Spirit Matters.* Charlottesville, VA: Hampton Roads Publishing Company, Inc., 2000.

Denise Levertov, *This Great Unknowing: Last Poems*. NY, NY: New Directions Publishing Corporation, 1999.
  Poems 1960-1967. NY, NY: New Directions Publishing Corporation, 1961.
Michael Lipske, "The True Nature of Chocolate," *National Wildlife*, the magazine of the National Wildlife Federation, Reston, VA, April/May 2003.
Al-Hafiz B.A. Masri, "Animals in Islam." Concern for Helping Animals in Israel, (CHAI) www.chai-online.org.
Barry McDonald, editor, *Seeing God Everywhere, Essays on Nature and the Sacred*. Bloomington, Indiana: World Wisdom, 2003.
Lynne McTaggart, *The Field: The Quest for the Secret Force of the Universe*. NY, NY: HarperCollins 2002.
Czeslaw Milosz, *The Collected Poems 1931-1987*. NY, NY: HarperCollins Publishers, 1988.
John P. Milton, *Sky Above, Earth Below*. study guide. Sounds True, Boulder Colorado, 1999.
Thomas Moore, editor, *The Education of the Heart*. HarperPerennial, New York, NY, 1997.
John Moyne and Coleman Barks, *Unseen Rain, Quatrains of Rumi*. Threshold Books, Putney, VT,1986.
John Muir, *The Eight Wilderness Discovery Books*. Seattle, WA:The Mountaineers, and Baton Wicks (UK), 1992.
Guy Murchie, *Music of the Spheres*. Cambridge, MA: The Riverside Press, 1961.(Currently published by Dover Publications)
Seyyed Hossein Nasr, "The Cosmos and the Natural Order" excerpted from *Islamic Spirituality: Foundations*, edited by Seyyed Hossein Nasr. NY, NY: The Crossroad Publishing Company, 1987.
"Sacred Science and the Environmental Crisis: An Islamic Perspective" by Seyyed Hossein Nasr, excerpted from *Islam and the Environment*, Edited by Harfiyah Abdel Haleem. London, England: Ta-Ha Publishers Ltd., 1998.
Nechaev and G.W. Jenkins, *The Chemical Elements, The Fascinating Story of their Discovery and of the Famous Scientists Who Discovered Them*, Norfolk, England: Tarquin Publications, 1997.
John G. Neihardt, *Black Elk Speaks*. Lincoln, Nebraska: University of

Nebraska Press, 1979.

Dr. Javad Nurbakhsh, *Traditions of the Prophet, Volume 2*, NY, NY: Khaniqah-Nimatullahi Publications, 1983.

Naomi Shihab Nye, *Nineteen Varities of Gazelles, Poems of the Middle East*. NY, NY: Greenwillow Books, 2002.

John O'Donohue, *Conamara Blues*. NY, NY: Doubleday, 2000.

Mary Oliver, *New and Selected Poems, Volume 2*. Boston, MA: Beacon Press, 2005.

F. David Peat, *Blackfoot Physics, A Native Journeying into the Native American Universe*. London, England: Fourth Estate, Ltd. 1996.

David Pitt-Brooke, Chasing Clayoquat, A Wilderness Almanac. Vancouver, B.C.: Raincoast Books, 2004.

Sandra Postel, *Pillar of Sand*. NY,NY: W.W. Norton & Company, Worldwatch Institute, 1999.

Ali, Aisha, and Alia Rafea, *Beyond Diversities: Reflections on Revelations*. Cairo, Egypt: Sadek Publishing, 2000.

Islam from Adam to Muhammad and Beyond. Sadek Publishing, Cairo, Egypt, reprinted as *Essential Islam* by The Book Foundation, Bristol England, 2004.

Fazlur Rahman, *Major Themes of the Qur'an,* Bibliotheca Islamica, Chicago, IL, 1980.

Kathleen Raine, *Selected Poems*. Hudson, NY: Lindisfarne Press, 1988.

Charles Recknagel, "Professor Fuat Sezgin." Washington, DC: Radio Free Europe/Radio Liberty, www.rferl.org, 2004.

Peter Reed and David Rothenberg, *Wisdom in the Open Air*. Minneapolis, Minnesota: University of Minnesota Press, 1993.

Rick Ridgeway, *The Big Open, On Foot Across Tibet's Chang Tang*. Washington, C.D. : National Geographic Society, 2004.

Rainer Maria Rilke, *Selected poems of Rainer Maria Rilke*, translated by Robert Bly, HarperCollins, New York, NY, 1981.

Peter Russell, *From Science to God*. The New World Library, Novato, CA. 2002.

May Sarton, *Collected Poems 1930-1993* by May Sarton. W. W. Norton & Company, Inc., 1993.

John Ralston Saul, *The Unconscious Civilization*. 1995 Massey Lectures.

Michael S. Schneider, *A Beginner's Guide to the Universe*. NY,NY:

HarperCollins Publishers, 1994.

Theodor Schwenk, *Sensitive Chaos, The Creation of Flowing Forms in Water and Art.* Rudolf Steiner Press, Sussex England, 1996.

Sa'd ud-Din Mahmud Shabistari, *The Garden of Mystery (Gulshan-i raz)*, Translated by Bob Darr. Sausalito, CA: Real Impressions, 1998.

Vandana Shiva, *Monocultures of the Mind.* Penang. Malaysia: Zed Books and Third World Network, 2000.

Theodor Schwenk, *Sensitive Chaos.* Sussex, England: Rudolf Steiner Press, 1996.

Sarah Simpson, "Regenerating the Heart", *Scientific American*, NY, NY: Scientific American, Inc., February 2003.

Doug Stewart, "Looking at Birds Through Creative Eyes" *National Wildlife,* Magazine of the National Wildlife Federation, Reston, VA, April-May 2003.

Allama Sir Abdullah Al-Mamun Al-Suhrawardy, *The Wisdom of Muhammad.* NY, NY: Citadel Press and Kensington Publishing Corp., 2001.

May Swenson, "Unconscious Came a Beauty" *American Poetry, Twentieth Century, Vol.2.* New York, NY: Literary Classics of the United States, 2000.

Henry David Thoreau, *Walden.*

Hildegard von Bingen, *Illuminations of Hildegard of Bingen* by Matthew Fox. Santa Fe, New Mexico: Bear & Company, 1985.

A.B.C. Whipple, *Planet Earth: Storm.* Alexandria, VA: Time-Life Books, 1982.

W.B. Yeats and Shree Purohit Swami, *The Ten Principal Upanishads.* NY, NY: Collier Books (Macmillan Publishing Co, Inc.), 1975.

Chief Yellow Lark (Lakota American Indian) *Prayers for Peace* 2002 Graphis, Inc. 307 Fifth Ave, NY, NY 10016, p.83.

Xenel Diary AH 1405/AD 1985, January-February.

At **The Book Foundation** our goal is to express the highest ideals of Islam and the Qur'an through publications, curricula, and other learning resources, suitable for schools, parents, and individuals, whether non-Muslims seeking to understand the Islamic perspective, or Muslims wanting to deepen their understanding of their own faith. Please visit our website: **thebook.org**

The Book of Revelations

*A Sourcebook of Themes
from the Holy Qur'an,*

Edited by Kabir Helminski
$33   £16.95   6 x 9"   508pp
1-904510-12-4

This book invites us to recognize and reflect upon the essential spiritual themes of the Qur'an. It offers 265 titled selections of ayats, presented in a fresh contemporary translation of high literary quality, with accompanying interpretations by Muhammad Asad, Yusuf Ali, and others. It is an essential sourcebook for Muslims and non-Muslims alike.

The Book of Character

*An Anthology of Writings on Virtue
from Islamic and Other Sources*
Edited by Camille Helminski
$33   £16.95   6 x 9"   484pp
1-904510-09-4

A collection of writings dealing with the qualities of our essential Human Nature: Faith and Trust; Repentance and Forgiveness; Compassion and Mercy; Patience and Forbearance; Modesty, Humility, and Discretion; Purity; Intention and Discernment; Generosity and Gratitude; Courage, Justice, and Right Action; Contentment and Inner Peace; Courtesy and Chivalry. From the Prophets Abraham and Moses, to the sages Confucius and Buddha, to the Prophet Muhammad, his wife, Khadija, and his companions Abu Bakr and 'Ali, through great saints like Rumi, and humanitarians like Florence Nightingale, Mother Theresa, and Martin Luther King, and even in the personal story of the bicyclist Lance Armstrong, we find stories and wisdom that will help us toward spiritual well-being.

The Book Foundation *has embarked on an important effort to develop books and teaching tools that are approachable and relevant to Muslims and non-Muslims.* ~**Shabbir Mansuri**, *Founding Director, Council on Islamic Education (CIE)*

The Book of Essential Islam
The Spiritual Training System of Islam
Ali Rafea,
with Aisha and Aliaa Rafea
$21   £10.95   6 x 9"   276 pp
1-904510-13-2

This book examines the main teachings and practices of Islam with lucidity and depth. It is a corrective to the distortions and misconceptions of Islam that abound. It can serve equally well to introduce non-Muslims to Islam, as well as to enhance Muslims understanding of their own faith. This book presents Islam as a spiritual training system that supports us in harmonizing ourselves with the Divine Order and thus with each other and our environment. It reveals the intent and inner significance of practices like ablution, ritual prayer, fasting, and pilgrimage.

The Fragrance of Faith
The Enlightened Heart of Islam
Jamal Rahman
$15.95 £9.95   6 x 9"   176pp
1-904510-08-6

The Fragrance of Faith reveals the inner Islam that has been passed down through the generations. Jamal is a link in this chain, passing along the message, just as he received it from his grandfather, a village wiseman in Bangladesh. We need reminders of this "enlightened heart of Islam" in our lives, our homes, and our schools. In Jamal Rahman's book Islam is alive and well. ~**Imam Feisal Abdul Rauf**, Author *Islam: A Sacred Law* and *What's Right With Islam*.

This heartfelt book is perfect for the classroom, whether in a Muslim context, or outside of it. It conveys a tradition of compassion and humor passed through one family that represents the best Islam has to offer. And Mr. Rahman is highly entertaining. ~**Michael Wolfe**, *The Hadj: An American's Pilgrimage to Mecca*, Producer of the PBS Documentary: *Muhammad: The Legacy of a Prophet*.

The Message of the Qur'an

by Muhammad Asad

- Newly designed and typeset
- Available in two formats: a single hardback volume,
  and a boxed set of six parts in paperback
  for ease of handling and reference
- Original artwork by the internationally renowned
  Muslim artist and scholar, Dr. Ahmed Moustafa
- A Romanised transliteration of the Arabic text
- A newly compiled general index

As the distinguished British Muslim, Gai Eaton, explains in a new Prologue to the work, there is no more useful guide to the Qur'an in the English language than Muhammad Asad's complete translation and commentary, and no other translator has come so close to conveying the meaning of the Qur'an to those who may not be able to read the Arabic text or the classical commentaries. Generous sponsorship has enabled the Foundation to offer this work at a very reasonable price for a publication of this exceptional quality.

Price: Hardback $55, £28, 39 Euros
Boxed set of 6 deluxe paperback volumes: $60, £33, 45 Euros
ISBN: Hardback 1-904510-00-0 Boxed set 1-904510-01-9
Hardback cover size: 8.5 x 11. Approximately: 1200 pages

To Order In the USA:
The Book Foundation: 831 685 3995
Bookstores: IPG 800 888 4741
In England: Orca Book Services 01202 665432

Or visit our website: TheBook.org

Lightning Source UK Ltd.
Milton Keynes UK
UKHW010637071021
391819UK00001B/6